THE LYLE OFFICIAL ARTS REVIEW 1991

While every care has been taken in the compiling of information contained in this volume, the publishers cannot accept any liability for loss, financial or otherwise, incurred by reliance placed on the information herein.

All prices quoted in this book are obtained from a variety of auctions in various countries during the twelve months prior to publication and are converted to dollars at the rate of exchange prevalent at the time of sale.

The publishers wish to express their sincere thanks to the following for their involvement and assistance in the production of this volume:

NICKY FAIRBURN (Art Editor)
EELIN McIVOR (Sub Editor)
ANNETTE CURTIS
TRACEY BLACK
LOUISE SCOTT-JONES
CATRIONA McKINVEN
GILLIAN EASTON
DONNA BONAR
JACQUELINE LEDDY
FRANK BURRELL
JAMES BROWN
EILEEN BURRELL
RICHARD SCOTT
FIONA RUNCIMAN

COVER ILLUSTRATIONS.
Golden Days by Edward Dufner (Sotheby's New York)
A Young Dandy on the beach by Lucien Hector Jonas (Sotheby's London)
Brigadier Gerard with Joe Mercer up by Keith Money (Christie's S. Ken.)
A Still Life of Butterflies, a bird's nest and fruit by Sebastian Wegmayr (Sotheby's London)
Rue de village animee by Maurice Vlaminck (Christie's)
Fishing boats, Brittany, by Hayley Lever, (Sotheby's New York)
Four Kings and a Knave by Thomas Blinks (Sotheby's London)
L'Arc de Triomphe, Paris by Eugene Galien Laloue (Christie's S. Ken.)
Idyll by Louis Welden Hawkins (Christie's London)

A CIP catalogue record for this book is available from the British Library.

ISBN 86248 - 135 - X

Copyright © Lyle Publications MCMXC
Glenmayne, Galashiels, Scotland.

Printed and bound by Butler & Tanner, Frome, Somerset.

THE

LYLE

OFFICIAL

ARTS

REVIEW 1991

COMPILED & EDITED BY
TONY CURTIS

Introduction

Published annually and containing details of thousands of oil paintings, watercolours and prints, The Lyle Official Arts Review is the most comprehensively illustrated reference work on the subject available at this time.

Each entry is listed alphabetically under the Artist's name for easy reference and includes a description of the picture, its size, medium, auctioneer and the price fetched at auction during the twelve months prior to publication.

As regards authenticity of the works listed, this is often a delicate matter and throughout this book the conventional system has been observed:

The full Christian name(s) and surname of the artist denote that, in the opinion of the auctioneer listed, the work is by that artist.

The initials of the Christian name(s) and the surname denote that, in the opinion of the auctioneer listed, the work is of the period of the artist and may be wholly or partly his work.

The surname only of the artist denotes that, in the opinion of the auctioneer listed, the work is of the school or by one of the followers of the artist or painted in his style.

The word 'after' associated with the surname of the artist denotes that, in the opinion of the auctioneer listed, the picture is a copy of the work of the artist. The word 'signed' associated with the name of the artist denotes that, in the opinion of the auctioneer listed, the work bears a signature which is the signature of the artist.

The words 'bears signature' or 'traces of signature' denote that, in the opinion of the auctioneer listed, the work bears a signature or traces of a signature which may be that of the artist.

The word 'dated' denotes that the work is dated and, in the opinion of the auctioneer listed, was executed at that date.

The words 'bears date' or 'inscribed' (with date) denotes that, in the opinion of the auctioneer listed, the work is so dated and may have been executed at about that date.

All pictures are oil on canvas unless otherwise specified. In the dimensions (sight size) given, the height precedes the breadth.

Although the greatest possible care has been taken to ensure that any statement as to authorship, attribution, origin, date, age, provenance and condition is reliable, all such statements can only be statement of opinion and are not to be taken as statements or representations of fact.

The Lyle Official Arts Review offers a unique opportunity for identification and valuation of paintings by an extremely broad cross section of artists of all periods and schools.

Unless otherwise stated descriptions are placed immediately underneath the relevant illustrations.

We firmly believe that dealers, collectors and investors alike will treasure this and subsequent annual editions of the Lyle Official Arts Review (published in September each year) as changing trends in the fluctuating world of art values are revealed.

Tony Curtis

Auction Acknowledgements

Anderson & Garland, Marlborough House, Marlborough Crescent, Newcastle upon Tyne.

Auktionsverket, Jakobsgatan 10 103-25 Stockholm, Sweden.

Australian Art Auctions, Suite 333, Park Regis, 27 Park Street, Sydney 2000, Australia.

Bearnes, Rainbow Avenue Road, Torquay, TQ2 5TG.

Biddle & Webb, Ladywood Middleway, Birmingham, B16 OPP

Bonhams, Montpelier Street, Knightsbridge, London, SW7 1HH.

Bruce D. Collins Fine Art Gallery, Box 113, Denmark, Maine, USA.

Christie's (International) SA, 8 Place de la Taconnerie, 1204 Geneva, Switzerland.

Christie's, 8 Kings Street, London, SW1Y 6QT.

Christie's, 502 Park Avenue, New York, NY 10022, USA.

Christie's, Cornelis Schuystraat 57, 1071 JG, Amsterdam, Netherlands.

Christie's (Monaco) S.A.M., Park Place, 98000 Monte Carlo, Monaco.

Christie's South Kensington Ltd., 85 Old Brompton Road, London SW7 3LD.

David Lay, The Penzance Auction House, Alverton, Penzance, Cornwall, TR18 4KE.

Du Mouchelles Art Galleries Co., 409 E. Jefferson Avenue, Detroit, Michigan 48226, USA.

Duran Sala de Arte y Subastas, Serrano 12, 28001 Madrid.

G.A. Key, Aylsham Salesroom, Palmers Lane, Aylsham, Norfolk, NR11 6EH.

Galerie Moderne, 3 Rue du Parnasse Bruxelles, Belgium.

Graves , Son & Pilcher, 71 Church Road, Hove, East Sussex, BN3 2GL.

Halifax Property Services, 53 High Street, Tenterden, Kent.

Henry Spencer & Sons, 20 The Square, Retford, Nottinghamshire, DN22 6DJ.

Hotel de Ventes Horta, 390 Chaussée de Waterloo (Ma Campagne), 1060 Bruxelles, Belgium.

Jean-Claude Anaf, Lyon Brotteaux, 13 bis place Jules Ferry, 69456 Lyon Cedex 06, France.

Kunsthaus am Museum, Drususgasse 1-5, 5000 Koln 1.

Lawrence Fine Art, South Street, Crewkerne, Somerset, TA18 8AB

Michael Newman, The Central Auction Rooms, St. Andrews Cross, Plymouth, PL1 3DG.

P. Herholdt Jensens Auktioner, Hammerichsgade 14, 1611 Copenhagen.

Phillips, Blenstock House, 7 Blenheim Street, New Bond Street, London, W1Y OAS.

Phillips, 65 George Street, Edinburgh, EH2 2JL.

Phillips Marylebone, Hayes Place, Lisson Grove, London, NW1 6UA.

Riddetts, Richmond Hill, Bournemouth.

Skinner Inc., Bolton Gallery, Route 117, Bolton, MA, USA

Sothebys, 34-35 New Bond Street, London, W1A 2AA.

Sothebys, 1334 York Avenue (at 72nd Street), New York NY 10021.

Sothebys Deutschland GmbH, Odeonsplatz 16, D8000 Munchen 22.

Sothebys Monaco Sporting, d'Hiver Place du Casino, Monte Carlo, MC 9800, Monaco.

W.R.J. Greenslade & Co., 13 Hammet Street, Taunton, Somerset, TA1 1RN.

W.H. Lane & Son, 65 Morrab Road, Penzance, Cornwall.

Woolley & Wallis, The Castle Auction Mart, Salisbury, Wiltshire, SP1 3SU.

ARTS
REVIEW 1991

I t's been another incredible year in the international Fine Art market. With the crazy sums parted with at the New York Impressionist sales in May '89, it seemed that the bubble must surely be on the point of bursting, and, indeed, ever since then the gloom and doom merchants/realists (depending on your point of view) have been predicting that this overheated market was on the verge of a terrible slump. Statistics were compiled to show that the Sotheby's Impressionist Index, which stood at 487 in May 1986, had risen to 1609 by December 1988, and already stood, before the latest New York sales, at around 2450. That means a rise of just under 500% in four years. Surely such rampant growth was unhealthy and totally unsustainable, as even spokesmen for the leading auction houses agreed. (Rather than a slump, however, they suggested that the boom would continue, simply moving to other areas, such as contemporary art.)

It seems they were simply hedging their bets, for, lo and behold, Messrs Christie's and Sotheby's again brought the art world to New

Vincent van Gogh (1853-1890) Portrait of Dr Gachet painted in June 1890, oil on canvas, 67 x 55.9cm. (Christie's New York) **$82,500,000 £49,107,142**

York in May 1990, with the lure of, among others, Van Gogh and Renoir, and proceeded to rewrite the record books once again. On May 15, van Gogh's portrait of Dr Gachet, painted shortly before the artist's death in 1890, was sold to a Japanese dealer bidding on behalf of a Japanese company for an all-time record of $75 million, almost doubling the lower estimate. The art world then held its breath to see if Sotheby's could do even better three days later, when they offered Renoir's familiar and delightful 'Au Moulin de la Galette'. It was estimated again at $40–50 million, and, in the event, it sold to the same dealer for $71 million. Thus at two strokes were all the rumours dispelled – that the market was falling back, and that the Japanese were deserting the auction rooms.

The same series of sales, too, saw new records for other artists. The highest ever price paid for a Chagall was achieved at Christie's when his 'Above the City' sold for $9 million. This was superceded almost immediately at Sotheby's when 'Anniversaire' sold, again to the Japanese, for $13.5 million. Modiglianis also did well, with a portrait of the artist's mistress

Jeanne Hebuterne selling at Christie's for $7.5 million and his 'Garcon a la veste bleue' fetching $10.5 million at Sotheby's a few days later.

Even a brief catalogue of such figures is likely to prove a mite indigestible for most of us, and it's hardly surprising that the prevalent images in the press are of gluttony and excess – 'the Impressionist binge', 'on the hog in New York', 'mad bid disease' to name but a few. It is perhaps worth considering just who is spending all this money and why. The two May sensations have doubtless already followed so many of their predecessors to their new homes in the Land of the Rising Sun, bought, we are told, by corporations, but as an investment, as a status symbol or what? It has been claimed that 'Sunflowers', bought for £24.2 million in 1987 and currently on public view at $2 a time in the Yasuda Fire and Marine Insurance Company in Tokyo, has already recouped more than half its purchase price in 'gate' money. If that is true then it has proved an investment indeed. However, even given that Japan is the most densely populated country on earth it would still mean that an awfully high percentage of the population would have queued to see it....

Pierre - Auguste Renoir 'Au Moulin de la Galette' oil on canvas (Sotheby's London)
$78,100,000 £46,488,095

Amedeo Modigliani (1884-1920) Jeanne Hebuterne con grande cappello, signed painted circa 1918, oil on canvas, 55 x 38cm. (Christie's New York)

Nor is buying at such levels without its problems. In October 1989 it was revealed that Sotheby's had staked the Australian millionaire Alan Bond to the tune of 50% of the £30 million plus purchase price of 'Irises'. Now Sotheby's make no secret of the fact that they are willing to offer loans to potential buyers, but what jarred in this case was the timing. Coming soon after the 1987 stock market crash it could be construed as a calculated attempt to lift a flagging market. The fact that Mr Bond had run into difficulties repaying the loan compounded the embarrassment, though the picture has now found a new home, for an undisclosed sum, in the Getty Museum.

As prices spiral, the major auction houses where these sensations take place have come in for a bit of flak. Certainly their profits have rocketed. Christie's have announced a pre-tax profit for 1989 of nearly £70 million, an increase of 58% on the previous year, with total sales exceeding £1.3 billion. Sotheby's pre-tax profits for the same period stand at over £117 million, an increase of 88%, with total sales at £1.8 billion. Both companies claim too that 1990 figures are already running in advance of the same period of the previous year. The trend seems worldwide, with auction sales in France for example producing a total of £892 million, a 56% increase over 1988. It may be human

nature to mistrust anyone who is seen to be doing too well, and the auction houses in the past year have been targeted by investigative reporters from both the press and television probing into their ethics and their practices.

Moving downmarket a little from the first rank of Impressionist masters, discerning collectors are now turning their attention to secondary painters. Now that the leaders are well out of the range of most pockets, there seems to be a growing preference for the first rate paintings by lesser artists rather than a mediocre example by a big name. There is a healthy private interest in this range too, and in the past year many records have been achieved by these artists. For example, at Sotheby's first Impressionist sale of 1990 in London, Gustave Loiseau's 'Le Verger au Printemps' fetched £85,000 against an estimate of £50–60,000. That hardy perennial Utrillo, despite all the

Gustave Loiseau, Le Verger au Printemps, signed, oil on canvas, 38.4 x 46cm. (Sotheby's)

Maurice Utrillo,Rue Saint Rustique,signed and inscribed Montmartre, oil on board laid down on panel, 41.5 x 50.5cm. (Sotheby's)

fakes and rumours of fakes, is still doing well too, thanks largely to a continuing Japanese interest. His 'Rue Ste Rustique' sold for £95,000 at the same auction.

Old Masters are of course a completely different market pursued, by and large, by a completely different clientele, and they have, until recently been somewhat neglected and undervalued. It is probably understandable that Japanese interest should be missing here, for Old Masters make demands on knowledge and understanding of European mythology, religion and imagery which are often too much for some Occidental let alone Oriental taste. Another problem has been that there are very few really first class ones around. In 1989 of course what was probably the Old Master of the decade, Pontormo's Cosimo, was sold in New York for $35.2 million and this may have had the effect of arousing the art world from its torpor in this field. Certainly since then there has been a noticeable quickening of interest in the middle range, of which there are a fair supply available.

Circle of Pierre Nicolas Huilliot, Roses, lilies, poppies, gladioli, an iris and other flowers in an urn with a bird of paradise on a branch below, 35 x 47in. (Christie's) **$12,705 £7,700**

Paul Sandby, R.A., A capriccio landscape said to be of Shrewsbury Castle, gouache, on paper laid on panel, 18in. x 24in. (Bearnes) **$25,575 £15,500**

Dutch 17th century still-lifes and flower pieces have sold well, for example, as have French 18th century paintings, which may well constitute the strongest growth area in this field. There are a good number of Breughels about, and these have done extremely well of late. Again, in this area, there is a sizeable private interest, and also a notable number of Italian buyers about, buying back their native artists. Old Masters have always been, and are still a difficult market however, and there can be hiccups, especially when estimates are set too high. Most major auction houses have been caught in this way at one time or another. Because of a dearth of good pictures around, they perhaps feel that they have to make extravagant promises to vendors in order to secure the pictures for sale. It often misfires, and a classic example of this was Rembrandt's masterpiece of St Peter Repentant, which was offered recently as the star of Christie's Old Masters sale in New York. Instead of breaking records, it failed to attract a single bid at $9 million.

John Hayes (19th Century), Fox terrier puppies and a tabby cat up to no good, signed 30 x 25in. (Christie's S. Ken.)   **$8,168 £4,950**

The bulk of 19th century paintings tend towards the more readily appreciable, and there is no doubt that many people, especially at the more modest end of the market, are buying for prettiness, with subject matter, be it children, animals, birds or pretty scenes, more important than the painter. Nevertheless, portraits, long in the doldrums, are beginning to find a market again, even if damaged and unretouched. If selling these, it is always better to frame them. A second hand frame costing £25 or so, can make a difference of as much as £150 on the sale value.

H. Wilhelmi, The bird's nest, oil on wood, signed, 36.5 x 28cm. (Kunsthaus am Museum)
$3,414 £2,069

William Henry Hunt, Young boy holding a candle, watercolour heightened with scratching out, signed, 25 x 20cm. (Sotheby's) **$17,204 £10,120**

Alfred de Breanski, Ben Vorlich, signed 74 x 126cm. (Henry Spencer)   **$34,020 £21,000**

Henry John Sylvester Stannard, Thatching a cottage by a duck pond, signed, watercolour heightened with bodycolour, 51 x 76cm. (Sotheby's)   **$16,698 £10,120**

Charles Sims, (1873 - 1928), Then The Fairies Ran Away With Their Clothes, signed, watercolour with bodycolour over traces of pencil, 25 x 32.5cm. (Phillips) **$11,000 £6,500**

Late Victorian artists such as de Breanski and Hunt continue to be popular. The auctioneers Henry Spencer recently sold a Breanski for £21,000 and a Ladell for £24,000. Cottage garden watercolours too are still finding a ready market.

Foreign 19th century painters have, however, enjoyed mixed fortunes. On one hand interest continues strong in the case of the Scandinavian painters. Sotheby's and Christie's held their annual round of Nordic sales in March, and they were generally considered a success, though characterised again by a high degree of selectivity. Buyers, it seems, will be tempted to go high on really good pictures, but will not be drawn on the second rate. Thus Anders Zorn's 'Les Baigneuses' set a new record for a Scandinavian painter when it sold to a Swedish dealer at Christie's for £1.6 million. At Sotheby's a few days later the £1 million

English School 1636, Portrait of Master Fortinsall aged five, oil on canvas, signed and inscribed, 43 x 35in. (Bonhams) **$13,200 £8,000**

mark was reached again when the Finnish artist Helene Schjerfbeck's 'The Dancing Shoe' sold for exactly that sum. The buyer in this case was also a Finn, which says something about the fidelity of Scandinavian dealers to works by their own native artists. In general, it seems that Nordic works tend to appeal to a Northern taste, with the British and the Americans being the other two nationalities who principally pursue them.

Anders Zorn, Les Baigneuses, oil on canvas, signed and dated 38¾ x 27in. (Sotheby's)

Helene Schjerfbeck Balskorna (The Dancing Shoe), oil on canvas, signed, 62 x 68cm. (Sotheby's)

Carl Holsoe (1863-1935),
In the dining room, signed,
33½ x 26½in. (Christie's)
$29,920 £18,700

Fernando Alvarez Sotomayor y Zaragoza,
The Weavers, signed, 39¼ x 43¼in.
(Christie's) **$158,950 £93,500**

On the other hand, a year ago, Spanish art of this period appeared to be entering a Golden Age, with numerous sales devoted entirely to Iberian works, and just about everything selling well. But, as so often happens, too many tried to climb onto the bandwagon, and there were soon too many pictures chasing too few buyers. Another contributory factor was that the Spanish trade and private buyers, who formed the backbone of purchasers of this material, were already tending to move into Spanish contemporary art. There were indeed some great moments, as, for example, when Ulpiano Checa y Sanz's 'Arc de Triomphe' sold for £350,000 at Christie's against an estimate of £60–80,000, but in general it was only the best of the best that raised much interest.

Approaching the contemporary art market by way of the Spaniards, it is worth noting that a number of such Spanish works sold well at

Antonio Saura, (b. 1930) Untitled, signed and dated, oil on canvas, 45.7 x 52.4cm.
(Christie's) **$101,400 £60,000**

Francisco Mateos, El Club, oil on canvas, signed, 80 x 100cm. (Duran, Madrid) **$12,548 £7,514**

Sotheby's in March. They were led by the Chilean Surrealist Roberto Matta's Nu cache par des arbres, which came in at £100,000. At Christie's around the same time a small oil by Antonio Saura dated 1960 made £60,000 against an estimate of £10–15,000.

This is typical of the way in which the contemporary art market is taking off, although, as we have seen, the predicted flight from the Impressionists has not yet taken place.

Bernard Buffet, Bouquet de roses, oil on canvas, signed,60 x 50cm.
(Jean-Claude Anaf Lyon-Brotteaux)   **$299,511 £179,348**

Pablo Picasso, Portrait of Jaime Sabartes, oil on canvas, signed, 19½ x 14¾in (Sotheby's)   **$3,630,000 £2,200,000**

Nevertheless, the contemporary art market has expanded at a dizzy speed and here too the pundits are warning of a possible levelling out, which is both normal and desireable, but may leave some people disappointed. The big names, such as Bacon, Pollock, Klein and Johns, seem definitely here to stay, but the question has to be asked, can it still be accurately called contemporary art, with many pieces now 30-odd years old? The term 'New contemporary art' is now being coined and this may well be the area to watch.

Well worth watching was the sale in November 1989 at Sotheby's in New York of Willem de Kooning's Interchange, an expressive description of which has been 'rather like a strawberry ice cream daubed on the Spanish flag'. In the catalogue it was estimated at $4–6 million, but the initial bidding rose at one step from $1.7 to $6 million. A battle ensued between a Swedish art investor and, yes you've guessed it, a Japanese bidder, who finally clinched the sale at $20.7 million, a record price for a living artist.

The work of Johns, de Kooning, Pollock and the like is now well enough established that there are no great head shakings any more when their pictures fetch incredible sums. What may be rather more difficult for some to swallow are the prices being paid now for so called 'pop art'.

Andy Warhol, Ten Portraits of Jews of the Twentieth Century, the set of ten signed and numbered screenprints in colours, all 40 x 32in. (Christie's East) $71,500 £41,684

Willem de Kooning, Interchange,
(Sotheby's New York)
$20,680,000 $13,039,092

Roy Lichtenstein, Torpedo Los! , oil on canvas. (Christie's New York) **$5,500,000 £3,516,150**

Robert Rauschenberg, Killdevil Hill, lithograph in red and blue, 1974-5, 680 x 2025mm.
(Christie's) **$38,500 £22,445**

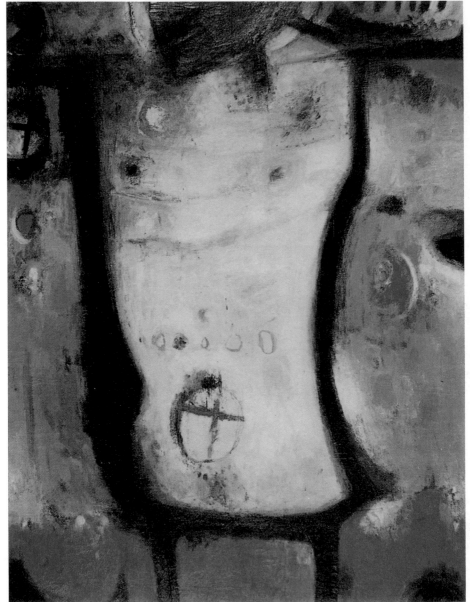

John Christoforou (England), Black Angel, signed, 76 x 50½in. (Bonham's) **$7,260 £4,400**

David Hockney, *A grand procession of Dignitaries in the semi-Egyptian style, signed, titled and dated 1961, oil on canvas, 84 x 144in. (Sotheby's)* $2,200,000 £1,294,117

Andy Warhol has got to be the high priest of this form, and whether you love it or hate it, there can be no doubt that he has reached beyond frontiers and broken down barriers in exactly the same way as Johns and Rauschenberg did twenty to thirty years before when they turned from the notion of art as remote and distanced from daily contemporary reality and reached for a form more closely aligned with the anxieties of daily existence and the increasing chaos threatening our perceptions and thought. In Warhol's work we are forced to contemplate the absurdity and emptiness of so much that we hold to be important in our cultural lives, and his obsession with the 'icons of death and glamour' lend his images a substance which make it impossible to disregard the significance of his contribution to the development of modern art.

In more general terms, the increasing interest in contemporary art seems based on broad and sound foundations which indicate that it will be more than just a passing phase. For one thing, of course, the Japanese are interested, particularly in abstract pieces dating from the 50s and 60s. Also a healthy number of specialist dealers are emerging, while apart from the likes of Christie's and Sotheby's, other auction houses, such as Bonhams, are setting up new departments

specially devoted to this area and are now holding regular sales of international post-war avant-garde art.

Theme sales continue popular with many auction houses. Some, like those timed to coincide with Crufts or the Chelsea Flower Show, have become fixed in the calendar as annual events. Others, one expects, will come and go as fashion dictates. Bonhams found a sure fire winner in November 1989 when they ran a sale devoted to the works of Sir William Russell Flint from a single private collection. It proved a resounding success, so much so, in fact, that they decided to repeat the experiment only six months later, this time drawing on items from a number of mainly private vendors.

W. Russell Flint, 'Clara Sprott', watercolour, signed, 10 x 12¾in. (Bonham's)
$91,280 £56,000

Laurent Gsell, The washerwomen, oil on canvas, signed, 80 x 100cm, (Jean-Claude Anaf Lyon-Brotteaux) **$8,500 £5,151**

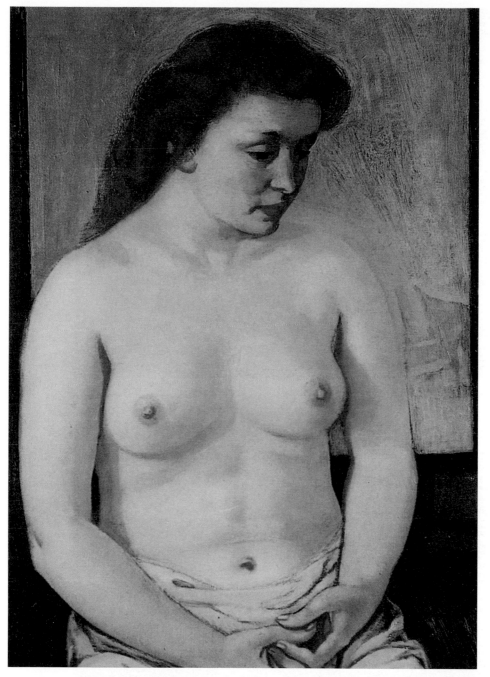

Leon Davos, Seated nude, oil on canvas, signed, 92x70cm.(Hotel de Ventes Horta) **$6,000** **£3,636**

The second sale was just about as successful as the first, with top price going to a small signed watercolour of Clara Sprott dated 1961 which sold for a new record for Flint of £56,000. This seems to be a mainly private market; we shall have to wait to see if it is judged capable of standing a third concentrated airing.

Finally, what's new in fakes? The short answer is quite a lot, and, in the light of Dr Gachet, quite an important lot too, for doubt has recently been cast by the Dutch born art historian Dr Walter Feilchenfeldt on the authenticity of three van Gogh self-portraits currently hanging in Oslo, New York and Connecticut. His investigations,

Dame Laura Knight, Lamorna Cove, signed, 19¼ x 23¼in. (Bearnes)$31,350 £19,000

J. Le Mayeur, Ray of sunshine, oil on canvas, signed, 120 x 99cm. (Hotel de Ventes Horta)
$47,999 £29,090

Elmyr De Hory, in the manner of Paul Gaugin, Tahitiennes, oil on board, bears facsimile signature and date 'Paul Gaugin, 98' 26 x 20in. (Bonhams)

which at least exonerated all other self-portraits from this stigma, will be published next year by the van Gogh Museum, and may well make headlines.

And last but not least, for really good fun, there is the 'honest' fake, which, it seems, you know about but buy regardless. After all, there's a chance that your dinner guests won't know the difference and will believe that really is a Gaugin/Renoir/Modigliani above the fireplace. Bonhams put on a sale of thirty such 'masterpieces' by Elmyr de Hory, with estimates of up to £8,000, and they did very well. It may seem a lot for a copy but then, in these stirring times, you'd still be saving up your pennies in heaven for a sniff of the real thing!

EELIN McIVOR

ARTS
REVIEW 1991

EDWIN AUSTIN ABBEY, R. A. (1852 – 1911) –
Potpourri – signed and dated 1899 l.r. - oil on canvas -
35 x 60¦in.
(Sotheby's)   **$130,900 £77,000**

WILLIAM ALBERT ABLETT –Portrait of a lady in a
green dress – signed and dated '05 – oil on canvas – oval
128 x 102cm.
(Sotheby's)   **$6,813   £4,180**

**MASTER WITH THE MONOGRAM AC - attributed
to** - Portrait de Femme - oil on panel - 35 x 26.5cm.
(Sotheby's)   **$49,474 £31,714**

JOHN ABSOLON – A rural landscape with two figures
conversing beside a cottage in the foreground – 24 x 34cm.
(Spencer's)   **$845   £500**

EMIL ADAM (1843 - 1924) - Sir James Miller's Dark
Bay Racehorse Rock Sand with jockey up - signed
Emil Adam 1904 and inscribed: Rock Sand - oil
on canvas - 89 x 115.5cm.
(Sotheby's)   **$25,872   £15,400**

ADAM

PATRICK WILLIAM ADAM, R.S.A. – Expectation –
signed and dated 1894; inscribed with title on a label on
the reverse – oil on canvas – 110 x 91.5cm.
(Sotheby's) **$20,207 £12,100**

PATRICK WILLIAM ADAM, R.S.A. – The drawing
room – signed and dated 1926 – oil on canvas – 114 x
68.5cm.
(Sotheby's) **$16,533 £9,900**

PATRICK WILLIAM ADAM, R.S.A. – The Great
Entrance, Palazzo Pitti, Florence – signed – oil on canvas –
77.5 x 57cm.
(Sotheby's) **$5,511 £3,300**

PATRICK WILLIAM ADAM, R.S.A. (1854-1929) –
The Morning Room – signed and dated 1916 – and
inscribed on the artist's label verso – oil on canvas –
76.2 x 94cm.
(Christie's) **$127,512 £75,900**

EDMUND ADLER – Feeding time – signed – oil on canvas – 56 x 77cm.
(Sotheby's) **$5,984 £3,520**

ALEXANDER ADRIAENSSEN (1587-Antwerp-1661) - A still life with artichokes in a silver gilt wine cistern beside a flagon, wine glasses and other silver objects - signed and dated Alex Adriaenssen F. 1647 - on canvas - 61.6 x 82.2cm.
(Phillips) **$57,800 £34,000**

EILEEN AGAR (b. 1903) - Lewis Carroll with Alice - signed lower right Agar - oil on canvas 23¼ x 35½in. Painted between 1960-62.
(Christie's) **$14,960 £8,800**

Circle of JACQUES LAURENT AGASSE (Geneva 1767 - London 1849) – A boy wearing a hat – pencil, charcoal and coloured chalks – 30.5 x 25.4cm.
(Lawrence) **$1,714 £1,045**

AIKMAN

CECIL CHARLES WINDSOR ALDIN (1870-1935) –
A Groom leading a Suffolk Punch – signed – watercolour
heightened with white over traces of pencil – 25.5 x 43cm.
(Phillips) **$1,467 £900**

CECIL CHARLES WINDSOR ALDIN - An Earnest
Entreat - signed twice and dated 1900 and '95 -
watercolour heightened with white - unframed -
36.5 x 53cm.
(Sotheby's) **$1,496 £880**

WILLIAM AIKMAN (1682-1731) – Portrait of William
Kent (1685-1748) – full length, standing, wearing a grey
waistcoat with an olive green surcoat and holding a palette
and brushes – oil on canvas – 197 x 104cm.
(Sotheby's) **$101,640 £60,500**

JOS ALBERT – A still life with apples and a pear on a
partly draped table – signed and dated lower right Jos
Albert 1917 – 54 x 67cm.
(Christie's) **$9,079 £5,710**

PIERRE ALECHINSKY – Goedendag – signed lower
left Alechinsky – and signed again and dated 1978 and
inscribed with title on the reverse – acrylics on paper laid
down on canvas – 66 x 52cm.
(Christie's) **$31,274 £19,669**

EDWIN ALEXANDER, A.R.S.A., R.A. (1870-1926) –
Seagulls on an Estuary – signed and dated lower left E
Alexander 1906 – watercolour and bodycolour on linen –
14 x 17in.
(Christie's) **$5,214 £3,300**

LOUIS HECTOR F. ALLEMAND (1840) – 'Old French
Town' - possibly Lyon – oil – signed and dated – label on
reverse – 19 x 19in.
(Graves Son & Pilcher) **$3,240 £2,000**

ARCHIBALD RUSSELL WATSON ALLAN, R.S.A. –
Feeding Sheep – signed – oil on canvas – 55 x 78cm.
(Sotheby's) **$2,388 £1,430**

HARRY EPWORTH ALLEN – The Timber Dump –
signed – tempera on board – 51 x 61cm.
(Phillips) **$38,870 £23,000**

SIR WILLIAM ALLAN, R.A., P.R.S.A. (1782-1850) –
An incident in the life of Napoleon – signed l.c. : William
Allan/pinx. 1848, and indistinctly inscribed on fragments
of old labels attached to the reverse – oil on canvas – 91 x
142cm.
(Sotheby's) **$32,395 £20,900**

HARRY EPWORTH ALLEN, R.B.A. (1894-1958) –
Landscape near Clifden, Connemara – signed lower left H
E Allen – oil on board – 18$^1/2$ x 23$^1/2$in.
(Christie's) **$15,642 £9,900**

ALLEN

THOMAS ALLEN (American, 1849-1924) – "A Dish of Lemons" – initialed – pastel on paper – 17¼ x 26½ in.
(Skinner) **$7,000 £4,192**

HELEN ALLINGHAM (1848-1926) – A Cottage Door – signed and inscribed as title on the reverse of the mount – pencil and watercolour heightened with white and touches of gum arabic – 17¼ x 14⅜ in.
(Christie's) **$55,110 £33,000**

HELEN ALLINGHAM, R.W.S. (Burton on Trent 1848 - Witley 1926) – 'Wash Day' – signed lower right: H. Allingham – watercolour – 24.2 x 19.1cm.
(Lawrence) **$5,412 £3,300**

HELEN ALLINGHAM, R.W.S. – Over the garden wall – signed – watercolour heightened with gum arabic and scratching out – 48 x 38cm.
(Sotheby's) **$59,840 £35,200**

HELEN ALLINGHAM – A child with her doll by a cottage gate – signed – watercolour – 24 x 19cm.
(Sotheby's) **$18,326 £10,780**

DENIS VAN ALSLOOT (circa 1599-Brussels 1628) –
The Baptism of Christ – on panel – 52.5 x 67.2cm.
(Phillips)   **$13,600   £8,000**

ALTMAN – Pastoral scenes, with figures, sheep and
cattle – gouache – a pair – both signed and dated 1791 –
each 19 x 25$^{1}/_{2}$in.
(Greenslades)   **$5,868   £3,600**

FRIEDRICH VON AMERLING – A young girl with her
prayer book – signed – oil on canvas – 96 x 74cm. –
Painted circa 1838-40
(Sotheby's)   **$13,244   £7,700**

LUIGI AMATO – At grandfather's – signed l.r. – oil on
canvas – 93 x 148cm.
(Sotheby's)   **$3,406   £1,980**

JACOPO AMIGONI (Venice 1675-1752 Madrid) – The
vision of Saint Theresa – on canvas – 102 x 86.5cm.
(Phillips)   **$13,600   £8,000**

ANDERSON

VICTOR COLEMAN ANDERSON (American, 1882-1937) – Keeping the Little Ones Dry/A Young Girl with Hen and Chicks – signed "Victor C. Anderson", l.r. - oil on board – 20 x 16in.
(Skinner) **$4,000 £2,453**

WILLIAM ANDERSON (1757-1837) – Frigates lying at anchor in a calm, with an Admiral of the Red beyond – signed l.l. :W.A. 1792 – oil on canvas – 34 x 47cm.
(Sotheby's) **$21,312 £13,750**

ANDERS ANDERSEN-LUNDBY – Cattle watering in an extensive landscape – signed – oil on canvas – 58.5 x 92cm.
(Sotheby's) **$4,114 £2,420**

ALEX DE ANDREIS – A guest at dinner – signed l.r. – oil on canvas – 64 x 80cm.
(Sotheby's) **$8,514 £4,950**

ALEX DE ANDREIS (late 19th Century) – A cavalier smoking a pipe – signed – 81 x 65.5cm.
(Christie's) **$1,771 £1,100**

FREDERICO ANDREOTTI – A good wine – signed – oil on canvas – 63.5 x 47.5cm.
(Sotheby's) **$17,765 £10,450**

FEDERICO ANDREOTTI (1847 - 1930) - The head of an Italian peasant woman - signed - 26.7 x 21.6cm. *(Christie's)* **$1,534 £990**

RICHARD ANSDELL (English, 1815-1885) – Feeding the Lamb – signed and dated 1852 – unframed – 66 x 100.3cm. *(Bonhams)* **$5,270 £3,400**

FILIPPO ANGELI, called FILIPPO NAPOLETANO (Naples circa 1590-1629 Rome) – Figures before a stream, a farmhouse beyond – on copper – 26 x 34.5cm. *(Phillips)* **$7,140 £4,200**

RICHARD ANSDELL, R.A. (1815-1885) – Mr. Thomas Clifton's Grey Hunter 'Gypsy' and dog 'Bowler' in a stable – signed l.r. : R.A. 1849 and inscribed on a label on the reverse – oil on canvas – 56 x 76.5cm. *(Sotheby's)* **$49,445 £31,900**

ANGLO-IRISH SCHOOL, 1703 – Portrait of Sir John Meade, bt. (1642-1707), with his daughter and his wife Elizabeth – emblazoned with coat of arms and dated: 1703 – oil on canvas – unframed – 123 x 150.5cm. *(Sotheby's)* **$16,434 £9,900**

RICHARD ANSDELL, R.A. – Pointers disturbing a brace of grouse – signed and dated 1884; indistinctly signed on a label on the stretcher – oil on canvas – 69 x 117cm. *(Sotheby's)* **$12,859 £7,700**

RICHARD ANSDELL, R.A. (1815-1885) – 'Retribution' – signed and dated 1876 – oil on canvas – 122 x 194cm. *(Phillips)* **$9,780 £6,000**

APPERLEY

GEORGE OWEN WYNNE APPERLEY (1884-1960) – The Death of Procris – signed and dated 1915 – watercolour and bodycolour – 77.5 x 133.3cm.
(Christie's)   **$93,775**   **£60,500**

KAREN APPEL – A Cat – signed and dated lower right C K Appel 51 – coloured crayons, watercolour and bodycolour on paper – 46.5 x 62.5cm.
(Christie's)   **$45,398**   **£28,552**

KAREN APPEL – Animal – signed and dated lower left Ck Appel 1950 – pencil, coloured crayons, watercolour and bodycolour on paper – 47 x 61cm.
(Christie's)   **$20,177**   **£12,690**

JAMES ARCHER – Taking the veil – signed with monogram and dated 1864 – 102 x 73cm.
(Christie's)   **$1,745**   **£1,045**

EDWARD ARDIZZONE, R.A. (1900-1978) – Bathers, Cap Ferrat No. 11 – signed with initials lower right EA – inscribed on the reverse – watercolour, pencil, pen and black ink – 8³/₄ x 10in.
(Christie's)   **$7,821**   **£4,950**

JUAN DE ARELLANO – A Still Life of Tulips, Roses, Peonies, Narcissi and other Flowers in a Basket on a stone Ledge – oil on canvas – 57.8 x 69.2cm.
(Bonhams)   **$32,200   £20,000**

GEORGE ARMFIELD – A terrier at a rabbit hole – signed – oil on board – signed and inscribed on the verso 'On the wall - Painted for my dear young friend Ida Rice. April 29 1877' – 20.5 x 25.5cm.
(Woolley & Wallis)   **$1,632   £960**

GEORGE ARMFIELD (fl. 1808-1893) – Spaniels flushing duck – signed and dated 1847 – 43.2 x 53.8cm.
(Christie's)   **$13,090   £7,700**

SEBASTIAN GESSA Y ARIAS (b. 1840) – Still life of a crayfish, glass, apple and cherries – indistinctly signed and dated 1865 (?) – on panel – 25.4 x 16.5cm.
(Christie's)   **$3,239   £2,090**

ATTRIBUTED TO GEORGE ARMFIELD – In the dog house – bears signature and date 1839 – oil on canvas – unframed – 81 x 110cm.
(Sotheby's)   **$4,225   £2,530**

ARMFIELD

GEORGE ARMFIELD (c. 1808-1893) – A Norfolk Terrier – signed with monogram – on panel – 25.4 x 20.3cm.
(Christie's) **$6,545 £3,850**

MAXWELL ARMFIELD – Madison Square Park – signed with monogrammed initials MA and inscribed NY, u.r. – oil on canvas – 86.2 x 76.3cm.
(Christie's) **$17,600 £11,000**

GEORGE ARMFIELD (c. 1808-1893) – A black and tan Cavalier King Charles Spaniel and a terrier in a Landscape – signed – 51.5 x 61cm.
(Christie's) **$14,212 £8,360**

G. ARMOUR (late 19th Century) – A token of love –
signed – unframed – 58.4 x 77.5cm.
(Christie's)   **$2,046**   **£1,320**

JOHN ARMSTRONG, A.R.A. (1893 - 1973) - Head of
a man - oil on canvas, laid down - initialled and dated
'41 - 9 x 6¼in.
(David Lay)   **$6,118**   **£3,800**

JOHN ARMSTRONG, A.R.A. – The Clown – signed
with initials and dated '59 – oil on hardboard – 23 x 13cm.
(Phillips)   **$2,112**   **£1,250**

ALWIN ARNEGGER (1883 - 1916) - An Alpine Mill
- board - signed - 41.8 x 52.8cm.
(Bonhams)   **$930**   **£600**

ARTHUR

REGINALD ARTHUR (fl. 1881-1896) – Rebecca –
signed and dated 1892 – 102 x 52cm.
(Christie's)   **$27,280   £17,600**

DAVID ADOLF ARTZ – Fishing for tiddlers – signed –
oil on canvas – 45 x 29.5cm.
(Sotheby's)   **$9,724   £5,720**

ALBERT ARTIQUE (late 19th Century) – Spring –
signed – 102 x 133cm.
(Christie's)   **$15,053   £9,350**

IURII PAVLOVICH ASNNENKOV (1889-1974) –
Portrait of Aleksandr Nikolaevich Tikhonov – signed in
Cyrillic and dated Iu. Annenkov 1922 – oil, collage, glass,
bell-push and 'enduit' on canvas – 67 x 58cm. –
Painted in 1922
(Christie's)   **$177,100   £110,000**

JOHN ATKINSON – A Horse Fair – signed – 36.5 x 47.5cm.
(Anderson & Garland) **$5,868 £3,600**

ALEXANDER AUSTIN – The card players – signed – 29.2 x 44.4cm.
(Christie's) **$861 £528**

GEORGE COPELAND AULT – The Kitchen Door – signed G. C. Ault and dated 29, l.r. – signed George C. Ault – dated 1929 and inscribed with title on the reverse – pencil on tan paper – 44 x 25.3cm.
(Christie's) **$1,980 £1,237**

ROBERT SARGENT AUSTIN, R.A. (1895-1973) – A Bedroom Interior – signed lower left Austin S. 36 – watercolour – 17³/₄ x 14in.
(Christie's) **$1,825 £1,155**

SAMUEL AUSTIN – Canal scene in Ghent – watercolour over pencil heightened with bodycolour with scratching out – 23 x 31cm.
(Sotheby's) **$2,525 £1,485**

AUTAL

BERKES AUTAL – "A Cold Winters Day, Paris" – signed – oil on canvas – 29³/₄ x 39¹/₂ in.
(Biddle & Webb)   **$7,950   £5,000**

LOUIS BAADER – The dogs' haircut – signed – oil on canvas – 37 x 45cm.
(Sotheby's)   **$3,784   £2,200**

AUGUSTE BACHELIN (1830 - 1890) - La Lecture au Jardin - signed and dated Bachelin 1873 - 130 x 82cm.
(Sotheby's)   **$14,696 £8,645**

MILTON AVERY – Seated Woman – signed Milton Avery and dated 1963, l.l. – gouache on paper – 76.2 x 56.5cm.
(Christie's)   **$17,600   £11,000**

THOMAS BRABAZON AYLMERR (1806-1856) – Shore scene with fisherfolk – signed – watercolour – 33.1 x 51.4cm.
(Lawrence)   **$1,960   £1,210**

FRANCOIS BACKVIS (mid 19th Century) – A still life with raspberries and roses in a vase – signed – on panel – 36 x 27cm.
(Christie's)   **$5,313   £3,300**

BAIL

JOHN HENRY FREDERICK BACON (1868-1914) – Portrait of a lady, seated on a chair, three-quarter length – signed and dated 83 – 142 x 112cm.
(Christie's) **$13,642 £8,580**

KATHERINE STANHOPE BADCOCK (Exh. 1889-90) – 'Carting Mangel' – signed and inscribed on label on reverse – oil on board – 12 x 16cm.
(Phillips) **$424 £260**

S.F.M. BADGER (American, 19th Century) – Catboat Under Way – signed and dated – oil on canvas – 22 x 36in.
(Skinner) **$12,000 £7,186**

STANLEY ROY BADMIN (1906-1989) – River Hill, Sevenoaks – signed and inscribed lower right S R Badmin River Hill, Sevenoaks – watercolour, bodycolour, pen and black ink – 14 x 16¼in.
(Christie's) **$4,171 £2,640**

DONALD BAIN – Last supper – signed – inscribed with title and dated 1944 on the reverse – oil on canvas – 69 x 71cm.
(Sotheby's) **$3,674 £2,200**

JOSEPH BAIL – Polishing the copper – signed – oil on canvas – unframed – 73 x 60cm.
(Sotheby's) **$9,460 £5,500**

BAILEY

PETER BAILEY (fl. late 19th Century) – Grouse –
signed and dated'98 – 40.5 x 61cm.
(Phillips) **$1,548 £950**

CHARLES THOMAS BALE (fl. 1866-1875) – Grapes, a
bird's nest and a jug; Grapes, oranges and a flagon – both
signed – 36 x 46cm.
(Christie's) **$3,498 £2,200**

CHARLES THOMAS BALE (fl. 1868-1875) –Still Life
of Pineapple, Melon, Grapes and other Fruit on a table –
signed – oil on canvas –57 x 75.5cm.
(Phillips) **$3,423 £2,100**

CHARLES THOMAS BALE – Still life of fruit – signed
and dated 1866 – oil on board – 30.5 x 41cm.
(Sotheby's) **$3,406 £2,090**

THOMAS C. BALE – A Mother and Child with Figures
driving Cattle across a Ford – signed with monogram and
dated 1866 – 25.4 x 20.3cm.
(Bonhams) **$852 £550**

ANTONIO BALESTRA, Attributed to (1666-Verona-
1740) – Constantine and soldiers standing before a statue
in a city – on canvas – 245 x 152.5cm.
(Phillips) **$12,225 £7,500**

ANTONIO BALESTRA (1666-Verona-1740) – Saint George and the dragon – on canvas – 64 x 44.5cm.
(Phillips) **$3,260 £2,000**

GIACOMO BALLA (1871-1958) – Grande Fiore Futurista – signed lower centre Futur balla – gouache on board – 29 x 36cm.
(Christie's) **$34,100 £22,000**

HURST BALMFORD – By The Fireside – on board – signed – inscribed on a label on the reverse – 21 x 17in.
(Bearne's) **$1,318 £780**

WILFRED WILLIAMS BALL – A mill in a wooded river landscape – signed with monogram – and dated '01 – watercolour over traces of pencil – unframed – 35.5 x 55.25cm.
(Woolley & Wallis) **$425 £250**

BESSIE BAMBER – Two seated cats – on milk glass – signed with initials and dated '08 – 5¹/₂ x 10¹/₂in.
(Bearne's) **$1,691 £950**

BARBARINI

EMIL BARBARINI – A village scene – signed – oil on canvas – 67 x 104cm.
(Sotheby's)   **$4,162**   **£2,420**

GIOVANNI BARBARO – Italian lakeside scene with figures – signed – watercolour – 29 x 19in.
(Biddle & Webb)   **$795**   **£500**

JEAN BARBAULT – Viarmes 1718-1762 Rome – Garde Suisse – oil on panel – 24 x 17cm.
(Sotheby's)   **$69,264**   **£44,400**

EDGAR BARCLAY (fl. 1868-1913) – Returning home, Stonehenge, Wiltshire – signed with monogram and dated 1891 – on panel – 40.5 x 76cm.
(Christie's) **$6,122 £3,850**

JOHN BARKER (1811-1886) – Keeping Guard – signed – 127 x 101.6cm.
(Christie's) **$8,415 £4,950**

THOMAS BARDWELL (1704-1767) – Portrait of a lady – three quarter length, standing, wearing Van Dyck costume and holding a feather – oil on canvas – 125 x 100cm.
(Sotheby's) **$9,889 £6,380**

GEORGE BARKER (19th Century) – Homeward bound – signed – watercolour – 26.5 x 41.5cm.
(Phillips) **$652 £400**

JOHN BARKER – Waiting for master – signed – oil on canvas – 76 x 63.5cm.
(Sotheby's) **$8,266 £4,950**

BARKER

WRIGHT BARKER – Calves in an orchard – signed – oil on canvas – 128 x 96cm.
(Sotheby's) **$4,776 £2,860**

MYRON BARLOW – New Shoes – signed Barlow, l.r. – oil on canvas – 75.5 x 75.5cm.
(Christie's) **$8,800 £5,500**

WRIGHT BARKER – Gossips – signed – oil on canvas – 76 x 96.5cm.
(Sotheby's) **$5,379 £3,300**

FRANCIS BARLOW (1626-1702) – A Spanish Pointer in a wooded landscape – oil on canvas – 102 x 133cm.
(Sotheby's) **$147,840 £88,000**

MARY B. BARNARD – The crofters daughters – signed – oil on canvas – 102 x 66cm.
(Sotheby's) **$10,103 £6,050**

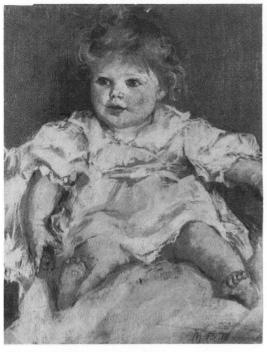

MARY B. BARNARD (1870-1946) – One Year Old –
signed and dated 1902 – pastel on linen – 61 x 50.8cm.
(Christie's) **$1,663 £990**

FELIX BARRIAS (1822-1907) – A beauty – signed and
dated Paris 87 – on panel – 22 x 15.8cm.
(Christie's) **$3,751 £2,420**

FREDERICK BARRY – Fisher children playing with a
crab – signed and dated 1856 – 30 x 48cm.
(Anderson & Garland) **$1,292 £760**

GEORGE HAMILTON BARRABLE – In a
conservatory – signed – oil on canvas – 107 x 61cm.
(Sotheby's) **$9,861 £6,050**

FREDERIC-AUGUSTE BARTHOLDI – The Statue of
Liberty – signed FA Bartholdi with initials conjoined, l.r. –
inscribed a*** cordial, l.l. – watercolour and pencil on
paper laid down on board – 13.2 x 21cm.
(Christie's) **$12,100 £7,562**

BARTHOLOMEW

VALENTINE BARTHOLOMEW – Fruit – bears signature and title on a label on the backboard – watercolour – 34 x 44.5cm.
(Sotheby's) **$2,057 £1,210**

H. FRANCIS BATE (1853-1950) – Stanpit Marsh, Hampshire – signed lower left Francis Bate – oil on board – 10 x 13in.
(Christie's) **$3,302 £2,090**

PIETRO BARUCCI – An obstinate donkey – signed and inscribed Roma l.r – oil on canvas laid down on board – 59 x 92cm.
(Sotheby's) **$13,244 £7,700**

SAMUEL BATEMAN – A passing storm, near Shiplake on the Thames – signed and dated 1894; signed – inscribed with title and dated 1894 on the reverse – oil on canvas – 61 x 108cm.
(Sotheby's) **$2,599 £1,59**

JACOPO BASSANO (1510/15-1592), Circle of – Portrait of a boy, bust length, wearing a white ruff – oil on canvas – 39 x 29cm.
(Phillips) **$3,703 £2,300**

DAVID BATES (British 1841-1921) – "Nr Bardon Tower, Wharfdale" – signed and dated 1904 and inscribed verso – watercolour heightened with bodycolour and scratching out – 35.5 x 51.5cm.
(Phillips) **$1,141 £700**

DAVID BATES – At Malvern Wells – watercolour –
signed and dated 1904 – 13³/₄ x 20¹/₄in.
(Bearne's)   **$3,560   £2,000**

DAVID BATES – Girl in a meadow – signed and dated
1890; with an oil sketch on the verso – oil on canvas – 61 x
91.5cm.
(Sotheby's)   **$14,344   £8,800**

BAUHAUS WORKSHOPS - Der Sieg der Farbe: P.
Mondriaan, Composition No. 1 - lithogram printed in
colours - 1924 - on stiff cream wove paper - signed
with initials PM in pen and black ink at the lower left
inside the image - extremely rare - printed Weimar.
1924 - published by the Photographische Gesellschaft,
Berlin - L.481 x 301mm., S.496 x 312mm.
(Christie's)   **$20,177   £12,690**

LUBIN BAUGIN (Pithiviers circa 1610-1663 Paris) –
Saint Jerome, seated reading in a cave – signed – on
copper – 48.5 x 34.7cm.
(Phillips)   **$13,600   £8,000**

CHARLES BAXTER – A billet doux – signed – oil on
canvas – 35.5 x 30.5cm.
(Sotheby's)   **$3,945   £2,420**

BAXTER

DAVID A. BAXTER – A Haymaking Scene –
watercolour – signed – 23.5 x 29.2cm.
(Bonhams) $520   £340

GIFFORD BEAL – Summer Outing – signed Gifford
Beal, l.r. – oil on canvas – 62 x 73cm.
(Christie's) $72,600   £45,375

CHARLES BAXTER, R.B.A. (1809 - 1879) - Reading
on the terrace - oil on canvas - 61 x 50.8cm.
(Christie's) $2,772   £1,650

GIFFORD BEAL – A street in Provincetown - signed
Gifford Beal and dated 20, l.r. - oil on canvas - 24 x
30in.
(Christie's) $28,600   £17,546

GIFFORD BEAL (1879-1956) – Figures on the beach – oil on board – 20.3 x 51.4cm. – Executed circa 1921-
23
(Sotheby's) $22,000   £14,013

REYNOLDS BEAL, ANA (1867-1951) – Montauk Point – etching accented with charcoal – 7³/₄ x 12¹³/₁₆in. (image) – ed. 28. – signed Reynolds Beal and dated 1941 lower right – titled lower left – unframed
(Bruce D. Collins)   **$660   £393**

GEORGE BEECHEY (fl. 1817-1832), Circle of – Portrait of a lady, standing three-quarter length, in a grey dress with a pink shawl and a grey bonnet – 147.3 x 116.8cm.
(Christie's)   **$2,510   £1,540**

ARTHUR EDWAINE BEAUMONT (American, 1879-1956) – Winter Dry Dock – signed "A. Beaumont" – scene with fishing boats (in oil) on the reverse – oil on board – 10³/₈ x 13⁷/₈in.
(Skinner)   **$1,200   £750**

ARTHUR EDWAINE BEAUMONT (American, 1879-1956) – Harbour View with Moored Boats – signed "Arthur Beaumont" l.r. – oil on canvas – 12 x 16in.
(Skinner)   **$1,400   £875**

ADRIAEN CORNELISZ BEELDEMAKER, Manner of – A young Man seated in a Landscape with two Greyhounds and a Spaniel, and two Dead Hares – oil on panel – 61 x 54cm.
(Bonhams)   **$1,369   £850**

OSIAS BEERT LE JEUNE, CIRCLE OF – Anvers 1622-1678 – Panier de Fleurs et Oiseaux sur un Entablement – oil on panel – 48.5 x 64cm.
(Sotheby's) **$36,281 £23,257**

JAN VAN BELCAMP (fl. 1625-1651) – Portrait of a lady – half length, wearing a white dress with a blue bodice and pink ribbons and pearls – oil on canvas – 74 x 63cm.
(Sotheby's) **$10,230 £6,600**

FRITZ BEINKE (1842-1907) – The naughty school boys – signed and inscribed – 65 x 54cm.
(Christie's) **$6,375 £3,960**

PETER BELA-MAYER (born 1888) – Covered bridge near Manchester, Vermont – oil on canvasboard – 25 x 30in. – signed Peter Bela-Mayer lower left
(Bruce D. Collins) **$5,225 £3,110**

ADOLFO BELIMBAU (b. 1845) – Portrait of a lady in a brown dress – on board – 17.8 x 13.8cm.
(Christie's) **$1,023 £660**

STUART HENRY BELL – 'Early Morning Whitburn' –
signed and dated 1887 – 49 x 75cm.
(Anderson & Garland) $1,156 £680

VANESSA BELL – The Garden at Charleston – signed –
watercolour – 63 x 47.5cm.
(Phillips) $6,400 £4,000

ALEXIS-SIMON BELLE (1674-Paris-1734) – Portrait
of Felix Calvert (1693-1755), of Albany Hall, half length,
in a long wig, a jabot and a burgundy-coloured robe – on
canvas – oval – 81.3 x 65.5cm.
(Phillips) $9,860 £5,800

VANESSA BELL – Still Life of Fruit on a Table Top –
signed – oil on canvas - 46 x 51cm.
(Phillips) $11,830 £7,000

GAETANO BELLEI (Italian, 19th Century) – Best
Friends – signed – 22.8 x 33cm.
(Bonhams) $2,325 £1,500

BELLIS

ANTONIO DE BELLIS, Attributed to (Active mid-17th Century) – Saint Cecilia – oil on canvas – 98.5 x 73cm.
(Phillips) **$14,580 £9,000**

GEORGE BELLOWS (1882-1925) – Portrait of Elizabeth Alexander – signed Geo. Bellows, l.r.; also titled Portrait of Elizabeth Alexander – oil on canvas – 135.3 x 109.2cm.
(Sotheby's) **$110,000 £70,064**

GEORGE BELLOWS (1882-1925) – Black House – inscribed Geo. Bellows/E.S.B. by Emma S. Bellows, the artist's wife, l.r. – oil on panel – 41.9 x 61cm. – Painted in 1924
(Sotheby's) **$44,000 £28,025**

GEORGE BELLOWS (1882-1925) – At the Dog Show – signed Geo. Bellows, l.r. – black crayon, India ink and collage on paper – 48.9 x 47.0cm.
(Sotheby's) **$22,000 £14,013**

ANTONIO BELLUCCI (1654-1726) – Belisarius – oil on canvas – 163.5 x 134cm.
(Phillips) **$23,490 £14,500**

FRANK MOSS BENNETT – The Falconer – signed and dated 1913 – oil on canvas – 66 x 54cm.
(Sotheby's) **$9,185** **£5,500**

GERRIT BENNER – A horse in a landscape – signed with initials lower right Bnr – gouache on paper – 76.8 x 55.5cm.
(Christie's) **$7,061** **£4,441**

FRANK MOSS BENNETT – His eminence's vintage – signed and dated 1935 – oil on canvas – 40.5 x 51cm.
(Sotheby's) **$16,137** **£9,900**

BENSON

AMBROSIUS BENSON, Follower of – The Mary
Magdalen – oil on canvas – 77 x 65cm.
(Phillips)   **$3,586   £2,200**

FRANK W. BENSON (1862-1951) - Geese in flight –
signed F. W. Benson and dated '23, l.l. – watercolour and
pencil on paper – 50.0 x 35.0cm.
(Sotheby's)   **$17,600   £11,210**

FRANK W. BENSON (1862-1951) – Portrait of a woman
– signed F. W. Benson and dated '99, u.l. – 66.0 x 55.8cm.
(Sotheby's)   **$137,500   £87,580**

JAN VAN DER BENT (1650-Amsterdam 1690) – A
herdsman and companion at a ford watering their livestock
– signed and dated 1657 – on canvas – 82 x 68.8cm.
(Phillips)   **$8,150   £5,000**

THOMAS HART BENTON (1889-1975) – Haystack –
signed Benton, l.r.; also inscribed Haystack and dated 1939
– tempera with oil glaze on linen mounted on panel –
61.0 x 76.2cm. – Painted in 1939
(Sotheby's)   **$341,000   £217,197**

THOMAS HART BENTON – Cotton Pickers – signed
Benton and dated 44, l.r. – oil and pencil on paper laid
down on board – 21 x 26cm.
(Christie's)   **$55,000   £34,375**

THOMAS HART BENTON (1889-1975) – Windmill
and water tank – signed Benton and dated '53, l.r.; also
inscribed Water Tank, oil/Thom. H. Benton on the backing
– oil on canvasboard – 50.8 x 69.9cm.
(Sotheby's)   **$154,000   £98,089**

BENTON

THOMAS HART BENTON (1889-1975) – Study for the
Lord is My Shepherd – oil on canvas – 21.0 x 16.5cm.
(Sotheby's) **$22,000 £14,013**

FRITS VAN DEN BERGHE (1883-1939) – Nature
morte avec Fleurs et Bol—Stilleven met Bloemen en Kop
– signed lower right F V Berghe – oil on canvas –
61 x 51cm. – Painted circa 1914
(Christie's) **$21,120 £13,200**

ROBERT BERENY – Noi porte – oil on canvas – signed
– 72 x 54cm.
(Mugyujtok Galeriaja Kft) **$779 £472**

**ETIENNE PROSPER BERNE-BELLECOUR (French,
1838-1910)** – Cavalryman Mending His Vest – signed and
dated 1896 – oil on panel – 14½ x 10in.
(Skinner) **$3,000 £1,796**

THERESA BERNSTEIN (American, b. 1895) – Sheep Meadow, Central Park, New York – partial signature – oil on canvas – 20^1/$_8$ x 25in.
(Skinner) **$3,500 £2,096**

EDWARD BIEDERMANN – 300th Anniversary Celebration of the Founding of Jamestown – signed EBiedermann with initials conjoined, l.r. – gouache, watercolour and pencil on tan paper laid down on board – 46.5 c 74cm.
(Christie's) **$6,600 £4,125**

LUCIEN BESSONNAT – Dappled light – signed and dated 1925 – oil on canvas – 80 x 99cm.
(Sotheby's) **$5,676 £3,300**

ALBERT BIERSTADT (1830-1902) – The ambush – signed with the artist's monogrammed signature ABierstadt, l.l. – oil on canvas – 76.2 x 128.3cm. – Painted circa 1870-75
(Sotheby's) **$528,000 £336,306**

VICTOR VAN BEYLEN – Pensive moments – signed – oil on canvas – 100 x 100cm.
(Sotheby's) **$3,740 £2,200**

ALBERT BIERSTADT (1830-1902) – Bavarian landscape – oil on canvas – 55.9 x 66cm.
(Sotheby's) **$24,200 £15,414**

BIERSTADT

ALBERT BIERSTADT (1830-1902) – Merced River, California – signed with the artist's monogrammed signature ABierstadt, l.r. – oil on paper mounted on canvas – 35.5 x 48.3cm.
(Sotheby's) **$45,100 £28,726**

REUBEN WARD BINKS (1860 - c. 1945) – Radiator of Solway, a Springer Spaniel – signed – inscribed and dated 1927 – watercolour and bodycolour – 24.7 x 33.1cm.
(Christie's) **$1,870 £1,100**

GEORGE CALEB BINGHAM (1811-1879) – Portrait of Reverend John Glanville – oil on canvas – 76.2 x 64.2cm. – Painted circa 1845
(Sotheby's) **$11,000 £7,006**

SAMUEL JOHN LAMORNA BIRCH (1869-1955) – Newlyn School – "Looking down Ledyr from Pontypont Bridge - a rocky Welsh river – signed and dated 1913 – oil on board – 10³/₄ x 14¹/₂in.
(W. H. Lane & Son) **$2,550 £1,500**

REUBEN WARD BINKS (1860 - c. 1945) – Champion Ashdell Shangetta, a Pekingese – signed – inscribed and dated 1923 – pencil and watercolour – 31.7 x 42.6cm.
(Christie's) **$4,114 £2,420**

SAMUEL JOHN LAMORNA BIRCH, R.W.S. – Cattle Drinking – signed and dated'99 – oil on panel – 22.5 x 27cm.
(Phillips) **$3,200 £2,000**

SAMUEL JOHN LAMORNA BIRCH, R.A., R.W.S.,
R.W.A. (1869-1955) – "The Farmyard, Treen, Cornwall" –
oil on canvas – lined – signed – inscribed and signed to
reverse – 12½ x 15½ in.
(David Lay)   **$3,220 £2,000**

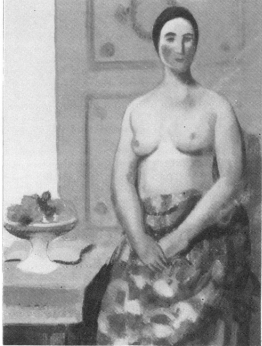

ROGER BISSIERE – 'Naked to the waist' – oil on canvas
– signed – 55 x 38cm.
(Jean-Claude Anaf)   **$17,333 £11,111**

SAMUEL JOHN LAMORNA BIRCH, R.A., R.W.S. –
'Seascape Sketch' – watercolour – signed and dated 1947 –
5 x 6¼ in.
(Bearne's)   **$640 £360**

WILLIAM MINSHALL BIRCHALL – 'A Cape Horner
of the Eighties' – watercolour with touches of white –
signed – inscribed and dated 1926 – 25.3 x 36.2cm.
(Bonhams)   **$1,142 £680**

CHARLES-EMMANUEL BISET (Malines 1633-after
1686 Breda) – 'Danae' – signed with initials C.E.B. and
dated, 1671 – on panel – 44 x 63.5cm.
(Phillips)   **$74,980 £46,000**

EDOUARD BISSON (born 1856) – A nymph – signed
and dated 1901 – 55.5 x 38cm.
(Christie's)   **$7,084 £4,400**

BIVEL

FERNAND BIVEL – A sleeping nude – signed and dated
'12 – oil on canvas – 64 x 99cm.
(Sotheby's)   **$5,610   £3,300**

FERNAND BIVEL - Before the ball – signed – oil on
canvas – 138 x 123cm.
(Sotheby's)   **$3,406   £1,980**

GERRIT WILLEM VAN BLAADEREN – A view in a
village in France on a sunny day – signed lower left G.W.
van Blaaderen – 120 x 100cm.
(Christie's)   **$4,539   £2,855**

OLIVE PARKER BLACK (American, 1868-1948) –
Pond Before a Farm, Spring – signed – oil on canvas – 16
x 24in.
(Skinner)   **$2,100   £1,257**

CHARLES HENRY BLAIR (fl. 1880-1900) – The Black
Kitten – signed and dated 1895 – oil on canvas –
50.8 x 38.2cm.
(Christie's)   **$7,762   £4,620**

WILLIAM KAY BLACKLOCK (1872-circa 1930) -
On the River Bank. The Ouse, Huntingdonshire -
signed and dated 15 - and inscribed on the reverse -
pencil and watercolour - 24½ x 29½in.
(Christie's)   **$48,411   £29,700**

WILLIAM KAY BLACKLOCK – Woman with a
parasol – signed – watercolour heightened with bodycolour
– 25.5 x 21cm.
(Sotheby's)   **$2,618   £1,540**

CHARLES BLACKMAN (b. 1928) – Approaching
Storm – signed – 48 x 72cm.
(Christie's)   **$8,019   £4,950**

EDMUND BLAMPIED (1886-1966) – Portrait of H. M.
Queen Mary – signed – oil on board – 44 x 34cm.
(Phillips)   **$4,238   £2,600**

BLANCH

ARNOLD BLANCH (American, 1896-1968) –"Outside the City" – signed "Arnold Blanch" – oil on canvas – 22 x 36in.
(Skinner) **$2,200 £1,375**

JULIUS VON BLASS (1855-1922) – Pienzgauer horses – signed and dated 1910 – 58 x 80cm.
(Christie's) **$7,084 £4,400**

JACQUES-EMILE BLANCHE (French, 1861-1942) – Kippers – signed and dated '27 – 33 x 41.3cm.
(Bonhams) **$853 £550**

TINA BLAU (Austrian 1845-1916) – Spring in the Vienna woods – signed – oil on canvas – 88 x 103cm.
(Sotheby's) **$36,520 £22,000**

HERRI MET DE BLES (Bouvignes circa 1480-circa 1550) - The sacrifice of Isaac - signed - with owl device - on panel - 33.5 x 43.5cm.
(Phillips) **$51,000 £30,000**

EUGEN VON BLASS (1843-1932) – Small talk – signed – on panel – 81 x 56cm.
(Christie's) **$88,660 £57,200**

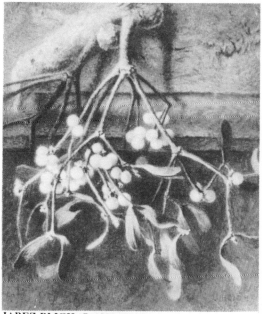

JABEZ BLIGH (fl. 1880-1891) – Mistletoe – signed twice – watercolour and bodycolour – 23.5 x 20cm.
(Phillips) **$1,548 £950**

THOMAS BLINKS – After a day's harvest – signed; signed and inscribed with title on the stretcher – oil on canvas – 40.5 x 51cm.
(Sotheby's) **$3,406 £2,090**

JAN FRANS VAN BLOEMEN, called ORIZZONTE (Antwerp 1662-1749 Rome) – An Italian wooded landscape, with travellers seated beside a path – on canvas – 34.2 x 43.5cm.
(Phillips) **$16,150 £9,500**

PIETER VAN BLOEMEN – Anvers 1657-1720 – Lecon D'Équitation – oil on canvas – 76 x 101cm.
(Sotheby's) **$90,703 £58,143**

ARNOLDUS BLOEMMERS (1792-1844) – Grape and other fruit with dahlias and game on a ledge – signed with monogram – 67.3 x 55.7cm.
(Christie's) **$8,525 £5,500**

ARTHUR MERRIC BLOOMFIELD (b. 1920) – Rosebud Landscape – signed and dated 1937 - on board – 24.7 x 27.3cm.
(Christie's) **$10,692 £6,600**

BLOOMFIELD

WILLIAM BOARDMAN – Hudson River Landscape –
signed Boardman, l.r. – oil on canvas – 84.5 x 123cm.
(Christie's) **$5,500 £3,437**

ARTHUR MERRIC BLOOMFIELD (b. 1920) –
Riverbank and Seagull – signed – on board –
30.5 x 20.3cm.
(Christie's) **$8,910 £5,500**

Attributed to PIETER DE BLOOT (1601/2-1658) –
Villagers dancing and revelling after a feast – oil on panel
– 24.8 x 41.3cm.
(Phillips) **$6,804 £4,200**

HENRY JOHN BODDINGTON (English, 1811-1865) –
A Country Lane – panel – signed and dated 1837 –
44.4 x 61cm.
(Bonhams) **$775 £500**

OSCAR FLORIANUS BLUEMNER – A Space Motive,
A New Jersey Valley – charcoal and graphite on paper laid
down on board – 77.5 x 104.2cm.
(Christie's) **$52,800 £33,000**

PIETER BOEL (Antwerp 1622-1674 Paris) – Dogs
resting beside dead game at the foot of a tree – on canvas –
94.5 x 122cm.
(Phillips) **$13,600 £8,000**

JACOB BOGDANI (Eperjes, Hungary-1724 London) –
Two wild muscovy ducks, a tufted domestic duck, a ruff
and other ducks by a pool – signed J. Bogdani – on canvas
– 72.5 x 124cm.
(Phillips) **$73,350 £45,000**

PAL BOHM (1839-1905) – A gypsy family – signed
and dated 1874 - on panel – 31.7 x39.3cm.
(Christie's) **$2,728 £1,760**

WILLIAM LOCKHART BOGLE – Prince Charles
Edward Stuart in the Cave of the Robbers of Glen
Moriston – signed and dated 1892 – oil on canvas – 132 x
188cm.
(Sotheby's) **$3,490 £2,090**

BOGGS

FRANK MYERS BOGGS – Pont St. Michel – signed – inscribed Paris and indistinctly dated; also titled Pont St. Michel and dated Paris 1922 on the stretcher – oil on canvas – 73.6 x 91.4cm.
(Sotheby's)   **$49,500 £31,132**

ATTRIBUTED TO JEAN-ALCIDE-HENRI BOICHARD (French, b. 1817) – The Fitting – signed – oil on panel – 21½ x 21½ in.
(Skinner)   **$2,800 £1,677**

PHILIP BOILEAU – A portrait of a young girl – signed and inscribed Paris – oil on canvas – 56 x 48cm.
(Sotheby's)   **$2,460 £1,430**

LOUIS-LEOPOLD BOILLY – La Bassée 1761-1845 Paris – Jeune Femme à la Guitare – oil on panel – 41.2 x 31.7cm.
(Sotheby's)   **$79,159 £50,743**

BOLOGNESE SCHOOL 17th C. – L'ange accoudé sur une Sépulture – oil on panel – 65 x 56cm.
(Sotheby's)   **$3,297 £2,114**

DAVID BOMBERG (1890-1957) – The Bathers, Tent Family – watercolour – 20¼ x 22in.
(Christie's)   **$6,778**   **£4,290**

GIUSEPPE BONITO, Attributed to – Portrait of a lady, bust length, wearing a red cape, believed to be Caterina Modella Romana, Baronessa Danmarca – oil on canvas – 48.2 x 36cm.
(Phillips)   **$3,703**   **£2,300**

DAVID BOMBERG (1890-1957) – Cuenca—Hueca Valley – signed and dated '34 – inscribed on the stretcher – oil on canvas – 77 x 66cm.
(Phillips)   **$45,640**   **£28,000**

ROSA BONHEUR – Sheep grazing – signed and dated '64 – oil on panel – 32 x 42cm.
(Sotheby's)   **$4,675**   **£2,750**

PIERRE BONNARD (1867-1947) – Jeune Fille au Corsage bleu – signed upper left Bonnard – oil on canvas – 48 x 35cm.
(Christie's)   **$290,691**   **£187,000**

BONNARD

PIERRE BONNARD – Jeune fille en bleu, A la rose – stamped with the signature – oil on canvas – 64 x 50cm. *(Sotheby's)* **$1,045,000 £657,233**

PIERRE BONNARD – Nu Rose, Tête Ombrée – stamped with signature – oil on canvas – 92 x 46cm. *(Sotheby's)* **$2,200,000 £1,383,648**

PIERRE BONNARD – Le Berger et le Chien (Ou le Ruisseau) – signed – oil on canvas – 117.5 x 70cm. *(Sotheby's)* **$1,540,000 £968,553**

ANNE BONNET (1908 - 1960) - Cap Sounion - signed lower left Anne Bonnet - gouache, pen and ink on paper - 48.3 x 59.1cm. - painted in 1958
(Christie's) **$11,440 £7,150**

CONSTANTINE BOONE (19th Century) – The
intercepted letter – on panel – 47 x 58.4cm.
(Christie's) **$2,557 £1,650**

ALFRED BORGE – Before the mirror – signed – oil on
canvas – 45 x 36cm.
(Sotheby's) **$6,433 £3,740**

**ARNOLD BOONEN, Circle of (1669-Dordrecht-
Amsterdam-1729)** - Three children releasing a
goldfinch standing by a ledge - traces of a signature
- on canvas - 39 x 33.5cm.
(Phillips) **$4,564 £2,800**

EDWARD BOREIN – The Meeting – signed Edward
Borein, l.r. – watercolour on paper laid down on board –
22.9 x 29.2cm.
(Christie's) **$11,000 £6,875**

ADOLPHE BORIE – Blue Feathered Hat – signed
Adolphe Borie, u.l. – oil on canvas – 50.8 x 40.7cm.
(Christie's) **$7,700 £4,812**

BORIONE

BERNARD LOUIS BORIONE – Tea for two – signed and inscribed Paris – oil on canvas – 63 x 52.5cm. *(Sotheby's)*   **$7,568   £4,400**

GIUSEPPE BORTIGNONI – Rival suitors – signed and dated Bologna 1907 – oil on canvas – 62.5 x 88.5cm. *(Sotheby's)*   **$7,480   £4,400**

CARLO BOSSOLI (Italian 1815-84) – A view of Nusretiye Mosque from the South, Constantinople – signed and dated 1846 – gouache – 44 x 58.5cm. *(Sotheby's)*   **$29,216   £17,600**

JOHANNES BORMAN (Active in The Hague-1658/59 Amsterdam) – A still life of fruit in a delft bowl, including peaches, oranges and grapes – bears monogram JDH F – on panel – 40.7 x 50.5cm. *(Phillips)*   **$44,200   £26,000**

ALFRED EDWARD BORTHWICK, R.S.A., P.R.S.W. – Princes Street, Edinburgh – signed – watercolour – 26 x 36cm. *(Sotheby's)*   **$2,755   £1,650**

JOHN BOSTOCK – The bouquet – watercolour over pencil – signed – 27$\frac{1}{4}$ x 19$\frac{1}{4}$in. *(Outhwaite & Litherland)*   **$1,458   £900**

GIUSEEPE BOTTANI (Cremona 1717 - 1784 Mantua) - The Angel appearing to Hagar - on canvas - 41.8 x 70.5cm.
(Phillips) $14,670   £9,000

GIUSEPPE BOTTANI 1717-1784 – Sainte-Catherine D'Alexandrie – oil on canvas – 62 x 52cm.
(Sotheby's) $4,946   £3,171

FRANCOIS BOUCHER, After – Cherubs – oil on canvas – 52.1 x 45.7cm.
(Bonhams) $6,118   £3,800

BOUDIN

EUGENE BOUDIN (1824-1898) – Bateaux dans la Baie, Douarnenez – signed – inscribed and dated lower right E Boudin Douarnenez—97 – oil on canvas – 55 x 90cm.
(Christie's) **$205,194 £132,000**

SAMUEL BOUGH, R.S.A. – Stirling Castle from the River Forth – signed and dated 1857 – oil on canvas – 49.5 x 70.5cm.
(Sotheby's) **$12,491 £7,480**

WILLIAM ADOLPHE BOUGUEREAU (French 1825-1905) - L'Amour au Repos - signed and dated 1891 - oil on canvas - 45 x 22.5cm.
(Sotheby's) **$27,390 £16,500**

GEORGE HENRY BOUGHTON – Falling Leaves – signed G. H. Boughton with initials conjoined, l.l. – oil on canvas – 60.6 x 40.6cm.
(Christie's) **$33,000 £20,625**

ETIENNE BOUHOT – The fire – signed and dated MDCCCXII – oil on canvas – 39.5 x 62cm.
(Sotheby's) **$4,675 £2,750**

**MICHEL BOUILLON (Ere near Tournai circa 1638-
after 1654)** – A still life with a vase of flowers on a table
next to a basket of vegetables, surrounded by an
assortment of fruit – on canvas – 95.8 x 141.5cm.
(Phillips) **$69,700 £41,000**

CYPRIEN BOULET – A sleeping nude – signed – oil on
canvas – 44.5 x 60cm.
(Sotheby's) **$2,270 £1,320**

**CHARLES EDOUARD BOUTIBONNE (French 1816-
97)** – Before the bath – signed and dated 1850 – oil on
canvas – 175 x 87cm.
(Sotheby's) **$43,824 £26,400**

**CORNELIS BOUTER also known as CAREL
VERSCHUUR** – Driving cattle along a country road –
signed C. Verschuur l.l – oil on canvas – 61 x 91cm.
(Sotheby's) **$7,568 £4,400**

**JACOB BOUTTATS, Attributed to (circa 1660-
Antwerp-circa 1700)** – The Garden of Eden – on canvas –
71.5 x 97cm.
(Phillips) **$20,400 £12,000**

BOUVARD

ANTOINE BOUVARD – On the Grand Canal, Venice –
signed – oil on canvas – 64 x 91cm.
(Sotheby's) **$14,025 £8,250**

ANTOINE BOUVARD (French, d. 1956) - Venice -
50.8 x 64.8cm.
(Bonhams) **$3,410 £2,200**

ANTOINE BOUVARD (died 1956) – Canale della
Giudecca con San Giorgio Maggiore – signed –
49.5 x 64.5cm.
(Christie's) **$8,500 £5,280**

ANTOINE BOUVARD – A Venetian canal – signed – oil
on canvas – 48 x 63cm.
(Sotheby's) **$7,190 £4,180**

**AUGUSTUS JULES BOUVIER, Attributed to (1827-
81)** - A mother and child comforting each other on
the foreshore before waves breaking on the cliffs -
monogrammed - watercolour - 8½ x 5in.
(W. H. Lane & Son) **$850 £500**

EDEN BOX (d. 1988) – The Deer Shelter – signed lower right E. Box – oil on canvas – 20 x 24in.
(Christie's) **$1,738 £1,100**

GUSTAVUS A. BOUVIER (exh. 1866-1884) – The Pagans worshipping the Golden Calf – watercolour heightened with gum arabic – 39.4cm. diameter.
(Christie's) **$932 £572**

GASTON BOUY (born 1866) - La robe jaune - signed and dated 1902 - charcoal and coloured chalks - 48 x 28cm.
(Christie's) **$3,945 £2,420**

JOHN R. BRABACH (1880-1981) – Village friends – signed John R. Grabach, l.l. – oil on canvas – 106.7 x 121.9cm.
(Sotheby's) **$28,600 £18,216**

JANE MARIA BOWKETT – Ironing lace – signed with monogram – oil on canvas – unframed – 61 x 48cm.
(Sotheby's) **$5,020 £3,080**

HERCULES BRABAZON BRABAZON (1821-1906) – A View of Venice across the Lagoon – signed with initials – watercolour and bodycolour over pencil – 14.5 x 21cm.
(Phillips) **$5,542 £3,400**

BRANGWYN

**SIR FRANK BRANGWYN, R.A., R.W.S., H.R.S.A.
(1867-1956)** – The Barbary Pirates – signed with initials –
charcoal and coloured chalks on buff-coloured paper –
43 x 81cm.
(Phillips) $2,608 £1,600

**SIR FRANK BRANGWYN, R.A., R.W.A.,H.R.S.A.
(1867 - 1956)** - The house on the corner - signed with
initials - oil on canvas laid down on panel - 44.5 x
55.2cm.
(Phillips) $11,410 £7,000

**SIDNEY LAWRENCE BRACKETT (American, 19th/
20th Century)** – A Captive Audience – signed "Sid.
Brackett" l.r. – inscribed on the reverse – oil on canvas –
29 x 22in.
(Skinner) $2,500 £1,563

BASIL BRADLEY (1842-1904) - English Setters in a
Highland landscape – signed and dated 1892 – pencil and
watercolour heightened with white – 29.8 x 43.8cm.
(Christie's) $3,740 £2,200

FERDINAND DE BRAECKELEER (1792-1883) –
Morning coffee – signed and dated 1853 – on panel –
52 x 65cm.
(Christie's) $8,501 £5,280

RICHARD BRAKENBURG (1650-1702/3) – A couple
dancing before Boers laughing and drinking in an interior –
oil on panel – 24.5 x 21cm.
(Phillips) $7,335 £4,500

Circle of LEONARD BRAMER (1596-1674) – St. Francis at prayer – oil on panel – 40 x 30.5cm.
(Phillips) **$8,424 £5,200**

OTTO BRANDT (1828-1892) – In the orchard – signed – 38 x 72cm.
(Christie's) **$4,427 £2,750**

ANTONIETTA BRANDEIS – A view near Venice – signed with monogram – oil on panel – 15 x 24cm.
(Sotheby's) **$4,488 £2,640**

ANTONIETTA BRANDIES (b. 1849) - The Doge's Palace, Venice: and St. Giorgio Maggiore, Venice - signed - on board - a pair - 17.8 x 22.8cm.
(Christie's) **$9,378 £6,050**

WARREN BRANDT (American, b. 1918) – "Irish and Poppies" – signed – identified on label Fischbach Gallery, New York on the reverse – oil on canvas – 50 x 40in.
(Skinner) **$1,100 £688**

BRANWHITE

GEORGES BRAQUE (1882-1963) – Fruits et Bol –
signed and dated lower left G. Braque 24 – oil on canvas –
20 x 64.5cm.
(Christie's)   **$478,786   £308,000**

CHARLES BRANWHITE – Cattle in a winter landscape
– signed and dated '55 – oil on canvas – 84 x 112cm.
(Sotheby's)   **$9,861   £6,050**

GEORGES BRAQUE – Les Roses – signed – oil on
board – 46 x 38cm.
(Sotheby's)   **$451,000   £283,648**

JOHN BRATBY, R.A. – Self Portrait With
Rhododendrons And Children - signed – oil on canvas
(Phillips)   **$1,152   £720**

JOHN BRATBY, R.A. (b. 1928) – Venice – signed lower
left Bratby – oil on canvas with impasto – 19 x 23^1/$_2$in.
(Christie's)   **$2,259   £1,430**

WILLIAM A. BREAKSPEARE - Portrait of a girl -
signed - oil on canvas - 40.5 x 27cm.
(Sotheby's) **$1,972 £1,210**

JOHN BRATBY, R.A. – Portrait of Spike Milligan –
signed and dated 1968 – inscribed by the sitter – oil on
canvas – 168 x 101cm.
(Phillips) **$2,880 £1,800**

WILLIAM A. BREAKSPEARE (1855-1914) – Sleeping
Beauty – signed – on panel – 18.5 x 28.3cm.
(Christie's) **$7,346 £4,620**

BREAKSPEARE

WILLIAM A. BREAKSPEARE (1855-1914) – The gypsy – signed – 59 x 38cm.
(Christie's) **$3,148 £1,980**

WILLIAM A. BREAKSPEARE (1855-1914) – A birthday toast – signed – on board – 35.5 x 26cm.
(Christie's) **$1,574 £990**

ALFRED DE BREANSKI, Snr. (1852-1928) – Near Luss, Loch Lomond – signed – and signed and inscribed on the reverse – 61 x 91.5cm.
(Christie's) **$29,733 £18,700**

ALFRED DE BREANSKI, Snr. – At sunset - Borrowdale – signed; signed and inscribed with title on the reverse – oil on canvas – 61 x 91.5cm.
(Sotheby's) **$20,207 £12,100**

ALFRED DE BREANSKI, Snr. (1852-1928) – Her Majesty's residence at Windsor, evening – signed with monogram and dated 1871 – and signed and inscribed on an old label on the reverse – 61.5 x 91cm.
(Christie's) **$7,346 £4,620**

ALFRED DE BREANSKI (1852-1928) – Grasmere, Westmoreland – signed – and signed and inscribed on the reverse – 40.7 x 55.8cm.
(Christie's) **$5,738 £3,520**

BREKELENKAM

ALFRED DE BREANSKI JUNIOR (—c. 1945) – 'Fyn-y-Groes, North Wales' – signed – title on label on reverse – oil on canvas – 61 x 91.5cm.
(Phillips) **$3,423 £2,100**

CAREL BREDAEL (1678-1733), Circle of – A cavalry engagement – oil on canvas – 32 x 42cm.
(Phillips) **$4,890 £3,000**

ALFRED DE BREANSKI, Snr. – The Trossachs – signed; signed and inscribed with title on the reverse – oil on canvas – 56 x 41cm.
(Sotheby's) **$4,776 £2,860**

ALFRED DE BREANSKI, Snr. (1852-1928) – The birches of Lodore – signed – and signed and inscribed on the reverse – 115 x 105cm.
(Christie's) **$17,490 £11,000**

QUIRYN GERRITSZ. VAN BREKELENKAM (Zwammerdam circa 1620-1668 Leiden) – A man and woman seated beside a table lit by candlelight – signed with initials QB and dated 1665 – on panel – 50 x 37cm.
(Phillips) **$30,600 £18,000**

BREMEN

JOHANN GEORG MEYER VON BREMEN (German 1813-86) – The young knitter – signed and dated 1853 – oil on canvas – 24 x 18cm.
(Sotheby's) **$16,434 £9,900**

HANS ANDERSEN BRENDEKILDE (1857-1920) – Portrait of the artist's niece, Gurli – signed – 37 x 31cm.
(Christie's) **$10,230 £6,600**

THORALD BRENDSTRUP (Danish, 1812-1883) – Figures amongst Roman Ruins – signed and inscribed on label on reverse – 33 x 47.6cm.
(Bonhams) **$1,318 £850**

JOHANN GEORG MEYER VON BREMEN (1813-1886) – A young student – signed and dated 1865 – and signed and inscribed Berlin on the reverse – 43 x 34.5cm.
(Christie's) **$17,050 £11,000**

JOHN BRETT, A.R.A. - Portmeirion - inscribed with title and dated 19 Aug 86 - oil on canvas - 18 x 35.5cm.
(Sotheby's) **$1,076 £660**

PIETER BREUGHEL the YOUNGER (1564-1638),
Studio of – The bird trap – inscribed with the collection
number 114 – oil on copper – 17.8 x 25.4cm.
(Phillips) $105,950 £65,000

ANTHONY DE BRIE – A portrait group of Lady
Bingley, daughter of Charles 2nd Viscount Halifax with
her daughters Marcia and Mary – signed and dated 1929 –
unframed – 128.3 x 102.8cm.
(Christie's) $4,776 £2,860

FREDERICK ARTHUR BRIDGMAN – Grandfather's
comfort – signed and dated 1878 – oil on panel – unframed
– 27 x 21cm.
(Sotheby's) $5,236 £3,080

FREDERICK ARTHUR BRIDGMAN (American
1847-1928) – Head of a caravan, Biskra, Algiers – signed
l.r. – oil on canvas – 76 x 118cm.
(Sotheby's) $43,824 £26,400

OTHMAR ANTON BRIOSCHI (1854-1912) – Lago de
Nemi – signed – 86 x 102cm.
(Christie's) $7,672 £4,950

BRISTOW

EDMUND BRISTOW (1787-1876) – An old man and his donkey – 40 x 50.8cm.
(Christie's) **$1,255 £770**

EDMUND BRISTOW – The blacksmiths – signed – 38.1 x 55.8cm.
(Christie's) **$1,653 £990**

ISAAK IZRAILOVICH BRODSKII (1883-1939) – Lenin in Red Square – signed in Cyrillic and dated lower right I. Brodskii 1924 – oil on canvas – 207 x 135cm. – Painted in 1924
(Christie's) **$17,710 £11,000**

RICHARD HENRY BROCK – Forty winks – signed – watercolour – 14¼ x 18in.
(Christie's) **$1,165 £715**

HORACE ASCHER BRODZKY (1885-1969) – Pedants – signed and dated '35 – signed – titled and dated 1935 on the reverse – on panel – 31.7 x 36.8cm.
(Christie's) **$6,772 £4,180**

MARION BROOM – Irises and Peonies in a glass Vase – watercolour – signed – 55.8 x 75cm.
(Bonhams)   **$1,390   £880**

HORACE ASCHER BRODZKY (1885-1969) – The Kilburn Nude – signed and dated '66 – titled twice and dated -66 twice on the reverse and signed on the reverse of the frame – 30.4 x 25.4cm.
(Christie's)   **$1,960   £1,210**

MARION BROOM – A Vase of mixed Summer Flowers including Peonies and Delphiniums – watercolour – signed – 77.5 x 55.8cm.
(Bonhams)   **$948   £600**

ALFRED CARL HARALD BROGE (born 1870) – By the sea – signed – 64 x 80cm.
(Christie's)   **$6,820   £4,400**

NICHOLAS ALDEN BROOKS (fl.c. 1880-1904) – An actual necessity – signed N. A. Brooks N.Y., l.r. – oil on panel – 17.8 x 22.9cm.
(Sotheby's)   **$26,400   £16,815**

ADRIAEN BROUWER – Oudenarde 1606-1638 – Les Mangeurs D'Huitres – oil on panel – 28 x 37cm.
(Sotheby's)   **$29,684   £19,028**

BROWN

DAVID BROWN (fl. late 19th Century) -'The Tug of War' – signed and dated 1880 – inscribed on reverse – oil on canvas – 30.5 x 46cm.
(Phillips)   **$782**   **£480**

JOHN APPLETON BROWN (American, 1844-1902) – White Island Light, New Hampshire – signed "J. Appleton Brown" – pastel on brown paper – 17$\frac{1}{2}$ x 13$\frac{1}{2}$in.
(Skinner)   **$1,900**   **£1,188**

SIR JOHN ALFRED ARNESBY BROWN, R.A. – Evening after Rain – signed – 24 x 38$\frac{1}{4}$in.
(Bearne's)   **$10,478**   **£6,200**

SIR JOHN ARNESBY BROWN, R.A. (1866-1955) – Dawn – signed lower left Arnesby Brown – oil on canvas – 27$\frac{1}{2}$ x 28$\frac{1}{2}$in. – Painted in 1914
(Christie's)   **$8,342**   **£5,280**

JOHN G. BROWN (1831-1913) – Fieldhand with scythe – signed J. G. Brown and dated Copyright 1909, l.l. – oil on canvas – 101.6 x 80.0cm.
(Sotheby's)   **$11,000**   **£7,006**

JOHN G. BROWN (1831-1913) – Thus perish the memory of our love – signed J. G. Brown and dated 1865, l.r. – oil on panel – 50.8 x 34.9cm. – Painted in 1865 (Sotheby's) **$82,500 £52,548**

NIGEL RODERICK BROWN – Tables Series VII – signed and dated '75 – also signed – titled and dated on the reverse – oil on board – 127 x 81cm. (Phillips) **$640 £400**

JOHN GEORGE BROWN – Crossing the Brook – signed J.G. Brown N.A. and dated 1877, l.l. – watercolour and pencil on paper laid down on board – 54.9 x 40.9cm. (Christie's) **$38,500 £24,062**

BYRON BROWNE – Seated Figure with Guitar – signed Byron Browne, u.l. – signed again – dated N.Y.C. September 1958 and inscribed Seated Figure on the reverse – oil on canvas – 66 x 50.5cm. (Christie's) **$4,400 £2,750**

BROWNELL

FRANKLIN P. BROWNELL (Canadian/American, b. 1857) – Seated Woman/A Tonal Portrait – signed and dated "F. Brownell '85" – oil on canvas – 24 x 19¾ in. *(Skinner)* **$750 £449**

ABRAHAM BRUEGHEL – Anvers 1631-1690 Naples – Composition aux Fleurs, Fruits et Personnages – oil on canvas – 196 x 170cm. *(Sotheby's)* **$82,457 £52,857**

PIERRE BRUEGHEL II, called the younger - Bruxelles 1564 - 1637 ou 38 Anvers - La Visite a la Ferme - oil on panel - 36.5 x 55cm.
(Sotheby's) **$164,914 £105,714**

PIETER BRUEGHEL II CALLED THE YOUNGER –
Vers 1564-1637 ou 38 – La Noce Villageoise – oil on
panel transferred on canvas – 72.5 x 118cm.
(Sotheby's) **$197,897 £126,857**

MARCEL BRUNERY (circa 1900) – The print collectors
– signed – on panel – 50.7 x 59.7cm.
(Christie's) **$14,492 £9,350**

LEON BRUNIN (1861-1949) – L'Été dans St Martin –
signed and dated 1887 – 98 x 124.5cm.
(Christie's) **$15,053 £9,350**

**PIETER BRUEGHEL THE YOUNGER (1564
Brussels-1638 Antwerp)** – 'Le Retour de la Kermesse' –
signed P. Brueghel – on panel – 41.5 x 57cm.
(Phillips) **$833,000 £490,000**

**PIETER BRUEGHEL THE YOUNGER, Circle of
(Brussels 1564-1638 Antwerp)** – The bird trap – on panel
– 38.5 x 54.5cm.
(Phillips) **$61,200 £36,000**

LEOPOLD BRUNNER the ELDER – A still life of
flowers and opera glasses – signed and dated 1843 – oil on
panel – 77 x 60cm.
(Sotheby's) **$47,300 £27,500**

BRUSSELMANS

JEAN BRUSSELMANS (1884 - 1953) - Retour du Travail - signed and dated lower right - oil on canvas - 115.6 x 110.2cm. - Painted in 1929.
(Christie's) **$211,200 £132,000**

JEAN BRUSSELMANS (1884 - 1953) - Marguerites et Delphiniums dans un Vase - signed and dated lower right Jean Brusselmans 1932 - oil on canvas - 74.3 x 54.6cm. - painted in 1932.
(Christie's) **$14,080 £8,800**

DE BRUSSES (late 19th Century) – The catch; and The accident – both signed – on panel – 21 x 26.8cm.
(Christie's) **$4,250 £2,640**

BERNARD BUFFET (b. 1928) – Le Phare – signed and dated upper left Bernard Buffet 67 – watercolour, brush and black ink on paper – 50 x 64cm. – Executed in 1967
(Christie's) **$47,740 £30,800**

BERNARD BUFFET (b. 1928) – Portrait de jeune Fille—Aniecse – signed and dated upper right Bernard Buffet 50 – gouache and black ink on paper laid down on canvas – 63 x 48cm. – Executed in 1950
(Christie's) **$32,395 £20,900**

BERNARD BUFFET - The circus, musical clowns - oil on canvas - signed and dated - 195 x 300cm.
(Jean Claude Anaf) **$993,854 £572,917**

KATE E. BUNCE – Gathering water – signed with monogram and dated '76 – indistinctly inscribed on the reverse – 67.3 x 49.5cm. *(Christie's)* **$1,826 £1,100**

RUPERT CHARLES WULSTEN BUNNY (1864-1947) – The White Parasol—A Sketch – inscribed 'Marie Tuck from Adelaide, Australia A Friend in Paris, France' – on board – unframed – 27 x 20cm. *(Christie's)* **$4,277 £2,640**

EDGAR BUNDY, A.R.A., R.I., R.B.A. (1862-1922) – A Bit of Banter – signed – oil on canvas – 45.5 x 61cm. *(Phillips)* **$2,445 £1,500**

BURBANK

ELDRIDGE AYER BURBANK (Am. 1858-1947) –
Chief Red Cloud, Sioux – oil on canvas board – signed E.
A. Burbank lower left – titled and dated upper left - Pine
Ridge, S. D. lower right – 12 x 9in.
(Bruce D. Collins) **$2,520 £1,575**

CHARLES BURCHFIELD (1893 - 1967) - Cold June
Evening - signed Chas. Burchfield and dated
l.r.; also titled Cold June Evening and dated June
19-1917 on the reverse - water colour on paperboard
- 55.9 x 45.7cm.
(Sotheby's) **$35,200 £22,420**

CHARLES BURCHFIELD - North wind in September –
signed with the artist's monogrammed initials; also titled
Northwind in September and dated 1948 on the reverse –
watercolour on paperboard – 65.4 x 88.8cm. –
Executed in 1948
(Sotheby's) **$99,000 £62,264**

CHARLES EPHRAIM BURCHFIELD - Autumn study -
conte crayon on paper - 34 x 49.5cm.
(Christie's) **$1,980 £1,222**

CHARLES EPHRAIM BURCHFIELD – Sunset –
signed Chas. Burchfield and dated 1917, l.r. – dated May
10, 1917 – numbered B-169 – gouache on paper –
55.8 x 45.7cm.
(Christie's) **$46,200 £28,875**

JOHN BAGNOLD BURGESS (1830-1897) – A Spanish beauty on a balcony – signed – on panel – 45.2 x 34.8cm. *(Christie's)* **$1,793** **£1,100**

RODNEY JOSEPH BURN, R.A. (b. 1899) – In the Surf – signed lower right R J Burn – oil on canvas – 25$^1/2$ x 22in. *(Christie's)* **$1,042** **£660**

JOHN BAGNOLD BURGESS, R.A. (1830-1897) – 'The Genius of the Family' – signed and dated 1881 – oil on canvas – 89 x 120cm.
(Phillips) **$30,970** **£19,000**

BURNE–JONES

SIR EDWARD COLEY BURNE-JONES, Bt., A.R.A. –
Study for "The call of Perseus" – sanguine, pencil and
white chalk, highlights on tinted paper – 33 x 30cm.
(Sotheby's) **$33,660 £19,800**

**SIR EDWARD COLEY BURNE-JONES, A.R.A.,
R.W.S. (1833-1898)** – A study of a Girl's Head – red chalk
– 24 x 14.5cm.
(Phillips) **$7,172 £4,400**

SIR EDWARD COLEY BURNE-JONES, Bt., A.R.A. –
Portrait of Georgiana, the artist's wife (Painted circa 1862-
3) – oil on canvas – 43 x 30.5cm.
(Sotheby's) **$7,172 £4,400**

ALEXANDER HOHENLOHE BURR –The Fairytale –
signed; signed and inscribed on the reverse – oil on board –
30.5 x 25.5cm.
(Sotheby's) **$1,561 £935**

GASTON BUSSIERE – A reclining nude – signed and dated 1926 – oil on canvas – 58 x 71cm.
(Sotheby's) $21,758 £12,650

THEODORE BUTLER (1861-1963) – East River – oil on canvas – 15 x 19in. – signed Butler lower right, titled verso
(Bruce D. Collins) $12,650 £7,529

THOMAS BUTTERSWORTH, Jnr. (fl. early 19th Century) – H.M.S. Philomel and Asia off Lisbon – signed l.r. : T. Buttersworth jun^r – oil on canvas – 29.5 x 40cm.
(Sotheby's) $9,207 £5,940

CABIANCA

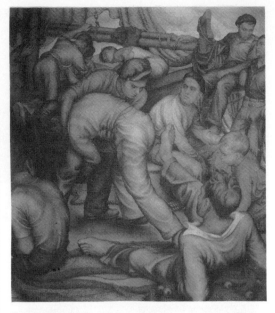

PAUL CADMUS – Mallorcan Fishermen – signed Paul
Cadmus – oil on canvas – 55.8 x 50.8cm.
(Christie's) **$154,000 £98,221**

VINCENZO CABIANCA (Italian 1827-1902) - A lovers'
meeting – signed and dated 1865 – watercolour –
58 x 29cm.
(Sotheby's) **$7,304 £4,400**

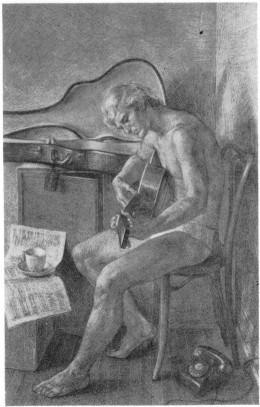

FLORENCE ST. JOHN CADELL – The new arrival –
signed – oil on canvas – 56 x 76cm.
(Sotheby's) **$2,939 £1,760**

PAUL CADMUS – Male Nude – signed twice Cadmus –
dated 55 and inscribed TS7, l.l. – pencil and egg tempera
on hand-toned paper – 24.4 x 38.1cm.
(Christie's) **$19,800 £12,628**

PAUL CADMUS – The Guitarist – signed Cadmus –
pastel on hand-toned paper – 62.8 x 45.7cm.
(Christie's) **$19,800 £12,628**

PAUL CADMUS – Hinky Dinky Parley Voo – signed
Paul Cadmus – oil and egg tempera on canvas laid down
on masonite – 91.4 x 91.4cm.
(Christie's)   **$93,500   £59,634**

PAUL CADMUS – Ballet Students – signed Paul Cadmus
– signed again and dated August 1943 on the reverse –
pencil on paper – 25.1 x 31.1cm.
(Christie's)   **$14,300   £9,121**

PAUL CADMUS – Male Nude – signed twice Cadmus – dated 55 and inscribed TS7, l.l. – pencil and egg
tempera on hand-toned paper – 24.4 x 38.1cm.
(Christie's)   **$19,800   £12,628**

CAHOON

ALEXANDER CALDER (1898-1976) – Hibou Blanc – signed with initials and dated 58 – mobile of painted sheet metal and rod – height 215.9cm – approximate span 381cm.
(Christie's) **$656,260 £418,000**

RALPH CAHOON (American, d. 1982) – A Fanciful Balloon Flight – signed "R. Cahoon" l.r. – oil on masonite – 28 x 22in.
(Skinner) **$5,500 £3,438**

WILLIAM JAMES CALLCOTT (fl. 1843-1896) – Shipping in a Stormy Sea – signed – watercolour heightened with bodycolour and scratching out – 38.5 x 56cm.
(Phillips) **$1,304 £800**

GUSTAVE CAILLEBOTTE – Houses along the Loing, Moret – oil on canvas – signed – 73 x 60cm.
(Jean-Claude Anaf) **$232,761 £149,206**

JOHN CALLOW – Unloading The Catch – unframed – 24 x 36in.
(Bearne's) **$2,197 £1,300**

WILLIAM CALLOW (1812-1908) – Durham from the River – signed and dated 1844 – watercolour over pencil – heightened with white and scraping out – 61.5 x 87.5cm.
(Phillips) **$11,084** **£6,800**

HENRY CALVERT (Darlton 1793 - Southport c. 1869) – A chestnut hunter and spaniels standing by a stone arch, a parkland beyond – signed and dated lower right: H. Calvert 1866 – oil on canvas – 44.4 x 59.6cm.
(Lawrence) **$5,232** **£3,190**

WILLIAM CALLOW (1812-1908) – A quiet Backwater – signed and dated 1877 – watercolour and bodycolour – 44 x 34cm.
(Phillips) **$3,586** **£2,200**

ARTURO CALOSCI (Italian, 1855-1926) – The Courtship – signed and inscribed Firenze – oil on canvas – 27.3 x 37.5cm.
(Christie's) **$2,957** **£1,760**

LEON GEORGES CALVES (French, b. 1848) – Peasant Girl with her Flock – signed – oil on canvas – 32 x 21½ in.
(Skinner) **$1,200** **£719**

CAMBIER

NESTOR CAMBIER – The dining room at Château Culbery-Court – signed – oil on board – 41 x 41cm.
(Sotheby's) **$8,415 £4,950**

DUNCAN CAMERON (fl. 1871 - 1900) - An extensive landscape with cattle by a stream on the edge of a wood - signed - 71.2 x 115cm.
(Christie's) **$1,703 £1,045**

JOSEPH DE CAMP – Portrait of a Young Lady – signed – oil on canvas – 33 x 27cm.
(Phillips) **$1,472 £920**

MOLLY CAMPBELL – "Mother's Darling" – pencil and watercolour – signed with initials in pencil – 13.3 x 19.1cm.
(Bonhams) **$474 £310**

MASSIMO CAMPIGLI (1895-1971) – Ville debout – signed and dated lower right Campigli 59 – inscribed with title on the reverse Ville debout – oil on canvas – 130 x 97cm.
(Christie's) **$290,691 £187,000**

GIUSEPPE CANELLA (Italian 1788-1847) – Paris, the Rue de Rivoli – oil on panel – 18 x 22.5cm.
(Sotheby's) **$25,564 £15,400**

SIMONE CANTARINI, attributed to - The Holy Family with St. John - on copper - octagonal - 22 x 16cm.
(Phillips) **$20,250 £12,500**

JOSEPH CARAUD (1821-1905) – The chamber maid – signed and dated 1868 – on panel – 46.5 x 31cm.
(Christie's) **$12,787 £8,250**

JACQUES FRANCOIS CARABAIN (1834-1892) – Piazza Cavalli, Piacenza – signed – and signed – inscribed and dated Bruxelles, 15 Sept 1894 on an old label on the reverse – 76 x 53cm.
(Christie's) **$13,282 £8,250**

JOSEPH CARAUD (1821-1905) – The new dress – signed – 82.5 x 69.8cm.
(Christie's) **$9,377 £6,050**

CARELLI

CARAVAGGIO, After - The card sharpers - unframed - 29¾ x 39in.
(Christie's) **$8,415 £4,950**

CONSALVO CARELLI (1818-1900) – A view from Posillipo with Vesuvius in the distance – signed and inscribed Napoli – on panel – 24.5 x 39.5cm.
(Christie's) **$13,981 £9,020**

GAB CARELLI – Dutch Harbour Scene with numerous boats and figures – signed – watercolour – 14 x 20in.
(G. A. Key) **$1,499 £980**

ARTHUR BEECHER CARLES - Woman and chair - signed Arthur Carles on the reverse - oil on panel - 23.9 x 18.7cm.
(Christie's) **$7,150 £4,206**

ARTHUR B. CARLES (1876-1952) – Reclining nude – signed Carles, l.r. – oil on canvas – 68.5 x 76.2cm. – Executed circa 1921
(Sotheby's) **$22,000 £14,013**

GIUSEPPE CARELLI (1858-1921) – Fishing boats in the bay of Naples – signed – 24 x 42.5cm.
(Christie's)   **$8,501   £5,280**

GEORGE F. CARLINE (1855-1920) – Arranging the peonies – signed and dated 1902 – 102 x 127.5cm.
(Christie's)   **$8,745   £5,500**

EMIL CARLSEN (1853-1932) – Copper kettle – signed Emil Carlsen and dated 1928, l.c. – oil on canvas – 74.9 x 68.6cm.
(Sotheby's)   **$66,000   £42,038**

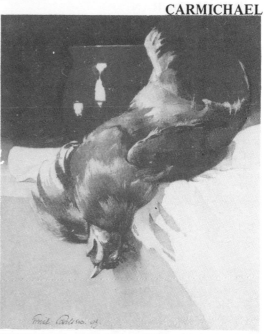

SOREN EMIL CARLSEN – Still Life with Cock and Pitcher – signed Emil Carlsen and dated 93, l.l. – watercolour on paper – 30.5 x 25.4cm.
(Christie's)   **$7,150   £4,469**

JOHN FABIAN CARLSON - Templed Hills - signed John F. Carlson. l.l. - oil on canvas - 124.5 x 149.5cm.
(Christie's)   **$22,000   £13,750**

JOHN WILSON CARMICHAEL – A Scottish burn - a cowherd watched by washer women – signed and dated 1845 – 50 x 60cm.
(Anderson & Garland)   **$1,190   £700**

CAROLUS–DURAN

EMILE AUGUSTE CAROLUS-DURAN – Portrait of
Edouard Manet – signed – oil on canvas – 64.7 x 54.6cm.
(Sotheby's) **$407,000 £255,975**

VITTORE CARPACCIO 1465-1525 – In the style of –
Portrait de Femme au Singe – oil on panel – 55.5 x 40cm.
(Sotheby's) **$19,788 £12,685**

SAMUEL S. CARR (American, 1837-1908) – Landscape
with Sheep – signed "S.S. Carr" l.l. – oil on canvas –
12 x 18in.
(Skinner) **$1,900 £1,188**

JOHN MULCASTER CARRICK – The Soidor, St.
Servan, Brittany – on board – signed and dated 1882 –
inscribed on the reverse – 8¼ x 13in.
(Bearne's) **$2,492 £1,400**

PIERRE CARRIER-BELLEUSE (French 1851-1933) –
Les Danceuses – signed – pastel on canvas – 90.5 x
71cm. *(Sotheby's)* **$13,150 £7,920**

ANTO CARTE (1886 - 1954) - L'Annonciation - signed lower right Anto Carte - oil on canvas - 79.4 x 99.6cm.
(Christie's) **$24,640 £15,400**

CLARENCE HOLBROOK CARTER (b. 1904)
Flower piece - signed and dated '31 - oil on canvas - 26 x 22in. *(Sotheby's)* **$3,850 £2,362**

DORA CARRINGTON (1893-1932) – Still Life with mixed Flowers – watercolour and pencil – unframed – 19½ x 13¾in.
(Christie's) **$4,866 £3,080**

W.J. CARROLL (late 19th Century) – The old, old story – signed – 91.5 x 71cm.
(Christie's) **$4,303 £2,640**

CLARENCE HOLBROOK CARTER (b. 1904) – Good crop – signed Clarence H. Carter and dated '42, l.r. – oil on canvas – 109.2 x 73.6cm.
(Sotheby's) **$38,500 £24,522**

CARTER

SYDNEY CARTER – Meeting in the field – signed and dated 1894 – 24 x 18in.
(Michael Newman) **$1,630 £1,000**

MARY CASSATT – Woman by a window feeding her dog – signed – oil, gouache and pastel on paper, laid down on canvas – 61.0 x 41.2cm.
(Sotheby's) **$797,500 £501,572**

MARY CASSATT (1844-1926) – Sara in a round-brimmed bonnet, holding her dog – signed Mary Cassatt, m.r. – pastel on paper – 55.9 x 41.2cm. – Executed circa 1901
(Sotheby's) **$165,000 £105,096**

MARY CASSATT (1844-1926) – Head of Julie, looking down – signed with the artist's initials M.C., l.r. – pastel on paper – 39.4 x 31.1cm. – Executed circa 1909
(Sotheby's) **$63,250 £40,287**

NICOLA CASSISA, Attributed to (Active Naples circa 1700) – A still life with a basket of assorted flowers, in a landscape, fruit lying nearby – on canvas – 61 x 95.5cm.
(Phillips) **$18,700 £11,000**

PETER CASTEELS, A follower of – A peacock and poultry in a formal garden – unframed – 82.5 x 115cm.
(Anderson & Garland) **$6,357 £3,900**

EDOUARD CASTRES (1838-1902) – In a Japanese garden – signed – on panel – 34.5 x 26cm.
(Christie's) **$12,397 £7,700**

GEORGE CATLIN (1796-1872) – Battle between Sioux and Sauk and Fox (Eastern Dakota) – oil on canvas – 65.4 x 81.3cm.
(Sotheby's) **$539,000 £343,312**

CLAUDIO CASTELUCHO (1870-1927) – The dancer – signed – unframed – 81 x 60cm.
(Christie's) **$2,302 £1,430**

PETER LA CAVE – Rustics in a cave with sheep and cows – signed: La Cave 1800 – pen and brown ink and watercolour over traces of pencil – 36.5 x 49cm.
(Sotheby's) **$1,870 £1,100**

CAWTHORNE

NEIL CAWTHORNE - Second from last at Stratford - signed and dated '80 - 20 x 30in.
(Christie's) **$1,165 £715**

PAUL CÉZANNE (1839-1906) – Au Bord de l'Eau – pencil and watercolour on paper – 33.3 x 50.2cm. – Executed circa 1895
(Christie's) **$375,100 £242,000**

JULIEN CELOS – House facades – oil on canvas – signed – 55 x 65cm.
(Galerie Moderne) **$1,490 £1,228**

CHARLES FERDINAND CERAMANO (Belgian 1829-1909) – A sheep dog and his flock – signed – oil on canvas – 138 x 228cm.
(Sotheby's) **$10,043 £6,050**

PAUL CÉZANNE – Fleurs dans un vase – oil on canvas – 46 x 55cm.
(Sotheby's) **$2,200,000 £1,383,648**

GIUSEPPE CESARI, IL CAVALIER D'ARPINO (1568-Rome-1640) – Leda and the swan – on slate – 19.3 x 25.3cm.
(Phillips) **$55,420 £34,000**

WILLIAM CHADWICK (1878-1962) – A stream by the farm – signed W. Chadwick, l.r. – oil on canvas – 61.0 x 76.3cm. – Painted circa 1916-17
(Sotheby's) **$27,500 £17,516**

MARC CHAGALL (1887-1985) – St. Paul de Vence, Peintre et Bouquet de Fleurs – signed lower right Chagall; signed again on the reverse Marc Chagall – oil on canvas – 65 x 50cm.
(Christie's)　　　　**$1,025,970　£660,000**

MARC CHAGALL (1887-1985) – Village aux deux Bouquets – signed lower right Marc Chagall; signed on the reverse Chagall – oil on canvas – 60 x 73cm.
(Christie's)　　　　**$1,367,960　£880,000**

MARC CHAGALL (1887-1985) – Le Coq vert et la Modèle – the estate stamp lower right Marc Chagall – oil on canvas – 30 x 61cm.
(Christie's)　　　　**$581,383　£374,000**

MARC CHAGALL (1887-1985) – Le Vent dans les Fleurs au Clair de Lune – signed lower left Chagall Marc – gouache and watercolour on paper laid down on board – 61.6 x 48.9cm.
(Christie's)　　　　**$392,150　£253,000**

MARC CHAGALL (1887-1985) – L'Enlèvement d'Europe – signed lower right Marc Chagall – gouache on paper – 50 x 65cm. – Executed circa 1927
(Christie's)　　　　**$306,900　£198,000**

CHALDERS

GEORGE CHALDERS – Figures Fishing from a Boat, in a Wooded River Landscape – panel – signed – 34.3 x 49.5cm.
(Bonhams) **$713 £460**

JAMES WELLS CHAMPNEY (American, 1843-1903) – "Saucy Jane"/Portrait of a Girl in a Red Bonnet – signed – identified on label on verso – oil on canvas – 12 x 10in.
(Skinner) **$550 £329**

JOHN CHALMERS – Fishing off the Scottish coast – signed and dated 1894 – oil on canvas – 68.5 x 107cm.
(Sotheby's) **$2,204 £1,320**

JOHN CHANCELLOR – 'From under their Noses' – signed – 23$^1/_2$ x 53in.
(Bearne's) **$40,750 £25,000**

HENRY BERNARD CHALON (1771-1849) – A Hunt Kennel – 29.2 x 37.5cm.
(Christie's) **$2,805 £1,650**

BRYANT CHAPIN (American, 1859-1927) – Still Life with Plums – signed and dated 1919 – oil on canvas – 18 x 24in.
(Skinner) **$6,500 £3,892**

BRYANT CHAPIN (1859-1927) – Fruit still life – oil on canvas – 12 x 16in. – signed Bryant Chapin and dated 1926 lower left – signed and dated on the reverse
(Bruce D. Collins)   **$7,150**   **£4,255**

REUBEN CHAPPELL (1870-1940) – The two masted schooner Bess Mitchell – water and body colour – signed – 14½ x 21½in.
(David Lay)   **$765**   **£450**

CHARLES C. CHAPIN – Morning on Upper Saranac Lake – signed C.H. chapin and dated 1882, l.l. – oil on canvas – 71 x 126.5cm.
(Christie's)   **$6,600**   **£4,125**

JOHN CHARLTON (1849-1917) – On the Scent – signed with monogram and dated 1877 – watercolour and bodycolour – 34.5 x 49.5cm.
(Phillips)   **$1,141**   **£700**

JOHN GADSBY CHAPMAN (American, 1808-1889) – "Italian Vintage" – unsigned – identified on loan/exhibition label from Lincoln House, Boston, on the reverse – oil on canvas – 16¾ x 13¼in.
(Skinner)   **$800**   **£500**

GEORGES CHARPENTIER (fl. 1880) – A view of the Cathedral Dieppe; and Dieppe harbour – both signed and inscribed – on board – a pair – 27.9 x 35.6cm.
(Christie's)   **$3,410**   **£2,200**

CHASE

WILLIAM MERRITT CHASE (1849-1916) – The consultation – signed Wm. M. Chase, l.l. – pastel on paper – 56.5 x 47.0cm.
(Sotheby's)   **$19,800   £12,611**

GEORGE CHINNERY (1774-1854) – Portrait of Francis Rawdon Hastings, 2nd Earl of Moria and 1st Marquess of Hastings (1754-1826) – full length, standing wearing Garter robes – oil on canvas – 87.5 x 57cm.
(Sotheby's)   **$17,050   £11,000**

H.T. CHAMIELINSKI (early 20th Century) – A troyka in a snowy street – both signed – a pair – 25.4 x 35.6cm. *(Christie's)*   **$3,069   £1,980**

CHRISTO

GEORGE CHINNERY, Attributed to - A lady standing full length, by a colonnade: a river landscape beyond - 24¾ x 19½in.
(Bearne's) **$19,560 £12,000**

IVAN CHOULTSE – A mountain river – signed – 25 x 20¾in.
(Bearne's) **$3,560 £2,000**

JOSEPH CHRETIEN (20th Century) – Sheep in a landscape – signed – unframed – 50.8 x 66.2cm.
(Christie's) **$1,534 £990**

CHRISTO (b. 1935) – The Gates (Project for Central Park, N.Y. City) – signed – inscribed with title and dated 1983 on the right panel – collage with coloured crayon, pencil, paper, fabric, chalk and photographs on paper – right panel 70 x 28cm. – left panel 70 x 56cm.
(Christie's) **$55,264 £35,200**

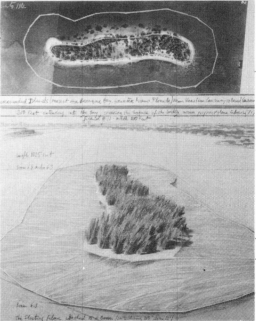

CHRISTO (b. 1935) – Surrounded Islands (Project for Biscayne Bay, Greater Miami, Florida) – signed – inscribed with title and dated 1982 on top panel – collage with coloured crayon, pencil, paper, fabric, gouache and photograph on card – top panel 28 x 70cm. – bottom panel 56 x 70cm.
(Christie's) **$103,620 £66,000**

CHRISTY

GUGLIEMO CIARDI – A view of the Giudecca, Venice – signed – oil on panel – 34.5 x 51.5cm. *(Sotheby's)*   **$15,895**   **£9,350**

HOWARD CHANDLER CHRISTY – The Same Old Yarn – signed Howard Chandler Christy – dated 1918 and inscribed To Byron and Virginia Ralston with best friendship, l.c. – inscribed with title, l.r. – watercolour, gouache and pencil on board – 88.9 x 64.1cm. *(Christie's)*   **$7,700**   **£4,812**

ANTONIO CIRINO (Italian/American, b. 1889) – The Stream in Winter – signed – oil on canvasboard – 8 x 10in. *(Skinner)*   **$1,100**   **£659**

HOWARD CHANDLER CHRISTY - Nude reclining - signed Howard C. Christy, l.l. - oil on canvas - 41.6 x 53.4cm. *(Christie's)*   **$22,000 £13,750**

EMMA CIARDI - Villa Gaia, Venice - signed and inscribed Venezia on the reverse - oil on panel - 14¼ x 14¾in. *(Sotheby's)*   **$13,448 £8,250**

ANTONIO CIRINO (Italian/American, 1889-1983) – Winter in the City – signed "A. Cirino", l.l. – oil on canvasboard – 7⁷/₈ x 9⁷/₈in. *(Skinner)*   **$1,349**   **£2,200**

ARTUS CLAESSENS, Attributed to (Active circa 1644) – A still life of black and white grapes in a silver gilt tazza, at the base lies a posy of flowers and a squirrel eating nuts – on panel – 66.2 x 56.5cm.
(Phillips) **$15,300 £9,000**

PAUL CITROEN - A portrait of the paintress H. van der Neut - de Wit as a young lady, full length, in a black dress with a camellia - signed lower left P. Citroen - 120 x 60cm.
(Christie's) **$4,792 £3,014**

PIER FRANCESCO CITTADINI (Milan 1616-1681 Bologna) – Portrait of a terrier dog with a red ribbon as a collar – on canvas – 34.5 x 33.5cm.
(Phillips) **$8,965 £5,500**

ANTHONY CLAESZ I, Circle of (1592-Amsterdam-1635) – A still life of a glass vase of assorted flowers standing on a stone ledge – on panel – 40.5 x 32cm.
(Phillips) **$8,150 £5,000**

OLIVER CLARE – Still life of primulas and lilac –
signed – oil on board – 15 x 22cm.
(Sotheby's)   **$5,199   £3,190**

A. CLAES-THOLOIS (b. 1883) - Nature morte -
signed and dated upper left A. Claes-Tholois
1920 - oil on panel - 50.2 x 50.2cm. - Painted in
1920.
(Christie's)   **$13,200   £8,250**

OLIVER CLARE (fl. 1853-1927) – Still life of grapes,
apples, a plum and a strawberry on a mossy bank – signed
and dated '94 – 20.3 x 24.2cm.
(Christie's)   **$1,076   £660**

GEORGE CLARE – A Still Life with Plums and
Strawberries by a Mossy Knoll – board – signed –
30.5 x 20.5cm.
(Bonhams)   **$403   £260**

VINCENT CLARE (Birmingham c. 1855-1930) –
Peaches and grapes in a wicker basket on a mossy bank;
Primroses and a birds' nest on a mossy bank – both signed
lower right: Vincent Clare – oil on canvas – 22.8 x 30.5cm;
a pair
(Lawrence)   **$4,330   £2,640**

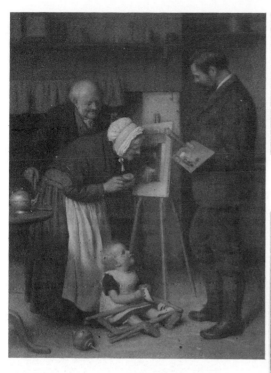

JOSEPH CLARK – My very image – signed and dated
1887 – oil on canvas – 89 x 68.5cm.
(Sotheby's)   **$14,702   £9,020**

SAMUEL JOSEPH CLARK (English, 19th Century) –
The Haycart – signed – 50.8 x 76.2cm.
(Bonhams)   **$1,705   £1,100**

EMILE CLAUS (1849 - 1924) - La Lys - signed lower
left Emile Claus - inscribed on the reverse Öktober -
oil on canvas - 93 x 73.5cm. - painted circa 1902.
(Christie's)   **$132,000 £82,500**

SAMUEL JOSEPH CLARK – Farm horses – signed –
oil on canvas – 76 x 63.5cm.
(Sotheby's)   **$2,869   £1,760**

EMILE CLAUS (1849 - 1924) - Les Meules - signed
lower right EC - oil on canvas laid on panel - 22.8
x 27.9cm.
(Christie's)   **$7,920   £4,950**

CLAUS

EMILE CLAUS (1849 - 1924) - Escorte sur la Tamise dans le Brouillard - signed, dated and inscribed lower left - oil on canvas - 92 x 57.1cm. - painted in 1918. *(Christie's)* **$29,920 £18,700**

SIR GEORGE CLAUSEN, R.A. (1852-1944) – Dutch Girl with Flowers – signed and dated lower left G. CLAUSEN 1878 – watercolour, bodycolour and pencil – 9 x 5³/₄in. *(Christie's)* **$1,651 £1,045**

SIR GEORGE CLAUSEN, R.A., R.W.S. (1852-1944) – The Breakfast Table – signed – oil on canvas – 46 x 36cm. *(Phillips)* **$42,380 £26,000**

HAROLD CLAYTON – A Still Life with Spring Flowers in a Jug upon a Ledge – signed – on canvas – 61 x 51cm. *(Bonhams)* **$4,108 £2,600**

SIR GEORGE CLAUSEN – Cottages and corn stoops –
signed – watercolour heightened with scratching out –
23 x 29cm.
(Woolley & Wallis) $1,224 £720

PAUL JEAN CLAYS (1819-1900) – On the Schelde –
signed – and signed – inscribed and dated Bruxelles 1865
on an old label on the reverse – on panel – 59.6 x 99cm.
(Christie's) $11,511 £7,150

Circle of **MARTIN VAN CLEVE (1560-1604)** – A
parable – inscribed 'Ocn Cruie Ick Hebbi Getalt dele hinne
Ick/Legghen Keren Wnre Ider Inn Spinnen Ons hinne...' –
oil on panel – tondo – 17cm. diam.
(Phillips) $1,458 £900

MARTEN VAN CLEVE – Anvers 1527-1581 – Le
Massacre des Innocents Dans un Paysage Hivernal – oil on
panel – 71 x 106cm.
(Sotheby's) $65,956 £42,286

JOOS VAN CLEVE, Circle of – The Holy Family; mid-
16th century - oil on panel – 9¼ x 14½in.
(Graves Son & Pilcher) $13,770 £8,500

MARTEN VAN CLEVE 1527 - 1581 - Circle of - La
Visite a la Ferme - oil on panel - 55 x 75cm.
(Sotheby's) $14,017 £8,985

CLIME

WINFIELD SCOTT CLIME (American, 1881-1958) –
Building of the Poseidon/A Harbour Scene – signed
"Winfield Scott Clime" l.l. – oil on canvasboard –
$8^{1}/_{2}$ x $10^{1}/_{2}$in.
(Skinner)   **$800   £500**

PIETER JACOBS CODDE, Attributed to (1599-Amsterdam-1678) – Elegant figures gathered around a
table draped with a red cloth – on panel – 37 x 56.6cm.
(Phillips)   **$10,595   £6,500**

H. BERNARD COBBE – A watched pot never boils –
signed – oil on canvas – 48 x 61cm.
(Sotheby's)   **$3,122   £1,870**

OSCAR CODDRON (1881-1960) – Le Port d'Ostende—
De Haven van Oostende – signed lower right Coddron –
and inscribed on the reverse Ostende Coddron – oil on
board – 68 x 58cm.
(Christie's)   **$14,080   £8,800**

FRANK COBURN (American, 20th Century) – Under
the Umbrella/Rainy Day on the Streets of San Francisco –
signed – oil on board – 20 x 15in.
(Skinner)   **$3,200   £1,916**

OSCAR CODDRON (1881-1960) – Femme aux deux
Lévriers—Vrouw met twee Windhonden – signed and
dated lower right Coddron 1917 – oil on canvas –
150.5 x 150.5cm. – Painted in 1917
(Christie's)   **$49,280   £30,800**

BILL COLEMAN – Reclining nude – oil on board –
signed – 61 x 96cm.
(Australian Art Auctions) **$2,425 £1,488**

OSCAR CODDRON (1881-1960) - Les Coquelieots -
signed lower left CODDRON - oil on canvas - 90.2 x
75cm.
(Christie's) **$17,600 £11,000**

WILLIAM STEPHEN COLEMAN – The fisherman's
children – signed with monogram – watercolour over
traces of pencil, heightened with bodycolour and stopping
out – 17 x 24cm.
(Woolley & Wallis) **$6,250 £4,000**

HENRY GEORGE COGLE (b. 1875) – Still life -
flowers – oil on canvas – signed – 19$\frac{1}{2}$ x 23$\frac{1}{2}$in.
(David Lay) **$542 £350**

GEORGE VICAT COLE, R.A. – Bisham – signed with
monogram and dated 1884 – oil on canvas – 91.5 x 145.
(Sotheby's) **$46,618 £28,600**

EVERT COLLIER – A vanitas still life with a violin,
incense burner, a globe, a casket of jewels and other items
– signed and dated 1696 – 39$\frac{1}{2}$ x 48in.
(Bearne's) **$48,060 £27,000**

COLLIER

EVERT COLLIER (Breda circa 1650-1702 Leyden) –
A trompe l'oeil, a quill pen, a seal, a comb, a pin cushion, a
document dated 1664, a medallion, a string of pearls, a
cameo, a paper knife, and other documents attached to a
letter-rack – inscribed on a book, anno 1664 – on canvas –
46 x 58.5cm.
(Phillips) **$49,800 £30,000**

Circle of EVERT COLLIER (circa 1680-1702) –
Cavaliers and their companions drinking and carousing in
a barn – bears initials and date 1699 – oil on canvas – 71 x
85cm.
(Phillips) **$7,776 £4,800**

IMOGEN COLLIER – Barrister – signed – inscribed
Barrister 1898 by Saalawyer on the reverse – 20 x 23¹/₂in.
(Michael Newman) **$530 £325**

ALBERT HENRY COLLINGS (1858-1910) – A Female
Nude seated on a Beach – signed – watercolour –
26.5 x 36.5cm.
(Phillips) **$1,467 £900**

CHARLES COLLINS – Cattle at rest by a windmill, in
an extensive landscape – signed and dated 1888 – oil on
canvas – 49.5 x 75cm.
(Woolley & Wallis) **$1,700 £1,000**

WILLIAM COLLINS, R.A. – 'Lord Charles & Lord
Thomas Pelham Clinton' and 'The Earl of Lincoln, Lady
Anna Maria & Lady Charlotte Pelham Clinton' – oils – a
pair – on panel and on canvas – 16¹/₂ x 13¹/₂in.
(Graves Son & Pilcher) **$8,100 £5,000**

CHARLES EDWARD CONDER (1868-1909) – Apple Blossom at Dennemont – on board – 13 x 13.6cm.
(Christie's) $3,208 £1,980

LOUIS COLSOUL (French, 20th Century) – 'Les Azalees' – signed – signed and inscribed on reverse – 100.4 x 80.6cm.
(Bonhams) $2,480 £1,600

JACQUELINE COMERRE-PATON – Idle moments – signed – oil on canvas – 130 x 190cm.
(Sotheby's) $7,106 £4,180

NICHOLAS MATTHEW CONDY (1818-1851) – The Cutter Iris off Plymouth – signed N.M. Condy 1845 and inscribed on the reverse: 'Iris Cutter/RYS/N.M. Condy Pinxt/Plymouth 1845 – oil on board – 34 x 44.5cm.
(Sotheby's) $22,176 £13,200

CHARLES EDWARD CONDER (1868-1909) – The Beach, Ferring Grange – signed – titled on an old label attached to the stretcher – 63.3 x 76.2cm.
(Christie's) $39,204 £24,200

ALBERT CONRAD – 'No more tick' – signed on the margin – 23 x 35in.
(Bearne's) $2,848 £1,600

CONSTABLE

EBENZER WAKE COOKE (1843-1926) – The Loggetta, St. Mark's, Venice – signed and dated 1901 – pencil and watercolour heightened with white – 15¼ x 21in.
(Christie's)   **$3,586   £2,200**

TITO CONTI (1842-1924) – An Italian beauty – signed – 52 x 41cm.
(Christie's)   **$9,377   £6,050**

JOHN CONSTABLE, R.A. (1776-1837) - Study of the artist's daughter Maria as Bo-peep – inscribed on the reverse: Minna as/Bo-peep-/painted by/J. Constable R.A. and: Done in Keppel Street/Decemb' 1 1820 – oil on millboard – 17.5 x 10.5cm.
(Sotheby's)   **$29,568   £17,600**

CONSTANT – Flute player with cat – signed and dated upper right Constant 50 – brush and black and brown ink and black chalk on paper – 46 x 51cm.
(Christie's)   **$21,185   £13,324**

DELBERT DANA COOMBS (American, 1850-1936) – "Study of Cows" – signed and dated 1921 – identified on label from the Portland Museum of Art – oil on canvas – 32¼ x 27¼ in.
(Skinner)   **$1,200   £719**

COLIN CAMPBELL COOPER (1856-1937) –
Columbus Circle, New York – signed Colin Campbell
Cooper, l.l.; also indistinctly inscribed and inscribed with
the artist's initials C.C.C. on the stretcher – oil on canvas –
63.5 x 76.2cm.
(Sotheby's) **$48,400 £30,828**

WILLIAM SIDNEY COOPER (fl. 1871-1908) –
Herding Sheep on a Village Lane – signed and dated 1883
– oil on canvas – 46 x 69cm.
(Phillips) **$1,222 £750**

WILLIAM SIDNEY COOPER (English, fl. 1871-1908)
– 'Christchurch, Hants' – signed and dated 1890 –
71 x 124.4cm.
(Bonhams) **$2,790 £1,800**

THOMAS SIDNEY COOPER, R.A. – Cattle and Sheep
in a water meadow – signed and dated 1872 – oil on
canvas – 76 x 109cm.
(Sotheby's) **$28,688 £17,600**

THOMAS SIDNEY COOPER, R.A. – Cattle in a water
meadow – signed and dated 1882 – oil on panel – 22.5 x
35.5cm.
(Sotheby's) **$4,303 £2,640**

ALEXANDER COOSEMANS – 17th Century Still Life
with grapes, melons and peaches, a blue and white Delft
bowl of blackberries in landscape – oil – signed –
23 x 32in.
(Graves Son & Pilcher) **$32,400 £20,000**

COPNALL

FERN I. COPPEDGE (1888-1951) – Sadler's shop at
Carversville, PA. – oil on canvas – 24 x 24in. – signed
Fern I Coppedge lower left
(Bruce D. Collins)   **$8,800 £5,238**

FRANK T. COPNALL (born 1870) – The Young Nelson
– signed and dated 1902 – oil on canvas – 134.5 x 71cm.
(Phillips)   **$1,956 £1,200**

LE CORBUSIER (CHARLES EDOUARD
JEANNERET) (1887-1965) – Femme nue se reposant –
signed lower right Le Corbusier 33 and inscribed, signed
and dated on the mount Georges Kirsch en souvenier d'un
accordeon bien Le Corbusier 3 Juillet 54 – black ink and
watercolour on paper – unframed – 30.7 x 20.9cm. –
Executed in 1933
(Christie's)   **$8,866 £5,720**

THERESA COPNALL - Sidalcea and other flowers' -
signed – on canvas – 61 x 51cm.
(Bonhams)   **$1,738 £1,100**

VITTORIO-MATTEO CORCOS (1859-1933) – A
beauty – signed – 68.5 x 43cm.
(Christie's)   **$19,481   £12,100**

JEAN-BAPTISTE DE CORNEILLE (1649-PARIS-
1695) – Proteus and Menelas – on canvas – 45 x 33cm.
(Phillips)   **$6,846   £4,200**

VITTORIO CORCOS (1859-1933) – La belle Epoque –
signed – 59 x 43cm.
(Christie's)   **$21,312   £13,750**

CORNEILLE – Les Amants passionement – signed and
dated lower left Corneille '74 – and signed and dated again
and numbered VIII – acrylic on canvas – 55 x 46cm.
(Christie's)   **$10,089   £6,345**

COROT

JEAN-BAPTISTE CAMILLE COROT – Fillette
Pensive – oil on canvas – 46.3 x 38.1cm.
(Sotheby's) **$880,000 £553,459**

CARLO CORRADINI (late 19th Century) – The
portrait – signed and dated Roma 1882 – on panel –
35.5 x 46.5cm.
(Christie's) **$4,250 £2,640**

JEAN BAPTISTE CAMILLE COROT (1796-1875) –
Une Rivière vue de haut entre les Arbres – signed lower
right Corot – oil on canvas – 24.4 x 27.6cm.
(Christie's) **$94,047 £60,500**

JEAN BAPTISTE CAMILLE COROT (1796-1875) –
Ronde d'Amours; Lever du Soleil – signed lower right
Corot – oil on canvas – 65 x 97cm.
(Christie's) **$940,472 £605,000**

HERMANN CORRODI – By the Nile – signed l.l and
inscribed Roma – oil on canvas – 72 x 43cm.
(Sotheby's) **$16,082 £9,350**

MASTER OF CORTEGES, attributed to – Actif en France au milieu du XVIIe siècle – Les Joueurs de Cartes – oil on canvas – 101 x 132cm.
(Sotheby's) $24,737   £15,857

EDOUARD CORTES (1882-1969) – La Place de la Madeleine, Paris – signed – on panel – 17 x 21.5cm.
(Christie's) $8,855   £5,500

EDOUARD CORTES (1882-1969) – Place de la Republique, Paris – signed – unframed – 33 x 46cm.
(Christie's) $13,299   £8,580

COSSIERS

ANDRE COTTAVOZ – The room – oil on canvas – signed – 25 x 42cm.
(Jean-Claude Anaf)   **$5,612   £3,598**

JAN COSSIERS (1600-1671), Circle of – Elegant ladies listening to a companion playing music – oil on copper – 37.5 x 31cm.
(Phillips)   **$5,796   £3,600**

NOEL JACK COUNIHAN (b. 1913) – Aboriginal Family outside Swann Hill – signed and dated '60 – on board – 76.2 x 92.1cm.
(Christie's)   **$30,294   £18,700**

GIOVANNI COSTA (1833-1903) – The young flower girl – signed – 128.5 x 76cm.
(Christie's)   **$22,165   £14,300**

GUTAVE COURBET – Paysanne au Madras – signed – oil on canvas – 60 x 73cm.
(Sotheby's)   **$605,000   £380,503**

FRANS COURTENS (1854-1943) – Shearing sheep –
signed and dated 1901 – 111 x 175cm.
(Christie's)   **$13,640   £8,800**

GUSTAVE COURBET (1819-1877) – Ophélie (La
Fiancée de la Mort) – signed lower left G Courbet – oil on
panel – 34.4 x 29cm.
(Christie's)   **$222,293   £143,000**

GUSTAVE COURTOIS – A young girl in a white dress –
signed and dated 1885 – oil on canvas – 45 x 36cm.
(Sotheby's)   **$3,784   £2,200**

ANGELO DE COURTEN – A good bargain – signed l.l
– oil on canvas – 131 x 86cm.
(Sotheby's)   **$8,514   £4,950**

E. IRVING COUSE (1886-1936) – Klikitat Indian with
pony – signed E. I. Couse, l.l. – oil on canvas –
66 x 82.6cm. – Executed circa 1897-98
(Sotheby's)   **$46,200   £29,427**

COUSE

MARMADUKE CRADOCK, Follower of – A hound chasing wild duck in a river landscape – 36.2 x 61.6cm.
(Christie's) **$2,869 £1,760**

E. IRVING COUSE "(1886-1936) – Indian by the fire – signed E. I. Couse, l.l. – oil on canvas – 61.6 x 74.3cm.
(Sotheby's) **$30,800 £19,618**

ROBERT MCGOWAN COVENTRY, A.R.S.A., R.S.W. – Dordrecht harbour – signed – watercolour heightened with bodycolour – 37 x 54cm.
(Sotheby's) **$2,020 £1,210**

EMILY CRAWFORD – Pussy's breakfast – signed and dated 1878; bears title on a label on the stretcher – oil on canvas – 30.5 x 25.5cm.
(Sotheby's) **$1,613 £990**

DAVID COX (Birmingham 1783-1859) – Harvesters – signed and dated lower centre: David Cox 1839 – watercolour – 16.5 x 22.8cm.
(Lawrence) **$2,706 £1,650**

RALSTON CRAWFORD – Sanford Tanks – signed Ralston Crawford, l.l. – watercolour, pen and black ink and pencil on paper laid down on board – 28.6 x 39.4cm.
(Christie's) **$15,400 £9,625**

ATTRIBUTED TO JOSEPH CRAWHALL, R.W.S. –
Mare and foal in Tangier – watercolour – 30.5 x 48.5cm.
(Sotheby's)   **$5,143   £3,080**

**THEODORE MORROW CRILEY (American, 1880-
1930)** – Figures Along the Stream – Estate monogram l.l. –
estate stamp on the reverse – oil on canvas – 16 x 12³⁄₄in.
(Skinner)   **$1,600   £1,000**

JOSEPH CRAWHALL, R.W.S. – A huntsman – signed
and dated '90 – watercolour over black ink – 30.5 x 25cm.
(Sotheby's)   **$11,940   £7,150**

CARLO ANTONIO CRESPI, Follower of – A still life
of fish and kitchen vessels upon a table – oil on canvas –
61 x 84cm.
(Phillips)   **$3,423   £2,100**

GEORGES CROEGAERT (born 1848) – A gypsy girl –
signed and inscribed Paris 1886 – on panel –
27.2 x 21.5cm.
(Christie's)   **$4,250   £2,640**

CROPSEY

JASPER FRANCIS CROPSEY (1823-1900) – Fort Putnam on the Hudson – signed J. F. Cropsey, l.r. – oil on canvas – 39.4 x 64.8cm.
(Sotheby's) **$82,500 £52,548**

JASPER FRANCIS CROPSEY – Hackensack Meadows in the Autumn – signed J. F. Cropsey and dated 1894, l.r. – watercolour and pencil on paper – 34 x 54.5cm.
(Christie's) **$17,600 £11,000**

JASPER FRANCIS CROPSEY – Autumn on the Delaware River – signed J. F. Cropsey and dated 1890, l.r. – oil on canvas – 17.8 x 33cm.
(Christie's) **$14,300 £8,937**

VILMOS PERLROTT CSABA – Ciganpar – tempera on paper – signed – 46 x 70cm.
(Mugyujtok Galeriaja Kft) **$974 £590**

ISTVAN CSOK – Tamar – oil on canvas – signed – 60 x 50cm.
(Mugyujtok Galeriaja Kft) **$5,188 £3,144**

ISTVAN CSOK – Sokac kislany - oil on canvas – signed – 60 x 50cm.
(Mugyujtok Galeriaja Kft) **$3,242 £1,965**

HENRY HADFIELD CUBLEY – The Village of Glencoe, Argyllshire – signed and dated 1889 – signed, inscribed and dated on the reverse – 23¹/₄ x 35¹/₄ in.
(Bearne's) **$3,204 £1,800**

F*** CUCANO – A Continental farmyard – signed – 35 x 47¹/₂ in.
(Bearne's) **$1,943 £1,150**

EDWARD CUCUEL – A Hot Day – signed Cucuel, l.r. – signed again on the stretcher – oil on canvas – 88.3 x 98.1cm.
(Christie's) **$19,800 £12,375**

CUCUEL

EDWARD CUCUEL – The Awakening – signed Cucuel, l.l. – signed again on the panel backing – oil on canvas laid down on panel – 72 x 80cm.
(Christie's) **$18,700 £11,687**

FREDERICK G.R. CUMING – Studio and Crescent Moon – signed and dated '69 – oil on board – 127 x 99cm.
(Phillips) **$2,704 £1,600**

EDWARD CUCUEL – Down the Garden Path – signed Cucuel, l.l. – oil on canvas – 61.3 x 76.5cm.
(Christie's) **$17,600 £11,000**

MAURICE CULLEN, R.C.A. (Canadian School, 1866-1934) – Cottage at Chembly – signed with monogram – oil on panel – 16 x 22cm.
(Phillips) **$2,934 £1,800**

M.L. CUROT-BARBEREL (fl. 1880) – Portrait of a young girl, in a blue dress and bonnet, with her pet dog – signed – pastel – 72 x 53cm.
(Christie's) **$2,558 £1,650**

CURRIER AND IVES (19th Century) – Camping in the woods "A good time coming" – large folio, hand coloured stone lithograph – 18³/₄ x 27¹/₂in.
(Bruce D. Collins)   **$3,850   £2,292**

CECIL E. CUTLER – A stroll in the park – signed and dated 1896 – watercolour over pencil heightened wirth bodycolour – unframed – 32 x 40cm.
(Sotheby's)   **$3,366   £1,980**

HIPPOLYTE DAEYE (1873-1952) - Baby - signed lower right DAEYE - oil on cnavas - 66 x 41cm. Painted in 1918.
(Christie's)   **$21,120 $13,200**

FRED DADE – Picking Flowers – signed indistinctly lower right Fred Dade 93 – oil on canvas – 13³/₄ x 9⁵/₈in.
(Christie's)   **$2,085   £1,320**

HENRI DAGNEAU – A Still Life with a potted Hydrangea before a Watering Can containing Gladiolo – signed and dated 1881 – on canvas – 66 x 54.5cm.
(Bonhams)   **$1,027   £650**

FRANCIS DANBY, A.R.A. (1793-1861) – The embarkation of Cleopatra on the Cydnus – This newly discovered picture was commissioned from Danby by William Hammond in 1843 – signed l.l. : F. Danby 1843 – 60 x 83cm.
(Sotheby's)   **$119,350   £77,000**

Circle of MICHAEL DAHL (?1659-1743) – Portrait of a young girl – full length, standing, wearing a green and silver dress with a basket of flowers and a lamb at her feet – oil on canvas, in a carved wood frame – 124 x 101cm.
(Sotheby's)   **$9,240   £5,500**

FRANCIS DANBY, A.R.A. (1793-1861) – A street in Tintern – inscribed on a label on the reverse: A Street in Tintern/F. Danby – oil on panel – 279 x 228cm.
(Sotheby's)   **$17,556   £10,450**

NATHANIEL DANCE, R.A. (1735-1811) – Portrait of
John Lee. Attorney-General (1733-1793) – half length,
wearing legal robes – signed u.l. N.D. p./1770 – oil on
canvas – 75 x 62cm.
(Sotheby's) **$5,968 £3,850**

WILLIAM DANIELL, R.A. (1769-1837) – Conway
Castle, North Wales – oil on canvas – 106 x 181.5cm.
(Sotheby's) **$44,330 £28,600**

WILLIAM DANIELL, R.A. (1769-1837) – A view of the
European factories at Canton in China – oil on canvas –
unlined, in original carved wood frame – 91.5 x 181cm.
(Sotheby's) **$1,182,720 £704,000**

BARTHOLOMEW DANDRIDGE (b. 1691), Circle of –
Portrait of a young boy, standing full length, holding a
shuttlecock and racket on a terrace by a balustrade –
152.4 x 101.7cm.
(Christie's) **$68,134 £41,800**

***CIRCLE OF HENRY PIERRE DANLOUX (1753-
1809)*** – Portrait of a gentleman with his wife and son – full
length, he seated wearing a blue coat, his wife a white
muslin dress, their son a white dress – oil on canvas –
69 x 50cm.
(Sotheby's) **$6,479 £1,180**

DANSAERT

LÉON DANSAERT – The Concert – signed – oil on panel – 36 x 26cm.
(Sotheby's) **$3,740 £2,200**

ANDREW DASBURG (1887-1979) – Finney Farm –
signed Dasburg, l.l. – oil on canvasboard – 33 x 40.6cm.
(Sotheby's) **$37,400 £23,821**

HUGO DARNAUT – A bridge over a river in a woody
landscape - signed - oil on board - 74.5 x 50.5cm.
(Sotheby's) **$3,740 £2,200**

**Studio of ANTONIS MOR VAN DASHORST, called
ANTONIO MORO (1517/21-1576/7)** – Portrait of an
officer of the Spanish forces, three-quarter length, his right
hand resting on his sword – oil on canvas – 109 x 77cm.
(Phillips) **$9,396 £5,800**

ARTURO D'ATRI – 'Young admirers' – signed - 82.5 x 51.5cm.
(Anderson & Garland) **$1,658 £975**

ALLEN DOUGLAS DAVIDSON – Model Resting – signed – oil on board – 38 x 30.5cm.
(Phillips) **$6,591 £3,900**

ETHEL DAVIES (Liverpool fl. circa 1910) – The Gossips – signed lower right: Ethel Davies – watercolour – 61.6 x 49.6cm.
(Lawrence) **$1,714 £1,045**

BESSIE DAVIDSON (1879-1965) – Still Life – signed – signed and inscribed on the reverse – on panel – 37.4 x 45.7cm.
(Christie's) **$16,038 £9,900**

DAVIS

DENHOLM DAVIS – Portrait of a lady — signed — oil on canvas — 30.5 x 25.5cm.
(Sotheby's) **$2,869 £1,760**

Circle of WILLIAM HENRY DAVIS – A Cow in an extensive Wooded Landscape – 55.3 x 76.2cm.
(Bonhams) **$1,914 £1,100**

STUART DAVIS (1894-1964) – Night Life – signed S. Davis, u.c.; also signed Stuart Davis, titled Night Life and dated 1962 on the stretcher – oil on canvas – 61.0 x 81.3cm.
(Sotheby's) **$880,000 £560,509**

STUART G. DAVIS (fl. 1893-1904) - An Arcadian idyll signed – 142.5 x 193.5cm.
(Christie's) **$32,395 £20,900**

WARREN B. DAVIS – The Green Glade – signed Warren Davis, l.r. – signed again and inscribed with title on the reverse – oil on canvas – 46 x 36cm.
(Christie's) **$2,200 £1,375**

WILLIAM DAVIS (1812-1873) – A field of corn – signed with initials – on board – 31.1 x 49.5cm.
(Christie's) **$6,996 £4,400**

WILLIAM M. DAVIS – Farmyard – signed W. M. Davis, l.r. – oil on canvas – 36 x 56.6cm.
(Christie's)   **$16,500   £10,312**

WALTER LOFTHOUSE DEAN (American, 1854-1912) – Wharves and Warehouses, Gloucester Harbor – signed - oil on canvas – 20 x 24¼ in.
(Skinner)   **$3,250   £1,946**

HENRY DAWSON – Evening on the coast – on board – 9¾ x 7¾in.
(Bearne's)   **$1,388   £780**

SCHOOL OF CHARLES DEAS (American, 1818-1867) – "Long Jakes" – unsigned – oil on canvas – 32 x 24in.
(Skinner)   **$7,000   £4,192**

HENRY THOMAS DAWSON – A continental harbour – signed and dated 1879 – 23⅔in x 36in.
(Bearne's)   **$11,036   £6,200**

JOSEPH DECKER (1853-1924) – The Red Admiral – signed J. Decker, u.r. – oil on canvas – 20.3 x 35.6cm. – Painted in the mid 1880's
(Sotheby's)   **$759,000   £483,439**

DEGAS

EDGAR DEGAS – Buste de femme – signed – oil on canvas – 55 x 36cm. – painted circa 1887-1890
(Sotheby's) **$907,500 £570,755**

EDGAR DEGAS - Femme en Peignoir bleu le torse découvert – stamped with the signature – oil on canvas – 92 x 42cm.
(Sotheby's) **$3,850,000 £2,421,384**

EDGAR DEGAS (1834-1917) – Duchesse de Montejasi-Cicerale – oil on canvas – 45 x 37.5cm. – Painted in Naples circa 1868
(Christie's) **$1,650,000 £1,033,890**

EUGENE DELACROIX (1798-1863) – Tête de Madame
Cave – pastel on paper – 31.5 x 25.5cm. –
Executed in 1846
(Christie's) **$88,660** **£57,200**

EDGAR DEGAS – Danseuses – signed – oil on canvas –
61 x 48cm.
(Sotheby's) **$3,630,000** **£2,283,019**

EUGENE DELACROIX (French 1798-1863) –
Cromwell at Windsor Castle – signed and stamped with the
EUGENE DELACROIX and assistants – Tobias and the collection mark of Dr. Justus Schmidt – watercolour over
angel – signed – oil on canvas – painted circa 1861 – pencil heightened with bodycolour and gum arabic –
39.5 x 31.5cm. 28 x 21cm.
(Sotheby's) **$22,440** **£13,200** *(Sotheby's)* **$80,344** **£48,400**

DELEN

PAUL DELVAUX (b. 1897) - St. Idesbald—
signed – dated and titled St Idesbald 4-9-45 P. Delvaux –
pen and black ink and watercolour on paper –
55.3 x 74.3cm. – Executed in 1945
(Christie's)   **$15,840**   **£9,900**

**DIRK VAN DELEN (Heusden 1605-1671
Arnemuyden)** – Two elegant figures standing in the hall
of a palace – signed and dated d.v. delen 1643 – on panel –
49.5 x 48cm.
(Phillips)   **$19,560**   **£12,000**

EDWIN WILLARD DEMING (American, 1860-1942)
– "Calling Moose" – signed with monogram – oil on
canvasboard – 12 x 15$^{1}/_{2}$ in.
(Skinner)   **$3,250**   **£1,946**

DAVIDA DELLEPIANE – A figure on a mountain at
dusk – signed l.r. and dedicated A l'ami Chabrol – oil on
canvas – 54 x 72.5cm.
(Sotheby's)   **$16,082**   **£9,350**

HIPPOLYTE CAMILLE DELPY – A washerwoman by
a river – signed; indistinctly dedicated Avec mes
meilleurs...Paris le 6 mars 1901, Eugénie Delpy – oil on
board – 16 x 27cm.
(Sotheby's)   **$3,553**   **£2,090**

ANDRÉ DERAIN (1880-1954) – Bateaux dans le Port,
Collioure – signed lower left a derain – oil on canvas –
72.2 x 91.5cm.
(Christie's)   **$9,575,720**   **£6,160,000**

GEORGES D'ESPAGNAT – Femme Jouant aux Cartes –
signed with the initials – oil on canvas – 60 x 73cm.
(Sotheby's) **$110,000 £69,182**

Follower of ALEXANDRE-FRANÇOIS DESPORTES
– A Marlborough Spaniel with the day's bag and a French
flintlock gun in the gardens of a country house –
76.2 x 97.7cm.
(Christie's) **$14,960 £8,800**

JULES ERNEST DEVAUX – The fishing corner of the
Ile Saint-Louis, Paris – signed – oil on canvas –
59.5 x 44.5cm.
(Sotheby's) **$4,675 £2,750**

**ALEXANDRE FRANCOIS DESPORTES (Champagne
1661-1743 Paris)** – A still life of dead game on a ledge
with a cat peering from behind an orange drape – on
canvas – 92 x 73cm.
(Phillips) **$65,200 £40,000**

ARTHUR DEVIS (1711-1787) – Portrait of the Reverend
Thomas D'Oyly with his wife, Henrietta Maria – both full
length, he seated wearing clerical dress and holding a
letter, she standing wearing a blue dress – oil on canvas –
73.5 x 61cm.
(Sotheby's) **$105,710 £68,200**

DEVIS

ARTHUR WILLIAM DEVIS (1762-1822) – Portrait of
Charles Russell Crommelin – full length, standing by a
tree, his Irish Setter by his feet, his residence beyond – oil
on canvas – 82.5 x 57.5cm.
(Sotheby's) **$71,610 £46,200**

JOHN ROBERT DICKSEE – Catherine Scott – signed
with monogram and bears monogram; signed and inscribed
with title on the reverse – oil on canvas – 42 x 34cm.
(Sotheby's) **$3,048 £1,870**

ROBERT HENRY DICKERSON (b. 1924) – Girl with
Clasped Hands – signed – pastel – 76.5 x 56.2cm.
(Christie's) **$1,426 £880**

ARTHUR VIDAL DIEHL (1870-1929) – Dockside – oil
on board – 10 x 7in. – signed A.V. Diehl lower left
(Bruce D. Collins) **$1,045 £622**

ADRIAEN VAN DIEST (1655-1704) – Prospect of Sprotborough Hall, near Doncaster, Yorkshire, the seat of Sir Godfrey Copley, from across the river Don – oil on canvas – 70 x 184cm. *(Sotheby's)* **$54,560 £35,200**

CHRISTIAN WILHELM ERNST DIETRICH, Manner of – The Wedding Feast – oil on canvas – 79 x 58.5cm.
(Bonhams)   **$1,932 £1,200**

JOHAN DIJKSTRA – A flower still life with gladioli in a glaze vase – signed lower left Johan Dijkstra – 80.5 x 60cm.
(Christie's)   **$2,775 £1,745**

DILLON

CHARLES DIXON, R.I. (1872-1934) – Shipping in Portsmouth Harbour – signed and dated 1890 – watercolour over pencil – 49.5 x 115.5cm.
(Phillips) **$2,445 £1,500**

FRANK DILLON, R.A. (1823-1909) - An Arab Courtyard – oil on canvas – 43 x 30.5cm.
(Phillips) **$1,141 £700**

HENRY JOHN DOBSON, R.S.W. – Asking a blessing – signed; bears title on a label attached to the backboard – oil on canvas – 40.5 x 51cm.
(Sotheby's) **$4,776 £2,860**

CHARLES DIXON, R.I. (1872-1934) – The busy Pool of London – signed and dated '04 – watercolour and bodycolour – 48.5 x 74cm.
(Phillips) **$9,454 £5,800**

CHARLES DIXON – "Greenwich Reach" – signed and dated 1913 – watercolour drawing – 11 x 31in.
(Riddetts) **$5,440 £3,400**

WILLIAM CHARLES THOMAS DOBSON, R.A. (1817-1898) – Meditation – signed with monogram and dated 1873 – watercolour – 52 x 41.5cm.
(Phillips) **$978 £600**

MARCO D'OGGIONO (1475-Oggiono-1549) -
Madonna and child – tempera on linen, laid down on panel
– 49.5 x 36cm.
(Phillips) **$61,940 £38,000**

CARLO DOLCI, Manner of – The Madonna – oil on
canvas – 121.5 x 99.5cm.
(Phillips) **$1,449 £900**

PIETER CORNELIS DOMMERSEN (1834-1908) –
Waiting for the ferry – signed and dated 1868 – on panel –
30 x 40cm.
(Christie's) **$8,500 £5,280**

WILLIAM R. DOMMERSEN – Scheveningen on the
Zuider Zee, Holland – signed – signed and inscribed on the
reverse – 19$^{1}/_{4}$ x 29$^{1}/_{2}$in.
(Bearne's) **$4,806 £2,700**

WILLIAM DOMMERSEN – Kampden on the Zuider
Zee – signed – inscribed on the reverse – 19$^{1}/_{2}$ x 29$^{1}/_{4}$in.
(Bearne's) **$5,518 £3,100**

DOMMERSEN

WILLIAM RAYMOND DOMMERSEN (died 1927) –
The Moses and Aaron church in the Jewish quarter of
Amsterdam – signed and dated 1884 – 39.3 x 59.6cm.
(Christie's) **$6,820 £4,400**

KEN DONE (20th Century) – Saturday 1982 – signed
and dated 1982 – unframed – 73.1 x 100.9cm.
(Christie's) **$5,702 £3,520**

KEES VAN DONGEN (1877-1968) – Mère et Enfant –
signed and inscribed lower right Van Dongen Deauville –
watercolour on paper – 61 x 49cm. – Executed in 1925
(Christie's) **$93,775 £60,500**

F.... R.... DONAT – A fisherman and his daughter – oil on
panel – a pair – each signed – each 18 x 9¹/₂in.
(David Lay) **$1,007 £650**

AUGUSTE DONNAY (1862-1921) – Un Sommet en
Automne à Mery-sur-Ourthe—Herfstlandschap te Mery-
sur-Ourthe – signed lower right Aug. Donnay – oil on
board – 42.5 x 68cm.
(Christie's) **$9,680 £6,050**

EDWIN DOUGLAS, R.S.A. (1848-1907) – The
Shepherd's trust — A Rough Collie – signed with initials
and dated '78 – 93 x 71cm.
(Christie's) **$14,025 £8,250**

GUSTAVE DORÉ (French 1832-83) – A mother and
child – signed – oil on canvas – 91 x 71cm.
(Sotheby's) **$51,128 £30,800**

EDWIN DOUGLAS, R.S.A. (1848-1947) – 'The First of
September' — An English Tricolour and a Gordon Setter
with a partridge – 127 x 160cm.
(Christie's) **$35,530 £20,900**

GERARD DOU, Follower of – An old woman chopping
onions by the light of a candle – oil on panel – 35 x 31cm.
(Phillips) **$2,934 £1,800**

ARTHUR WESLEY DOW (American, 1857-1922) –
The Blue Boat – signed – oil on canvas – 26 x 36in.
(Skinner) **$42,000 £25,150**

DOWNIE

PATRICK DOWNIE, R.S.W. – Ploughing – signed and dated 1924 – gouache – 38 x 55cm.
(Sotheby's) **$1,653   £990**

PATRICK DOWNIE, R.S.W. – Evening- The foot of Smithhills Paisley – signed with monogram; signed – inscribed with title and dated 1887 on a label on the stretcher – watercolour heightened with bodycolour – 24.5 x 34cm.
(Sotheby's) **$1,837   £1,100**

DELAPOER DOWNING – Pondering a next move – signed – oil on canvas – 51 x 76cm.
(Sotheby's) **$3,586   £2,200**

CHRISTIAAN LODEWIJK WILLEM DREIBHOLZ (1799-1874) – Fishing boats in choppy seas – signed – on panel – 33.5 x 47cm.
(Christie's) **$4,250   £2,640**

ALFRED DE DREUX, Attributed to – Spaniel in a landscape – signed with initials – oil on canvas – 116.8 x 83.8cm.
(Sotheby's) **$12,100   £7,610**

GEORGE W. DREW (1875-?) – Coast of Maine – oil on canvas – 12 x 24in. – signed George W. Drew lower right
(Bruce D. Collins) **$1,650   £982**

DAVID CLYDE DRIDAN (b. 1932) – The Coorong, South Australia – signed – titled on the reverse – on board – 69.2 x 89.5cm.
(Christie's)   **$3,029 £1,870**

CLAUDE MARIE DUBUFE – A portrait of an elegant lady – signed – oil on canvas – 130 x 97cm.
(Sotheby's)   **$4,114 £2,420**

ADOLPHE HENRI DUBASTY (French, 1814-1884) – The Tambourine Girl – panel – signed and dated 1868 – 40.7 x 33cm.
(Bonhams)   **$1,860 £1,200**

JEAN DUBUFFET (1901-1985) – Site aleatoire avec un personnage – signed and dated 82 – acrylic and paper collage on paper mounted on canvas – 67 x 100cm.
(Christie's)   **$138,160 £88,000**

GUY PENE DUBOIS – The Circus Tent – signed Guy Pène duBois, l.r. – oil on panel – 51 x 63.7cm.
(Christie's)   **$137,500 £85,937**

CHARLES DUDLEY – Gathering flowers in a meadow – signed – oil on canvas – 37 x 53.5cm.
(Sotheby's)   **$4,841 £2,970**

DUEZ

ERNEST-ANGE DUEZ (French 1843-96) – The Pont Neuf, Paris – signed and dated Paris 1884 – oil on canvas – 64 x 80cm.
(Sotheby's)   **$58,432**   **£35,200**

RAOUL DUFY (1877-1953) – Les Arbres verts à l'Estaque – signed lower right R. Dufy – oil on canvas – 81 x 65cm.
(Christie's)   **$273,592**   **£176,000**

PREFETE DUFFAUT (Haitian, b. 1929) – "Jacmel Haiti" (A Harbour View) – signed and titled "Prefete Duffaut..." l.c. – oil on masonite – 24 x 20in.
(Skinner)   **$1,000**   **£625**

RAOUL DUFY (1877-1953) – Chevaux devant les Ecuries, Deauville – signed lower right Raoul Dufy – watercolour and gouache on paper – 56 x 76.5cm.
(Christie's)   **$98,890**   **£63,800**

WILLIAM DUFFIELD (1816-1863) – Portrait of the Hon. Frederick Villiers (1815-1871), with his sisters Lady Sarah and Lady Clementina Villiers – all full length, wearing historical costumes – signed l.l: William Duffield/ 1840 – oil on canvas – 100 x 124cm.
(Sotheby's)   **$30,690**   **£19,800**

GASPAR DUGHET, Attributed to, called GASPAR POUSSIN (1615-Rome-1675) – A landscape in the Campagna – on canvas – 74 x 98cm.
(Phillips)   **$11,050**   **£6,500**

THOMAS R. DUNLAY (American, 20th Century) –
Summer Meadow, Williamstown – signed and dated
"Thomas R. Dunlay '78" – oil on canvas   16 x 20in.
(Skinner)   **$5,500   £3,293**

MARY DUNCAN (1885- c. 1967) – "Still Life with
Globe" – oil on board   signed – inscribed to reverse –
17 x 14½in.
(David Lay)   **$217   £140**

BRIAN JAMES DUNLOP (b. 1938) – Cattle Market,
Victoria – signed – titled on the reverse – watercolour and
bodycolour – 50.1 x 60.3cm.
(Christie's)   **$3,564   £2,200**

DUNLOP

RONALD OSSORY DUNLOP – A full length portrait of
a lady in a pink dress – signed 'Dunlop' – oil on canvas –
82 x 59cm.
(Woolley & Wallis) **$1,190 £700**

HARVEY T. DUNN – The Old Miner – signed with
monogrammed initials HTD and dated 24, u.r. – signed
Harvey Dunn – dated April 1925 and inscribed Ladies
Home Journal on the reverse – oil on canvas – 77 x 101cm.
(Christie's) **$8,800 £5,500**

JOSEPH DUNN of Worcester (English, 1806-1860) – A
Pointer in a Landscape – signed and dated '57 –
33 x 48.3cm.
(Bonhams) **$853 £550**

ROBERT SPEAR DUNNING – Peaches in a Glass Bowl
– signed R. S. Dunning, l.r. – oil on canvas –
28.5 x 32.3cm.
(Christie's) **$8,800 £5,500**

ROBERT SPEAR DUNNING (1829-1905) – Still life:
Peach, pear and grapes – signed R. S. Dunning and dated
'97, l.r.; also signed R. S. Dunning, P....and dated 1897 on
the reverse – oil on canvas – 19.0 x 28.5cm.
(Sotheby's) **$23,100 £14,713**

**Attributed to FRANCOIS LEONARD DUPONT (1756-
1821)** – A still life of a vase of flowers upon a draped
ledge beside a bowl of fruit with sheet music and a
recorder at its foot – oil on panel – 74 x 57cm.
(Phillips) **$7,452 £4,600**

BERNARD DUNSTAN, R.A. – Dressing in front of Door 1 – signed with initials bottom left: BD – oil on board – 44.4 x 30.5cm.
(Lawrence)   **$4,330 £2,640**

PAUL MICHEL DUPUY – A young girl in a straw hat - signed; stamped with the cachet de vente on the reverse – oil on canvas – 54.5 x 32cm.
(Sotheby's)   **$4,730 £2,750**

BERNARD DUNSTAN, R.A. (b. 1920) – The Bathroom – signed with initials lower left BD – pastel – 13¾ x 11in.
(Christie's)   **$2,781 £1,760**

LYLE DURGIN (American, 19th/20th Century) – Portrait of a Woman – signed and dated "Lyle Durgin '87" – oil on canvas – 52 x 32in.
(Skinner)   **$1,500 £938**

DURRIE

GEORGE HENRY DURRIE (1829-1863) – At the mill, winter – signed G. H. Durrie and dated N. Haven 1858, l.r. – oil on canvas – 66 x 91.4cm.
(Sotheby's) **$264,000 £168,153**

GEORGE HENRY DURRIE – Winter Farmyard – signed G. H. Durrie and dated 1862, l.l. – oil on board – 20.3 x 32cm.
(Christie's) **$16,500 £10,312**

ABRAHAN VAN DYCK (1635-Amsterdam-1672) – Portrait of a young woman, half length in profile, wearing a Burgundian hat – on panel – 71 x 57cm.
(Phillips) **$11,050 £6,500**

PAUL DUVERGNE – A North African fort – signed and dated Paris '84 – oil on canvas – 96.5 x 130cm.
(Sotheby's) **$4,675 £2,750**

ANTON VAN DYCK 1599-1641 – Follower of – Portrait du Collectionneur d'art Anversois Antonius Cor-Nélissen (1565-1639) – oil on panel – 26 x 21cm.
(Sotheby's) **$7,421 £4,757**

ROBERT EADIE, R.S.W. – Princes Street from the Royal Scottish Academy looking east – signed – watercolour over black chalk on buff paper – 37 x 55cm. *(Sotheby's)* **$6,796 £4,070**

JOAN KATHLEEN HARDING EARDLEY, R.S.A., S.S.A. (1921-1963) – A Samson Girl – pastel on glass paper – 26.7 x 22.2cm. *(Christie's)* **$11,088 £6,600**

JOAN KATHLEEN HARDING EARDLEY, R.S.A. – Field in Summer II – oil on board – 109 x 121cm. *(Sotheby's)* **$22,044 £13,200**

JOAN KATHLEEN HARDING EARDLEY, R.S.A., S.S.A. (1921-1963) – A Glasgow Tenement – oil on canvas – unframed – 75 x 67.2cm. – and verso, A similar view *(Christie's)* **$18,480 £11,000**

JOAN KATHLEEN HARDING EARDLEY, R.S.A. – Boy in a blue jersey – signed – pastel – 50 x 37cm. *(Sotheby's)* **$23,881 £14,300**

171

EARL

RALPH EARL, Attributed to – Self Portrait – signed – dated 1774 and inscribed done by himself – oil on paper laid down on canvas – 66.0 x 50.8cm.
(Sotheby's)   **$8,250**   **£5,189**

SIR ALFRED EAST, R.A. (1849-1913) – In the Roman Campagna – signed and dated 1904 – 124.5 x 183cm.
(Christie's)   **$16,197**   **£10,450**

CHARLES H. EBERT – The Village Pump – signed Ebert, l.l. – signed again on the reverse and on the stretcher – oil on canvas – 63.5 x 76.2cm.
(Christie's)   **$8,800**   **£5,500**

GEORGE WHARTON EDWARDS – The Flemish Lacemaker – signed George Wharton Edwards and inscribed ©, l.r. – gouache, pastel and pencil on brown paper laid down on board – 43.8 x 32.5cm.
(Christie's)   **$9,900**   **£6,187**

LIONEL EDWARDS – The Bullfight – signed – inscribed "Spain", and dated 1910 – charcoal and pen and ink, heightened with white – 37 x 55cm.
(Phillips)   **$2,535**   **£1,500**

MARIE EGNER (Austrian 1850-1940) – Prickly pears in the corner of a terrace – signed – oil on canvas – 30 x 40cm.
(Sotheby's)   **$10,956**   **£6,600**

ERNEST H EHLERS – The coming of Spring – on board – signed – 9½ x 13½in.
(Michael Newman)   **$1,467   £900**

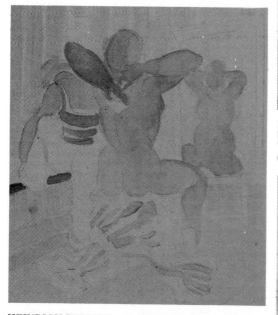

HEINRICH EHMSEN – In the bathing hut – watercolour and pencil – 49 x 39cm.
(Sotheby's)   **$1,758   £1,034**

ELISABETH VON EICKEN – A Birch Wood – signed – 67.9 x 99cm.
(Bonhams)   **$372   £240**

EMILE EISMAN-SEMENOWSKY – An Oriental beauty – signed – signed – authenticated and dated avril '89 on a label on the reverse – oil on panel – 32.5 x 24cm.
(Sotheby's)   **$6,054   £3,520**

GEORGE SAMUEL ELGOOD (1851-1943) – "Genoa" – signed – inscribed with title and dated 1891 – watercolour heightened with bodycolour and scratching out over pencil – 31.5 x 25.5cm.
(Phillips)   **$3,260   £2,000**

EDWIN ROMANZO ELMER – White Magnolias in a
Glass Pitcher – oil on canvas – 43.5 x 39cm.
(Christie's)   **$7,700   £4,812**

ARTHUR ELLIS (1856-1918) – A moment's thought –
signed – 61 x 51cm.
(Christie's)   **$26,235   £16,500**

JOHN ELLYS (c. 1701-1757) – Portrait of Mrs Hester
Booth, the dancer (1680-1773) – full length, standing on a
stage, wearing a harlequin dress – oil on canvas, in a
carved wood frame – 122 x 89cm.
(Sotheby's)   **$121,968   £72,600**

HENRY HETHERINGTON EMMERSON – My ladye
faire – signed with monogram; bears title on a label on the
backboard – oil on canvas laid on board – 105 x 74cm.
(Sotheby's)   **$2,331   £1,430**

JOHN EMMS – The Keeper - Partridge season – signed
and dated 1895 – oil on canvas – 94 x 79cm.
(Sotheby's) **$13,777 £8,250**

LYDIA FIELD EMMETT (American, born 1866) –
Portrait of a Young Girl, full length, seated – signed – oil
on canvas – 158.2 x 107cm.
(Phillips) **$8,476 £5,200**

JOHN EMMS and GEORGE CHESTER – Harvest
time in Surrey – signed and inscribed Figures by J. Emms
and G. Chester 1878; inscribed with title on the reverse –
oil on canvas – unframed – 91.5 x 152cm.
(Sotheby's) **$3,586 £2,200**

JOHN EMMS (1843-1912) – The Otter hunt; The
Fisherman's friend; and The day's bag - one signed –
19.1 x 15.2cm. – three in a common frame
(Christie's) **$10,285 £6,050**

JOHN EMMS – Mares and foals grazing – signed and
dated '04 – oil on canvas – 61 x 84cm.
(Sotheby's) **$4,662 £2,860**

EMMS

JOHN EMMS – English Setter with game – signed – oil on canvas – 35 x 44cm.
(Sotheby's)   **$5,694   £3,410**

ROSALIE M. EMSLIE (1854-1932) – Resting – signed – oil on canvas – 43 x 53.5cm.
(Phillips)   **$3,749   £2,300**

JOHN EMMS – Breaking cover – This depicts Henry Powell pulling down a fence at New Park Enclosure – signed – oil on canvas – 71 x 114cm.
(Sotheby's)   **$24,205   £14,850**

JOHN EMMS – Into the kennel – signed – oil on canvas – 26 x 36cm.
(Sotheby's)   **$1,972 £1,210**

ENGLISH SCHOOL (c. 1730-35) – A portrait of John Buchanan, Esq., Younger of Lenney, died 1735, half length, in a green gold braided coat, holding a rose – inscribed – painted oval – oil on canvas – 54.6 x 39.4cm.
(Christie's)   **$3,326   £1,980**

ENGLISH SCHOOL, circa 1800 – The Barber's shop – on copper – 36.8 x 52.1cm.
(Christie's)   **$4,488   £2,640**

AUGUSTUS WILLIAM ENNESS (b. 1876) – Tower Bridge, London – signed and dated 1910 – 25.3 x 35.6cm.
(Christie's)   **$4,303   £2,640**

JAMES ENSOR (1860-1949) – Rotondités—Rondheid – signed lower right ENSOR – and signed again on the reverse Ensor – inscribed on the stretcher Rotondités – oil on canvas – 50.8 x 60.9cm.
(Christie's)   **$123,200   £77,000**

SVEN ERIXSON – Sverre in white hat – signed and dated – 54 x 66cm.
(AB Stockholms Auktionsverk)   **$15,780   £9,681**

DELPHIN ENJOLRAS (French b. 1875) – The billet doux – signed – pastel – 70 x 51cm.
(Sotheby's)   **$8,217   £4,950**

MAURITS CORNELIS ESCHER – Day and Night (B. & L.303) – woodcut printed in black and ochre-grey – 1938 – on thin Japan – signed in pencil and inscribed eigen druk – S487 x 773mm.
(Christie's)   **$11,602   £7,297**

ESSELENS

JACOB ESSELENS (1626-Amsterdam-1687) –
Fishermen on a beach with their catch – on canvas –
109.5 x 148.5cm.
(Phillips)   **$22,820   £14,000**

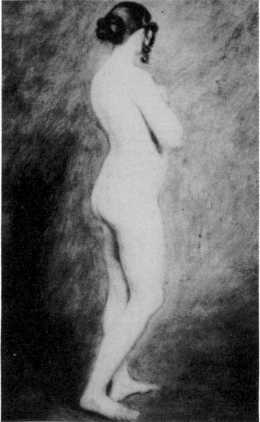

GUSTAV ESSIG – Portrait of two men – signed – oil on
canvas – 130 x 100cm.
(Sotheby's)   **$14,655   £8,620**

WILLIAM ETTY – A standng female nude – signed – a
sketch – on board – unframed – 35.5 x 20.3cm.
(Christie's)   **$913   £550**

PRINS EUGEN (Swedish 1865-1947) – A view of Södra Landet – signed and dated 1902; signed and titled on the backboard – charcoal and watercolour on paper laid down on canvas – 59 x 73.5cm.
(Sotheby's)   **$13,695   £8,250**

FREDERICK JAMES McNAMARA EVANS (fl. 1886-1930) – Anxious Moments – signed and dated 1888 – titled and signed on reverse label – watercolour – 54.5 x 35.5cm.
(Phillips)   **$4,890   £3,000**

DE SCOTT EVANS (S. S. DAVID), Attributed to – The Doctor's Prescription – oil on canvas – 23 x 16cm.
(Christie's)   **$18,700   £11,687**

FRANS VAN EVERBROECK – Grappe de Raisins – oil on canvas – 82 x 55cm.
(Sotheby's)   **$16,490 £10,571**

EVERGOOD

PHILIP EVERGOOD (1901-1973) – Aftermath – signed Philip Evergood, l.r.; also titled Aftermath on a piece of wood attached to the stretcher – oil on canvas – 94.5 x 124.5cm.
(Sotheby's) **$24,200 £15,414**

ADRIANUS EVERSEN (1818-1897) – A village scene – signed – on panel – unframed – 25.5 x 32cm.
(Christie's) **$2,834 £1,760**

ADRIANUS EVERSEN (Dutch 1818-97) – A busy street scene – signed – oil on panel – 56 x 74cm.
(Sotheby's) **$43,824 £26,400**

FRANCES EWAN (Exh. 1892-1929) – "Jim" a young sailor – oil on canvas – signed – artist's label to reverse – 35½ x 29½in.
(David Lay) **$775 £500**

FRANCES EWAN (Exh. 1892-1929) – "St. Ives Harbour, Low Tide" – oil on canvas – signed – artist's label to reverse – 31½ x 39in.
(David Lay) **$2,325 £1,500**

FRANCES EWAN (Exh. 1892-1929) – "High Tide, St. Ives Harbour" – oil on canvas – signed – artist's label to reverse – 25 x 31in.
(David Lay) **$2,945 £1,900**

FABIO FABBI (1861-1946) – The harem – signed – pencil and watercolour heightened with white – 44.5 x 29.2cm.
(Christie's) **$1,194   £770**

HANS EWORTH (fl. 1540-c. 1573), Follower of – Portrait of Sir Edward Montagu (d. 1557) – three quarter length, seated, wearing a black tunic and cap and a fur lined cloak – oil on panel – 96.5 x 71cm.
(Sotheby's) **$9,240   £5,500**

ADOLPH SOPHUS AAGE EXNER (1870-1951) - In the inn – signed and dated 1910 – 79 x 103.5cm.
(Christie's) **$5,313   £3,300**

FABIO FABBI (Italian 1861-1946) In the courtyard of the harem – signed – oil on canvas – 59 x 77.5cm.
(Sotheby's) **$21,912   £13,200**

FABIO FABBI (Italian 1861-1946) – Harem girls – signed – oil on canvas – unframed – 93 x 73cm.
(Sotheby's) **$18,260   £11,000**

FABRY

EMILE FABRY (Belgian 1865-1966) – A Faun playing a pipe – oil on canvas – unframed – 132 x 116cm.
(Sotheby's) **$11,869 £7,150**

PETER FAES (1750-1814), Attributed to – A still life of assorted flowers including lilies, tulips and roses in a terracotta vase upon a marble table – with strengthened initials – oil on canvas – 84 x 77cm.
(Phillips) **$9,780 £6,000**

FRANCES C* FAIRMAN** – A portrait of a black and white, long-haired dog – signed and dated 1902 – 51 x 65cm.
(Anderson & Garland) **$1,735 £1,020**

THOMAS FAED, R.A., H.R.S.A. – A fishergirl – signed and dated 1866 – oil on board – 17.5 x 11.5cm.
(Sotheby's) **$2,571 £1,540**

GEORGE FALL – Lichfield Cathedral – signed – watercolour – 5¹/₄ x 8in.
(Christie's) **$351 £209**

HENRI FANTIN-LATOUR – Pêches – signed – oil on
canvas – 19.4 x 24cm.
(Sotheby's)   **$242,000   £152,201**

HENRI FANTIN-LATOUR – Roses – signed – oil on
canvas – 48.5 x 43.5cm.
(Sotheby's)   **$825,000   £518,868**

HENRI FANTIN-LATOUR – Zinnias – signed and dated
91 – oil on canvas – 50 x 59cm.
(Sotheby's)   **$1,430,000   £899,371**

HENRI FANTIN-LATOUR (1836-1904) –
Chrysanthemes – signed upper left Fantin 71 – oil on
canvas – 31.8 x 20.3cm.
(Christie's)   **$102,597   £66,000**

HENRI FANTIN-LATOUR - Roses – signed and dated
81 – oil on canvas – 21.2 x 24.8cm.
(Sotheby's)   **$275,000   £172,956**

FARGUE

PAULUS CONSTANTIN LA FARGUE (1729-1782) –
Views of Huis Ten Bosch, near the Hague – traces of a
signature – oil on panel – 30.5 x 43.5cm.
(Phillips)   **$8,910**   **£5,500**

JOSEPH FARQUARSON, R.A. (1846-1935) – At the
piano – signed – 43 x 33cm.
(Christie's)   **$10,043**   **£6,050**

JOSEPH FARQUHARSON (1846-1935) – The artist's
garden – signed – 46.5 x 30.5cm.
(Christie's)   **$6,121**   **£3,850**

JOSEPH FARQUHARSON, R.A. – The road to Loch
Maree – signed; bears title on the reverse – oil on canvas –
61 x 91.5cm.
(Sotheby's)   **$15,614**   **£9,350**

ROBERT FARREN (Exh. 1880-90) – Children with a
Donkey on a Cliff Top – signed and dated 1889 – oil on
canvas – 61 x 91.5cm.
(Phillips)   **$4,075**   **£2,500**

ROBERT FARRIER (1796-1879) – A tale of the war –
signed – and signed and inscribed on the reverse – on panel
– 43.7 x 34.3cm.
(Christie's)   **$3,586 £2,200**

EDGARD PIETER FARASYN – Portrait of a young girl
wearing a straw wide brimmed hat, leaning on a grassy
bank picking wild flowers – signed – inscribed Anvers and
dated 1878 – 80 x 59.5cm.
(Spencer's)   **$2,041 £1,300**

JOHN FAULKNER, R.H.A. – Honiley, Kenilworth –
watercolour – signed and inscribed – $17^{1}/_{2}$ x $28^{1}/_{4}$in.
(Bearne's)   **$2,225 £1,250**

T. FARRIER (late 19th Century) – The pet rabbits –
signed – 56 x 50.5cm.
(Christie's)   **$5,247 £3,300**

HANS VON FABER DU FAUR – Racing on the beach –
signed and dated 3.X.1919 – signed with the initials –
watercolour, gouache and brush and indian ink –
20.5 x 24cm.
(Sotheby's)   **$3,810 £2,241**

FAURE

EUGENE FAURE (1822-1879) – The flower girl –
signed – 199.5 x 99cm.
(Christie's) $24,794   £15,400

WILLIAM GOWE FERGUSON (1632-1695 London) –
A hanging partridge – bears false signature – on canvas –
54.5 x 41.5cm.
(Phillips) $6,520   £4,000

MARY FEDDEN – The Cake – signed and dated 1978 –
numbered "17" and inscribed on a label on the reverse – oil
on canvas – 51 x 71cm.
(Phillips) $5,915   £3,500

CHRISTIAN JANE FERGUSSON – Shawhead
Spougray – signed; signed on the reverse and bears title on
a label on the reverse – oil on panel – 65 x 77cm.
(Sotheby's) $1,496   £935

JOHN DUNCAN FERGUSSON, R.B.A. (1874-1961) –
The Village, Saint Palais, near Royan – signed – inscribed
and dated March 1943 on label verso – charcoal and
watercolour – 22.3 x 27.9cm.
(Christie's)   **$11,088   £6,600**

JOHN DUNCAN FERGUSSON, R.B.A. (1874-1961) –
Bather on the rocks, Antibes – signed and dated 1950 verso
– oil on board – 23.2 x 19.1cm.
(Christie's)   **$20,328   £12,100**

JOHN DUNCAN FERGUSSON – Portrait of a girl –
signed and dated 1914 on the reverse – oil on board – 35 x
28cm.
(Sotheby's)   **$16,533   £9,900**

FERNELEY

JOHN FERNELEY, Snr. (1782-1860) – A Chestnut Pony with a Greyhound in a landscape – signed J. Ferneley/Pinx'/1809 – oil on canvas – 69.5 x 90cm.
(Sotheby's) **$14,784 £8,800**

JOHN FERNELEY, Jnr. - Gralloching Stag - oil on canvas – 76 x 63.5cm.
(Sotheby's) **$9,552 £5,720**

NUNZIO FERRAJUOLI (1661-1735) – Cattle watering in a stream beside a mill in a mountainous landscape – signed and inscribed on reverse – oil on canvas – 40.5 x 51.5cm. – and companion
(Phillips) **$5,670 £3,500**

FERRARA SCHOOL, 2nd half 16th century – Mariage Mystique de Saint Catherine – oil on panel – 42 x 27cm.
(Sotheby's) **$148,423 £95,442**

ORAZIO DEI FERRARI 1605-1657 – Atrributed to – Sujet d'histoire ancienne – oil on canvas – 11 x 97cm.
(Sotheby's) **$6,595 £4,228**

CIRRO FERRI (1634-1689), Circle of – The Madonna – oil on canvas – 74 x 61.5cm.
(Phillips) **$1,467 £900**

ANTON FIDLER (fl. 1825-1855) – Grapes, peaches, plums and other fruit with birds on a ledge – signed and dated 1884 – 23.5 x 74cm.
(Christie's) **$15,053 £9,350**

HARRY FIDLER – Cattle in a watermeadow – signed – oil on canvas – 61 x 81.25cm.
(Woolley & Wallis) **$2,040 £1,200**

BENJAMIN EUGENE FICHEL (1826-1895) – The recital – signed and dated 1853 – on panel – unframed – 26.5 x 21cm.
(Christie's) **$2,834 £1,760**

WALTER FIRLE (1859-1929) – A good book – signed – on board – 49.5 x 63.5cm.
(Christie's) **$7,084 £4,400**

FISCHER

AUGUST FISCHER (1854-1921) – A street scene, Lugano – signed and dated Lugano 86 – on board – 47.5 x 37cm.
(Christie's) **$4,250 £2,640**

PAUL FISCHER (Danish 1860-1934) – A street scene in Copenhagen – signed – oil on panel – 39 x 32.5cm.
(Sotheby's) **$8,765 £5,280**

PAUL FISCHER (Danish 1860-1934) – A flower market in Copenhagen – signed – oil on canvas – 56 x 73cm.
(Sotheby's) **$47,476 £28,600**

PAUL FISCHER (Danish 1860-1934) – On the beach –
signed – oil on canvas – 94 x 126cm.
(Sotheby's) **$32,868 £19,800**

PAUL FISCHER – The Marie Kirke, Helsingor – signed;
titled on a label on the frame – oil on canvas – 69 x 89cm.
(Sotheby's) **$6,732 £3,960**

PAUL FISCHER (Danish 1860-1934) – Figures in the
snow, Copenhagen – signed – oil on canvas – 55.5 x 73cm.
(Sotheby's) **$36,520 £22,000**

PAUL FISCHER – Figures in Kongens Nytorv,
Copenhagen – signed – oil on panel – 20 x 25cm.
(Sotheby's) **$10,406 £6,050**

PAUL FISCHER (Danish 1860-1934) – A rendez-vous
on the pier – signed – oil on canvas – 38 x 54cm.
(Sotheby's) **$10,043 £6,050**

FLEETWOOD-WALKER

SIR WILLIAM RUSSELL FLINT, R.A., P.R.W.S., R.S.W., R.O.I. (1880-1969) – Two Together – signed – and signed and inscribed verso – watercolour – 37.5 x 54cm.
(Christie's) **$25,872 £15,400**

BERNARD FLEETWOOD-WALKER, R.A., R.W.S. – At the Farm – signed – pencil and watercolour – 32 x 27.5cm.
(Phillips) **$1,690 £1,000**

SIR WILLIAM RUSSELL FLINT, R.A., P.R.W.S. – Sketching at Shandos – signed – watercolour – 37 x 56cm.
(Sotheby's) **$23,881 £14,300**

SIR WILLIAM RUSSELL FLINT, R.A., P.R.W.S. (1880-1969) – Fellow Creatures – signed – inscribed with title on the reverse – also signed and inscribed on the backboard - watercolour and bodycolour – 33 x 49cm.
(Phillips) **$24,450 £15,000**

SIR WILLIAM RUSSELL FLINT, R.A., P.R.W.S. (1880-1969) – Blue and Silver – signed – signed and inscribed on the backboard – watercolour and bodycolour – 33 x 61cm.
(Phillips) **$40,750 £25,000**

SIR WILLIAM RUSSELL FLINT, R.A., P.R.W.S. – A Study for "Models for Goddesses" – signed – titled and inscribed, "To my friend Geoffrey Holme" – coloured crayon – 18 x 25.5cm.
(Phillips) **$8,788 £5,200**

SIR WILLIAM RUSSELL FLINT, R.A., P.R.W.S. (1880-1969) – Figures in a Spanish Interior – signed – also signed and inscribed on the backboard – watercolour heightened with white – 30 x 21.5cm.
(Phillips) $5,542 £3,400

LAVINIA FONTANA – Bologne 1552-1614 Rome – Nativité – oil on canvas – 38 x 32cm.
(Sotheby's) $24,737 £15,857

DONALD H. FLOYD (Exh. 1914-40) – Preparing fishing boats – oil on canvas – signed and dated 1921 – 13½ x 17½in.
(David Lay) $465 £300

FRANCESCO FONTEBASSO (1709-1769) – Rebecca at the well – oil on canvas – 60.5 x 46.5cm.
(Phillips) $11,084 £6,800

LAI FONG – A ship on a stormy sea – signed – inscribed 'Calcutta' and dated 1905 – 23¼ x 35¼in.
(Bearne's) $1,744 £980

FREDERICK FRANCIS FOOTTET (1850-1935) – street scene at dusk - signed lower left Foottet - oil on canvas – 40 x 50in.
(Christie's) $6,083 £3,850

FOPPA

VINCENZO DA FOPPA – Les Anges Musiciens – oil on panel – 14 x 20cm.
(Sotheby's)   **$115,440**   **£74,000**

Style of ELIZABETH FORBES – Woman in sunlight – oil on canvas – 44 x 34in.
(David Lay)   **$4,340**   **£2,800**

PATRICK LEWIS FORBES – Holly Hill, Hampstead – watercolour – signed and inscribed "looking down on Holly Hill" verso – 18.8 x 26.7cm.
(Bonhams)   **$887**   **£580**

STANHOPE ALEXANDER FORBES (1857-1947) – Newlyn School – "The Farm Worker" – signed – oil on canvas board – $12^1/_2$ x $7^1/_2$in.
(W. H. Lane & Son)   **$4,080**   **£2,400**

EUGENE FRANCOIS FOREL (late 19th Century) – Lutteurs de foire – signed and dated 1886 – and signed – inscribed and dated 1886 on the reverse – 81 x 101cm.
(Christie's)   **$13,640**   **£8,800**

CHARLES FORSTER, Jr. – Two fishergirls with their catch – indistinctly signed – watercolour over pencil with bodycolour – 57.5 x 47.5cm.
(Sotheby's) **$1,122 £660**

BERNARD FOSTER (19th Century) – Homeward Bound – signed – watercolour heightened with bodycolour over traces of pencil – 23 x 32.5cm.
(Phillips) **$487 £300**

MYLES BIRKET FOSTER, R.W.S. – Bridge near Dartmouth, Devon – signed with monogram; bears title on a label on the backboard – watercolour heightened with bodycolour – 19 x 24cm.
(Sotheby's) **$1,683 £990**

ETTORI FORTI (19th Century) – Rustic courtship – signed and inscribed Roma – on panel – 40.6 x 25.4cm.
(Christie's) **$4,092 £2,640**

MYLES BIRKET FOSTER – Figures on a terrace above the sea – with studio stamp – pencil and watercolour – unframed – 5 x 7in.
(Christie's) **$739 £462**

FOSTER

WILLIAM FOSTER – Feeding time – signed – watercolour – 30.5 x 42cm.
(Sotheby's) **$1,683 £990**

TSUGUJI FOUJITA (1886-1968) – Fillette au Chat – signed – inscribed and dated lower right Foujita Paris 1950 – signed again – inscribed and dated on the stretcher Paris 1950 Foujita – oil on canvas – 33 x 24cm.
(Christie's) **$273,592 £176,000**

LEONARD TSUGUHARU FOUJITA – The Women – one of a set of five (orig. six) etching and aquatints printed in colours on china paper, published by Editions Apollo, Paris circa 1930 – signed and numbered
(Jean-Claude Anaf) **$140,317 £89,947**

TSUGUJI FOUJITA (1886-1968) – Youki endormie – signed and dated lower right Foujita 1931 – and again in Japanese – watercolour, pen and ink on paper – 42.5 x 32.5cm.
(Christie's) **$170,500 £110,000**

TSUGUJI FOUJITA (1886-1968) – Portrait de jeune Femme – signed – inscribed and dated centre left Foujita Rio de Janerio 1933 – watercolour, pen and black ink on paper – 42 x 32cm. – Executed in 1933
(Christie's) **$102,300 £66,000**

GEORGE FOX – A game of crib – signed – oil on panel
– 23 x 30.5cm.
(Sotheby's) **$2,152 £1,320**

EDWIN M. FOX (fl. 1830-1870) – Mr. Falkner on a dark
bay hunter with his two greyhounds and a dead hare, at
Foxrock, Co. Kildare – signed and dated 1869 –
63.5 x 76.2cm.
(Christie's) **$5,738 £3,520**

ETHEL CARRICK FOX (1872-1952) – Market Day,
Caudebec – signed and inscribed on an old exhibition label
attached to the stretcher – 50.7 x 60.9cm. –
Painted circa 1903
(Christie's) **$39,204 £24,200**

FOX

HENRY CHARLES FOX – Cattle watering –
watercolour – signed – 9³/₄ x 13³/₄in.
(Bearne's) $516 £290

MARCANTONIO FRANCHESCHINI, Follower of –
The Triumph of Galatea – oil on canvas – 83 x 103.5cm.
(Phillips) $11,084 £6,800

HENRY CHARLES FOX (1860-C. 1913) – A Huntsman
and Hounds on a Sussex Track – signed and dated 1909 –
watercolour and bodycolour – 36 x 53cm.
(Phillips) $1,141 £700

FRANS FRANCKEN III (1607-Antwerp-1667) – The
interior of a picture gallery – signed and dated D ²ffranck .
IN . f 1636 – on panel – 52 x 77.5cm.
(Phillips) $57,050 £35,000

EDWARD REGINALD FRAMPTON – St. Dorothea –
signed and indistinctly dated – watercolour over pencil
heightened with bodycolour and gold paint –
49.5 x 44.5cm.
(Sotheby's) $19,635 £11,550

SALVATORE FRANGIAMORE (1853-1915) – A good
book – signed and inscribed Roma – 68.5 x 54.5cm.
(Christie's) $7,438 £4,620

HARRY FRECKLETON – Pushing The Boat Out – signed – 25 x 29in.
(Bearne's) **$3,887 £2,300**

ALEXANDER FRASER, R.S.A. –The morning catch – signed with initials A. F. – oil on panel – 35.5 x 49.5cm.
(Sotheby's) **$6,813 £4,180**

CIRCLE OF ALEXANDER GEORGE FRASER, Snr., A.R.S.A. – The hunter's return – oil on panel – 44 x 54.5cm.
(Sotheby's) **$2,388 £1,430**

GEORGE AUGUSTUS FREEZOR – Old friends – signed and dated 186- – oil on canvas – unstretched – 53 x 41cm.
(Sotheby's) **$6,813 £4,180**

ROBERT WINTER FRASER (fl. 1870-1899) – On the Thames; and After a rainy day – signed and dated '92 – with inscriptions on labels on the reverse – pencil and watercolour – 33 x 30.5cm.
(Christie's) **$3,407 £2,090**

JANE FREILICHER (American, 20th Century) – "Green and Grey"/A Landscape – signed – identified on label Fischbach Gallery, New York on the reverse – pastel on paper – 38^1/$_2$ x 49^1/$_2$in.
(Skinner) **$950 £594**

FRENCH

LEONARD FRENCH – Double Cruicform – enamel – signed verso – 26 x 21cm.
(Australian Art Auctions)   **$1,213**   **£744**

PAL FRIED – Three ballerinas – signed – oil on canvas – 75.5 x 60cm.
(Sotheby's)   **$2,270**   **£1,320**

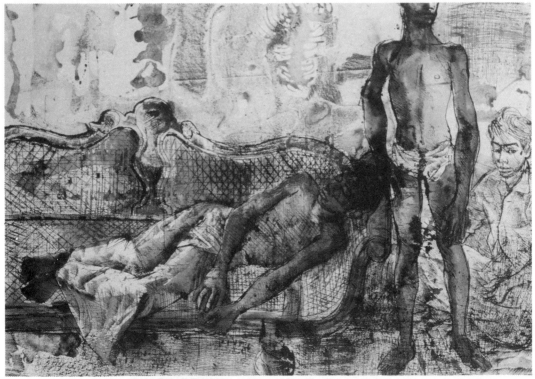

DONALD STUART LESLIE FRIEND (1915-1989) - The Verandah Sofa - signed and inscribed - pen, black and blue ink, watercolour and coloured chalks - 71.7 x 105.4cm. *(Christie's)*
$16,038 £9,900

NILAUS FRISTRUP – A courtyard behind San Gregorio, Venice – signed with initials and dated '75 – signed and indistinctly inscribed...Venedig on the stretcher – oil on canvas – 30.5 x 31cm.
(Sotheby's) **$11,352 £6,600**

FREDERICK C. FRIESEKE (1874-1939) – Woman before a mirror – signed F. C. Frieseke, l.l. – oil on canvas – 81.3 x 65.4cm. – Painted circa 1902-1903
(Sotheby's) **$82,500 £52,548**

ARTHUR B. FROST – Gun shy – signed – watercolour and gouache on paper – 40.6 x 59.6cm.
(Sotheby's) **$57,750 £36,321**

WILLIAM POWELL FRITH, R.A. (1819-1909) –
Study of Miss Mortimer holding a parasol – canvas laid down on board – 25.5 x 20.2cm.
(Christie's) **$11,082 £7,150**

ROGER FRY – A Mediterranean Church – oil on card – 39 x 52cm.
(Phillips) **$3,040 £1,900**

FULTON

DAVID FULTON, R.S.W. – Morning, Saddell Ferry,
Kintyre – signed; bears title on a label attached to the
frame – oil on canvas – 71 x 91.5cm.
(Sotheby's)   **$7,715**   **£4,620**

ETHEL GABAIN – The Yellow Gloves – signed – oil on
canvas – 41 x 52cm.
(Phillips)   **$4,640**   **£2,900**

SAMUEL FULTON – Jack Russell Terrier – signed – oil
on canvas – 38 x 28cm.
(Sotheby's)   **$6,245**   **£3,740**

JAN FYT 1611-1661 – Circle of – Nature Morte au
Gibier, Lièvre et Légumes – oil on canvas – 77 x 115cm.
(Sotheby's)   **$23,088**   **£14,800**

PIETRO GABRINI – An elegant lady by a piano –
signed l.l and dated ROMA 1903 – oil on canvas –
unframed – 131 x 90cm.
(Sotheby's)   **$3,406**   **£1,980**

FRANS GAILLIARD (1861-1932) – Claquedents –
signed lower right Franz Gailliard – signed again and
inscribed at the back F. Gailliard "CLAQUEDENTS" RUE
ROYALE 41 BRUXELLES – watercolour heightened with
white on board – 69.7 x 83.7cm.
(Christie's)   **$6,138**   **£3,960**

FRANS GAILLIARD (1861-1932) - La Kermesse -
signed lower right F. Gailliard - pastel on paper laid
on canvas - 38.1 x 45.7cm.
(Christie's) **$7,040 £4,400**

THOMAS GAINSBOROUGH, R.A. (1727-1788) –
Rocky wooded landscape with mounted drover, horses
watering at a trough and distant village and mountains – oil
on canvas – 123 x 99cm.
(Sotheby's) **$1,201,200 £715,000**

THOMAS GAINSBOROUGH, R.A. (1727-1788) –
Portrait of Giles Phillips of washbrook, Suffolk – half
length, wearing a blue coat edged with gold – indistinctly
inscribed Giles Philips(?) – oil on canvas, in a painted oval
– unframed – 61 x 51cm.
(Sotheby's) **$26,796 £15,950**

GAINSBOROUGH

THOMAS GAINSBOROUGH, R.A. (1727-1788) –
Portrait of Louis-Edmond Quentin de Richebourg,
Chevalier de Champcenetz (1760-94) – half length,
wearing a dark blue coat – oil on canvas – oval – 68 x
55cm.
(Sotheby's) **$119, 350 £77,000**

THOMAS GAINSBOROUGH, R.A. (1727-1788) –
Portrait of Miss Elizabeth Tyler (1739-1821) – half length,
seated, wearing a blue silk dress edged with pearls and a
gold embroidered sash – oil on canvas – 73.5 x 61cm.
(Sotheby's) **$51,150 £33,000**

JAKOB EMMANUEL GAISSER – The midday meal –
signed – oil on canvas – 94 x 118cm.
(Sotheby's) **$22,704 £13,200**

THOMAS GAINSBOROUGH, R.A. (1727-1788) –
Portrait of William Northey (1722-1770) – half length,
wearing a red coat and waistcoat – oil on canvas, in a
painted oval – 74.5 x 62cm.
(Sotheby's) **$13,860 £8,250**

PIETER GALLIS, Circle of (1633-Hoorn-1697) – A
swag of flowers, in a stone niche – on panel –
26.8 x 35.7cm.
(Phillips) **$7,140 £4,200**

GAETANO GANDOLFI –San Matteo Della Decima
1734-1802 Bologne – Sainte Famille – oil on basic canvas
– 87 x 69cm.
(Sotheby's) **$72,562 £46,514**

KARL GAMPENRIEDER (born 1860) – Ready for the
ball – signed and dated 83 – 114.5 x 74.5cm.
(Christie's) **$20,460 £13,200**

GAETANO GANDOLFI 1734-1802 – Circle of –
Portrait d'homme - oil on canvas - 69 x 55cm.
(Sotheby's) **$4,121 £2,642**

MAURO GANDOLFI – Bologne 1764-1834 – Portrait de
Jeune Fille – oil on canvas – 42 x 33cm.
(Sotheby's) **$46,176 £29,600**

GARBER

DANIEL GARBER – Sally – signed Daniel Garber – dated 1933 – and inscribed To Sally, l.l. – charcoal and chalk on buff paper – 55.2 x 45.5cm.
(Christie's) **$1,100 £687**

WILLIAM BISCOMBE GARDNER – Children fishing – signed – watercolour – 25 x 14.5cm.
(Sotheby's) **$2,057 £1,210**

DANIEL GARBER – Tohickon Bridge – signed Daniel Garber, l.r. – signed again – dated 1923 and inscribed with title on the reverse – oil on board – 46 x 51cm.
(Christie's) **$23,100 £14,437**

WILLIAM FRASER GARDEN, Attributed to – A View across a Common towards a Village and Parish Church – watercolour – bears signature and date 1912 – 17.8 x 26.8cm.
(Bonhams) **$643 £420**

VALENTINE THOMAS GARLAND (fl. 1868-1903) – A stranger in their midst - signed and dated 1893 – watercolour heightened with white and gum arabic – 25.4 x 34.3cm.
(Christie's) **$7,106 £4,180**

MICHEL GARNIER – Ne a Saint-Cloud et actif en France a la fin du XVIIIe siecle – La Jeune Fille Punie – oil on canvas – 44.5 x 54cm.
(Sotheby's) $230,880 £148,000

ANNIBALE GATTI – John Milton with Galileo in his observatory – signed – oil on canvas – 80 x 117cm.
(Sotheby's) $7,106 £4,180

ARTHUR JOSEPH GASKIN – Psyche – inscribed on the reverse – tempera on panel – 52.7 x 38.7cm.
(Sotheby's) $5,610 £3,300

PAUL GAUGUIN – Vaches au bord de la mer – signed and dated 86 – oil on canvas – 75 x 112cm.
(Sotheby's) $3,960,000 £2,490,566

GAULD

DAVID GAULD, R.S.A. – Ayrshire calves – signed –oil on canvas – 102 x 128cm.
(Sotheby's)   **$13,777   £8,250**

DAVID GAULD, R.S.A. (1865-1936) – 'Three Calves' – signed – oil on canvas – 61 x 76cm.
(Phillips)   **$4,564   £2,800**

ARTHUR W. GAY – Preparing a farmhorse – oil on board – signed – 6 x 7¹/₂in.
(David Lay)   **$465   £300**

WALTER GAY – The Fencing Lesson – signed Walter Gay, l.l – oil on canvas – 68.6 x 108.5cm.
(Christie's)   **$8,800   £5,500**

LUDWIG GEDLEK (born 1847) – The Jewish community in Lotch, near Warsaw, receiving the message of the Austrian Emperor – signed and inscribed Wien – on panel – 53 x 41cm.
(Christie's)   **$4,250   £2,640**

LUDWIG GEDLEK (born 1847) – Returning from the raid – signed and inscribed Wien – on board – 59 x 100cm.
(Christie's)   **$7,438   £4,620**

MABEL GEAR – West Highland Terriers – signed – oil on panel – 28 x 41cm.
(Sotheby's) **$3,306 £1,980**

MARTEN JOSEF GEERAERTS (1707-1791) – David before Saul – oil on canvas – 138 x 117cm.
(Phillips) **$5,474 £3,400**

HENRI JULES GEOFFROY – Children with a bag of sweets – signed – oil on canvas – 53.5 x 37cm.
(Sotheby's) **$15,136 £8,800**

LILLIAN GENTH – Nude in the woods – signed L. Genth, 1.1 – oil on canvas – 75.5 x 99.5cm. *(Christie's)* **$7,700 £4,812**

GEORGE

ERIC GEORGE (born 1881) –The Bathers – signed – dated III, 1927 – oil on canvas – 76 x 99cm.
(Phillips) **$3,260 £2,000**

VESPER GEORGE (American, 1865-1934) –
Gentleman Playing a Piano – signed and dated "Vesper L.
George '94" – oil on canvas – 27 x 33in.
(Skinner) **$6,500 £3,892**

MARGUERITE GERARD - Grasse 1761-1873 Paris -
Les Tourterelles – oil on canvas – 44.8 x 36.2cm.
(Sotheby's) **$72,562 £46,514**

THEODORE GERARD (1829-1895), Circle of –
Feeding the birds – with monogram and the date 1879 –
38.2 x 30.4cm.
(Christie's) **$853   £550**

MAESTRO GERARDO – La Tentation de Saint Antoine
Abbé – tempera on panel – 120 x 160cm.
(Sotheby's) **$24,737   £15,857**

GERMAN SCHOOL, 19th Century – Teasing the Baby
– panel – indistinctly signed – 39.4 x 49.5cm.
(Bonhams) **$2,480   £1,600**

GERMAN SCHOOL, early 20th Century – A man
feeding pigeons – 89 x 127.5cm.
(Christie's) **$1,816   £1,142**

GERMAN SCHOOL. early 19th Century – An Italian
family feasting in the country – oil on canvas –
57.5 x 85cm.
(Sotheby's) **$9,029   £5,280**

GESTEL

MARCUS GHEERAERTS the YOUNGER (1561-1636), Circle of – Portrait of a lady – three-quarter length wearing a fine white ribbed blouse with decorated green skirt, a pearl and ruby head band and holding a fan – oil on panel – 130 x 81cm.
(Sotheby's) **$15,708 £9,350**

LEO GESTEL – Meisje met bont – signed upper right Leo Gestel – and signed again and inscribed with title on the backboard of the frame – pastel on paper – 71 x 53cm.
(Christie's) **$4,035 £2,538**

LEO GESTEL – Bloemen in tinnen kan, no. 1 – signed lower left Leo Gestel – and signed again and inscribed with title on the reverse – 71 x 63cm.
(Christie's) **$19,167 £12,055**

MARCUS GHEERAERDTS THE YOUNGER (1561-1635) – Portrait of Frances, Countess of Richmond – half length, wearing a richly embroidered dress – oil on panel – in a carved wood frame – 58.5 x 43cm.
(Sotheby's) **$34,100 £22,000**

NAPOLEON FRANCOIS GHESQUIERE (1812-1862)
- The Fiddler - signed - on panel - unframed - 43 x 34cm.
(Christie's)   **$5,313**   **£3,300**

J A GIBBS – "The Dream" – signed and dated 1882 –
watercolour – 22 x 18in.
(G. A. Key)   **$536**   **£350**

GEORGE GIBBS (American, 1870-1942) –
"Marigolds"/Woman Tending Flower Beds – signed –
pastel on mounted paper – 33 x 21½ in.
(Skinner)   **$3,250**   **£1,946**

JOHN GIFFORD – A break for lunch – signed – oil on
canvas – 76 x 63.5cm.
(Sotheby's)   **$2,939**   **£1,760**

JOSÉ BENLLIURE Y GIL (1855-1914) – A good story
– signed – on panel – 38 x 54cm.
(Christie's) **$110,825 £71,500**

JAN PAUWEL GILLEMANS LE VIEUX – Anvers
1618-1675 – Nature Morte aux Fruits dans une Coupe en
Faïence – oil on panel – 28.5 x 38cm.
(Sotheby's) **$61,018 £39,114**

MINNIE F.W. GILBERT (fl. 1889) – 'Medora' – signed
and inscribed on an old label on the stretcher –
40.6 x 30.5cm.
(Christie's) **$2,152 £1,320**

**JAN PAUWEL GILLEMANS, THE YOUNGER
(1651-Antwerp-1704)** – A still life consisting of a swag of
fruit with a parrot and a monkey in an ornamental garden –
bears signature J. P. Gillemans – on canvas –
35.5 x 48.5cm.
(Phillips) **$11,050 £6,500**

VICTOR BA==GABRIEL GILBERT (1847-1933) –
The Pantheon, Paris – signed and dated Le Pantheon 89 –
on panel – 17 x 25cm.
(Christie's) **$7,438 £4,620**

BARTHEL GILLES – At the kiosk – signed – tempera
on panel – 86 x 64cm.
(Sotheby's) **$46,896 £27,586**

SIR WILLIAM GEORGE GILLIES, R.S.A., R.A., R.S.W. – Beached boats – signed – oil on canvas – 62 x 84cm.
(Sotheby's) **$17,451 £10,450**

BALDOMERO GALOFRÉ Y GIMENEZ (1849-1902) – Horse breakers during the Feria – signed – on panel – 34 x 48cm.
(Christie's) **$54,780 £33,000**

CLAUDE GILLOT, Follower of – Procession of a disgraced husband wearing his cuckold horn hat – pen and ink – 7³/₄ x 13¹/₂in.
(Graves Son & Pilcher) **$551 £340**

LEON GIRAN-MAX – On the way to the masked ball - signed – oil on canvas – 47 x 84cm.
(Kunsthaus am Museum) **$1,955 £1,150**

FILIPPO GIUNTOTARDI (1768-1831) – The Forum, Rome - signed with initials – 80 x 159cm.
(Christie's) **$51,150 £33,000**

J.H. GILREU – Farm chicken – signed – 91.5 x 71.2cm.
(Christie's) **$5,984 £3,740**

FAUST GIUSTO (late 19th Century) – Porte Saint Denis, Paris – signed – 45.7 x 76.2cm.
(Christie's) **$12,751 £7,920**

GLACKENS

WILLIAM J. GLACKENS – Washington Square and A Cafe Scene: A double-sided pastel – signed W. Glackens, l.l. – pastel and pencil on tan paper – 25.4 x 36.8cm. *(Christie's)* **$22,000 £13,750**

WILLIAM J. GLACKENS (1870-1938) – Lenna feeding a rabbit – oil on canvas – 33.6 x 25.4cm. – Painted in 1918 *(Sotheby's)* **$52,800 £33,631**

JOHN HAMILTON GLASS, A.R.S.A. (1820-1885) – A Whinny Bank – signed – watercolour heightened with white – 49 x 74.5cm. *(Phillips)* **$816 £480**

WILLIAM J. GLACKENS (1870-1938) – Bath House, Bellport – oil on canvas – 66 x 81.3cm. – Painted in 1914 *(Sotheby's)* **$517,000 £329,299**

WILLIAM J. GLACKENS (1870-1938) – Nude bathers – oil on canvas – 31.8 x 39.4cm. *(Sotheby's)* **$41,800 £26,624**

ARMIN GLATTER – Piros ruhas no – signed – oil on canvas – 44 x 34cm. *(Mugyujtok Galeriaja Kft)* **$1,216 £737**

WILFRED GABRIEL DE GLEHN, R.A. (1870-1951) –
The Mill Pond – signed – oil on canvas – 63.5 x 76cm.
(Phillips)   **$11,818   £7,250**

ALFRED AUGUSTUS GLENDENING, Snr. – Harvest
in Sussex – signed with initials and dated '80 – oil on
canvas – 101.5 x 153cm.
(Sotheby's)   **$7,530   £4,620**

ALFRED GLENDENING, Jnr. – Arranging flowers –
signed with monogram and dated 1897 – watercolour –
74 x 49cm.
(Sotheby's)   **$4,675   £2,750**

ALFRED AUGUSTUS GLENDENING, Jnr. (d. 1907)
– Thoughts far away; and The morning walk – both signed
with monogram and dated 1887 – a pair – 59.6 x 29.2cm.
(Christie's)   **$4,662   £2,860**

GLENDENING

ALFRED GLENDENING, Jnr. – Taming a dove – signed with monogram and dated 1895 – watercolour heightened with bodycolour – 46 x 23cm.
(Sotheby's) **$2,805 £1,650**

ERNST JEAN JOSEPH GODFRINON (1878-1927) – Vase de Chrysanthemes et Parasol—Vaas met Chrysanten en Parasol – signed and dated lower right E. Godfrinon 1917 – oil on canvas – 55 x 70cm. – Painted in 1917
(Christie's) **$44,000 £27,500**

FREDERICK E. J. GOFF (1855-1931) – "Blackfriars Bridge" and "Westminster" – watercolour – a pair – each signed – 6¼ x 4¾in.
(David Lay) **$2,334 £1,450**

LUDWIG GLOSS – A scientific discovery – signed – oil on panel – unframed – 55.5 x 47cm.
(Sotheby's) **$15,136 £8,800**

FREDERICK E. J. GOFF - The Monument - signed and inscribed – watercolour heightened with white – 6 x 4½in.
(Christie's) **$967 £572**

ARISTIDE GOFFINON - A still life of peonies in a vase – signed – oil on canvas – 79 x 99cm.
(Sotheby's)   **$5,610   £3,300**

VINCENT VAN GOGH – L'Homme est en Mer – oil on canvas – 66 x 51cm.
(Sotheby's)   **$7,150,000   £4,496,855**

VINCENT VAN GOGH (1853-1890) – Le vieil If – oil on canvas – 92 x 72.4cm. – Painted in October, 1888
(Christie's)   **$20,350,000   £12,751,310**

THOMAS GOOCH (1750-1802) – Portrait of a gentleman with his Bay Hunter in the grounds of a country house – oil on canvas – 49.5 x 59cm.
(Sotheby's)   **$16,632   £9,900**

VINCENT VAN GOGH (1853-1890) – Nature morte aux Pinceaux dans un Pot à Fleurs – oil on canvas – 31.5 x 41.5cm.
(Christie's)   **$307,884   £198,000**

FREDERICK GOODALL – A Shepherd with his Flock in an Oasis – signed with monogram – 30.5 x 61cm.
(Bonhams)   **$1,479   £850**

GOODALL

FREDERICK GOODALL, R. A. (1822-1904) - 'The Rising of the Nile' - signed with monogram and dated 1866 - oil on panel - 41 x 69cm. *(Phillips)* **$5,623 £3,450**

JOHN EDWARD GOODALL (London fl. 1877-1891) – Ennui – signed lower right: J. Edwd. Goodall – watercolour – 34.3 x 50.8cm. *(Lawrence)* **$2,706 £1,650**

ALBERT GOODWIN (1845-1932) – Sheep grazing below Corfe Castle – signed and dated 1923 and inscribed indistinctly "...day the Lord hath made" – watercolour and bodycolour with pencil and chalk – 35.5 x 55cm. *(Phillips)* **$5,868 £3,600**

ALBERT GOODWIN (1845-1932) – "Corfe Castle" – signed and inscribed – pen and ink – watercolour and bodycolour – 32 x 51cm. *(Phillips)* **$7,498 £4,600**

ALBERT GOODWIN, R.W.S. – Sunset, Beachy Head – signed and inscribed with title – oil on board – 24 x 32cm. *(Sotheby's)* **$5,020 £3,080**

ALBERT GOODWIN (1845-1932) – Horse and Cart below Corfe Castle – signed and dated '95 – watercolour and bodycolour and pen and ink – 23.5 x 32.5cm. *(Phillips)* **$3,912   £2,400**

ARTHUR CLIFTON GOODWIN (American, 1864-1929) – "T Wharf South Side Looking Towards Ames Building" – signed – pastel on tan paper – 13 x 19¹/₂ in. *(Skinner)* **$6,000   £3,593**

ALBERT GOODWIN R.W.S – "Amalfi" – signed and dated 1893 – watercolour drawing – 10 x 13in. *(Riddetts)* **$5,760   £3,600**

ARTHUR CLIFTON GOODWIN (American, 1864-1929) – Wharf in Winter, Boston – unsigned – inscribed "A.C. Goodwin..." on verso – oil on canvas – 14 x 18in. *(Skinner)* **$12,000   £7,186**

ARTHUR CLIFTON GOODWIN (American, 1864-1929) – Bench by the Frog Pond, Boston Common - signed "A. C. Goodwin", l.l. – signed and dated"A. C. Goodwin 07" – pastel on ochre paper – 12¹/₄ x 18³/₄in. *(Skinner)* **$16,000   £9,815**

GOODWIN

ARTHUR CLIFTON GOODWIN (American, 1864-1929) – "Louis Kronberg in his Studio" – signed "A. C. Goodwin", l.c. – identified on label from the Vose Galleries, Boston, on the reverse – oil on canvas – 22 x 28in.
(Skinner)   **$15,000   £9,202**

FREDERICK GORE – Path to Mausanne I – signed and dated '52 – also signed and dated and inscribed on the stretcher – oil on canvas – 51 x 61cm.
(Phillips)   **$7,098   £4,200**

ARTHUR CLIFTON GOODWIN (American, 1864-1929) – House on the Neponset River – signed – pastel on tan paper – 21 x 24in.
(Skinner)   **$3,250   £1,946**

ARTHUR CLIFTON GOODWIN (American, 1864-1929) – Quincy Market, Winter – signed – oil on canvas – 25 x 30in.
(Skinner)   **$10,000   £5,988**

IVAN SILYCH GORIUSHKIN-SOROKOPUDOV (1873-1954) – The Maiden at Prayer – signed in Cyrillic lower right – gouache and watercolour on paper – 127.4 x 94cm. – with frame
(Christie's)   **$38,962   £24,200**

AARON HARRY GORSON – Pittsburgh Factories – oil on canvas – 41.3 x 48cm.
(Christie's)   **$9,350   £5,844**

GRANDGERARD

COLIN GRAEME (late 19th Century) – Two game dogs in a Highland landscape – signed and dated 88 – 51 x 76cm.
(Christie's) $6,996 £4,400

LAUREYS GOUBAU (op. 1651-1670), Attributed to – A peasant lighting his pipe from coals, seated at a table before a window – oil on panel – 36.5 x 27.5cm.
(Phillips) $3,260 £2,000

ANNE MARIE GRAHAM (b. 1925) – The Opening Speech – signed – on board – 36.8 x 26.7cm.
(Christie's) $1,337 £825

A. L. GRACE (fl. late 19th Century) – The China Cupboard – signed – oil on canvas – 61 x 51cm.
(Phillips) $1,141 £700

LUCIEN-HENRY GRANDGÉRARD – Irène Endormie – signed; titled on a label on the reverse – oil on panel – 46 x 55cm.
(Sotheby's) $3,740 £2,200

GRANDKOVSKII

NIKOLAI KARLOVICH GRANDKOVSKII (1864-1907) – Russian Fair – signed in Cyrillic and dated lower right N. Grandkovskii 1883 – oil on canvas – 86 x 108cm.
(Christie's) **$23,023 £14,300**

DOUGLAS STANNUS GRAY (1890-1959) – Still Life of Roses in a Glass Vase – signed and dated 1930 – oil on canvas – 53 x 33.5cm.
(Phillips) **$2,445 £1,500**

DUNCAN GRANT – Odalisque – watercolour and gouache over pencil – 15 x 15cm.
(Phillips) **$2,240 £1,400**

GENNARO GRÉCO 1663-1714 – Vue d'un Port Méditerranéen – oil on canvas – 96 x 134cm.
(Sotheby's) **$26,386 £16,914**

EMILE GRAU-SALA – Regatta at Deauville – oil on canvas – signed – 73 x 54cm.
(Jean-Claude Anaf) **$49,524 £31,746**

PIETER FRANSZ DE GREBBER (Haarlem circa 1600-1653) – The denial of Saint Peter – on canvas – 105 x 147.5cm.
(Phillips) **$21,190 £13,000**

CHARLES GREEN (1840-1898) – Children playing with a wagon on a woodland lane – signed and dated 1862 – watercolour heightened with white – 15.2 x 20.3cm.
(Christie's) **$1,793 £1,100**

KATE GREENAWAY (1846-1901) – The Little Miss – signed – inscribed 'For Olivers Friend' and dated 1894 – watercolour over pencil – 15 x 11cm.
(Phillips) **$782 £480**

JOSIAH GREEN (fl. 1862-1868) – The little mountebank of Bretange – signed and dated 1864 – and indistinctly inscribed on the reverse – 46 x 61cm.
(Christie's) **$9,619 £6,050**

ROLAND GREEN – Ducks and drakes (on a lake) – watercolour and gouache – 25.5 x 35.5cm.
(Woolley & Wallis) **$323 £190**

ROBERT DUCKWORTH GREENHAM – Studio Corner – signed and dated '46 – also signed and inscribed on a label on the reverse – oil on board – 76 x 50.5cm.
(Phillips) **$2,400 £1,500**

GREENHAM

ROBERT DUCKWORTH GREENHAM (1906-1975) –
A Day at the Beach – signed with initials – oil on board –
38 x 51cm.
(Phillips)   **$3,260**   **£2,000**

ROBERT GREENHAM, R. A. (1906-1975) A Hampstead Street - signed and dated - oil on board - 23 x
19in.
(Christie's)   **$2,847**   **£1,705**

FRANK GRESLEY - Figures sitting on the banks of a
River, a Weir and Village Buildings beyond – watercolour
– signed – 29.2 x 39.3cm.
(Bonhams)   **$2,448**   **£1,600**

FRANK GRESLEY – Bluebell Glade – watercolour –
signed and dated 1915 – 22 x 15^1/$_2$in.
(Bearne's)   **$2,690**   **£1,650**

JEAN-BAPTISTE GREUZE 1725-1805 – Follower of –
L'Enfant Architecte – oil on canvas – 52 x 44.5cm.
(Sotheby's)   **$4,947**   **£3,171**

JEAN-BAPTISTE GREUZE – Tournus 1725-1805 Paris – Portrait de Jeune Fille – oil on panel – 47 x 32.5cm.
(Sotheby's) **$32,983 £21,143**

BORIS DMITRIEVICH GRIGORIEV (1886-1939) - Portrait of Carlos Herrera of Toledo – signed lower right Grigorieff – inscribed on stretcher Carlos Herrera Chanoine de Tolèdo – oil on canvas – 72.7 x 59.7cm.
(Christie's) **$7,969 £4,950**

JOHN ATKINSON GRIMSHAW – Eveleigh, Forge Valley – signed and dated 1877; signed and inscribed with title on the reverse – oil on board – 29 x 45cm.
(Sotheby's) **$53,790 £33,000**

BORIS DMITRIEVICH GRIGORIEV (1886-1939)- Portrait of a Lady wearing a patterned Scarf – signed lower right Boris Grigoriev – oil on canvas – 65.4 x 52.5cm.
(Christie's) **$8,855 £5,500**

JOHN ATKINSON GRIMSHAW (1836-1893) – The moated grange – signed and inscribed on the reverse – 49 x 76.5cm.
(Christie's) **$5,247 £3,300**

JOHN ATKINSON GRIMSHAW – Glasgow – signed and inscribed sp-8; signed and inscribed with title and sp/8 on the reverse – oil on canvas – 30.5 x 46cm. *(Sotheby's)* **$60,962 £37,400**

JOHN ATKINSON GRIMSHAW (1836-1893) – November morning – signed and dated 1886 – 61 x 91.5cm. *(Christie's)* **$54,560 £35,200**

ANTHONY GROSS, R.A. (b. 1905) – Street in North Africa – signed and dated lower left Anthony Gross 55 – signed again and inscribed on the reverse Road in Bolivia – oil on canvas – 17¹/₂ x 20¹/₂in. *(Christie's)* **$1,390 £880**

EMILE A. GRUPPE (1896-1978) – Unloading the nets – oil on canvas – 24 x 20in. – signed Emile A. Gruppe lower right *(Bruce D. Collins)* **$4,510 £2,684**

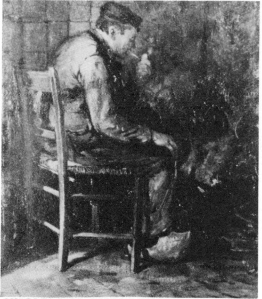

CHARLES PAUL GRUPPE (American, 1860-1940) –
Smoking a Pipe Before the Fire – signed – oil on canvas –
18³/₄ x 15¹/₄ in.
(Skinner)   **$950   £569**

EMILE ALBERT GRUPPE (American, (1896-1978) -
"Cloudy Day Gloucester"/"Arnold's Wharf Seine Nets
Drying" – signed "Emile A. Gruppe" l.l. – oil on
canvasboard – 16 x 20in.
(Skinner)   **$1,400   £875**

EMILE ALBERT GRUPPE (American, 1896-1978) –
"Mending the Nets" – signed – identified on label on verso
– oil on canvas – 16 x 20in.
(Skinner)   **$3,600   £2,156**

O. LOUIS GUGLIELMI (1906-1956) – Still life with
mask – signed Guglielmi and dated '31, u.l. – oil on canvas
– 51.4 x 41.3cm.
(Sotheby's)   **$34,100   £21,719**

EMILE ALBERT GRUPPE (American, 1896-1978) –
"Sugaring, Vermont" – signed - oil on canvas – 30 x 36in.
(Skinner)   **$9,000   £5,389**

RENE GUIETTE (1893-1976) - Les Joueurs de Cartes
- signed and dated lower right Rene Guiette/28 -
gouache on paper - 58 x 43cm.
(Christie's)   **$14,960   £9,350**

GUIETTE

RENÉ GUIETTE (1893-1976) – Intérieur au Personnage double—Interieur met dubbel Personage – signed and dated lower right René Guiette 19 avril/1941 – gouache on paper – 68 x 46cm. – Executed in 1941
(Christie's)   **$15,840   £9,900**

PAUL GUIGOU - L'Entrée de la Rivière à Lourmarin – signed and dated '67 – oil on canvas – 71.7 x 117.5cm.
(Sotheby's)   **$253,000   £159,120**

PAUL GUIGOU – Paysage aux Bords de la Durance – signed and dated '68 – oil on panel – 22.3 x 47.2cm.
(Sotheby's)   **$104,500   £65,723**

ALFRED GUILLOU (French, 19th Century) – White Lace – signed "Alf Guillou" u.l. – oil on panel – 11³/₄in x 8³/₈in. – framed
(Skinner)   **$1,300   £813**

WILLIAM GUNNING-KING – The Feed Seller – signed – 59.7 x 41.9cm.
(Bonhams)   **$930   £600**

WILLIAM GUNNING-KING – The Farmer's Orders –
signed – 43 x 46.9cm.
(Bonhams)   **$1,705   £980**

WILLIAM GUNNING-KING – Feeding the Flock –
signed – 41.9 x 45.8cm.
(Bonhams)   **$1,317   £850**

WILLIAM GUNNING–KING - Feeding the Pigs - signed and dated 1925 - 43 x 47.6cm.
(Bonhams)   **$1,392   £800**

GUTERBOCH

LEOPOLD GÜTERBOCH (d. 1881) – The bather –
signed – 39.3 x 31.7cm.
(Christie's)   **$2,899   £1,870**

JUAN BATTISTA GUZMAN (late 19th Century) – The
farewell – signed and dated Barcelona 1890 –
139.7 x 87cm.
(Christie's)   **$7,438   £4,620**

SEYMOUR JOSEPH GUY – Portrait of a Lady – signed
SJ Guy N.A. with initials in monogram and dated 1866, l.r.
– oil on canvas – 26 x 21cm.
(Christie's)   **$5,500   £3,437**

CARL HAAG – The sportsman – signed and dated 1851 –
watercolour heightened with white – 18 x 21in.
(Christie's)   **$968   £605**

LOUIS HAGHE (1806-1885) – The Temple of Venus at Pompeii – signed – inscribed and dated 1850 – watercolour – 18.1 x 25.6cm.
(Lawrence) **$891 £550**

EDWARD MATHEW HALE – Naked to the World – signed and dated 1882 – oil on panel – 46 x 56cm.
(Sotheby's) **$2,868 £1,760**

CARL HAAG (1820-1915) - Bedouin from the Sinai on Camel's back - signed and dated 1858 and also signed - inscribed and dated Dez. 7th 1858 verso - watercolour over pencil - 49.5 x 34.5cm.
(Phillips) **$2,200 £1,350**

MAURITZ FREDERIK HENDRIK DE HAAS – Fishing at Sunset – signed M.F.H. de Haas with artist's device and dated 75, l.l. – oil on canvas – 31.1 x 51.1cm.
(Christie's) **$7,700 £4,812**

ARTHUR HACKER (fl. 1878-1893) – Making friends – signed and dated 1889 – 45.7 x 61cm.
(Christie's) **$6,545 £3,850**

LILLIAN WESTCOTT HALE (1881-1963) – Agnes Doggett as a bride – oil on canvas – 76.8 x 63.5cm.
(Sotheby's) **$14,300 £9,108**

HALE

PHILIP LESLIE HALE (1865-1931) – Lady in black – oil on board – 91.5 x 76.2cm.
(Sotheby's) **$16,500 £10,510**

HARRY HALL (c. 1813-1882) – Mr. Sylvester's Dark Bay Racehorse with jockey in an extensive landscape – oil on canvas – 56.5 x 74.5cm.
(Sotheby's) **$18,480 £11,000**

ANDRÉ HALLET (1890-1959) – Vue d'Aarschot le long du Canal—Gezicht op Aarschot langs het Kanaal – signed and dated lower right A. Hallet '23 – oil on panel – 50.3 x 60.3cm. – Painted in 1923
(Christie's) **$7,920 £4,950**

HARRY HALL (1814-1882) – Stockwell, a Chestnut racehorse with Notman up, on a racecourse – oil on canvas – 49 x 65cm.
(Sotheby's) **$20,460 £13,200**

SAMUEL T. HALPERT (American, 1884-1930) – Table Top Still Life with Fruit – signed – oil on cardboard mounted on plywood – 15 x 18in.
(Skinner) **$2,600 £1,557**

J*** HALLIDAY - H.R.H. Prince of Wales at a battue Sandringham – signed – watercolour heightened with bodycolour – arched top – 43 x 38cm.
(Sotheby's) **$9,185 £5,500**

LETITIA M. HAMILTON, R.H.A. – Donegal Landscape – signed with initials – and also signed with initials on the stretcher   oil on canvas   56 x 66cm.
(Phillips) **$9,920 £6,200**

LETITIA M. HAMILTON, R.H.A. – Donkey and Turf Cart in the Bog – signed with initials – also inscribed on the reverse – oil on panel – unframed – 31.5 x 37cm.
(Phillips) **$11,520 £7,200**

LETITIA M. HAMILTON, R.H.A. – The Turf Cutter's Donkey – signed with initials – also signed with initials on the reverse – oil on canvas – 51 x 41cm.
(Phillips) **$23,200 £14,500**

LETITIA HAMILTON, R.H.A. (1878-1964) - In the Paddock – signed with initials – oil on canvas – 56 x 66cm.
(Phillips) **$30,970 £19,000**

HAMILTON

PHILIP FERDINAND DE HAMILTON (Brussels 1664-1750 Vienna) – A still life of dead game lying on a bank in a landscape, with finches and a woodpecker in the foreground – on canvas – 43 x 51.5cm.
(Phillips) **$9,350 £5,500**

JAN HAMKENS – The Deer Hunt – signed – oil on canvas – 150 x 87cm.
(Sotheby's) **$7,480 £4,400**

WILLIAM HAMILTON, R.A. (1751-1801) – Rowena and Vortigern – Vortigern, a fifth century British leader fell in love with Rowena, a Saxon Princess – signed l.r. : W. Hamilton R. A. 179? – oil on canvas – 200 x 150cm.
(Sotheby's) **$93,775 £60,500**

WILLIAM HAMILTON R.A. (1751-1801) – David Declaring His Will – bears inscription 'Hamilton R.A.' on reverse – 62.8 x 76cm.
(Christie's) **$3,740 £2,200**

WILLIAM HAMMER – A still life of fruit and a wine glass – signed; inscribed and dated 1848 on the reverse – oil on canvas – 40 x 32cm.
(Sotheby's) **$3,366 £1,980**

CHARLES HANCOCK (1802-1877) – A Bay Hunter in an open landscape – oil on canvas – 110.5 x 148cm. *(Sotheby's)* **$18,480 £11,000**

VILHELM HAMMERSHØI (Danish 1864-1916) – A study of a male nude from the back – charcoal – 42.5 x 28.5cm. – Executed circa 1884 in P. S. Krøyer's studio *(Sotheby's)* **$8,217 £4,950**

ADRIAEN HANNEMAN (1603-1671), Studio of – Portrait of Charles II – full length, wearing a leather jerkin and breast plate, a garter sash and badge – oil on canvas – 126 x 100cm. *(Sotheby's)* **$16.632 £9.900**

ARTHUR HENRY KNIGHTON HAMMOND, R.I., R.O.I. (Nottingham 1875-Seaborough 1970) – A Gypsy Girl – signed and inscribed lower right: A gypsy girl, Knighton Hammond – watercolour – 57.2 x 37.4cm. *(Lawrence)* **$758 £462**

HERMAN WENDELBORG HANSEN – Leader of the Herd – signed H. W. Hansen, l.r. – watercolour on paper laid down on board – 49 x 73.5cm. *(Christie's)* **$6,050 £3,781**

HANSEN

JOSEF THEODOR HANSEN (1848-1912) – Il Canale della Misericordia, Venice – signed and dated 1894 – on panel – 15 x 27cm.
(Christie's) **$7,084 £4,400**

SIGVARD HANSEN – Ruins at Ravello, Italy – signed and dated Ravello-1926 – oil on canvas – 68.5 x 98cm.
(Sotheby's) **$6,811 £3,960**

CHARLES MARTIN HARDIE – A lady feeding pigeons in a walled garden – signed and dated 1901 – oil on canvas – 71 x 71cm.
(Woolley & Wallis) **$4,727 £2,900**

MARY E. HARDING (fl. 1880-1903) – Winding the skein – signed and inscribed on an old label on the reverse – on panel – 25 x 20cm.
(Christie's) **$4,897 £3,080**

HEYWOOD HARDY, A.R.W.S., R.P.E. (1843-1933) – The Stirrup Cup – signed – oil on canvas – 46 x 61cm.
(Phillips) **$17,930 £11,000**

HEYWOOD HARDY – Grouse shooting – signed and dated 1892 – oil on canvas – 75 x 103cm.
(Sotheby's) **$55,110 £33,000**

HEYWOOD HARDY, A.R.W.S. – In the aviary – signed and dated 1877 – oil on canvas – 94.5 x 143cm.
(Sotheby's)   **$44,825   £27,500**

JAMES HARDY, Jnr. – The day's bag – signed and dated '80 – watercolour heightened with bodycolour – 73.5 x 61cm.
(Sotheby's)   **$38,577   £23,100**

WILLIAM J. HARDY (Late 19th Century) – A tug of war – signed and dated 1891 – and signed, inscribed and dated 1891 on the reverse – on board – 23 x 18cm.
(Christie's)   **$2,057   £1,210**

HARLAMOFF

ALEXEI ALEXEIVICH HARLAMOFF (Russian 1848-1915) – A portrait of a young girl with a red shawl – signed – oil on canvas – 46 x 35.5cm.
(Sotheby's) **$43,824 £26,400**

HENRI JOSEPH HARPIGNIES – Figures by a pond – signed – oil on canvas – 17 x 29cm.
(Sotheby's) **$3,740 £2,200**

Attributed to J. HARRIS (mid 19th Century) – In the classroom – indistinctly signed – 51 x 51cm.
(Christie's) **$5,597 £3,520**

HENRI JOSEPH HARPIGNIES (French 1819-1916) – The young fishing party - signed twice – oil on canvas – 127 x 69cm.
(Sotheby's) **$36,520 £22,000**

WILLIAM E. HARRIS (English, fl. 1883-1891) – Eton College from the River – signed and dated '90 – 22 x 30cm.
(Bonhams) **$1,550 £1,000**

CHARLES HARMONY HARRISON – Fine Broadland Scene with Fishermen Fishing from a Rowing Boat, Sailing Boats in Background – signed and dated 1886 – watercolour – 15 x 19in.
(G. A. Key) **$4,805** **£3,100**

JOHN CYRIL HARRISON (1898-1985) – Studies of Eagles – signed – grisaille – 44.5 x 34.5cm.
(Phillips) **$3,562** **£2,185**

CHARLES H. HARRISON – By the Blyth, Suffolk – signed – inscribed and dated 1894 – watercolour heightened with white – 10$\frac{1}{2}$ x 16$\frac{1}{4}$in.
(Christie's) **$2,045** **£1,210**

JOHN CYRIL HARRISON – Golden Eagle in flight – signed – watercolour heightened with bodycolour – 55 x 73.5cm.
(Sotheby's) **$3,490** **£2,090**

JOHN CYRIL HARRISON – Pheasants in flight – watercolour – signed – 13 x 9in.
(Bearne's) **$2,366** **£1,400**

241

HARTMAN

GERTRUDE HARVEY (Exh. 1915-39) – A bowl of flowers – oil on panel – signed R.A. and artist's labels to reverse – 20 x 15$^1/_2$in.
(David Lay)   **$2,737   £1,700**

C. BERTRAM HARTMAN – New York Canyon – signed C. Bertram Hartman, l.r. – signed again and inscribed with title on the reverse – watercolour on paper – 55.5 x 37.7cm.
(Christie's)   **$3,300   £2,062**

C. BERTRAM HARTMAN – Autumn – signed C. Bertram Hartman, l.l. – oil on canvas – 61 x 76.5cm.
(Christie's)   **$4,950   £3,093**

HAROLD HARVEY – Audir Lane, Paul Hill, Newlyn – signed and dated 1917 - oil on canvas – 51 x 41cm.
(Phillips)   **$11,830   £7,000**

HAROLD HARVEY (1874-1941) – Interior, woman with parrott – oil on canvas – signed and dated '16 – 17½ x 17½in.
(David Lay)   **$4,830   £3,000**

HAROLD HARVEY – Mounts Bay, Cornwall – signed and dated '28 – 17¾ x 15¾in.
(Bearne's)   **$8,450   £5,000**

HAROLD HARVEY (1874-1941) – Fishing for Bullcod, Larrigan Rocks – signed and dated '07 – oil on canvas – 30.5 x 40.5cm.
(Phillips)   **$40,750   £25,000**

HARVEY

HAROLD HARVEY (1874-1941) - "Steady", boys fishing off Newlyn - oil on canvas – signed and inscribed – traces of artist's label to reverse – 40 x 50in.
(David Lay)   **$34,100   £22,000**

J. D. H. HARVEY (Australian) – Factory and Offices at Melbourne – signed and dated '53 – watercolour, pencil and coloured chalks – 42 x 75cm.
(Phillips)   **$507   £300**

JOHN RABONE HARVEY (English, d. 1933) – Ducks by a Pond – panel – signed – 24.8 x 31.8cm.
(Bonhams)   **$651   £420**

WILLIAM STANLEY HASELTINE – Fishing Boats, Venice – signed W. S. Haseltine and dated 82, l.r. – oil on canvas – 34.9 x 62.8cm.
(Christie's)   **$14,300   £8,937**

ERNEST WILLIAM HASLEHURST - A Sussex garden
– watercolour and bodycolour heightened with white –
unframed – 15^1/$_2$ x 20^3/$_4$in.
(Christie's)   **$528   £330**

CHILDE HASSAM (1859-1935) – Dock scene,
Gloucester – signed Childe Hassam and dated 1896, l.r. –
oil on canvas – 61 x 50.8cm.
(Sotheby's)   **$770,000   £490,446**

ERNEST WILLIAM HASLEHURST - A summer garden
by a thatched cottage – watercolour heightened with
bodycolour and white – unframed – 14^3/$_4$ x 20^7/$_8$in.; and a
similar watercolour by the same artist
(Christie's)   **$1,936   £1,210**

CHILDE HASSAM (1859-1935) – Early evening, Union
Square – signed Childe Hassam and dated 1902 (?), l.r. –
oil on canvas – 50.8 x 61.0cm.
(Sotheby's)   **$330,000   £210,191**

CHILDE HASSAM (1859-1935) – Nymph on a rocky
ledge – signed Childe Hassam and dated 1886, l.r. – oil on
canvas – 35.5 x 29.3cm.
(Sotheby's)   **$37,400   £23,822**

HASSAM

CHILDE HASSAM – Horse drawn cabs at evening – signed and inscribed N.Y. – watercolour and gouache on paper – 34.2 x 43.8cm.
(Sotheby's)   **$990,000**   **£622,642**

HANS HASSENTEUFEL (born 1887) – A Spanish beauty – signed and dated München 1926 – 81 x 60.5cm.
(Christie's)   **$3,365**   **£2,090**

CHILDE HASSAM (1859-1935) - The Old Brush House, Cos Cob – signed Childe Hassam and dated 1902, l.l. – pastel on paper – 43.8 x 54.6cm.
(Sotheby's)   **$187,000**   **£119,108**

FREDERICK CHILDE HASSAM – Idle Hours – signed F. Childe Hassam and dated 1882, l.l. – watercolour on paper laid down on board – 26 x 37.5cm.
(Christie's)   **$33,000**   **£20,625**

JAMES HAYLLAR – Une matelotte – signed – signed and inscribed on the artist's label on the reverse – watercolour – 10 x 7¹/₄in.
(Christie's)   **$1,450   £858**

DOROTHY WEBSTER HAWKSLEY – The fair Rebecca – signed – pencil, pen and brown and black ink and watercolour heightened with white – unframed – 10⁵/₈ x 6³/₈in.
(Christie's)   **$710   £418**

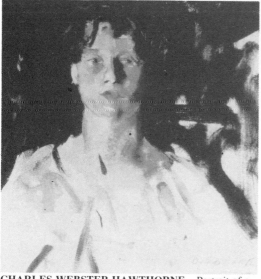

CHARLES WEBSTER HAWTHORNE – Portrait of a Woman – signed By Chas. W. Hawthorne, l.r. – oil on canvas – 61 x 56cm.
(Christie's)   **$4,400   £2,750**

JAMES HAYLLAR – Primroses – signed with monogram and dated 1861 – oil on panel – 20 x 15cm.
(Sotheby's)   **$2,869   £1,760**

HAYLS

JOHN HAYLS (d. 1679), Attributed to – Portrait of a lady moyer, half length, as St. Catherine – in a carved and giltwood frame – 76.2 x 63.5cm.
(Christie's) **$1,972 £1,210**

ARTHUR HAYWARD – St. Ives harbour – signed - 15 x 21in.
(Bearne's) **$7,824 £4,800**

ARTHUR HAYWARD – Smeaton Pier, St Ives – signed and titled on the reverse – oil on board – 25.5 x 35cm.
(Phillips) **$6,720 £4,200**

EDWARD HAYTLEY (Preston fl. 1740-1761) – Portrait of a gentleman – seated small full length, wearing black costume, holding a book, in a landscape, a menagerie beyond – oil on canvas – 50.1 x 35.6cm.
(Lawrence) **$9,922 £6,050**

EDWARD JOSEPH HEAD – Naval tales – signed – oil on canvas – 66 x 51cm.
(Sotheby's) **$4,662 £2,860**

ERICH HECKEL (1883-1970) – Mädchen - signed –
dated and titled lower right Erich Heckel 12 Madchen –
gouache on paper – 34 x 27cm. - Executed in 1912
(Christie's) **$68,200 £44,000**

THOMAS FRANK HEAPHY (1813-1873) – A Spanish
Beauty – signed and numbered '12' on reverse – oil on
canvas – 97 x 71cm.
(Phillips) **$2,771 £1,700**

ERICH HECKEL (1888-1962) – Am Strand – signed –
dated and inscribed lower right Am Strand, Heckel '26 –
watercolour and charcoal on paper – 54.5 x 68cm. –
Executed in 1926
(Christie's) **$23,870 £15,400**

HEARNE

THOMAS HEARNE (1744-1817) – The Old Cheese-cake House, Hyde Park – watercolour over pencil – 25.5 x 34cm.
(Phillips)   **$2,608   £1,600**

ERICH HECKEL (1888-1962) – Zircus Akrobat – signed and inscribed on the reverse with a dedication – coloured crayons and black ink on a postcard – 14 x 9cm. – Executed circa 1909.
(Christie's)   **$11,935 £7,700**

WILLEM CLAESZ. HEDA (1594-Haarlem-1680) – Still life with roemer, ham and a covered flagon, on a table covered by a white cloth – signed and dated 1639 – on panel – 57.5 x 82.5cm.
(Phillips)   **$272,000   £160,000**

CORNELIS DE HEEM (1631-Leiden-1695) – A still life of fruit and a glass of wine resting on a blue cloth draped over a stone ledge – on canvas – 27.2 x 37.4cm.
(Phillips)   **$42,500   £25,000**

GERRET WILLEMSZ HEDA (c. 1620-Haarlem-c. 1702) – A still life, with a pewter jug, wine glass, a pewter plate with a chopped herring and onions, resting on a table – signed and dated Gerret Heda 1646 – on panel – 69 x 58.5cm.
(Phillips)   **$53,790   £33,000**

CORNELIS DE HEEM (1631-1695) – A still life with fruit and chestnuts upon a stone ledge draped with a brocaded blue cloth – oil on canvas – 30 x 38cm.
(Phillips)   **$210,600   £130,000**

CORNELIS DE HEEM (Leyden 1631-1695 Antwerp) –
A still life, a wine glass, a delft bowl on its side from
which tumbles fruit, a melon, bunches of grapes, with
hazel nuts and roses scattered on a green drape covering a
ledge nestling in a stone niche - signed C. de Heem f. – on
canvas – 38.8 x 51.5cm.
(Phillips) **$407,500 £250,000**

GERRIT VAN HEES (1629-Haarlem-circa 1702) – A
milkmaid crossing a brook in a woodland landscape
– bears signature J. Ruysdael – on panel – 46.3 x 58.7cm.
(Phillips) **$8,840 £5,200**

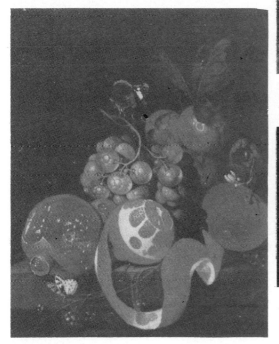

DANIEL VAN HEIL (1604-1662) – The burning of Troy
– oil on canvas – 56 x 76.5cm.
(Phillips) **$2,282 £1,400**

DAVID DE HEEM (1570-Utrecht-1632) – Still life of
fruit, including a pomegranate, lemon, orange and grapes
lying on a ledge – signature strengthened? – on canvas –
32 x 26.2cm.
(Phillips) **$27,200 £16,000**

EGBERT VAN HEEMSKERK – Fete villageoise –
oil on canvas – 89.5 x 115cm.
(Sotheby's) **$13,193 £8,457**

Circle of JOHANN-ERNST HEINSIUS (1740-1812) –
Portrait of a lady, half length, her dress decorated with
pearls and a bow – pastel – an oval – 64.5 x 54.5cm.
(Phillips) **$9,720 £6,000**

RUDOLF HELLWAG - A view of Santa Marie Della Salute - signed and dated 1894 - oil on canvas – 83 x 111cm. *(Sotheby's)*   **$5,610   £3,300**

PIET VAN DER HEM – A lady in a white dress watering the roses in a garden by a statue – signed lower right Piet van der Hem – 72.5 x 52cm.
(Christie's)   **$2,270   £1,428**

WILLIAM HEMSLEY (born 1819) – The young artist – signed – on board – 21 x 16cm.
(Christie's)   **$4,262   £2,750**

CHARLES NAPIER HEMY R.A., R.W.S. (1841-1917)
– "Waiting for the tide" – oil on canvas – initialled and
dated 1892 – 13½ x 20in.
(David Lay)   **$2,790   £1,800**

**CHARLES COOPER HENDERSON (Chertsey 1803-
1877)** – 'A Halt for the Mail Coach' – pen and watercolour,
heightened with gouache – 13.9 x 20.9cm.
(Lawrence)   **$722   £440**

JEAN-JACQUES HENNER – A seated nude by a pond –
signed – oil on panel – 27 x 19cm.
(Sotheby's)   **$2,805   £1,650**

JOSEPH MORRIS HENDERSON, R.S.A. – Arran from
Kintyre – signed – signed and inscribed on the reverse –
17¾ x 24in.
(Bearne's)   **$3,380   £2,000**

JEAN JACQUES HENNER (1829-1905) – An auburn
beauty – signed – on board – 27 x 21.5cm.
(Christie's)   **$1,594   £990**

HENNINGSEN

ERIK HENNINGSEN – A moonlit rendez-vous – signed with monogram and dated 1899 – oil on canvas laid down on board – 35 x 27cm.
(Sotheby's) **$2,460 £1,430**

EDWARD LAMSON HENRY – A Philadelphia Doorway – signed E. L. Henry and dated 82, u.r. – oil on panel – 24 x 19cm.
(Christie's) **$13,200 £8,250**

ROBERT HENRI – Volendam, Gray House – signed Robert Henri, l.l. – oil on panel – 19 x 25cm.
(Christie's) **$5,500 £3,437**

EDWARD LAMSON HENRY(1841-1919) – Examining illustrations by the fire – inscribed Sentiment....d'après Nature/fait en 1872/ELH on the reverse – oil on board – 16.5 x 24.8cm.
(Sotheby's) **$28,600 £18,217**

GEORGE HENRY, R.A., R.S.A., R.S.W. – Portrait of Florence Janet Brookes (née Adair) – signed and dated 1905 – inscribed on the reverse – oil on canvas – 103 x 76cm.
(Phillips) **$720 £450**

FREDERICK HENRY HENSHAW – Travellers by a
sunlit villa – on panel – signed – Collection: Mayor A. C.
Hart – 22³/₄ x 16¹/₂in.
(Bearne's) **$3,560 £2,000**

WILSON HEPPLE (English, 1854-1937) – A Head
Study of a bay hunter – signed and dated 1895 –
45.8 x 35.6cm.
(Bonhams) **$651 £420**

GEORGE HEPPER (fl. 1866-1868) - Two Terriers and a
Tabby Cat by a chair – signed and dated 1866 –
42.5 x 52.1cm.
(Christie's) **$3,366 £1,980**

WILSON HEPPLE – 'Waiting for some milk' – signed
and dated 1919 – 25 x 35.5cm.
(Anderson & Garland) **$2,689 £1,650**

EDWARD BENJAMIN HERBERTE (fl. 1860-1893) –
Full cry – signed and dated 1886 – 45.5 x 35.5cm.
(Christie's) **$1,399 £880**

EDWARD BENJAMIN HERBERTE (fl. 1860-1893) –
Outside the inn – signed and dated 1879 – 61 x 91.5cm.
(Christie's)   **$4,372   £2,750**

LÉON HERBO – Salomé – signed and inscribed
Bruxelles - Salomé – oil on canvas – 106 x 81cm.
(Sotheby's)   **$5,236   £3,080**

ROBERT HERDMAN, R.S.A. – Beatrice - Rome –
signed with monogram and dated '69; signed and inscribed
with title on a label on the stretcher – oil on canvas – 85 x
70cm.
(Sotheby's)   **$12,859   £7,700**

HERMANSEN

LUDWIG HERMANN (German 1812-1881) – Ober Wesel, Rhine – signed and dated 1871 – oil on canvas – 64 x 94cm.
(Sotheby's) **$13,695 £8,250**

ROBERT HERDMAN, R.S.A., R.S.W. – Arran fern gatherer – signed with monogram and dated 1864 – watercolour heightened with white and scratching out – 19 x 12cm.
(Sotheby's) **$2,431 £1,430**

LUDWIG HERMANN (1812-1881) – A view of Konigsberg – signed and dated 1847 – 65 x 94cm.
(Christie's) **$10,980 £6,820**

SALI HERMAN (b. 1898) – Droving – signed and dated 74 – 30.4 x 38.1cm.
(Christie's) **$11,583 £7,150**

SALI HERMAN (b. 1898) – The Ginger Plant – signed – 96.5 x 142.2cm.
(Christie's) **$30,294 £18,700**

OLAF AUGUST HERMANSEN – Roses in a glass vase – signed with monogram and dated 1880 – oil on canvas – 38.5 x 29cm.
(Sotheby's) **$9,082 £5,280**

HERMANSEN

OLAF AUGUST HERMANSEN (1849-1897) – Roses in
a vase, peaches, nuts and a melon on a marbled ledge –
signed with monogram and dated 1891 – 50 x 71.5cm.
(Christie's)   **$15,004   £9,680**

**Circle of JOHN FREDERICK HERRING, Jnr. (1820-
1907)** – Plough horses and pigs in a stable yard – on board
– unframed – 20.2 x 26.1cm.
(Christie's)   **$1,255   £770**

JOHN FREDERICK HERRING, Jnr. – Farmyard scene
– oil on panel – 32 x 40cm.
(Sotheby's)   **$8,606   £5,280**

DANIEL HERNANDEZ (Peruvian, 1856-1932) –
Lovers – board – signed – unframed – 46.6 x 33.5cm.
(Bonhams)   **$4,650   £3,000**

JOHN FREDERICK HERRING, Jnr. – Perplexed –
bears signature – oil on board – 30 x 46cm.
(Sotheby's)   •   **$8,068   £4,950**

JOHN FREDERICK HERRING, Jnr. – A farmyard –
signed – oil on canvas – 41 x 61cm.
(Sotheby's)   **$16,137   £9,900**

JOHN FREDERICK HERRING, Snr. (1795-1865) –
Beeswing, a Dark Bay Racehorse, standing in a stable –
signed l.r.: J. F. Herring Senr., 1842 – oil on canvas –
71 x 91.5cm.
(Sotheby's)   **$77,616**   **£46,200**

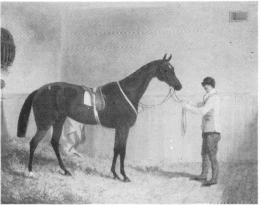

JOHN FREDERICK HERRING, Snr. (1795-1865) –
Alice Hawthorn held by a jockey in a stable – signed l.r. :
J.F. Herring Snr/1844 and inscribed: Alice Hawthorn – oil
on canvas – 70 x 90cm.
(Sotheby's)   **$68,200**   **£44,000**

JOHN FREDERICK HERRING, Snr. (1795-1865) –
Feeding the horse – signed J. F. Herring Snr/1846 – oil on
canvas – 140 x 109.5cm.
(Sotheby's)   **$388,080**   **£231,000**

JOHN FREDERICK HERRING, Snr. (1795-1865) – A
donkey, with its foal, and ducks in a landscape – signed
l.c. : J.F. Herring 1883 – oil on canvas – 33 x 43cm.
(Sotheby's)   **$86,955**   **£56,100**

HERRING

JOHN FREDERICK HERRING, Snr. (1795-1865) –
Colonel Peel's Slane, with A. Pavis up, on a racecourse –
signed l.r. : J.F. Herring 1838 – oil on canvas – 62.2 x
76.2cm.
(Sotheby's) **$93,775 £60,500**

JOHN FREDERICK HERRING, Snr. (1795-1865) –
Deer in a park – signed l.r. : J.F. Herring: Senr. 1855 – oil
on panel – 26.5 x 31.5cm.
(Sotheby's) **$31,542 £20,350**

ARTHUR HEYER (1872-1931) – Persian kittens –
signed – canvas laid down on board – 48.5 x 69cm.
(Christie's) **$3,188 £1,980**

ARTHUR HEYER – A colourful ball – signed – oil on
canvas – 57.5 x 77.5cm.
(Sotheby's) **$5,610 £3,300**

HANS HERRMANN (1813-Hamburg-1890) – A still
life of flowers in a glass vase upon a stone plinth with
peaches resting at its foot – signed H. Herrmann and dated
1844 – on canvas – 70.8 x 52cm.
(Phillips) **$40,800 £24,000**

ADRIAAN-JOSEF HEYMANS (1839-1921) – La Mine;
Environs de Charleroi—De Mijn in de omgeving van
Charleroi – signed lower left AJH – oil on canvas –
81 x 72cm. excluding painted frame – 115 x 96cm.
including painted frame – Painted circa 1892
(Christie's) **$52,800 £33,000**

ALDRO THOMPSON HIBBARD – Jefferson, Vermont
– signed A. T. Hibbard, l.r. – oil on canvas –
61.6 x 81.5cm.
(Christie's) **$9,350 £5,844**

SIR HANS HEYSEN (1877-1968) – The Picnic – signed
twice and dated 1905 1917 – 122.2 x 92cm.
(Christie's) **$231,660 £143,000**

THOMAS HICKEY (1741-1824) – A young boy with his
Aya – oil on canvas – 136 x 168cm.
(Sotheby's) **$17,050 £11,000**

ALDRO T. HIBBARD, NA (1886-1972) – Spring thaw –
oil on canvas – 24 x 29in. – signed A. T. Hibbard lower
left
(Bruce D. Collins) **$6,050 £3,601**

ALDRO T. HIBBARD, NA (Am. 1886-1972) – Rushing
stream, N.H. – oil on canvas laid down – signed A. T.
Hibbard lower right – titled on the reverse –
17$\frac{1}{2}$ x 23$\frac{1}{2}$in.
(Bruce D. Collins) **$2,530 £1,581**

GEORGE ARTHUR HICKIN – Farmyard fowl – signed
– oil on canvas – 61 x 51cm.
(Sotheby's) **$3,945 £2,420**

261

HICKS

GEORGE ELGAR HICKS (1824-1914) – Family accounts – signed – 30.5 x 25.5cm.
(Christie's)   **$6,996**   **£4,400**

P. HILLIER (late 19th Century) – A winter river landscape with figures skating – signed and dated 1875 – 61 x 99cm.
(Christie's)   **$11,594**   **£7,480**

TRISTRAM HILLIER, R.A. – Eggs and Apples – signed – titled on the reverse – oil on board – 20.5 x 38cm.
(Phillips)   **$2,535**   **£1,500**

TRISTRAM HILLIER (b. 1905) – The Indian Ocean from Plettenberg 1976 – signed and dated lower left Hillier 76 – oil on canvas – 13^1/$_2$ x 19^1/$_2$in.
(Christie's)   **$5,214**   **£3,300**

ROBERT ALEXANDER HILLINGFORD (1825-1904) – Baron Munchhausen relating his adventures – signed with monogram – 43.5 x 66.5cm.
(Christie's)   **$13,992**   **£8,800**

LAURA COOMBS HILLS (American, b. 1859) – "A White Jar of Flowers" – signed – pastel on tan paper – 23^3/$_4$ x 19^1/$_2$ in.
(Skinner)   **$21,000**   **£12,575**

LAURA COOMBS HILLS (American, 1859-1952) –
"Hollyhocks in the Sunshine" – signed – pastel on tan
paper – 20⁵/₈ x 14³/₈ in.
(Skinner)   **$41,000   £24,551**

FRED HINES – The rustic bridge – signed and dated
1897 – on board – 38.7 x 60.9cm.
(Christie's)   **$1,187   £715**

THEODORE HINES – Near the lock, Mapledurham –
signed; signed and inscribed with title on the reverse – oil
on canvas – 51 x 76cm.
(Sotheby's)   **$2,510   £1,540**

HANS HILSOE – An interior – signed and indistinctly
inscribed – oil on canvas – 63 x 53cm.
(Sotheby's)   **$6,358   £3,740**

HERMANN HIRSCH (1861-1934) – Au plein air –
signed and dated 98 – on board – 31 x 41cm.
(Christie's)   **$10,626   £6,600**

CLAUDE RAGUET HIRST – A Gentleman's Table – signed Claude Raguet Hirst and inscribed
N.Y.,l.r. – oil on canvas – 45.7 x 81.2cm. *(Christie's)*   **$44,000 £27,500**   1252

SAMUEL HIRSZENBERG – A self portrait with a muse
– signed and dated 1890 – oil on canvas – 60 x 77.5cm.
(Sotheby's)   **$4,114   £2,420**

JOHN HITCHENS – Red Depths and Blue – signed –
titled and dated 1967 on reverse – oil on canvas –
71 x 77cm.
(Phillips)   **$1,440   £900**

HAROLD HITCHCOCK – Italian Landscape – signed
with monogram and dated 1956 – watercolour and
bodycolour – 50.8 x 76.2cm.
(Phillips)   **$1,600   £1,000**

FRANK HOBDEN – Footsteps – signed – 61 x 91.4cm.
(Bonhams)   **$1,305   £750**

KASPAR VAN DEN HOECKE, (d. circa 1648) –
Bouquet de Fleurs – oil on copper – 36 x 28cm.
(Sotheby's) **$173,160 £111,000**

M*** HOFNER (?) – A young woman in feathered hat –
indistinctly signed and dated 1888 – on panel – 25 x 20cm.
(Anderson & Garland) **$867 £510**

CARL HOFER – Standing nude in front of a window –
signed twice with the initials – gouache – 34 x 24.5cm.
(Sotheby's) **$14,069 £8,276**

M*** HOFNER (?) – A young woman wearing a
jewelled skull-cap – indistinctly signed and dated 1889 –
on panel – 25 x 20cm.
(Anderson & Garland) **$816 £480**

WILLIAM HOGARTH, Follower of – Election entertainment – on panel – 46.3 x 61.6cm.
(Christie's)   **$627   £385**

WILLIAM HOGARTH, Follower of – Portrait of William Thirkeld son of Rev. Taylor Thirkeld and Dorothy Bacon, standing three quarter length – in a painted oval – 74.9 x 63.4cm.
(Christie's)   **$3,048   £1,870**

RUDOLF HÖGER (1878-1928) – On the veranda – signed – 53 x 79.5cm.
(Christie's)   **$2,834   £1,760**

WILLIAM HOGARTH (1697-1764) – Portrait of a gentleman – three-quarter length, seated, wearing a grey coat with pink lining, his right arm resting on a table – oil on canvas – 84.5 x 68.5cm.
(Sotheby's)   **$196,057   £126,500**

ABEL HOLD (fl. 1849-1871) – A Dead Pigeon – signed and dated 1866 – oil on canvas – 42 x 55cm.
(Phillips)   **$848   £520**

JAMES HOLLAND (1799-1870) – Portrait of the Langford family in their drawing room – The picture shows Edward William Langford of Blackheath with his wife and their daughter Anne Elizabeth who subsequently married Charles Shirreff in 1852 – oil on canvas – 59.5 x 82cm.
(Sotheby's)   **$52,855   £34,100**

JAMES HOLLAND (1799-1870) – The Piazzetta, Venice – signed with monogram and dated 1855 – on panel –32 x 46.5cm.
(Christie's)   **$6,996 £4,400**

HOLYOAKE

WINSLOW HOMER (1836-1910) – The initials – signed Homer and dated '64, l.l. – oil on canvas – 40.6 x 31.1cm.
(Sotheby's) **$880,000 £560,510**

ROWLAND HOLYOAKE (English, 19th/20th Century) – A Young Beauty – panel – signed and dated '12 – 29.8 x 17.6cm.
(Bonhams) **$1,473 £950**

ABRAHAM DANIELSZ HONDIUS (Rotterdam 1625-1695 London) – Two hounds attacking a heron on a riverbank – signed Abraham Hondius – on panel – 25.5 x 34.5cm.
(Phillips) **$13,855 £8,500**

WINSLOW HOMER – Yacht in a cove, Gloucester – signed and dated 1880 – watercolour on paper – 22.8 x 33.0cm.
(Sotheby's) **$209,000 £131,447**

GERRIT HONDIUS (American, 1891-1970) – Fruit Stalls, New York City – signed "G. Hondius" u.r. – oil on canvas – 50 x 40in. – framed
(Skinner) **$1,000 £625**

NATHANIEL HONE, R.A. (1718-1784) – Portrait of David Garrick (1717-1779) – half length, wearing a red coat – oil on canvas – 63.5 x 54.5cm.
(Sotheby's)   **$35,850**   **£23,100**

BERNARD DE HOOG (Dutch, 1867-1943) – Interior Scene – signed – oil on canvas – 11 x 9in.
(Skinner)   **$2,000**   **£1,198**

NATHANIEL HONE, R.A. (1718-1784) – Portrait of a young girl with her Pomeranian dog – oil on canvas – 49 x 40cm.
(Sotheby's)   **$13,640**   **£8,800**

BERNARD DE HOOG – Mother and children – signed l.r. – oil on canvas – 37.5 x 28cm.
(Sotheby's)   **$3,784**   **£2,200**

BERNARD DE HOOG - The sewing lesson - signed - oil on canvas - 29 x 38.5cm.
(Sotheby's)   **$13,090 £7,700**

BERNARD DE HOOG (Dutch, 1867-1943) – The Happy
Family – signed – 50.8 x 40.6cm.
(Bonhams)   **$11,625   £7,500**

**SAMUEL VAN HOOGSTRATEN, Circle of (1627-
Dordrecht-1678)** – A boy standing in a window niche
lighting a lantern from a candle – on canvas – 38 x 29.5cm.
(Phillips)   **$9,860   £5,800**

JOHN HORACE HOOPER – Backwater, Wargate on Thames – signed; signed and inscribed with title on the reverse – oil on canvas – 62 x 107cm.
(Sotheby's) **$8,668 £4,950**

JOHN HOPPNER, R.A. (1758-1810) – Portrait of Louisa Reid (1786-1879) – half length, wearing a crimson dress decorated with a jewelled brooch, a flowing black shawl draped over her right shoulder – oil on canvas – 75 x 62cm.
(Sotheby's) **$11,088 £6,600**

W. G. HOOPER – "The Gift", with elderly gentleman and young girl at cottage door – oil on canvas – signed and dated 1894 – in gilt frame – 24^1/$_2$ x 33^1/$_2$in.
(Riddetts) **$880 £550**

JOHN HOPPNER, R.A. (1758-1810) – Portrait of Jane, Countess of Westmorland as hebe – oil on canvas – in a carved wood frame – 73 x 65cm.
(Sotheby's) **$51,150 £33,000**

JOHN HOPPNER, R.A. (1758-1810) – Portrait of George John Frederick Sackville, later 4th Duke of Dorset (1793-1815) – full length, standing in the grounds of Buckhurst Castle, wearing a grey suit and white shirt – oil on canvas – 141 x 116cm.
(Sotheby's) **$36,960 £22,000**

HOPPNER

JOHN HOPPNER, R.A. (1752-1810) – Portrait of Sir John Osborn, Bt. (1772-1848) of Chicksands Priory, Bedfordshire – half length, wearing a brown coat with red lined collar and white neck cloth, a landscape beyond – oil on canvas – 75 x 62cm.
(Sotheby's)   **$66,528   £39,600**

GWENDOLINE MARY HOPTON – A Walk in the Tuileries – signed – oil on board – 19 x 24cm.
(Phillips)   **$1,267   £750**

JAN JOSEF HOREMANS THE ELDER (1682-Antwerp-1759) – Elegant figures dancing on a terrace – on canvas – 67 x 83.2cm.
(Phillips)   **$15,300   £9,000**

JAN JOSEF HOREMANS – A sick Man surrounded by his Family, ministered to by an Angel – and three companion pictures – a set of four – oil on canvas – 48.3 x 58.4cm.
(Bonhams)   **$20,930   £13,000**

GEORGE W. HORLOR (fl. 1849-1891) – 'What will he do with it?' — Two Drop-eared Skye Terriers and a black and tan puppy with a hedgehog – signed and dated 1883 – and signed, inscribed and dated 1882 on the reverse – 43.2 x 53.3cm.
(Christie's)   **$13,090   £7,700**

EDWARD ATKINSON HORNEL, R.O.I. (1864-1933) – Balloons in the woods – signed and dated 1916 – oil on canvas – 63.5 x 76.2cm.
(Christie's)   **$62,832   £37,400**

EDWARD ATKINSON HORNEL – Feeding the ducks –
signed and dated 1918 – oil on canvas – 62 x 51cm.
(Sotheby's) **$33,066 £19,800**

EDWARD ATKINSON HORNEL – Spring in the wood
– signed and dated 1919 – oil on canvas – 61 x 51cm.
(Sotheby's) **$18,370 £11,000**

EDWARD ATKINSON HORNEL – Wearing a spring garland – signed and dated 1917; inscribed with title
on the stretcher – oil on canvas – 64 x 77cm.
(Sotheby's) **$29,392 £17,600**

HORNEL

EDWARD ATKINSON HORNEL – On the shore, Brighouse Bay, Kirkcudbright – signed and dated 1918 – oil on canvas – 51 x 61cm.
(Sotheby's) **$29,392 £17,600**

EARLE HORTER – Tabletop Abstraction – signed E. Horter, l.r. – oil on panel – 50.8 x 61cm.
(Christie's) **$66,000 £41,250**

L*** HOUBAER – At the Ball – signed – oil on canvas – 138 x 80cm.
(Sotheby's) **$4,675 £2,750**

GEORGE EDWARD HORTON – On the beach at Scheveningen – signed – 34 x 25cm.
(Anderson & Garland) **$782 £460**

ARNOLD HOUBRAKEN, Follower of – Vortumnus and Pomona – oil on canvas – 128 x 102cm.
(Phillips) **$5,474 £3,400**

GEORGE HOUSTON, R.S.A., R.S.W. – Rhododendrons
– signed – watercolour on canvas – 93 x 72cm.
(Sotheby's) $3,674 £2,200

HUBERTUS VAN HOVE (Dutch, 1814-1865) – The
Interruption/An Interior Genre Scene – signed and
indistinctly inscribed "H.v. Hove..." – oil on canvas – 28 x
25in.
(Skinner) $2,200 £1,317

**JOHN RENNIE McKENZIE HOUSTON, R.S.W.
(1856-1932)** – A woman with her children amongst corn
stooks – signed – watercolour – 58.4 x 46cm.
(Christie's) $3,511 £2,090

FELICIE WALDO HOWELL (American, b. 1897) –
"The Approaching Shower"/Boats in Gloucester Harbor –
signed and dated 1921 – gouache on tan paper – 24¼ x
18¼in.
(Skinner) $9,500 £5,689

HOWSE

GEORGE HOWSE – The Clock Tower, St. Alban's, Hertfordshire – signed on old label attached to backboard – watercolour over pencil heightened with touches of bodycolour – 40 x 52cm.
(Sotheby's)   **$4,488   £2,640**

WILLIAM R. HOYLES – Springtime at Rhuddlan, Near Rhyl - A girl holding a basket, standing beside the gate of a thatched cottage – signed – 25 x 39cm.
(Spencer's)   **$2,106   £1,300**

INEZ HOYTON (1903-1983) – Untitled – signed on the canvas overlap – Inez Hoyton – oil on canvas – 20 x 24in.
(Christie's)   **$1,303   £825**

HEINRICH HUBNER (German b. 1869) – Autumn sunshine – signed; titled in German on a label on the stretcher – oil on canvas – 84 x 69cm.
(Sotheby's)   **$7,304   £4,400**

LEONART HUBNER (Active circa 1752) – A still life with a pumpkin, cabbages, celery, parsnips, carrots and potatoes upon the ground beneath a tree – oil on canvas – 70 x 88cm.
(Phillips)   **$15,390   £9,500**

LOUIS HUBNER (fl. 1740-1769) – Duckwing game cock, chickens, pigeons and a bullfinch in a landscape – oil on canvas – 98 x 123.5cm.
(Sotheby's)   **$11,935   £7,700**

THOMAS HUDSON (1701-1779), Follower of – Portrait of a gentleman, seated half length, in a brown coat and blue turban – in a carved and giltwood frame – 83.8 x 73.7cm.
(Christie's) **$3,945 £2,420**

ARTHUR HUGHES (1832-1915) – Faith – signed – and signed and inscribed on an old label on the reverse – on panel – 48 x 35.5cm.
(Christie's) **$10,844 £6,820**

THOMAS HUDSON (1701-1779) – Portrait of Mrs. Binford – three quarter length, standing, wearing a pink dress and holding gloves – oil on canvas, in a carved wood frame – 126 x 101.5cm.
(Sotheby's) **$18,480 £11,000**

EDWIN HUGHES (English, 19th Century) – 'Tired Out'/Portrait of an Armourer – signed and dated 1875 – oil on canvas – 16¼ x 12¼in.
(Skinner) **$700 £419**

HUGHES

TALBOT HUGHES (English, 1869-1942) – The Recital
– panel – signed and dated 1891 – 35.6 x 45.8cm.
(Bonhams) **$9,300** **£6,000**

ABRAHAM HULK (1813-1897) – A river estuary with
fishing vessels – signed – on panel – 17.8 x 26.6cm.
(Christie's) **$12,751** **£7,920**

WILLIAM HUGHES – A Still Life of Grapes and
Apples attended by a Butterfly – panel – signed and dated
'82 – 22.8 x 30.5cm.
(Bonhams) **$2,170** **£1,400**

JACOB VAN HULSDONCK (1582-1647) – A still life
of fruit in a wan-li bowl upon a stone ledge, with cherries
and plums scattered around – oil on panel – 40 x 52.5cm.
(Phillips) **$56,700** **£35,000**

WILLIAM HUGHES – Still life of an apple, pineapple
and grapes on a mossy bank – signed and dated 1863 –
24.2 x 44.5cm.
(Christie's) **$876** **£528**

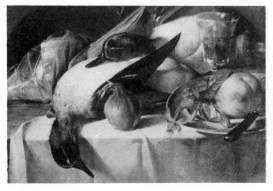

WILLIAM HUGHES – Still life with Teal – signed with
initials and dated August 1861 – oil on canvas laid on
board – 29 x 39cm.
(Sotheby's) **$3,306** **£1,980**

HUNGARIAN SCHOOL – Cleopatra – oil – 90 x 60cm.
(Mugyujtok Galeriaja Kft) **$1,297** **£786**

TOM HUNN (fl. 1878-1908) – At the Garden Gate – signed – watercolour over pencil – 27.5 x 37cm.
(Phillips) $652   £400

ALFRED WILLIAM HUNT (1830-1896) – "Rhine, Steam Tugs with Barges" – signed also inscribed verso – watercolour and bodycolour with scratching out – 18.5 x 27cm.
(Phillips) $6,800   £4,000

CHARLES HUNT (English, 1803-1877) – Dressing Up – signed and dated 1869 – 31.1 x 21cm.
(Bonhams) $1,163   £750

CHARLES HUNT - In the dock - signed and dated '76 - oil on canvas - 61 x 91.5cm.
(Sotheby's) $16,137 £9,900

HUNT

CHARLES HUNT – 'Horspittal for Woonded Solgers home from Egipt' – signed and dated '86 – 23¼ x 35¼in.
(Bearne's) **$14,240** **£8,000**

CHARLES HUNT – The fortune teller – signed and dated1869 – oil on canvas – 46 x 71cm.
(Sotheby's) **$6,275** **£3,850**

EDGAR HUNT – Chickens and doves in a farmyard – signed and dated 1907 – 17½ x 13½in.
(Bearne's) **$20,470** **£11,500**

EDGAR HUNT (1876-1953) – Feathered Friends – signed and dated 1932 – 35.5 x 28cm.
(Christie's) **$14,866** **£9,350**

EDGAR HUNT – A duck pond – signed and dated 192(4?) – 19 x 27cm.
(Anderson & Garland) **$22,100** **£13,000**

WALTER HUNT (1861-1941) – Farmyard friends – signed and dated 1910 – canvas laid down on panel – 45.7 x 61cm.
(Christie's) **$12,593** **£7,920**

WALTER HUNT – Waiting to be fed – signed and dated
'83; signed and inscribed with title on the reverse – oil on
canvas – 36 x 46cm.
(Sotheby's) **$12,909 £7,920**

WILLIAM HENRY HUNT – Plums – signed –
watercolour over pencil with bodycolour – 20 x 28cm.
(Sotheby's) **$2,244 £1,320**

Circle of WILLIAM HENRY HUNT – Gathering
Primroses – watercolour and pastel heightened with
bodycolour and scratching out – 49 x 39.5cm.
(Phillips) **$1,467 £900**

EMIL HÜNTEN – Frederick the Great in battle – signed
and dated 1865 – oil on canvas – 79.5 x 91cm.
(Sotheby's) **$12,155 £7,150**

GEORGE LESLIE HUNTER (1877-1931) – The kitchen dresser, Larkhall – signed – watercolour – 45.7 x 38.1cm.
(Christie's)   **$7,762**   **£4,620**

GEORGE LESLIE HUNTER – Man standing on a jetty – signed – brush and black ink and pastel – 30.5 x 9.5cm.
(Sotheby's)   **$2,755**   **£1,650**

LOUIS BOSWORTH HURT – A herd of highland cattle – indistinctly signed – oil on canvas – 76 x 63.5cm.
(Sotheby's)   **$2,689**   **£1,650**

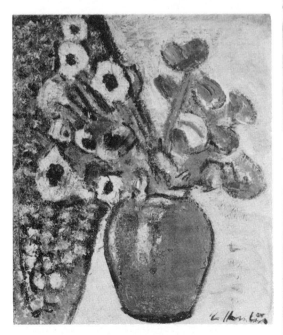

GEORGE LESLIE HUNTER – Flowers in a vase – signed – oil on board – 46 x 38.5cm.
(Sotheby's)   **$22,044**   **£13,200**

LOUIS BOSWORTH HURT – Mists of the morning – signed – oil on canvas – 51 x 76cm.
(Sotheby's)   **$20,619**   **£12,650**

LOUIS BOSWORTH HURT – In Skye, hills of the Isle of Mist – signed and dated 1885 – oil on canvas – 76 x 63.5cm.
(Sotheby's) **$11,022 £6,600**

ROBERT GEMMELL HUTCHISON, R.S.A., R.S.W. – Girl sitting on a lobster creel – oil on canvas – 61 x 46cm.
(Sotheby's) **$36,746 £22,000**

LOUIS BOSWORTH HURT (English, 1856-1929) – 'Through the Pass of Awe' – signed and dated 1904 – inscribed on reverse – 61 x 101.6cm.
(Bonhams) **$28,675 £18,500**

LOUIS BOSWORTH HURT (1856-1929) – Highland Cattle in a mountainous landscape – signed and dated 1880 – 76 x 122cm.
(Christie's) **$34,980 £22,000**

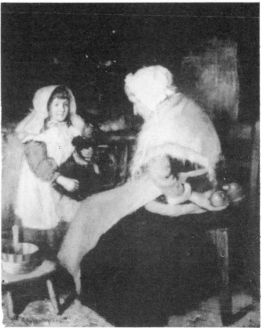

ROBERT GEMMELL HUTCHISON – 'Which hand?' – signed – 42 x 34.5cm.
(Anderson & Garland) **$13,692 £8,400**

ROBERT GEMMELL HUTCHISON, R.S.A., R.S.W., R.O.I (1855-1936) – Amongst the dunes – signed – oil on canvas – 45.7 x 35.5cm.
(Christie's)   **$22,176   £13,200**

ROBERT GEMMELL HUTCHISON, R.S.A., R.S.W., R.O.I. (Edinburgh 1855-1936) –A Quiet Pastime – signed with initials bottom right and bearing signature: R. G. Hutchison – oil on canvas – 34.2 x 24.2cm.
(Lawrence)   **$1,173   £715**

ROBERT GEMMELL HUTCHISON, R.S.A.,R.S.W. – In tow – signed – oil on canvas – 36 x 53cm. *(Sotheby's)*   **£34,903 £20,900**

ROBERT GEMMELL HUTCHISON, R.S.A., R.S.W. – Playing horsie – signed – oil on canvas – 34 x 46.5cm.
(Sotheby's) $14,696 £8,800

ROBERT GEMMELL HUTCHISON, R.S.A., R.S.W. – Children with a toy boat – signed – oil on canvas – 35.5 x 43cm.
(Sotheby's) $17,451   £10,450

ROBERT GEMMELL HUTCHISON, R.S.A., R.W.S. – Christmas decorations – signed – oil on canvas – unframed – 102 x 76cm.
(Sotheby's) $8,817   £5,280

WILLIAM HENRY FLORIO HUTCHISSON (1773-1857) – The reception of Lord Amherst by Rup Lal Mallick – oil on canvas – 102 x 150.5cm.
(Sotheby's) $103,488   £61,600

HUYSMANS

J B HUYSMANS – Arab market – on wood – signed – 40 x 50cm.
(Galerie Moderne) **$10,533 £6,666**

GEORGE INNESS (1825-1894) – The commencement of the Galleria (Rome, the Appian Way) – signed G. Inness – dated 1870 and inscribed Rome, l.r. – oil on canvas – 77.5 x 115.5cm.
(Sotheby's) **$40,700 £25,924**

RUDOLPH IHLEE – Provencal Village – oil on canvas – 38 x 45.5cm.
(Phillips) **$1,440 £900**

INNOCENTI (late 19th Century) – Banditti playing cards in a woodland – signed – on panel – 35.6 x 45.7cm.
(Christie's) **$938 £605**

GERELY IMRE – "School Outing - Picnic in the woods" – signed – oil on canvas – 24 x 32in.
(Biddle & Webb) **$5,406 £3,400**

LAWRENCE IRVING – Unloading Gravel at Whitstable Harbour – acrylic on canvas – 46 x 61cm.
(Phillips) **$760 £450**

JOSEF ISRAELS (Dutch, 1824-1911) – Mother and Daughter by the Hearth – signed – oil on canvas - 14^1/$_8$ x 10^1/$_4$ in.
(Skinner)   **$1,100**   **£659**

EGILL JACOBSEN – Den gule Mand -The Yellow Man – signed with initials E.J. and dated 77 on the reverse – 116 x 89cm.
(Christie's)   **$21,185**   **£13,324**

ITALIAN SCHOOL,18th Century – Landscape with figures – oil on canvas – 37 x 47cm
(Galerie Moderne)   **$3,049**   **£1,930**

SIGISMUND IVANOWSKI – Window Shopping – oil on canvas – 50.8 x 81.2cm.
(Christie's)   **$6,050**   **£3,781**

EGILL JACOBSEN – Komposition med maske – with the name and the date E. Jacobsen 1963 on the stretcher – 98 x 80cm.
(Christie's)   **$15,132**   **£9,517**

JACOBSEN

ANTONIO NICOLO GASPARO JACOBSEN – Three
Masted Rigger Great Western – signed Antonio Jacobsen
and dated 1916, l.r. – oil on board – 44.7 x 76.5cm.
(Christie's)   **$11,000   £6,875**

ALFRED JACOMIN – Sunday afternoon in the
Luxembourg Gardens, Paris – signed – oil on panel –
45.5 x 38cm.
(Sotheby's)   **$9,350   £5,500**

**ALEXANDER JAKOLEFF (East European late 19th
Century)** – The artist's model – signed – oil on canvas –
98 x 74cm.
(Sotheby's)   **$14,608   £8,800**

Follower of DAVID JAMES – Man Overboard!, Shipping off a Coastline, with sailors rowing and a Gentleman swimming – bears signature and date 1877 – 76.2 x 127cm.
(Bonhams)   **$348   £200**

ALEXANDER JAMIESON – Dieppe Harbour – signed; signed and dated 1904 on the reverse – bears title on a label on the stretcher – oil on canvas – 99 x 140cm.
(Sotheby's)   **$17,451   £10,450**

DAVID JAMES – A coastal view – signed - 18¹/₄ x 41¹/₄in.
(Bearne's)   **$2,934   £1,800**

DAVID JAMES (fl. 1900-1913) – When the tide is out, Pimn Bay, Cornwall – signed – and inscribed on the reverse – 63 x 127.5cm.
(Christie's)   **$6,296   £3,960**

ALEXANDER JAMIESON – A quiet corner, Bruges – signed – oil on canvas – 73.5 x 94cm.
(Sotheby's)   **$2,020   £1,210**

WILLIAM JAMES (fl. 1754-1771) – View of the Thames looking towards St. Pauls from the gardens of Somerset House – oil on canvas – 74 x 126cm.
(Sotheby's)   **$96,096   £57,200**

WILLEM GEORGE FREDERICK JANSEN (Dutch, 1871-1949) – Seaweed gatherers on the Dutch coast – signed – oil on canvas – 73.7 x 94cm.
(Christie's)   **$6,468   £3,850**

JANSSENS

HIERONYMOUS JANSSENS (1624-1693) – Elegant figures playing games in an interior – oil on canvas – 47.2 x 63.5cm.
(Phillips) $6,440 £4,000

GUSTAV JEAN JAQUET (1846-1909) – A beauty – signed – on panel – 33 x 24cm.
(Christie's) $8,525 £5,500

JIERONYMOUS JANSSENS (1624-1693) – Cavaliers and ladies seated on a balcony before dancing figures – oil on canvas – 81.5 x 63cm.
(Phillips) $3,586 £2,200

ZDZISLAW JASINSKI (late 19th Century) – Advice on the good life – signed and inscribed München – 36.2 x 52.6cm.
(Christie's) $3,542 £2,200

RUDOLF ALFRED JAUMANN (born 1859) – The trophy – signed and dated München 1887 – 44 x 35.5cm.
(Christie's) **$2,656 £1,650**

GEORGES JEANNIN (1841-1925) – Roses in a vase – signed and dated '94 – on panel – 45.7 x 36.8cm.
(Christie's) **$4,433 £2,860**

CECIL JAY – The letter – signed – oil on canvas – 66 x 43cm.
(Sotheby's) **$15,136 £8,800**

CHARLES JERVAS (c. 1675-1739) – Portrait of Thomas Pelham Holles, 1st Duke of Newcastle (1693-1768) – full length, wearing Garter Robes – oil on canvas – in a carved wood frame – 204 x 145cm.
(Sotheby's) **$9,377 £6,050**

JESPERS

FLORIS JESPERS (1889-1963) - Le Schelte - De Schelde - signed lower right Floris Jespers and inscribed indruk on the reverse - oil on canvas - 79 x 104cm. - Painted in 1919.
(Christie's) $24,640 £15,400

FLORIS JESPERS (1889-1965) – Deux Visages—Twee Gezichten – signed lower left Jespers, verre églomisé – 40 x 30.2cm. – Painted circa 1923
(Christie's) $19,360 £12,100

FLORIS JESPERS (1889-1965) – Le Mirroir vert—De groene Spiegel – signed and dated lower right Floris Jespers 1917 – signed - dated and inscribed on the reverse Floris Jespers '17 'Groene spiegel' – oil on canvas – 120 x 89.5cm. – Painted in 1917
(Christie's) $105,600 £66,000

CLARENCE JOHNSON – Back road to Clarensville – signed – oil on canvas – 50.8 x 61.0cm.
(Sotheby's)   **$13,200 £8,302**

AUGUSTUS JOHN, O.M., R.A. (1878-1961) – Portrait of a bearded Man wearing a Hat – pencil – 10 x 7in.
(Christie's)   **$5,909 £3,740**

CLARENCE JOHNSON – Summer landscape – signed – oil on canvas – 91.4 x 101.5cm.
(Sotheby's)   **$121,000 £76,101**

AUGUSTUS JOHN, O.M., R.A. (1878-1961) – Head of Dorelia – signed – pencil – 29 x 24.5cm.
(Phillips)   **$37,490 £23,000**
AVERY JOHNSON (born 1906) – Deer Isle Vista – watercolour - 20 x 27½in. – signed Avery Johnson lower right
(Bruce D. Collins)   **$1,980 £1,178**

EDWARD KILLINGWORTH JOHNSON, R.W.S. – The third volume – signed and dated 1884 – watercolour heightened with bodycolour and gum arabic – 33 x 41cm.
(Sotheby's)   **$13,090 £7,700**

JOHNSON

HENRY JAMES JOHNSTONE (1826-1884) – The young Mussel Gatherer – signed – watercolour – 25 x 17.5cm.
(Phillips) $4,564 £2,800

EDWARD KILLINGWORTH JOHNSON, R.W.S. – Gathering lavender – signed – watercolour heightened with bodycolour – 34 x 21.5cm.
(Sotheby's) $9,724 £5,720

EDWARD KILLINGWORTH JOHNSON, R.W.S.
- The third volume - signed and dated 1884 - watercolour heightened with bodycolour and gum arabic - 33 x 41cm.
(Sotheby's) $13,090 £7,700

HENRY JAMES JOHNSTONE – A new pasture – signed watercolour – 25.5 x 18cm.
(Sotheby's) $4,675 £2,750

ANTONIO JOLI (c. 1700-1777) – Prospect of London from a Colonnade with a distant view of St. Paul's and Old London Bridge – oil on canvas – 104 x 114.5cm.
(Sotheby's)   **$443,300   £286,000**

CHARLES JONES – Sheep on a Highland crag – on panel – signed with monogram and dated '73 – signed and dated 1873 on the reverse – 15¼ x 21½in.
(Bearne's)   **$7,298   £4,100**

CHARLES JONES, R.C.A. (1836-1892) – Startled — A Royal and three hinds – signed with monogram and dated 1866 – oil on canvas – lunette – 111.7 x 101.5cm.
(Christie's)   **$14,784   £8,800**

FRANCIS COATES JONES (1857-1932) – A candlelight romance – signed Francis C. Jones, l.l. – oil on canvas – 55.2 x 75.6cm.
(Sotheby's) **$27,500 £17,516**

LUDOLPH DE JONGH, Circle of – Portrait of a cavalier in a landscape – oil on panel – 22.5 x 18.5cm.
(Phillips) **$612 £380**

PAUL JONES (fl. late 19th Century) – Terriers Rabbiting on a Heath – signed and dated 1880 – oil on canvas – 23 x 30.5cm.
(Phillips) **$978 £600**

O.R. DE JONGH (20th Century) – A Dutch canal with figures and boats – signed – 63.5 x 86.4cm.
(Christie's) **$1,535 £990**

CLAUDE DE JONGH, Attributed to – Figures standing by the Temple of Vesta, Rome – oil on panel – unframed – 21.5 x 27.9cm.
(Bonhams) **$1,711 £1,100**

JOHAN BARTHOLD JONGKIND – Le Canal de L'Ourcq, Aisne – signed and dated 1872 – oil on canvas – 27.3 x 38.7cm.
(Sotheby's) **$66,000 £41,509**

Circle of JACOB JORDAENS (1593-1678) – Neptune with a prancing horse – oil on canvas – 85 x 137cm.
(Phillips)   **$5,184   £3,200**

JACOB JORDAENS – Anvers 1593-1678 – Silène – oil on canvas – 118 x 147cm.
(Sotheby's)   **$69,264   £44,400**

MANUEL AMELL Y JORDA (born 1840) – The new sash – signed and indistinctly dated – 66.5 x 48.5cm.
(Christie's)   **$5,667   £3,520**

HANS JORDAENS III after HENDRICK GOLTZIUS, Attributed to (Anvers 1595-1644) – The Adoration of the Magi – unframed – oil on copper – 45.2 x 34.3cm.
(Lawrence)   **$9,922   £6,050**

PIO JORIS (1843-1921) – The flower seller – signed – 22 x 16cm.
(Christie's)   **$4,959   £3,080**

JUTZ

CARL JUTZ (1838-1916), Attributed to – Duck by a
pond – with signature – on panel – 19 x 24.7cm.
(Christie's) **$3,4100   £2,200**

FREDERIK HENDRIK KAEMMERER – The young
harpist – signed l.l. – oil on canvas – unframed –
60.5 x 35cm.
(Sotheby's) **$13,244   £7,700**

GYULA KARDOS – A gift from the sea – signed and
dated 1887 – oil on canvas – 193 x 51cm.
(Sotheby's) **$6,622   £3,850**

ANNE-PIERRE DE KAT (1881-1968) – Portrait d'Homme – indistinctly signed and dated lower right 1922 – the artist's studio stamps on reverse – oil on canvas – 72.3 x 58.4cm.
(Christie's) **$5,280 £3,300**

LEE LUFKIN KAULA (19th/20th Century) – Woman seated – oil on canvas – 24 x 20in. – unsigned
(Bruce D. Collins) **$12,100 £7,202**

ANGELICA KAUFFMANN, R.A. (1741-1807) – Portrait of Louise Henrietta Campbell, later Lady Abinger – full length, seated in an interior, wearing a white dress with a green shawl, holding a pen and sheaf of drawings – oil on canvas – 74 x 61cm.
(Sotheby's) **$19,404 £11,550**

ARNE KAVLI (1878-1970) – A summer's day, Grimstad – signed – 81 x 70cm.
(Christie's) **$34,100 £22,000**

C. J. KEATS – "Abbeville" and "Orleans" – pair of watercolours – signed – 20 x 12½in.
(Biddle & Webb) **$1,059 £650**

FELIX KELLY (b. 1916) – Capriccio – signed lower right Felix Kelly – gouache – 8½ x 6in.
(Christie's) **$869 £550**

BERNHARDT KEILHAU, CALLED MONSU BERNARDO - Helsingborg 1624-1687 Rome - Vendeur de Pains et Femme Allaitant Son Enfant - oil on canvas - 140 x 177cm.
(Sotheby's) **$46,176 £29,600**

**SIR GERALD KELLY, K,V.C.O., P.R.A., R.H.A.
(1879-1972)** – Saw Ohn Nyun III – dated lower left Dec 23
1931 – inscribed on the reverse – oil on board –
15¼ x 11¼in.
(Christie's)   **$3,824   £2,420**

ROBERT KEMM (fl. 1874-1885) – An Andalusian folk
group – signed – 71.2 x 91.4cm.
(Christie's)   **$7,531   £4,620**

CECIL KENNEDY – Bowl of Freesias and Anemones –
signed – oil on canvas – 46 x 61cm.
(Phillips)   **$5,070   £3,000**

ROBERT KEMM (fl. 1874-1885) – The fair slave –
signed – 76 x 50.5cm.
(Christie's)   **$6,996   £4,400**

CECIL KENNEDY – A Study of white Roses in a Bowl
upon a Lowboy – signed – on canvas – 40.5 x 51cm.
(Bonhams)   **$11,060   £7,000**

EDWARD SHERARD KENNEDY – Strolling acrobats "En route" – signed; signed and inscribed with title on the reverse – oil on canvas – 63.5 x 100cm.
(Sotheby's)   **$3,227   £1,980**

WILLIAM KENNEDY – Children and Rabbits – signed – oil on canvas – 51 x 61cm.
(Sotheby's)   **$5,143   £3,080**

CECIL KENNEDY – A Still Life with red, orange and yellow Nasturtiums in a glass Vase – signed – on canvas – 61 x 51cm.
(Bonhams)   **$8,216   £5,200**

CECIL KENNEDY – A Still Life with red, yellow and orange Chrysanthemum Blooms and Bramble in a green-glazed Vase – signed – on panel – 76 x 63.5cm.
(Bonhams)   **$6,004   £3,800**

ROCKWELL KENT (1882-1971) – Starry night – wood engraving – edition 1750 – signed Rockwell Kent lower right – 7 x 5in., with margins
(Bruce D. Collins)   **$627 £385**

ROCKWELL KENT - Motherhood - signed Rockwell Kent, l.r. - dated 1913, l.l. - oil on canvas - 82 x 106.8cm. *(Christie's)* **$22,000 £13,750**

JOHN DALZELL KENWORTHY – Laura – signed and inscribed with title – oil on canvas – 91.5 x 61cm. *(Sotheby's)* **$6,454 £3,960**

HERMANN KERN – The young violinist – signed – oil on canvas – 78 x 54.5cm. *(Sotheby's)* **$7,190 £4,180**

KERR

GEORGE COCHRANE KERR – An Estuary Landscape with Shipping, a Town beyond – signed – unframed – 76.2 x 127cm.
(Bonhams) **$1,479 £850**

JAN VAN KESSEL (1626-1679) – A still life with grapes and plums on a china plate beside a bowl of raspberries, with other fruit scattered nearby, on a table – oil on copper – 16.5 x 21.8cm.
(Phillips) **$17,820 £11,000**

JAN VAN KESSEL, Manner of – A still life of tulips, narcissi and roses in a glass upon a ledge – oil on panel – 48.5 x 32cm.
(Phillips) **$4,238 £2,600**

JAN VAN KESSEL –Anvers 1626-1679 – Singe Renversant un Panier de Fruits – oil on copper – 23.5 x 31cm.
(Sotheby's) **$65,965 £42,285**

FERNAND KHNOPFF (1858-1921) – Tête de Femme – signed with monogram lower centre FK. interlaced in a three-lobed clover – dedicated at the bottom to Sir Edward Burne-Jones from Fernand Khnopff – pencil on paper – 23 x 15cm.
(Christie's) **$102,300 £66,000**

GEORGE GOODWIN KILBURNE – 'A Pinch of Snuff'
– signed – 35 x 52cm.
(Anderson & Garland)   **$3,230**   **£1,900**

GEORGE GOODWIN KILBURNE – Laying for tea –
signed – watercolour heightened with scratching out –
53 x 38cm.
(Sotheby's)   **$3,366**   **£1,980**

GEORGE GOODWIN KILBURNE, Jnr. — Home
brewed – signed; bears title on a label on the reverse – oil
on panel – 18 x 25.5cm.
(Sotheby's)   **$2,867**   **£1,760**

**GEORGE GOODWIN KILBURNE (English, 1839-
1924)** – A Game of Chess – signed – 45.8 x 35.6cm.
(Bonhams)   **$7,440**   **£4,800**

GEORGE GOODWIN KILBURNE (1839-1924) – The
Minuet – signed – pencil and watercolour with touches of
white heightening – 9 x 13¼in.
(Christie's)   **$5,020**   **£3,080**

KILBURNE

GEORGE GOODWIN KILBURNE (1839-1924) –
Confidences – signed – pencil and watercolour –
26.1 x 31.1cm.
(Christie's)   **$3,048**   **£1,870**

GEORGE GOODWIN KILBURNE (1839-1924) – A
Wayside Prayer – signed – watercolour – 24 x 16cm.
(Phillips)   **$945**   **£580**

GEORGE GOODWIN KILBURNE – 'The Despised
Gifts' – signed – 23 x 34cm.
(Anderson & Garland)   **$2,295**   **£1,350**

GEORGE GOODWIN KILBURNE (1839-1924) – A
mother peeling an orange for her little girl – signed –
pencil and watercolour – 35.6 x 25.4cm.
(Christie's)   **$7,172**   **£4,400**

HENRY JOHN YEEND KING – A break from
haymaking – signed – oil on canvas – 61 x 91.5cm.
(Sotheby's)   **$9,324**   **£5,720**

HENRY JOHN YEEND KING, R.B.A. (1855-1924) –
'The Sand Garden, Ballaterson' – signed – inscribed and
dated 1915 – oil on board – 39.5 x 29cm.
(Phillips) **$5,705 £3,500**

HENRY JOHN YEEND KING (English, 1855-1924) –
'Mary the Maid of the Inn' – panel – signed – signed and
inscribed on label on reverse – 43.2 x 32.4cm.
(Bonhams) **$2,325 £1,500**

HENRY JOHN YEEND KING (1855-1924) – A young
girl, with cattle on a path outside a village – signed –
60.9 x 91.4cm.
(Christie's) **$5,020 £3,080**

PAUL KING – Returning Fishermen – signed Paul King
and dated Concarneau, 1929, l.r. – oil on canvas –
64 x 76.5cm.
(Christie's) **$8,800 £5,500**

HENRY JOHN YEEND KING – Day dreams – signed –
oil on canvas – 46 x 61cm.
(Sotheby's) **$15,240 £9,350**

HENRY JOHN KINNAIRD – View near Salisbury –
signed and inscribed with title – watercolour heightened
with bodycolour – 25.5 x 37cm.
(Sotheby's) **$3,366 £1,980**

KINNAIRD

HENRY JOHN KINNAIRD – A Sussex hay field – An extensive rural landscape with figures resting beside a hay cart – signed and inscribed – 37 x 53cm.
(Spencer's)   **$6,422**   **£3,800**

JOSEPH KIRKPATRICK (1872-?) – "Sark C.I." – signed and inscribed – watercolour – 25.5 x 35.5cm.
(Phillips)   **$1,711**   **£1,050**

ADOLF KIRSTEIN (1814-1873) – A frozen winter landscape with skaters by a castle near Strassburg – signed – 68 x 87cm.
(Christie's)   **$7,438**   **£4,620**

MOISE KISLING – Portrait of a woman with a red corsage – oil on canvas – signed and dated 65 x 54cm.
(Jean-Claude Anaf)   **$47,046**   **£30,158**

MOISE KISLING – A still life with a rose, an arum, tulips and irises in a vase, on a table – signed lower right Kisling – 65 x 50cm.
(Christie's)   **$88,272**   **£55,517**

L*** KLAUS – An argument – signed – oil on panel – unframed – 26 x 21cm.
(Sotheby's)   **$2,244   £1,320**

CLARA KLINGHOFFER (1900-1970) – Head of a Girl – signed and dated lower right C Klinghoffer March 1928 – oil on canvas – 14 x 10in.
(Christie's)   **$956   £605**

PAUL KLEE (1879-1940) – Die Schattige – signed upper centre Klee – dated, numbered and titled on the Artist's mount 1939E15 die Schattige – watercolour on paper – 29.5 x 20.5cm. – Executed in 1939
(Christie's)   **$221,650   £143,000**

JOHANN BERNARD KLOMBECK – Figures on a path by a stream – signed and dated 1850 – oil on panel – 30.5 x 25.5cm.
(Sotheby's)   **$14,960   £8,800**

GEORGE KNAPTON (1698-1778) –Portrait of a Murrough O'Brien, 5th Earl of Inchiquin – half length, wearing a white tunic with gold braid and an ermine lined cloak – inscribed on the stretcher with the identity of the sitter – oil on canvas – 75 x 62cm.
(Sotheby's)   **$13,640   £8,800**

SIR GODFREY KNELLER, Follower of – Portrait of a lady, seated three-quarter length, in a brown dress and a blue wrap – with inscription Lady Bishop wife to 1ˢᵗ Lᵗ Cecil and with signature – 127 x 161.7cm.
(Christie's)   **$2,689   £1,650**

LUDWIG KNAUS (1829-1910) – A girl wearing a straw hat – signed with initials and dated 1862 – oil on canvas – 49.5 x 38.2cm.
(Lawrence)   **$1,693   £1,045**

SIR GODFREY KNELLER, Bt (1646-1723) and Studio – Portrait of Charles Fitzroy, 2nd Duke of Grafton, when a boy – full length, standing, wearing yellow classical dress with a blue mantle – inscribed l.r. by a later hand: The Lord Euston/Sir G. Kneller. Pinx. 1685 – oil on canvas, in a carved wood frame – 121 x 99.5cm.
(Sotheby's)   **$15,708   £9,350**

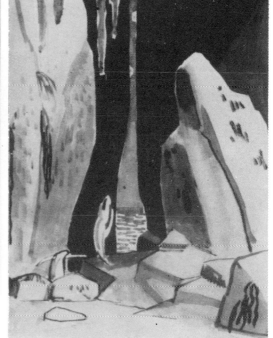

SIR GODFREY KNELLER, Follower of – Portrait of a gentleman, standing three-quarter length, wearing armour – 121.9 x 97.8cm.
(Christie's)   **$1,793**   **£1,100**

DAME LAURA KNIGHT (1877-1970) – Newlyn School – "Sketch" for "Sealwomen" (Act 1) - a woman before seal cave, Nanjizel Beach, Cornwall – signed and inscribed – watercolour and pencil – 13$\frac{1}{2}$ x 9$\frac{1}{2}$in.
(W. H. Lane & Son)   **$3,200**   **£2,000**

DAME LAURA KNIGHT, D.B.E., R.A. – Dancing Couples – signed – inscribed, "Krasnapolski, Amsterdam" – and dated 2 Aug. 1925 – pencil – 35 x 25cm.
(Phillips)   **$1,920**   **£1,200**

DAME LAURA KNIGHT, D.B.E., R.A. – Sunlight on a Cornish Stream – signed – 29$\frac{3}{4}$ x 29$\frac{3}{4}$in.
(Bearne's)   **$45,630**   **£27,000**

KNIGHT

LAURA KNIGHT – Children seated on rocks by Sea –
signed – watercolour – 11 x 14in.
(G. A. Key) **$3,978 £2,600**

HAROLD KNIGHT (1874-1961) – Newlyn School –
Horse and cart at the water's edge before shipping – signed
– oil on canvas – 22 x 30in.
(W. H. Lane & Son) **$8,000 £5,000**

DAME LAURA KNIGHT, R.A. (1877-1970) – Betty
Renwick dressing a Doll – pencil – 7 x 9¹/₂in.
(Christie's) **$3,824 £2,420**

HAROLD KNIGHT, R.A. (1874-1961) – Clifftop View,
Cornwall – signed – oil on canvas – unframed –
101 x 128cm.
(Phillips) **$12,225 £7,500**

DANIEL RIDGWAY KNIGHT – Courtship – signed
Ridgway Knight, l.l. – oil on canvas – 46.2 x 38.2cm.
(Christie's) **$8,250 £5,156**

FREDERICK J. KNOWLES – By the river – signed –
oil on canvas laid on board – unframed – 27.5 x 38cm.
(Sotheby's) **$2,510 £1,540**

JOHN KOCH – Portrait of Dora Koch Before the Piano –
signed Koch, l.l. – oil on canvas – 76.8 x 66.7cm.
(Christie's)   **$24,200   £14,756**

JOHN KOCH – Portrait of My Mother – signed Koch and
dated '65, l.r. – oil on canvas – 61 x 50.8cm.
(Christie's)   **$2,200   £1,375**

JOHN KOCH - Bacchanal – signed Koch, l.r. – oil on canvas – 180.3 x 210.2cm.
(Christie's)   **$16,500   £10,312**

KOCH

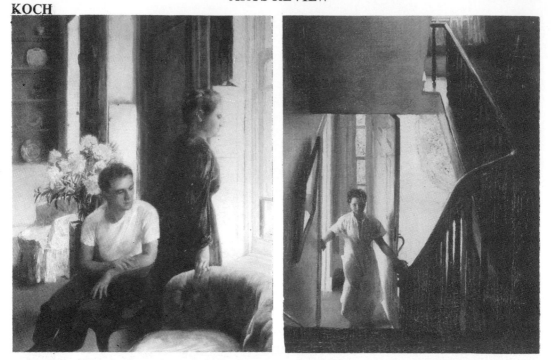

JOHN KOCH – The Window – signed Koch, l.l. – oil on canvas – 51.4 x 41cm.
(Christie's)   **$16,500   £10,312**

JOHN KOCH – On the Stairs – signed Koch, l.r. – oil on canvas laid down on masonite – 31.7 x 24.2cm.
(Christie's)   **$7,480   £4,675**

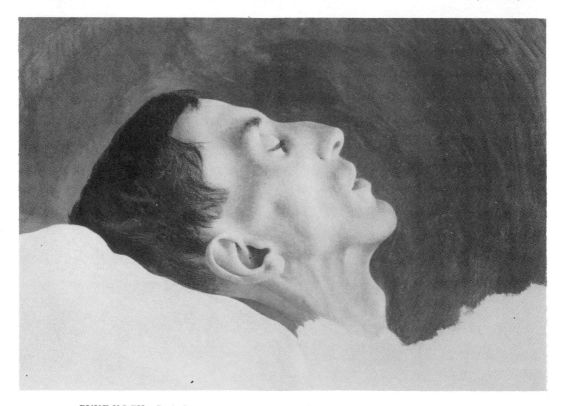

PYKE KOCH – Dode Jongen – tempera on canvas laid down on panel – 35.5 x 38cm.
(Christie's)   **$19,167   £12,055**

HUGO WILHELM GEORG KOCKE (1875-1956) – On the quayside – signed and dated 1929 – 125.7 x 175.2cm.
(Christie's)   **$7,084   £4,400**

HERMANUS KOEKKOEK (1815-1882) – Shipping in choppy sea off a coast – signed – 39.4 x 52cm.
(Christie's)   **$13,640   £8,800**

FRIEDRICH KOKO-MICOLETZKY – A reclining nude on a sofa – signed – oil on canvas – 76 x 95cm.
(Sotheby's)   **$1,703   £990**

RUDOLF KONOPA (1864-1938) – An interior with a lady reading by a window – signed – on panel – 31 x 41cm.
(Christie's)   **$6,198   £3,850**

BAREND CORNELIS KOEKKOEK (Dutch 1803-62) – Logging on an icy stream – signed and dated 1851 l.l.; authenticated with the artist's seal on a label on the stretcher – oil on canvas – 73 xz 92cm.
(Sotheby's)   **$131,472   £79,200**

WILLEM GILLISZ KOOL (1608/9 - 1666) – A dune landscape with a horse-drawn cart approaching fisherfolk displaying their catch – oil on panel – 39 x 61cm.
(Phillips)   **$8,150   £5,000**

KOPMAN

BENJAMIN KOPMAN (American, 1887-1965) – The Music Room – signed "Kopman", l.l. – signed and dated "Kopman '45" on the reverse – oil on canvas – 23 x 31in.
(Skinner) **$475 £291**

EMIL A. KRAUSE – "Dunnelly Castle" – watercolour – signed and inscribed – 34.3 x 52.2cm.
(Bonhams) **$1,224 £800**

BRUNO KRAUSKOPF – Three figures – signed – oil on canvas – 89 x 71cm.
(Sotheby's) **$3,517 £2,068**

BRUNO KRAUSKOPF – Mother and child – signed – oil on panel – 70 x 55cm.
(Sotheby's) **$2,931 £1,724**

WILHELM VIKTOR KRAUSZ – A glimpse of the artist at work in a courtyard – signed – oil on canvas – 117 x 98cm.
(Sotheby's) **$2,805 £1,650**

LEON KROLL (American, 1884-1974) – "Dennison Road (Girl with Guitar)" – signed and dated 1961 – oil on panel – 30 x 25in.
(Skinner) **$22,000 £13,174**

LOUIS KRONBERG (American, 1872-1964) – "Behind the Scenes — Two Dancers in Orange and Green" – signed "Louis Kronberg" – monogrammed and on the reverse, inscribed and dated "Boston 1920" – oil on canvas – 34 x 30in.
(Skinner) **$3,000 £1,840**

LOUIS KRONBERG (American, 1872-1964) – "Ballet Girl" – signed and dated "Louis Kronberg 1914" with monogram
(Skinner) **$1,800 £1,125**

LOUIS KRONBERG (American, 1872-1964) – "The End of the Ballet" – signed "Louis Kronberg", l.r. – identified on labels on the reverse and inscribed "N.Y. April 1939" on the reverse – oil on canvas – 28 x 24in.
(Skinner) **$2,500 £1,470**

KUEHNE

MAX KUEHNE (1880-1968) – Gloucester harbour –
signed Kuehne and dated '12, l.r. – oil on canvasboard –
49.5 x 61cm.
(Sotheby's) **$33,000 £21,019**

YASUO KUNIYOSHI – Cripple Creek, Colorado –
signed Kuniyoshi, u.r. – signed again – dated 1941 and
inscribed with title on the backing – gouache on gessoed
masonite – 25.5 x 40.5cm.
(Christie's) **$57,200 £35,750**

J. KURESVELT? (late 19th Century) – An elegant
woman in a winter woodland – signed – canvas laid down
on board – oval – 92.7 x 73.7cm.
(Christie's) **$1,023 £660**

WALT KUHN – Dancer with Red Plume – gouache on
paper laid down on paper – 63.5 x 32.7cm.
(Christie's) **$8,800 £5,500**

EDUARD KURZBAUER (1840-1879) – Discovered –
signed – 79 x 105cm.
(Christie's) **$10,271 £6,380**

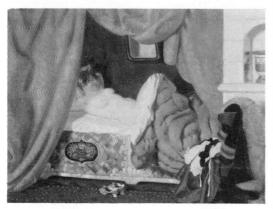

EDUARD KURZBAUER – The card players – signed and dated 1877 München – oil on panel – 46 x 65cm. *(Sotheby's)* **$7,106 £4,180**

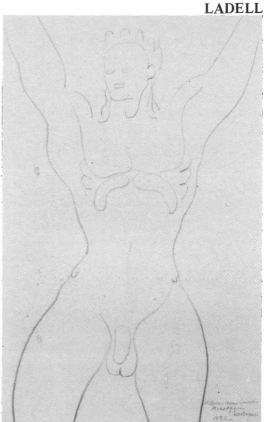

GASTON LACHAISE – Male Nude – signed G Lachaise – dated 1932 and inscribed A Mon ami Lincoln Kirstein – pencil on paper – 45.7 x 29.8cm. *(Christie's)* **$8,250 £5,262**

BORIS MIKHAILOVICH KUSTODIEV (1878-1927) – Reclining Nude in Bed – signed in Cyrillic and dated, B. Kustodiev, 1919 – oil on canvas – 35 x 47.4cm. *(Christie's)* **$33,649 £20,900**

CHARLES EUPHRASIE KUWASSEG Jnr. (1838-1904) – An alpine village on a river – signed and dated 1870 – on board – 29 x 46cm. *(Christie's)* **$7,084 £4,400**

EDWARD LADELL – A Still Life with Grapes, Nuts and Peaches beside a Roemer and an ivory Box upon a marble Ledge – signed with monogram – on canvas – 43 x 35.5cm. *(Bonhams)* **$34,760 £22,000**

LADELL

EUGENE LAMBERT, Follower of – Kittens in a basket; and The Monkey's lunch interrupted – 39.5 x 31.5cm. – a pair
(Christie's)   **$3,740 £2,200**

ELLEN LADELL – Still life with fruit and a glass of wine – bears monogram – oil on canvas laid on board – 40.5 x 30.5cm.
(Sotheby's)   **$3,945 £2,420**

CHRISTOFELL JANSZ VAN DER LAMEN (1606/15-1651) – An elegant company seated in an interior – oil on panel – 49 x 64.5cm.
(Phillips)   **$13,770 £8,500**

ELLEN LADELL – Still life with fruit, birds and a bird's nest – signed – oil on canvas – 46 x 36cm.
(Sotheby's)   **$6,813 £4,180**

WILLIAM B. LAMOND – A gathering storm – signed – oil on canvas – 72 x 103cm.
(Sotheby's)   **$4,776 £2,860**

WILLIAM B. LAMOND – The Main Street, Auchmithie
– signed – oil on canvas – 35.5 x 46cm.
(Sotheby's)   **$7,715   £4,620**

NICOLAS LANCRET, Manner of – An Allegory of
Summer with Gardeners watering a Flower Bed beside a
Fountain – oil on canvas – 88.9 x 77.5cm.
(Bonhams)   **$7,728   £4,800**

PIERRE FRANC LAMY (1855-1919) – An exotic
beauty – signed – 73.5 x 61cm.
(Christie's)   **$8,501   £5,280**

SIR EDWIN HENRY LANDSEER, R.A. – A Husky dog
– signed with initials – oil on canvas – unstretched – 12.5 x
14.5cm.
(Sotheby's)   **$2,689   £1,650**

LUDWIG LANCKOW - Still life with grapes – signed –
oil on board – 33 x 42cm.
(Kunsthaus am Museum)   **$2,210   £1,300**

SIR EDWIN HENRY LANDSEER, R.A. – Neptune,
the property of W. Ellis Gosling, Esq. – signed with initials
and dated 1824 – oil on canvas – 150 x 197cm.
(Sotheby's)   **$577,500   £363,208**

LANGKER

SIR ERIK LANGKER (1898-1982) – Still Life – signed
– unframed – 76.2 x 60.9cm.
(Christie's)   **$5,346   £3,300**

WALTER LANGLEY – A Cornish Fisherman – signed –
.watercolour – 33 x 25cm.
(Phillips)   **$1,267   £750**

WALTER LANGLEY, R.W.A. (1852-1922) – While the
Boats are Away – signed – oil on canvas – 61 x 51cm.
(Phillips)   **$42,380   £26,000**

WALTER LANGLEY (1852-1922) – Newlyn School –
A young woman in a pensive mood wearing a white apron,
seated in a kitchen beside a table – watercolour –
20 x 14^1/2in.
(W. H. Lane & Son)   **$7,392   £4,400**

MARK WILLIAM LANGLOIS – Girls in a meadow –
signed – 29¼ x 19¼in.
(Bearne's) **$4,806 £2,700**

NICOLAS DE LARGILLIERE – Paris 1656-1746 –
Jeune Femme en Flore – oil on canvas – 81 x 65cm.
(Sotheby's) **$19,789 £12,685**

**J.J. LANSDALE after GEORGE ROMNEY (late 19th
Century)** – Lady Hamilton – signed – inscribed and dated
1881 – 96.7 x 71.2cm.
(Christie's) **$1,524 £935**

NICOLAS DE LARGILLIERE – Paris 1656-1746 –
Portrait de la Duchesse de Berry – oil on canvas – 139 x
105cm.
(Sotheby's) **$65,966 £42,286**

LARIONOV

MICHEL LARIONOV – Chevaux sur la Colline – signed; also signed and titled on the reverse – oil on canvas – 79 x 105.4cm.
(Sotheby's)   **$121,000   £76,101**

LEE LASH (1864-1935) – Wall Street – signed Lee Lash, l.r. – oil on canvas – 127.0 x 152.4cm. – Painted in 1935
(Sotheby's)   **$66,000   £42,038**

LOUIS LASSALLE (French, b. 1915) – The Young Musicians – signed and dated '67 – 46.4 x 38cm.
(Bonhams)   **$2,945   £1,900**

LOUIS ALBERT ARTHUR LATAPIE – La Fenêtre a Toulon – signed upper right Latapie – and with inscription on a label on the reverse – 54 x 73cm. – Executed circa 1929
(Christie's)   **$5,549   £3,490**

MAURICE-QUENTIN DE LATOUR 1704-1788
–Portrait de Femme – pastel – 36.5 x 29cm.
(Sotheby's) **$4,122 £2,643**

MARIE LAURENCIN (1885-1956) – Portrait de jeune
Fille au Collier – signed upper right Marie Laurencin –
watercolour on paper – 29 x 24cm.
(Christie's) **$68,200 £44,000**

CHARLES JAMES LAUDER, R.S.W. – Statue of Allan
Ramsay, Edinburgh – signed and inscribed – watercolour –
47 x 32cm.
(Sotheby's) **$2,020 £1,210**

MARIE LAURENCIN (1885-1956) – Tête de Femme au
Collier de Perles – signed lower right Marie Laurencin –
watercolour on paper – 40 x 36cm.
(Christie's) **$24,335 £15,700**

LAVERY

SIR JOHN LAVERY, R.A., R.S.A., R.H.A., P.R.P., H.R.O.I., N.P.S., N.S., I.S. (1856-1941) – Summer Afternoon – signed and dated 1886 – and inscribed on label verso – oil on canvas – 27.3 x 27.3cm.
(Christie's) **$12,936 £7,700**

SIR JOHN LAVERY, R.S.A. (1836-1941) – Half length portrait of Eileen Lavery (the Artist's daughter) – oil on canvas – 26 x 20in.
(W. H. Lane & Son) **$2,320 £1,450**

SIR JOHN LAVERY, R.A., R.S.A., R.H.A. (1856-1941) – Portrait of Miss Nora Maclean, long bust length – signed and inscribed twice – oil on canvas board – 40.5 x 25cm.
(Phillips) **$10,595 £6,500**

ANDREW LAW – 'Chrysanthemums' – signed – also signed and inscribed on a label on the frame – on canvas – 71 x 51cm.
(Bonhan.) **$2,844 £1,800**

ALFRED KINGSLEY LAWRENCE, R.A. (1893-1978) – Pellegrina Clarke wearing a Pink Dress – signed lower left Lawrence – oil on canvas – 36 x 28¼in.
(Christie's)   **$1,390   £880**

SIR THOMAS LAWRENCE, Follower of – Portrait of a lady, quarter length, in a blue and white dress, a gold chain around her neck – oval – 55.8 x 44.4cm.
(Christie's)   **$1,614   £990**

CECIL GORDON LAWSON (1851-1882) – Strayed – signed and dated 1875 – 63.5 x 58.5cm.
(Christie's)   **$4,373   £2,750**

JACOB LAWRENCE – The Wedding – signed Jacob Lawrence and dated 48, l.r. – tempera on gessoed board – 51 x 61cm.
(Christie's)   **$44,000   £27,500**

SIR THOMAS LAWRENCE, P.R.A. (1769-1830) – Portrait of Mrs. Clement Kynnersley – half length, seated, wearing a white dress tied with a black sash – indistinctly inscribed by a later hand on a label attached to the stretcher – oil on canvas – 77 x 63.5cm.
(Sothe'y's)   **$102,300   £66,000**

LAWRENCE

WILLIAM GOADBY LAWRENCE – Lake and stream fishing: A pair of paintings – each signed; each also signed and inscribed Red Bank, New Jersey on the stretchers – oil on canvas – 45.7 x 61.0cm.
(Sotheby's) **$9,350 £5,881**

ERNEST LAWSON (American, 1873-1939) – "Winter Landscape" - signed – oil on canvas – 20 x 24in.
(Skinner) **$45,000 £26,946**

GREGORIO LAZZARINI, Circle of (1655-Venice-1730) – The good samaritan – on canvas – 189 x 148cm.
(Phillips) **$16,300 £10,000**

BENJAMIN WILLIAMS LEADER, R.A. – A quiet valley amongst the Welsh hills – signed and dated 1860 – oil on canvas – 91 x 71.5cm. *(Sotheby's)* **$16,137 £9,900**

EDWARD LEAR (1812-1888) – View of Hardwar – signed l. with monogram – oil on canvas – 37.5 x 23cm.
(Sotheby's) **$81,840 £52,800**

JEANNE-PHILIBERTE LEDOUX – Paris 1767-1840 Belleville – Portrait de Jeune Fille – oil on canvas – 42.5 x 32.5cm.
(Sotheby's) **$18,965 £12,157**

EDWARD LEAR – Trichoglossus Swainsonii – signed – titled and inscribed 'plate 20' – watercolour over touches of pencil, heightened with traces of gum arabic – 18 x 11.5cm.
(Woolley & Wallis) **$17,115 £10,500**

DORIS LEE (1905-1983) – Johnnie Appleseed – signed Doris Lee, l.r. – oil on canvas 91.5 x 106.7cm. – Painted in 1944
(Sotheby's) **$33,000 £21,019**

HIPPOLYTE LECOMTE (1781-1857) – The students of the École Polytechnique rescuing the crucifix and other sacred objects from the Chapel of the Tuileries Palace in 1848 – signed and dated 1848 – 48.3 x 63.5cm.
(Christie's) **$5,313 £3,300**

WILLIAM LEE-HANKEY (1869-1952) - At Anchor, La Rochelle – signed lower left W. Lee-Hankey – oil on panel – 8½ x 11½in.
(Christie's) **$7,821 £4,950**

LEE-HANKEY

WILLIAM LEE-HANKEY (1869-1952) – Woman on
the Quayside, Etaples – signed – oil on canvas –
66 x 19cm.
(Phillips)   **$5,705   £3,500**

DERWENT LEES (1885-1931) – Trees in Provence –
signed and dated 1911 – oil on panel – 25.5 x 25.5cm.
(Phillips)   **$6,194   £3,800**

CHARLES LEES, R.S.A (1800-1880) – The snowball
fight – signed and indistinctly dated 63(?) – unframed –
127 x 101.5cm.
(Christie's)   **$27,984   £17,600**

ALEXIS DE LEEUW – The Haycart – signed – oil on
canvas – 59 x 85cm.
(Sotheby's)   **$3,366   £1,980**

ALEXIS DE LEEUW (fl. 1848 - 1883) – Winter fuel – signed and dated 1868 – 60.5 x 91cm.
(Christie's)   **$7,870   £4,950**

CARL PETER LEHMANN – Huntsmen in the mountains of Hardanger – signed – oil on canvas – 90 x 124cm.
(Sotheby's)   **$5,984   £3,520**

EUGENE ERNEST LEFEBVRE (1850-1889) – Still life with cherries – signed – on panel – 47 x 61cm.
(Christie's)   **$5,667   £3,520**

CHARLES RODOLPHE LEHMANN – A young peasant girl – signed and dated Roma MDCCCLXII – oil on panel – 46 x 37cm.
(Sotheby's)   **$7,106   £4,180**

ALEXANDER LEGGETT – Kelp burners – signed; signed – inscribed with title and dated 1880 on the reverse – oil on canvas – 51 x 76cm.
(Sotheby's)   **$5,511   £3,300**

CHARLES LEICKERT – A frozen river landscape – signed – oil on canvas – 41 x 76cm.
(Sotheby's)   **$11,352   £6,600**

LEICKERT

CHARLES HENRI JOSEPH LEICKERT – A riverside village in summer – signed and dated '66 – oil on panel – 18 x 26.5cm.
(Sotheby's) $11,220 £6,600

WILLIAM ROBINSON LEIGH (1866-1955) – Pool at Oraibi – signed W. R. Leigh and dated N.Y. 1917, l.l. – oil on canvas – 56.5 x 71.7cm.
(Sotheby's) $187,000 £119,108

FREDERIC, LORD LEIGHTON, P.R.A. (1830-1896) – Rizpah – 143.5 x 132.5cm.
(Christie's) $136,400 £88,000

SIR PETER LELY (1618-1680) – Portrait of Richard and Anne Gibson – full length, he wearing a red tunic and cape, she wearing a grey gown with a russet cloak – oil on canvas – 165 x 122cm.
(Sotheby's) $71,720 £44,000

SIR PETER LELY (1618-1680) – Portrait of Dorothy Mason – three quarter length, seated, wearing a yellow dress, a landscape beyond – oil on canvas – 125 x 100cm.
(Sotheby's) $48,048 £28,600

Circle of SIR PETER LELY (Saest 1618 - London 1680) – Portrait of a girl said to be Lady Elizabeth Spelman – bears inscription top left: Lady Eliz[th] Spelman – oil on canvas – 127.1 x 101.6cm.
(Lawrence)   **$8,840   £5,390**

GEORGES LEMMEN (1865-1916) – La Baigneuse—De Baadster – the studio stamp on the reverse – oil on canvas – 64.2 x 32.4cm.
(Christie's)   **$19,360   £12,100**

GEORGES LEMMEN (1865-1916) – Femme au Chapeau—Vrouw met Hoed – signed with monogram lower left – oil on board laid on panel – 50.8 x 34.2cm.
(Christie's)   **$21,120   £13,200**

GEORGES LEMMEN (1865-1916) –Toits à Uccle— Daken te Ukkel – the studio stamp lower right – oil on paper laid down on board – 40 x 57.2cm. – Painted circa 1890
(Christie's)   **$79,200   £49,500**

GEORGES LEMMEN (1865-1916) - La Baigneuse avec son Chien - De Baadster met Hondje
- signed with monogram lower left - oil on panel - 45.7 x 55.8cm. *(Christie's)* **$17,600 £11,000**

MARIE-VICTOIRE LEMOINE – Paris 1754-1820 –
Portrait Présumé de Madame de Genlis – oil on canvas –
60 x 50cm.
(Sotheby's) **$59,369   £38,057**

**FRANZ-SERAPH VAN LENBACH (Schrobenhausen
1836-Munich 1904)** – Portrait of Mrs Horace Helyar,
afterwards Lady Savile, head and shoulders – charcoal
heightened with pastel and chalks – 59.6 x 44.5cm.
(Lawrence) **$902   £550**

ROBERT LENKEWICZ – `A triple portrait of a girl's head – on board – signed – 20 x 29½in.
(Michael Newman)   **$367   £225**

MICHEL-NICOLAS-BERNARD LEPICIE – Paris 1735-1784 – Nature Morte avec sculpture antique, Globe Terrestre et Livres – oil on canvas – 45 x 35.5cm.
(Sotheby's)   **$97,299   £62,371**

STANISLAS LÉPINE – La Place de la Concorde – signed – oil on canvas – 26.6 x 40.6cm.
(Sotheby's)   **$77,000   £48,428**

LEONEL (late 19th Century) – The market place, Seville – signed and dated 1875 – on panel – 23 x 35.5cm.
(Christie's)   **$6,198   £3,850**

MICHEL NICOLAS BERNARD LEPICIÉ, Attributed to (1735-Paris-1784) – The bird cage – on canvas – oval – 31 x 25.5cm.
(Phillips)   **$27,200   £16,000**

ADOLPHE ALEXANDRE LESREL (late 19th Century) – The connoisseurs – signed and dated 1895 – on panel – 37 x 30cm.
(Christie's)   **$7,672   £4,950**

LESSORE

HELEN LESSORE – Lyndhurst Gardens – signed – also inscribed on a label on the reverse – oil on canvas – 103 x 76cm.
(Phillips)   **$3,042**   **£1,800**

AUGUSTE LÉVEQUE (Belgian 1864-1921) – Bacchanalia – signed – oil on canvas – 96.5 x 127cm.
(Sotheby's)   **$54,780**   **£33,000**

ADRIENNE LESTER (Early 20th Century) – Kittens with a butterfly in a summer garden – signed – 49.6 x 60.4cm.
(Christie's)   **$7,480**   **£4,400**

HAYLEY LEVER (1876-1958) – Main Street, Nantucket – signed Hayley Lever and dated 1928. l.r. – oil on canvas – 64.1 x 76.1cm.
(Sotheby's)   **$23,100**   **£14,713**

JOHN LEVACK – A young poacher – signed and dated 1855 – oil on canvas – 81 x 63.5cm.
(Sotheby's)   **$7,715**   **£4,620**

RICHARD HAYLEY LEVER, NA, Attributed to (1876-1958) – Monhegan Island Dock – oil on canvas – 23 x 26in. – unsigned
(Bruce D. Collins)   **$9,900**   **£5,893**

RICHARD HAYLEY LEVER, R.B.A. (1876-1955) – A yacht moored in Penzance harbour – oil on board – signed – 15 x 19in.
(David Lay) **$3,381 £2,100**

RICHARD HAYLEY LEVER – Yachts Leaving Marblehead – signed Hayley Lever, l.l. – oil on canvas – 61 x 91.4cm.
(Christie's) **$18,700 £11,687**

RENAUD LEVIEUX 1625-1690 –Vierge à L'Enfant et Saint Jean-Baptiste – oil on canvas – 72 x 56cm.
(Sotheby's) **$16,490 £10,571**

LEVRAC-TOURNIERES

MAURICE LEVIS – A view of the Fortress of Mombasa, Sultanat of Zanzibar – signed – titled and dedicated A Maître Jullemier de tout coeur – oil on canvas – 48.5 x 59cm.
(Sotheby's) **$5,610 £3,300**

DIMITRI GRIGORIEVITCH LEVITSKI – Kiev 1735-1822 Saint-Petersbourg – Portrait de Grégoire Nikolaewitch Teploff (1711-1779) – oil on canvas – 90 x 72cm.
(Sotheby's) **$52,772 £33,828**

ROBERT LEVRAC-TOURNIERES 1667-1752 – Portrait d'un Gentilhomme – oil on canvas – 104 x 79cm.
(Sotheby's) **$5,772 £3,700**

LEVY

RUDOLF LEVY – Dahlias in a blue vase – stamped with the Nachlaß mark on the reverse – oil on canvas – 74 x 60.5cm.
(Sotheby's) **$18,758 £11,034**

JÓHN FREDERICK LEWIS, Follower of – An Arab beauty – 76.2 x 63.5cm.
(Christie's) **$717 £440**

EDMUND DARCH LEWIS (1835-1910) – Boating on the Lake – oil on canvas – 30 x 50in. – signed Edmund D. Lewis and dated 1871 lower right
(Bruce D. Collins) **$4,400 £2,619**

JAMES LEWIS CA – Cairndhu Park – signed – watercolour – 23 x 45cm.
(Sotheby's) **$2,388 £1,430**

OTTO THEODORE LEYDE, R.S.A., R.S.W. – The Conspirators – signed and dated 1889 – watercolour heightened with white – 54 x 43cm.
(Sotheby's) **$2,388 £1,430**

ALFRED LEYMAN – A street in Dartmouth – watercolour – signed and dated '10 – 21¼ x 14¼in. *(Bearne's)* **$890 £500**

JOSEPH CHRISTIAN LEYENDECKER – At Your-Service – signed JCLeyendecker with initials in monogram, l.r. – oil on canvas – 54.6 x 50.8cm. *(Christie's)* **$28,600 £17,875**

LÉON LHERMITTE (1844-1925) – Harandiers au bord de la Marne: effet de soleil – signed and dated 1919 – pastel – 66 x 90cm. *(Christie's)* **$37,510 £24,200**

ANDRE LHOTE (1885-1962) - Nu Couche - signed upper right A. Lhote - oil on canvas - 81 x 105cm. *(Christie's)* **$255,750 £165,000**

LIANORI

PIETRO DI GIOVANNI LIANORI (Bolognese, active 1400) – The Crucifixion – on panel – gold ground – 67 x 50.8cm.
(Phillips) **$97,800 £60,000**

CHARLES SILLEM LIDDERDALE – Lost in thought – signed with monogram and dated '81 – oil on canvas – 104 x 78cm.
(Sotheby's) **$11,116 £6,820**

PIETRO LIBERI DIT LIBERTINO' ATTRIBUTED TO - Padoue 1614-1687 Venise -
Suzanne et les Vieillards - oil on canvas - 210 x 250cm. *(Sotheby's)* **$36,281 £23,257**

DIETRICH WILHELM LINDAU, Follower of – A woman in an Italianate landscape – on panel – 46.3 x 38.1cm.
(*Christie's*)   **$1,705   £1,100**

CHARLES SILLEM LIDDERDALE – A serving girl – signed with monogram and dated 1891 – oil on canvas – 77 x 51cm.
(*Sotheby's*)   **$4,482   £2,750**

CHARLES SILLEM LIDDERDALE – A farm girl – signed with monogram – oil on canvas – 46 x 35.5cm.
(*Sotheby's*)   **$5,558   £3,410**

JOHAN ERIK LINDH (1793-1865) – The knitting lesson – signed – 76.7 x 59.7cm.
(*Christie's*)   **$5,667   £3,520**

LINDSAY

THOMAS LINDSAY, N.W.S. (1793-1861) – "Dingle Scene on the Brook...near Hay, Brecon" – signed – inscribed and dated 1848 – watercolour over pencil with scratching out – 40 x 40cm.
(Phillips) **$359 £220**

JOHN LINNELL (1792-1882) – The white cow – signed J. Linnell/1856 – oil on canvas – 44.5 x 59.5cm.
(Sotheby's) **$14,784 £8,800**

LADY BLANCHE LINDSAY (1844-1912) - Portrait of a lady, small quarter-length, wearing black costume – signed with mongram – watercolour – 25.4 x 19.6cm.
(Lawrence) **$962 £594**

NORMAN ALFRED WILLIAM LINDSAY (1879-1969) – Toilet – aquatint – signed – titled and numbered 20 26 45 in pencil – 16 x 14cm.
(Christie's) **$1,604 £990**

JEAN ETIENNE LIOTARD (1702-1789), Circle of – Portrait of John Montagu, Fourth Earl of Sandwich (1718-1792) – full length seated wearing Turkish dress attended by two Turkish ladies and taking coffee – oil on canvas – 180 x 155.5cm.
(Sotheby's) **$133,056 £79,200**

After JEAN ETIENNE LIOTARD – The chocolate girl – oil on canvas – 86 x 58cm.
(Phillips) **$2,898 £1,800**

HENRY LIVENS – Still life in a basket – signed – oil on canvas – 41 x 51cm.
(Sotheby's) **$2,151 £1,320**

JOHANNES LINGLEBACH (Frankfurt 1622-1674 Amsterdam) – A hawking party – signed Linglebach – on panel – 31.6 x 38.2cm.
(Phillips) **$42,380 £26,000**

SIR JAMES DROMGOLE LINTON, P.R.I., H.R.S.W. (1840-1916) – 'Thanksgiving' – signed with initials – oil on panel – 36 x 25.5cm.
(Phillips) **$13,040 £8,000**

DOROTHEA M. LITZINGER (American, 1889-1925) – Landscape through Rhododendron Blossoms – unsigned – artist's name inscribed on the reverse – oil on canvas – 40 x 42in.
(Skinner) **$4,800 £3,000**

LODGE

GEORGE EDWARD LODGE – Eagle on a Blue Hare –
signed and dated 1949; bears title on a label on the
backboard – watercolour heightened with bodycolour – 50
x 64cm.
(Sotheby's)   **$4,225 £2,530**

GEORGE EDWARD LODGE – A ten pointer and hinds
at Inchnacardoch – signed – oil on canvas – 33 x 51cm.
(Sotheby's)   **$6,980 £4,180**

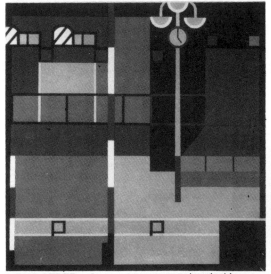

LOU LOEBER – Spoorwegovergang – signed with
initials and dated lower right L.L. '32 – and signed and
dated again and inscribed with title on the reverse – on
board – 81.5 x 81.5cm.
(Christie's)   **$11,097 £6,979**

WILLIAM LOGSDAIL (1859-1944) – St. Martins-in-
the-field – signed and dated 88 – 41 x 31cm.
(Christie's)   **$45,474 £28,600**

WILLIAM LOGSDAIL (1859-1944) – The Great Court,
Trinity College, Cambridge – signed – on board –
41 x 31cm.
(Christie's)   **$1,399 £880**

LAMBERT LOMBARD (1506-1566), Circle of – The Lamentation – oil on panel – arched top – 55.5 x 49.5cm.
(Phillips) **$3,586 £2,200**

WILLIAM LOGSDAIL – St. Mary's in the Strand – oil on canvus – unframed – 76.5 x 36cm.
(Sotheby's) **$3,227 £1,980**

GUSTAVE LOISEAU – Le Mairie d'Osny – signed and dated 1906 - oil on canvas – 50 x 61cm.
(Sotheby's) **$93,500 £58,805**

PIETRO LONGHI (1709 Venice-1785) – The fruit seller – inscribed: Per Doge/Sier/Franc-Loredan/Padre de Pov...within a sculptured wreath on a pillar. — Per Piovan/ in San Trovaso/D. Zuawne Farinato/de? ann? – on canvas – 61 x 49.5cm.
(Phillips) **$416,500 £245,000**

LONGPRE

WALDEMAR LORENTZON – Spanish washerwoman – signed – 100 x 80cm.
(Kvalitetsauktion)   **$18,147**   **£11,133**

PAUL DE LONGPRE – Poinsettia – signed P. de Longpre, l.l. – watercolour and pencil on paper – 55.5 x 45.5cm.
(Christie's)   **$4,950**   **£3,093**

JACOB VAN LOO, Attributed to (Sluys 1614-1670 Paris) – A young sheperd and shepherdess seated in a landscape – on canvas – 136 x 128cm.
(Phillips)   **$97,800**   **£60,000**

THOMAS LOSIK (1849-1896) – The miniature – oil on canvas – 24 x 18in. – signed T. Losik lower right
(Bruce D. Collins)   **$1,760**   **£1,047**

ROBERT ELMER LOUGHEED (American, b. 1910) –
"Retour on Village near Ft. Janvier, P. Que"/The Sleigh
Ride – signed – oil on canvasboard – 12 x 16in.
(Skinner)   **$2,500   £1,497**

FRANK W. LOVEN – A Winter Stream – signed F. W.
Loven and dated 1915, l.l. – oil on canvas – 76.5 x 102cm.
(Christie's)   **$5,720   £3,575**

KATHERINE LOVELL - Summer Afternoon - signed K. Lovell, l.r. - oil on canvas -
46 x 55.9cm.
(Christie's)   **$3,850   £2,406**

LOVERIDGE

CLINTON LOVERIDGE (American, 1824-1902) – An Afternoon of Skating – signed "C. Loveridge" l.r. – oil on board – 6 x 12in.
(Skinner) **$2,100 £1,313**

CHARLES LOW (circa 1860-circa 1920) – The watering Place, Evening – signed – and inscribed on the reverse of the mount - pencil and watercolour – 9¼ x 15⅛in.
(Christie's) **$3,568 £2,200**

MAXIMILIEN LUCE (1858-1941) – Un Jardin au Grèsillon, Poissy – signed and dated lower left Luce 94; signed – dated and inscribed on the stretcher Maximilien Luce 1894 Un Jardin au Gresillon – oil on canvas – 50 x 64cm.
(Christie's) **$427,487 £275,000**

ALAN LOWNDES (1921-1978) – The Swings – signed and dated lower left – inscribed and dated on reverse The Swings 16¾ x 12¼ St Ives Jan 1965 – oil on board – 12¼ x 16¼in.
(Christie's) **$2,259 £1,430**

ASCANIO LUCIANI (d. 1706) – A lady swooning before classical ruins attended by weeping women – signed Ascanius Lucianus – oil on canvas – 102.5 x 136cm.
(Phillips) **$6,846 £4,200**

EDWARD GEORGE HANDEL LUCAS (1861-1936) – The Chapel of the Old Archbishop's Palace, Croydon – signed and dated 1880 – and signed and inscribed on the reverse and also on board – 23 x 30.5cm.
(Christie's) **$6,479 £4,180**

EDUARD LUCKE – Still life with mushrooms – oil on canvas – signed – 60 x 60cm.
(Galerie Moderne) **$661 £421**

GEORGE LUKS – Trout Fishermen, Berk Hills – signed
– watercolour on paper – 35.5 x 50.8cm. –
Painted circa 1928
(Sotheby's)   **$9,900   £6,226**

FERDINAND LUIGINI – La Péniche – signed – oil on
panel – 21.5 x 27cm.
(Sotheby's)   **$1,683   £990**

JOHN LUKE, R.U.A. (born 1906) The Carnival – signed
– oil on board – 41.5 x 53cm.
(Phillips)   **$40,750   £25,000**

FREDERIK CHRISTIAN LUND – A vegetable seller –
signed and dated Roma 1863 – oil on canvas – 45 x 36cm.
(Sotheby's)   **$4,114   £2,420**

WILLIAM LUKER (fl. 1851-1889) – An Arab
encampment at sunset – signed – 45 x 56cm.
(Christie's)   **$3,323   £2,090**

THOMAS LUNY – Fishermen landing – signed –
9 x 13in.
(Bearne's)   **$5,408   £3,200**

LUNY

THOMAS LUNY (1759-1837) – Cornwallis's retreat from De Joyeuse, 1795 – signed l.l. : Luny 1834 – oil on canvas – 59.5 x 84.5cm.
(Sotheby's)   **$28,985**   **£18,700**

FRANCIS LYMBURNER (1916-1972) – Black Stockings – pen, black ink and grey wash – 32.4 x 38.1cm.
(Christie's)   **$1,426**   **£880**

CHARLES HENRY AUGUSTUS LUTYENS – "Gang forward" – Winner of the Two Thousand Guinea Stakes in 1873 – signed – oil on canvas – 102 x 127cm.
(Sotheby's)   **$9,861**   **£6,050**

PHILIP LYFORD – The Stubborn Child – signed Philip Lyford, l.r. – oil on canvas – 69 x 61.3cm.
(Christie's)   **$3,300**   **£2,062**

JOHN ABERNETHY LYNAS-GRAY (1869-?) – The new Kitten – signed and dated 1918 – also on reverse – watercolour and bodycolour – 26 x 17cm.
(Phillips)   **$2,037**   **£1,250**

RAYMOND LYNDE – A cuddly companion – signed –
oil on canvas – 77 x 63.5cm.
(Sotheby's) $14,344 £8,800

ANDREW MACARA (b. 1944) – The Swimming Pool –
signed and dated lower right Andrew Macara 1987 – oil on
canvas – 29¹/₄ x 35¹/₄in.
(Christie's) $2,607 £1,650

ROBERT WALKER MACBETH, R.A., R.W.S. – Girls
fishing on a quay, Douarnenez – signed with monogram
and dated '78 – oil on canvas – 52 x 96.6cm.
(Sotheby's) $8,606 £5,280

CORNEILLE DE LYON, d. circa 1514 – Attributed to -
Portrait D'homme – oil on panel – 21.2 x 16.5cm.
(Sotheby's) $8,246 £5,286

**WILLIAM STEWART MacGEORGE, R.S.A. (1861-
1931)** – The Goldfish Bowl – indistinctly signed – oil on
canvas – 61 x 50.8cm.
(Christie's) $10,164 £6,050

McBEY

JAMES McBEY – Portrait of a seated woman – signed and dated July 1927 – watercolour – 20 x 17cm.
(Sotheby's)   **$2,571   £1,540**

SAMUEL McCLOY – By the sea – signed with monogram – watercolour – 54 x 37cm.
(Sotheby's)   **$4,488   £2,640**

HAROLD McCULLOCH, R.S.A. – Gathering firewood – signed; indistinctly inscribed on the stretcher – oil on canvas – 40.5 x 61cm.
(Sotheby's)   **$6,980   £4,180**

WILLIAM McCANCE – Man reading – signed and dated 1927 – pen and ink – 20 x 16.5cm.
(Sotheby's)   **$5,511   £3,300**

TOM McEWAN R.S.W. – Study for 'Granny's Kitchen' – signed – inscribed with title and dated 1901 on reverse – oil on canvas – 25.5 x 30.5cm.
(Sotheby's)   **$2,939   £1,760**

MACHATSCHECK

WILLIAM STEWART MacGREGOR, R.S.A. – Girls amidst blossom – signed – oil on canvas – 40.5 x 50.5cm. *(Sotheby's)* **$20,207 £12,600**

ROBERT MacGREGOR, R.S.A. – The duet – signed and dated 79 – oil on canvas – 46 x 61cm. *(Sotheby's)* **$9,185 £5,500**

ROBERT McGREGOR, R.S.A. – Homeward at the close of day – signed – oil on canvas – 61 x 46cm. *(Sotheby's)* **$3,306 £1,980**

FELIX MACHATSCHECK (German b. 1863) – Potsdamerplatz, Berlin at dusk – signed and dated Berlin '99 – oil on canvas – 118 x 156cm. *(Sotheby's)* **$32,868 £19,800**

FLORENCE MACKAY - Feeding the ducks - signed and dated 1917 - 5¾ x 8¾in.
(Outhwaite & Litherland)   **$4,212   £2,600**

AUGUST MACKE – Coloured forms – stamped with the
Nachlaß mark N 82 and inscribed August Macke, Farbige
Formule, Aquarelle 1913 on the backboard – watercolour –
30 x 26cm.
(Sotheby's)   **$52,758   £31,034**

ADOLF MACKEPRANG – Stag and hinds – signed –
140 x 108cm.
(P. Herholdt Jensen)   **$9,547   £5,857**

CHARLES RENNIE MACKINTOSH (1868-1928) –
Boultenère, c. 1924-1927 – signed with initials – and
inscribed possibly by the hand of his wife on label verso –
watercolour – 44.7 x 44.7cm.
(Christie's) **$221,760 £132,000**

BESSIE MacNICOL – The lilac sun bonnet – signed – oil
on canvas – 41 x 31cm.
(Sotheby's) **$30,310 £18,150**

DANIEL MACLISE, R.A. (1806-1870) – May – signed
with monogram – on panel – 40.5 x 31.5cm.
(Christie's) **$8,745 £5,500**

ROBERT RUSSELL MacNEE – Loading the cart –
signed and dated 34 – oil on canvas – 41 x 61cm.
(Sotheby's) **$5,878 £3,520**

PAUL MAK (PAUL IVANOV) – Self Portrait – signed
and dated in the lower right corner MAK 1953 – pencil and
gouasche heightened with gold on paper – 33 x 24cm.
(Christie's) **$4,604 £2,860**

MARY LIZZIE MACOMBER (American, 1861-1916)
– "The Music Stand Central Park N.Y. City" – signed – oil
on canvas – 8 x 10in.
(Skinner) **$1,600 £958**

WILLIAM McTAGGART, R.S.A., R.S.W. – Chums –
oil on panel – 40.5 x 30.5cm.
(Sotheby's) **$18,370 £11,000**

WILLIAM McTAGGART, R.S.A., R.S.W. – Lazing on
the grass – signed – oil on board – 23 x 35cm.
(Sotheby's) **$10,103 £6,050**

SIR WILLIAM MacTAGGART, P.R.S.A. – Still life
with Hyacinths – signed and indistinctly dated – oil on
board – 51 x 61cm.
(Sotheby's) **$3,490 £2,090**

SIR WILLIAM MacTAGGART, P.R.S.A. – From my
window – signed – oil on canvas – 91.5 x 76cm.
(Sotheby's) **$14,696 £8,800**

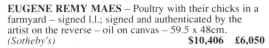

M. McWROE – Head and shoulder portrait of a young lady – signed with initials – watercolour – 21 x 16¹/₂in. *(Biddle & Webb)* **$1,828 £1,150**

EUGENE REMY MAES – Poultry with their chicks in a farmyard – signed l.l.; signed and authenticated by the artist on the reverse – oil on canvas – 59.5 x 48cm. *(Sotheby's)* **$10,406 £6,050**

JAN MADDEN (American, 20th Century) - View of Gloucester Harbor - signed - oil on canvas - 25¼ x 30in. *(Skinner)* **$1,800 £1,078**

MAGRITTE

RENÉ MAGRITTE (1898-1967) – La Découverte de Feu
– signed upper right Magritte – oil on canvas –
34.5 x 40.5cm.
(Christie's)   **$290,691   £187,000**

EDMUND MAHLKNECHT (1820-1903) – By the lake –
signed and dated Wien 863 – 74 x 101cm.
(Christie's)   **$15,345   £9,900**

THOMAS MAIDMENT (Exh. 1905-38) – "Pudding Bag
Lane" – watercolour – 15 x 11in.
(David Lay)   **$558   £360**

MAIN FRANKEN SCHOOL, 1st quarter 16th century
– Saint Cyriaque Exorcisant la Princesse Arthémie, saint
Philippe Apôtre, Saint Bartholomé, Saint Christophe – oil
on panel – 150 x 180cm.
(Sotheby's)   **$79,158   £50,742**

LEO MALEMPRE – Young goatherds – signed – oil on
canvas – 53 x 66cm.
(Sotheby's)   **$5,199   £3,190**

WILLIAM HENRY MANDER (English, fl. 1880-1922)
– 'The Upper Lake, Capel Cruig, N. Wales' – signed and
dated '87 – 55.8 x 97.2cm.
(Bonhams)   **$1,240   £800**

WILLIAM HENRY MANDER – "The Valley of the Llugny" – signed and dated 13 - oil painting – 19 x 30in. *(G. A. Key)* **$8,050 £5,000**

E. MALLINSON – Village scene with mother and child beside a rose clad cottage in the foreground – signed and dated 1920 – 37 x 45cm. *(Spencer's)* **$3,564 £2,200**

ANTONIO MARIA DE REYNA MANESCAU (1859-1937) – A view of Venice with the Dogana – signed – on board – 33 x 72cm. *(Christie's)* **$21,312 £13,750**

JAMES BOLIVAR MANSON (1879-1945) – Summer Flowers – signed lower left J B Manson – oil on canvas - 19 x 15in. *(Christie's)* **$4,866 £3,080**

CHARLES MALFROY (born 1862) – A Mediterranean port – signed – unframed – 60 x 91.5cm. *(Christie's)* **$4,959 £3,080**

EDOUARD MANET (1832-1888) – La rue Mosnier aux drapeaux – signed and dated bottom left Manet 1878 – oil on canvas – 65.5 x 81cm. - Painted in 1878 *(Christie's)* **$26,400,000 £16,542,240**

MANN

ALEXANDER MANN, R.O.I. (1853-1908) – 'Kaid Maclean, Instructor General to the Infantry Forces of the Sultan of Morocco' – signed – also signed and inscribed on label on reverse – oil on canvas – 130 x 89cm.
(Phillips) $2,282 £1,400

MISS M. MANNING (late 19th Century) – The guitar player – signed and dated 1890 – 61 x 46cm.
(Christie's) $22,308 £13,200

WILLIAM MANNERS, R.B.A. (fl. 1889-c. 1910) – Shipping on a river – signed and dated 1885 – oil on canvas – 30.5 x 45.5cm.
(Phillips) $1,141 £700

GIOVANNI MANSUETI – Venise Aprés 1450-vers 1527 – Le Baptéme du Christ – oil on panel – 65.5 x 53cm.
(Sotheby's) **$32,983 £21,142**

DAVID DE LA MAR (French, 19th/20th Century) – Shepherdess with Goat – signed – oil on canvas – 28¹/₂ x 19in.
(Skinner) **$550 £329**

GIACOMO MANTEGAZZA (1853-1920) – The proposal – signed and inscribed Milano – on panel – 46 x 37cm.
(Christie's) **$10,626 £6,600**

ANDRÉ MARCHAND – La femme verte – signed lower left André Marchand – and signed again and inscribed with title and Paris on the reverse – 80.5 x 65cm.
(Christie's) **$13,114 £8,248**

MARCHESE

GIUSEPPE MARCHESE (1699-1771) – The departure of Aeneas – oil on canvas – 104.8 x 137.5cm.
(Phillips)   **$15,485   £9,500**

WILLIAM HENRY MARGETSON – A Young Lady in Medieval Costume Reading by a Stream – panel – signed and inscribed on label on reverse – 40.7 x 29.8cm.
(Bonhams)   **$1,085   £700**

MRS MARIS MARGITSON (fl. 1857-1864) – Still Life of Peaches, Grapes, Pears and a Pineapple in a Basket on a Table – signed and dated 1879 – oil on canvas – 52 x 68cm.
(Phillips)   **$2,934   £1,800**

SZANTHO MARIA – Three quarter length portrait study of a pretty young girl holding a bunch of roses – oil on canvas – signed – 39 x 31in.
(Biddle & Webb)   **$4,890   £3,000**

ANTONIO MARICINI – The Piazza Majo Casaniciola – signed and inscribed – watercolour heightened with white – $13^3/4$ x $21^1/4$in.
(Christie's)   **$1,703   £1,045**

MICHELE MARIESCHI – Venise 1710-1743 – Le Palais Ducal et les Prisons vus Depuis le Bassin de Saint Marc – oil on canvas – 55 x 82.5cm.
(Sotheby's)   **$325,371   £208,571**

RAFFAELLO MARINO – Sur le quai voltaire – signed l.l – oil on canvas – 25.5 x 24cm.
(Sotheby's)   **$14,190   £8,250**

JOSÉ MARIN-BALDO (1826-1891) – Au jardin du Luxembourg, Paris – signed and dated 90 – 46 x 32.5cm.
(Christie's)   **$10,230   £6,600**

JACOB MARIS – A view of Marlotte, France – signed and dated '64; titled on a label on the stretcher – oil on canvas – 20.5 x 30.5cm.
(Sotheby's)   **$10,846   £6,380**

MARINO MARINI (1901-1980) – Cavaliero – signed lower right Marino – gouache, brush and black ink heightened with white on paper – 86.5 x 61.5cm.
(Christie's)   **$64,790   £41,800**

CARL MARKO, Jnr. – A meeting on the road – signed and dated 1879 – oil on canvas – 41 x 56cm.
(Sotheby's)   **$3,740   £2,200**

MARQUES

D*** MARQUÉS – The dancer – signed and dated 1941 – oil on canvas – unframed – 181 x 145cm.
(Sotheby's) **$3,406 £1,980**

REGINALD MARSH (1898-1954) – Man and woman on a bench and Four women on the boardwalk: A double-sided work – signed Reginald Marsh and dated 1947, l.r. recto – Chinese ink on paper – 34.3 x 48.2cm.
(Sotheby's) **$13,200 £8,407**

REGINALD MARSH – The Flying Concellos – tempera on panel – 24.4 x 28.7cm.
(Christie's) **$22,000 £13,750**

ALBERT MARQUET - Houses at Arceuil - oil on canvas - signed - 27 x 35cm.
(Jean-Claude Anaf) **$84,190 £53,968**

JEAN BAPTIST MARTIN I, called MARTIN DES BATAILLES (1659-1735) – A nobleman, believed to be Louis XIV, surveying the Battlefield at Valenciennes – oil on canvas – 38 x 46cm.
(Phillips) **$4,5360 £2,800**

ALEXANDRE CHARLES MASSON (late 19th Century) – Danae in a shower of gold – signed – 51 x 74cm.
(Christie's) **$2,479 £1,540**

JOHN MARTIN (1789-1854) – Arundel Castle – signed l.r. : J. Martin – oil on canvas – 30 x 44.5cm.
(Sotheby's) **$109,120 £70,400**

GERTRUDE MARTINEAU – Loch Tay, Perthshire – watercolour heightened with white – 23 x 53cm.
(Sotheby's) **$1,010 £605**

Circle of JAN MASSYS (1509-1575) – A hurdy gurdy player – inscribed 'Nov Schoon Lynken Herdy Myne' – oil on panel – 46 x 36cm.
(Phillips) **$3,888 £2,400**

FRANK HENRY MASON – A Naval patrol leaving harbour – watercolour heightened with bodycolour – signed – 9³/₄ x 13³/₄in.
(Bearne's) **$945 £580**

JOHANNES HENDRIK VAN MASTENBROECK – A view of a Dutch riverside town – signed and dated 1919 – oil on canvas – 26.5 x 34cm.
(Sotheby's) **$9,350 £5,500**

MASTER

MASTER OF 1518 – Portrait de Ferdinand de Hongrie – oil on panel – 46 x 33.5cm.
(Sotheby's) **$32,983 £21,143**

LEONA SZEGEOY MASZAK (Hungarian, early 20th Century) – The Models – signed – unframed – 68.6 x 50.8cm.
(Bonhams) **$2,015 £1,300**

PAUL MATHIEU (1872-1932) – Peupliers le long du Canal—Populieren langs het Kanaal – oil on board – 40 x 55.2cm.
(Christie's) **$17,600 £11,000**

PAUL MATHIEU (1872-1932) – L'Etang aux Peupliers—Poel met Populieren – signed and dated lower right Paul Mathieu 21 – oil on canvas – 60 x 81.5cm. – Painted in 1921
(Christie's) **$44,000 £27,500**

PAUL MATHIEU (1872-1932) – Exile à Ste Adresse—In Ballingschap te Ste Adresse – signed – dated and inscribed Paul Mathieu Ste Adresse 1915 – oil on panel – 39.4 x 54.6cm. – Painted in 1915
(Christie's) **$63,360 £39,600**

HENRI MATISSE – Tête de Femme (Lorette) – signed – oil on panel – 22 x 16cm.
(Sotheby's) **$660,000 £415,094**

HENRI MATISSE – Femme à L'Ombrelle Rouge, Assise de Profil – signed – oil on canvas – 81 x 65cm.
(Sotheby's) **$12,375,000 £7,783,019**

PAOLO DE MATTEIS, Follower of – Adam and Eve mourning over Abel – oil on canvas – 79.5 x 116cm.
(Phillips) **$724 £450**

HENRI MATISSE (1869-1954) – Nu assis dand l'Atelier – signed lower right Henri Matisse – oil on canvas board – 42 x 33.5cm. – Painted circa 1917-18
(Christie's) **$1,619,750 £1,045,000**

JAMES MATTHEWS – A Garden at West Lavington, Sussex – watercolour – signed and inscribed – 24.8 x 35cm.
(Bonhams) **$1,264 £800**

J.H. MAY (mid 19th Century) – Still life of Lily-of-the-Valley and Violets on a mossy bank – signed and dated 1867 – and signed and inscribed on an old label on the reverse – 25 x 20cm.
(Christie's) $1,524 £935

GABRIEL CORNELIUS VON MAX – A bust-length Portrait of a Bearded Gentleman, possibly a self-portrait painted oval – signed twice – inscribed 'Prag 1869' – 45.7 x 33.7cm.
(Bonhams) $263 £170

JOHN MAXWELL, R.S.A. – Figure in a landscape – signed and dated 1950 – ink and watercolour – 30.5 x 55cm.
(Sotheby's) $11,022 £6,600

ARTHUR JOSEPH MEADOWS (1843-1907) – 'On the Maas, W. Scheidam' – signed – also signed, inscribed and dated 1879 on label on reverse – oil on canvas – 34.5 x 61cm.
(Phillips) $3,749 £2,300

REUBEN MEDNIKOFF – Cromer Medley – signed – dated "May 24 1949-7 – pen and ink – unframed – 29 x 40cm.
(Phillips) $507 £300

JAMES EDWIN MEADOWS (1828-1888) – A country lane with a horse and cart – 60 x 100.2cm.
(Christie's) $6,646 £4,180

G. MEEKYN – 'Old Bridlesmithgate, Corner of St. Petersgate, Nottingham' – signed and dated 1879 - inscribed on the reverse – 39.5 x 29cm.
(Spencer's) $1,099 £700

SIR JOHN MEDINA (1659-1710) – Portrait of two children – full lengths, one seated on a rock with a lamb at her feet, the other standing wearing a silver dress and holding a garland of flowers – signed c.r.: J. Medina 1697 – oil on canvas, in a carved wood frame – 122 x 114cm.
(Sotheby's) $10,164 £6,050

DORA MEESON (1869-1955) – In the Farmyard – signed – 40 x 49.8cm.
(Christie's) $1,782 £1,100

MEIJER

SAL MEIJER – A Saxon Farmhouse, Blaricum, with a cat in the front, a churchspire beyond – signed lower left Sal Meyer – on panel – unframed – 50 x 40cm.
(Christie's) **$3,026 £1,903**

ARTHUR MELVILLE, R.W.S., A.R.S.A., R.S.W. – Kurrachee – signed – inscribed with title and dated 1883 – watercolour heightened with bodycolour – 37 x 54cm.
(Sotheby's) **$18,370 £11,000**

ANDREW W. MELROSE – Summer in the Lehigh Valley, Pennsylvania – signed with monogrammed initials AM, l.l. – signed Melrose – dated 79 and inscribed with title on the reverse – oil on canvas – 56 x 35.5cm.
(Christie's) **$5,500 £3,437**

MORTIMER MENPES (1860-1938) – The pot seller – signed with monogram – on panel – 17 x 11cm.
(Christie's) **$2,274 £1,430**

CIRCLE OF PHILIP MERCIER (1689-1760) – Temptation – oil on canvas – unframed – 82.5 x 101cm. *(Sotheby's)* **$17,902 £11,550**

PHILIP MERCIER (1689-1760) – Portrait of Martha Lowther – three-quarter length, wearing a white dress and holding a rose – oil on canvas – 90 x 70cm. *(Sotheby's)* **$12,936 £7,700**

GABRIEL METSU, After – Old man selling poultry – oil on panel – 38.5 x 31cm. *(Phillips)* **$2,898 £1,800**

PHILIP MERCIER (1689-1760) – Portrait of Sir William Lowther and his second wife, Catherine Ramsden – full length, standing, Swillington House beyond – signed l.r.: Ph. Mercier/1742 – oil on canvas – 244 x 151cm. *(Sotheby's)* **$48,048 £28,600**

JEAN METZINGER – Still life with fruit, a loaf of bread, a geranium, a jug, a bowl, a bottle of wine and a letter, on a partly draped wooden table – signed and dated lower left J. Metzinger 10-23 – 60 x 81cm. *(Christie's)* **$90,794 £57,103**

DIETHELM MEYER (1840-1884) – The afternoon nap – signed – 70 x 57cm.
(Christie's)   **$8,501   £5,280**

PIERRE MIGNARD, After – Portrait of Louis XIV – unframed – oil on canvas – 81.3 x 64.8cm.
(Bonhams)   **$1,208   £750**

A. MICHEL (fl. c. 1880) – Shipping on a river; A quayside – both signed lower left: A. Michel – oil on canvas – 48.9 x 64.7cm; a pair
(Lawrence)   **$5,953   £3,630**

GEORGES MICHEL – A windmill in a stormy landscape – oil on canvas – 67.5 x 98cm.
(Sotheby's)   **$12,155   £7,150**

PIERRE MIGNARD (Troyes 1612-1695 Paris) – Portrait of a lady, three-quarter length, seated, her left hand beside a small vase containing jasmine, in her right hand she holds a spray of the same flower – on canvas – 130 x 98cm.
(Phillips)   **$13,600   £8,000**

ABRAHAM MIGNON – Francfort-sur-le-Mein |640-1679 – Vase de Fleurs et Fruits sur un Entablement – oil on canvas – 52 x 42.5cm.
(Sotheby's)   **$362,811   £232,571**

FRED MILLARD (Exh. 1882-1910) – Newlyn School – "He loves me, he loves me not" - girl pulling petals from a daisy in an orchard – signed – oil on canvas relined – 30 x 20in.
(W. H. Lane & Son)   **$12,920   £7,600**

ATTRIBUTED TO JAMES MILLAR (fl. 1763-1805) – Portrait of Miss Mary Robinson of Durham – full length, standing, wearing a white dress, green sash, and holding flowers – oil on canvas – 125.5 x 85cm.
(Sotheby's)   **$11,935   £7,700**

JOHN MILLER (b. 1911) – Venice, April Afternoon Light – signed lower right John Miller – oil on canvas – 28¹/₂ x 41in.
(Christie's)   **$1,912   £1,210**

MILLOT

HENRI MILLOT, b. 1756 – Portrait D'Officier – oil on canvas – oval – 83 x 65cm.
(Sotheby's)   **$4,947**   **£3,171**

JOHN MACLAUCHLAN MILNE, R.S.A. – Mediterranean shore – signed – watercolour over black chalk – 38 x 28cm.
(Sotheby's)   **$4,776**   **£2,860**

JOHN MacLAUCHLAN MILNE, R.S.A. - The North end of Loch Long and the village Arrocher - signed and dated '52 - oil on canvas - 38 x 55.5cm. *(Sotheby's)*   **$11,940**   **£7,150**

RICHARD EDWARD MILLER – The Artist's Wife –
signed Miller, l.l. – oil on panel – 34.9 x 26.4cm.
(Christie's) **$18,700 £11,687**

FRANCIS DAVID MILLET (American, 1846-1912) –
Young Woman with an Urn – oil on canvas – 14¼ x
10½ in.
(Skinner) **$3,100 £1,856**

J. W. MILLIKEN – 'Evening after rain, Bruges' and 'The
Fishmarket, Bruges' – Street scenes with numerous figures
in the foreground – signed – a pair – unframed –
17 x 25cm.
(Spencer's) **$2,619 £1,550**

ROBERT W. MILLIKEN – The sunken butt – signed
and inscribed with title – watercolour heightened with
white – 63 x 101cm.

RICHARD EDWARD MILLER (1875-1943) – The Sun
room – signed Miller, l.l. – oil on panel – 61.0 x 55.9cm.
(Sotheby's) **$220,000 £140,127**

(Sotheby's) **$1,928 £1,155**

MILORADOVICH

SERGEI DMITRIEVICH MILORADOVICH (1851-1943) – Patriarch Nikon – signed in Cyrillic lower centre S. Miloradovich – oil on canvas – 90.2 x 125.7cm.
(Christie's) $46,046 £28,600

JUAN CARRENO DE MIRANDA, Attributed to – The Madonna of the Moon – oil on canvas – 65.5 x 50cm.
(Phillips) $2,275 £1,300

JOAN MIRO (1893-1983) – Composition – signed lower right Miro – black wash and coloured crayons on paper – 65 x 52cm.
(Christie's) $110,825 £71,500

376

ERNEST GABRIEL MITCHELL R.B.S.A. (b. 1859) –
A rest from harvesting – watercolour – signed –
11 x 15½in.
(David Lay) **$1,240 £800**

PAULA MODERSOHN-BECKER – Mother and child –
confirmation of authenticity written by Otto Modersohn,
May 1924 – oil on board – 72.5 x 54.5cm.
(Sotheby's) **$140,689 £82,758**

JAMES CAMPBELL MITCHELL, R.S.A. – Landing
the catch – signed and indistinctly dated – oil on board –
31 x 36cm.
(Sotheby's) **$2,388 £1,430**

WILLIAM FREDERICK MITCHELL – The iron clad
Gunboat 'Sultan' – watercolour heightened with white –
signed and dated 1878 – numbered 993 – 24.8 x 36.2cm.
(Bonhams) **$638 £380**

PAULA MODERSOHN-BECKER – The red house – oil
on canvas laid down on board – 44.5 x 36cm.
(Sotheby's) **$58,620 £34,482**

MODIGLIANI

AMEDEO MODIGLIANI (1884-1920) – Giovane Donna
– signed lower right Modigliani – brown wash pen and
black ink heightened with white on paper – 48.2 x 33.6cm.
– Executed circa 1917-1918
(Christie's) **$204,600 £132,000**

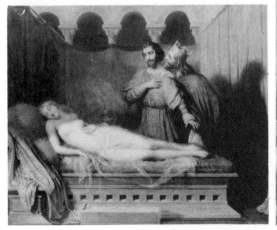

CHARLES MOENCH – King Candaule and Gygès by
the Queen's bed – signed and dated 1846 – oil on canvas –
59 x 71cm.
(Sotheby's) **$5,610 £3,300**

JOHN HENRY MOLE (1814-1886) – A Rest by the
Way – signed and dated 1867 – watercolour heightened
with bodycolour – 17.5 x 29cm.
(Phillips) **$2,282 £1,400**

BARTHOLOMEUS MOLENAER (Active circa 1640)
– Boers gathered around a table in an interior – signed with
initials – oil on panel – 24 x 20.5cm.
(Phillips) **$4,050 £2,500**

KLAES MOLENAER (1540-1589) – A winter landscape
with figures walking beside a stream running beside a
village – oil on panel – 47 x 36cm.
(Phillips) **$6,804 £4,200**

CARL MOLL (Austrian 1861-1945) – A still life of a lobster, asparagus and lemons – signed and dated '92 – oil on canvas – 77 x 115cm.
(Sotheby's) **$14,608 £8,800**

ACHILLE MOLLICA (fl. 1870-87) – The duet – signed and inscribed Napoli – canvas laid down on board – 94 x 75cm.
(Christie's) **$4,604 £2,860**

JOOS DE MOMPER THE YOUNGER (1564-Antwerp-1635) – Mountainous landscape with figures on a path – on panel – 33.3 x 55.3cm.
(Phillips) **$59,500 £35,000**

JOOS DE MOMPER (1564-Antwerp-1635) – A mountainous landscape with a church in the valley and figures on a path before a chateau – executed circa 1600 – on canvas – 108 x 143cm.
(Phillips) **$48,900 £30,000**

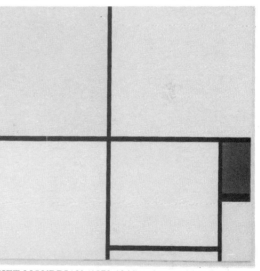

PIET MONDRIAN (1872-1944) – Composition C with Red and Grey– signed with initials and dated in red lower right PM 32; label on the reverse inscribed by the artist Composition C – oil on canvas – mounted in the artist's original white-painted strip frame and original back frame – 50.2 x 50.4cm.
(Christie's) **$4,958,855 £3,190,000**

PIET MONDRIAN – Landscape – signed lower right Piet Mondriaan – oil on paper laid down on board – 24 x 38.5cm. – Executed circa 1905-1907
(Christie's) **$20,177 £12,690**

MONET

CLAUDE MONET – La Berge à Argenteuil – signed and
dated 77 – oil on canvas – 60.4 x 73.4cm.
(Sotheby's) **$6,600,000 £4,150,943**

CLAUDE MONET – Meules, Effet de Neige, Le Matin –
signed and dated 91 – oil on canvas – 65 x 100cm.
(Sotheby's) **$8,525,000 £5,361,635**

CLAUDE MONET – Cobeas – oil on canvas –
118.5 x 37cm.
(Sotheby's) **$605,000 £380,503**

CLAUDE MONET – Perdrix et Becasse – signed – oil on
canvas – 61 x 51cm. – Painted in 1872
(Sotheby's) **$671,000 £422,013**

CLAUDE MONET – Bords de la Seine, un Coin de Berge
– signed and dated 81 – oil on canvas – 82 x 60cm.
(Sotheby's) **$3,740,000 £2,352,201**

CLAUDE MONET – Faisans, Becasses et Perdrix -
signed – oil on canvas – 89 c 68.5cm.
(Sotheby's) **$1,760,000 £1,106,918**

CLAUDE MONET – Nature morte, Poires et raisins – signed – oil on canvas – 45.8 x 56cm.
(Sotheby's) **$1,650,000 £1,037,736**

MONET

CLAUDE MONET – Promenade (Esquisse) – oil on canvas – 102 x 75cm.
(Sotheby's) **$1,430,000   £899,371**

ADOLPHE FRANCOIS MONFALLET (1816-1900) – Bubbles – signed and with the date 1856 – on panel – 32.5 x 24cm.
(Christie's) **$2,643   £1,705**

CLAUDE MONET (1840-1926) – Camille et Jean Monet au Jardin d'Argenteuil – the studio stamp lower right Monet – and on the reverse Monet – oil on canvas – 131 x 97cm.
(Christie's) **$5,984,825   £3,850,000**

JEAN BAPTIST MONNOYER, Studio of (Lille 1634-1699 London) – Still life of flowers in a vase upon a table – on canvas – 56 x 43.5cm.
(Phillips) **$21,190   £13,000**

PEDER MØNSTED – A winter's day in Dyrehave –
signed and dated Jagersborg Dyrehave 1929 – oil on
canvas – 49 x 69cm.
(Sotheby's) **$7,946 £4,620**

PEDER MØNSTED (1859-1941) – In the shadow of an
Italian Pergola. A warm afternoon in Anacapri – signed
and dated Capri 1884 – 122.5 x 96cm.
(Christie's) **$81,840 £52,800**

PEDER MØNSTED (Danish 1859-1941) – At the well –
signed and dated Fr Minge 1920 – oil on canvas –
69 x 95.5cm.
(Sotheby's) **$23,738 £14,300**

PEDER MØNSTED – Hellebaek – signed – dated 1897
and inscribed Hellebaek l.l – oil on canvas – 80 x 119cm.
(Sotheby's) **$30,272 £17,600**

PEDER MØNSTED (1859-1941) – First snow – signed
and dated Bröndbyvester 1923 – 46.5 x 61.5cm.
(Christie's) **$14,492 £9,350**

PEDER MØNSTED (Danish 1859-1941) – Unloading
stone from a barge at Ouchy – signed and dated Ouchy
1887 – oil on canvas – 51.5 x 87cm.
(Sotheby's) **$14,608 £8,800**

MONTALD

ANTONIO MATTEO MONTEMEZZO (1841-1898) –
Feeding the geese – signed and inscribed München –
60 x 89cm.
(Christie's) **$17,391 £11,220**

CONSTANT MONTALD (1862-1944) – Bouquet de
Lys—Lelies – signed and dated lower right C. Montald 43
– oil on canvas – 89.5 x 69.8cm. – Painted in 1943
(Christie's) **$11,440 £7,150**

ALFRED MONTAGUE (fl. 1832-1883) – Little gleaners
– signed and indistinctly dated – 100.3 x 139.8cm.
(Christie's) **$6,646 £4,180**

CONSTANT MONTALD (1862-1944) - L'Aveugle—De Blinde - signed and dated lower
right C. Montald '16 - gouache on board - 80 x 97.1cm. - Executed in 1916.
(Christie's) **$22,880 £14,300**

ADOLPHE MONTICELLI – Musical entertainment – signed – oil on panel – 33 x 26cm.
(Sotheby's) **$12,716** **£7,480**

FANNIE MOODY, S.W.A. (b. 1861 - c. 1948) – Canny little Scots – signed and signed and inscribed on the reverse – pastel – unframed – 30.5 x 66cm.
(Christie's) **$2,431** **£1,430**

BARLOW MOORE – 'Emerald', off Osborne Bay, I.O.W. – signed and inscribed – watercolour over pencil; heightened with scratching out – 44.5 x 62.25cm.
(Woolley & Wallis) **$1,700** **£1,000**

JOHN MOORE OF IPSWICH - Moonlight, Aldeburgh Beach – oil on panel – 28 x 38cm.
(Sotheby's) **$3,765** **£2,310**

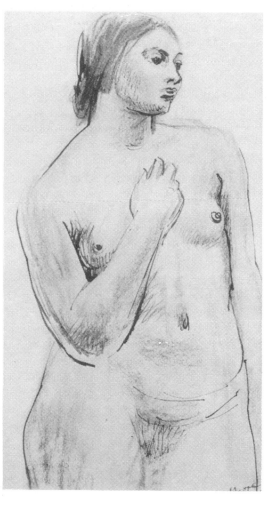

HENRY MOORE, O.M., C.H. (1898-1986) – Standing Figure – signed lower right Moore 27 – brush and black ink and soft pencil on paper – 37 x 22.9cm. – Executed in 1927
(Christie's) **$17,050** **£11,000**

MORA

FRANCIS LUIS MORA – Trapeze Artists – signed F. Luis Mora, l.l. – oil on canvas – 120 x 89.5cm. *(Christie's)* **$30,800 £19,250**

EDWARD MORAN (1829-1901) - Bringing in the catch – signed Edward Moran, l.l. – oil on canvas – 98.4 x 67.3cm. *(Sotheby's)* **$28,600 £18,217**

EDWARD MORAN – Early Morning – signed Edward Moran and dated 1873, l.l. – oil on canvas – 45 x 73cm. *(Christie's)* **$35,200 £22,000**

THOMAS MORAN (1837-1926) – Sunset after a storm – signed with the artist's monogrammed signature TMoran, N.A. – and dated 1901, l.l. – oil on canvas – 76.2 x 101.6cm. *(Sotheby's)* **$187,000 £119,108**

THOMAS MORAN – A Summer Morning Coast – oil on canvas laid down on board – 30.6 x 45.7cm. *(Christie's)* **$17,600 £11,000**

PAUL CHARLES CHOCARNE MOREAU (French 1855-1931) – Young pedlars by the Pont des Arts, Paris – signed - oil on canvas – 87 x 112cm.
(Sotheby's)   **$21,912 £13,200**

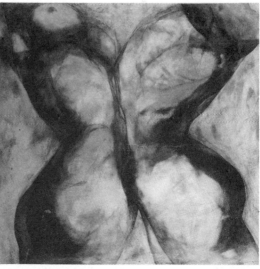

PAULUS MOREELSE 1571-1638 – Attributed to – Cérès – oil on canvas – 64 x 49.5cm.
(Sotheby's)   **$4,122 £2,642**

SERVANDO CABRERA MORENO – La Leyenda Negra – signed and dated lower right Cabrera Moreno '77 – and signed and dated again and inscribed with title on the reverse – 201 x 201cm.
(Christie's)   **$1,412 £888**

MORENO

SERVANDO CABRERA MORENO – Muchacha de Buenavista – signed and inscribed with title on the reverse – 50 x 89cm.
(Christie's)   **$908**   **£571**

L. MORETTI (19th Century) – Istanbul from Asia — signed and dated 1873 – 80 x 130cm.
(Christie's)   **$7,672**   **£4,950**

FRED MORGAN – The farmer's daughter – signed and inscribed with title on the backboard – watercolour heightened with bodycolour – 51 x 35.5cm.
(Sotheby's)   **$2,244**   **£1,320**

GEORGE MORLAND – Gypsy encampment – oil on panel – 30 x 38cm.
(Woolley & Wallis)   **$2,805**   **£1,650**

FREDERICK MORGAN (1856-1927) – Mother's darling – signed – 81 x 56cm.
(Christie's)   **$15,741**   **£9,900**

GEORGE MORLAND – The Farmer's Cottage — a kitchen interior – signed – 17½ x 23½in.
(Bearne's)   **$17,800**   **£10,000**

GEORGE MORLAND (1762-1804) – Rough haired dogs
– signed G. Morland. 1792 – oil on canvas – 44 x 57.5cm.
(Sotheby's) **$21,252 £12,650**

ROBERT EDWARD MORRISON (1852-1925) – The
mandolin player – signed and dated 1895 – 91.5 x 71cm.
(Christie's) **$3,227 £1,980**

ROBERT MORLEY – A portrait of a terrier – signed –
oil on canvas – 76 x 63.5cm.
(Woolley & Wallis) **$6,846 £4,200**

ALBERTO MORROCCO, R.S.A. – Siesta – signed;
signed and inscribed with title on a label on the frame – oil
on board – 51 x 58.5cm.
(Sotheby's) **$1,653 £990**

ANNA MARY ROBERTSON (GRANMA) MOSES –
Hills of New England – signed Moses, l.l. – dated ca. 1939
and inscribed with artist's number 20 on the artist's label
affixed to the reverse – oil on board – 35.5 x 41.7cm.
(Christie's) **$63,800 £39,875**

GEORGE L.K. MORRIS – Baroque – signed Morris, l.r.
– signed George L. K. Morris – dated 1938 and inscribed
with title on the reverse – oil on canvas – 45.7 x 64cm.
(Christie's) **$19,800 £12,375**

MOSLER

TOM MOSTYN (1864-1930) – Landscape, Peace –
signed lower left Mostyn – oil on canvas – 19³/₄ x 26¹/₂in.
(Christie's)   **$3,823   £2,420**

HENRY MOSLER – Woman in a Bonnet – signed Hy
Mosler – dated 1892 and inscribed Pnt. Paris, u.l. – oil on
canvas – 33 x 24cm.
(Christie's)   **$4,180   £2,612**

**GILLIS MOSTAERT THE ELDER (Hulst 1534-1598
Antwerp)** – A winter landscape, with a procession of
figures approaching a village – on panel – 71.8 x 99.3cm.
(Phillips)   **$136,000   £80,000**

WILLIAM SIDNEY MOUNT (1807-1868) – The
residence of the Honorable William H. Ludlow – signed
W. S. Mount and dated '59, l.l.; also signed with the artist's
intitals W.S.M. – dated July 1859 – oil on panel –
22.9 x 30.5cm.
(Sotheby's)   **$71,500   £45,541**

J* C* MOURAT – The Confession – signed and dated '78
– 68.2 x 55.5cm.
(Bonhams)   **$957   £550**

LOUIS FAIRFAX MUCKLEY (exh. 1889-1914) –
Summer – signed, watercolour heightened with white –
29 x 20½in.
(Christie's)   **$4,171 £2,640**

ALPHONSE MUCHA (Czech 1860-1934) – A portrait of
a woman – signed and dated '30 – pencil and coloured
crayon and bodycolour – 58.5cm. high
(Sotheby's)   **$29,216 £17,600**

FREDERICK MULHAUPT (1874-1939) – Stilling
winds – signed Mulhaupt, l.r. – oil on canvas –
127.5 x 151.8cm.
(Sotheby's)   **$26,400 £16,815**

MULLER

EUGENE ROBERT MULLER – A portrait of a child with a bird – signed and dated 1852 – oil on canvas – 80.5 x 65cm.
(Sotheby's)   **$5,298**   **£3,080**

WILLIAM JAMES MULLER (1812-1845) – Rowing boat crossing a river – signed l.r. W. Muller 1840 – oil on canvas – 21.5 x 41cm.
(Sotheby's)   **$7,161**   **£4,620**

WILLIAM JAMES MULLER – The Young Anglers – watercolour – signed and dated '49 – 14³/₄ x 11¹/₂in.
(Bearne's)   **$783**   **£440**

WILLIAM JAMES MULLER – Cairo – A street scene with numerous colourful market stalls, and mosques and minarets beyond – signed – inscribed and dated 1843 – 43 x 34cm.
(Spencer's)   **$2,835**   **£1,750**

EMILE MUNIER – Playing with the kitten – signed and dated 1893 – oil on canvas – 45.5 x 30.5cm.
(Sotheby's) **$47,300 £27,500**

SIR ALFRED MUNNINGS, P.R.A. - Before the start, Newmarket – signed - oil on board - 45.7 x 55.9cm.
(Sotheby's) **$231,000 £145,283**

SIR ALFRED J. MUNNINGS, P.R.A. – Brightworthy Ford near Withypool – on panel – signed – signed, inscribed and dated 1942 on the reverse – 19½ x 23½in.
(Bearne's) **$13,528 £7,600**

SIR ALFRED MUNNINGS, P.R.A. (1878-1959) – The Coming Storm – signed lower left A. J. Munnings – oil on canvas – 40 x 50in.
(Christie's) **$563,200 £352,000**

SIR ALFRED MUNNINGS, P.R.A. (1878-1959) – The Old Thatcher, Bob Riches – signed and dated lower right A. J. Munnings 1908 – oil on canvas – 30 x 40in.
(Christie's) **$299,200 £187,000**

MUNNINGS

SIR ALFRED MUNNINGS, P.R.A. (Mendham 1878-Dedham 1959) – The Horsefair – signed and dated lower left: A. J. Munnings 1902 – watercolour – 23.4 x 32.4cm.
(Lawrence)   **$63,140   £38,500**

HENRY TURNER MUNNS – Neapolitan coral seller – signed – signed and inscribed on the reverse – 35¹/₂ x 23¹/₂in.
(Bearne's)   **$2,225   £1,250**

LOUIS MURATON (fl. 1887-1901) – The photographer – signed – 177.1 x 127cm.
(Christie's)   **$10,626   £6,600**

Manner of MURILLO – Taking favours – oil on canvas –
81.25 x 100cm.
(Woolley & Wallis)   **$2,210   £1,300**

SIR DAVID MURRAY, R.A., H.R.S.A., R.S.W., R.W.S.
– The reed cutter – signed and dated 86 – oil on canvas –
41 x 74cm.
(Sotheby's)   **$34,903   £20,900**

JOSÉ BRANCO Y MURILLO – A still life with melon,
artichoke and fruit – signed – oil on canvas – 45 x 52.5cm.
(Sotheby's)   **$5,676   £3,300**

F. SYDNEY MUSCHAMP (fl. 1870-1903) – Feeding the
doves – signed with a monogram – 71 x 85cm.
(Christie's)   **$5,597   £3,520**

JOHN FRANCIS MURPHY – Sycamores – signed
Francis Murphy, l.l. – oil on canvas – 68.5 x 104.5cm.
(Christie's)   **$8,800   £5,500**

F. SYDNEY MUSCHAMP (fl. 1870-1903) – The dance –
signed – 50.8 x 76.2cm.
(Christie's)   **$1,076   £660**

MUSCHAMP

FRANCIS SYDNEY MUSCHAMP – A tangle – signed and dated 1897 – oil on canvas – 51 x 76cm.
(Sotheby's) **$8,965 £5,500**

PIETRO MUTTONI called PIETRO DELLA VECCHIA (1605-1678) – The presentation in the temple – oil on canvas – 80 x 118cm.
(Phillips) **$7,172 £4,400**

FRANCOIS ETIENNE MUSIN (1820-1888) – Sailing vessels in stormy seas – signed – 52 x 76cm.
(Christie's) **$8,501 £5,280**

HERMAN VAN DER MYN (1684-1741) – Portrait of a money changer seated beside a table – signed – oil on canvas – 76 x 63cm.
(Phillips) **$2,415 £1,500**

MARTHA DARLAY MUTRIE (1824-1885) – Still life of Hyacinths, Orchids and other flowers in a pot on a stone ledge – 81.5 x 61cm.
(Christie's) **$3,586 £2,200**

FRANS NACKAERTS – Children singing and dancing in a circle – signed lower left F. Nackaerts – 73 x 90cm.
(Christie's) **$7,061 £4,441**

PAUL JACOB NAFTEL (1817-1891) – The River Dochart in spate at Killin, Perthshire – signed and dated 1873 and extensively inscribed on an old label on the reverse – watercolour – 44.4 x 81.4cm.
(Lawrence)   **$1,426**   **£880**

JOHN GEORGE NAISH – South side of the Gull Rock (Serpentine). Mullion Cove, Cornwall – canvas – signed – 29³/₄ x 49³/₄in.
(Outhwaite & Litherland)   **$972**   **£600**

ALBERT NAMATJIRA (1902-1959) – Behind Simpson's Gap – signed – pencil and watercolour – 29.8 x 24.9cm.
(Christie's)   **$4,277**   **£2,640**

JOHN NASH, R.A. – Landscape with Houses – signed – anotated with artist's notes – inscribed "to Norah" – watercolour over pencil – 25 x 35cm.
(Phillips)   **$1,267**   **£750**

ATTRIBUTED TO ALEXANDER NASMYTH – View on the coast of Ayrshire – inscribed with title on reverse – oil on canvas – 45 x 58cm.
(Sotheby's)   **$6,980**   **£4,180**

ALEXANDER NASMYTH (1758-1840) - A prospect of London, seen from the Earl of Cassilis's Privy Garden, with Waterloo Bridge – inscribed on the relining: painted by/Alex Nasmyth/Edinburgh 1826 – oil on canvas – 139.5 x 208.5cm.
(Sotheby's)   **$579,700**   **£374,000**

PATRICK NASMYTH (1787-1831) – Wooded lane by the sea – signed l.r.: Patk Nasmyth/1828 – oil on panel – 42 x 56cm.
(Sotheby's)   **$27,720**   **£16,500**

NASON

JEAN-MARC NATTIER – Paris 1685-1765 – Portrait D'un Gentilhomme – oil on canvas – 145 x 113cm.
(Sotheby's) **$138,750 £79,285**

PETER NASON (c. 1612-1689) – Portrait of a lady, said to be Henrietta, daughter of Charles I – half length, wearing a white satin dress with a fur stole – signed l.r. : P (in monogram) Nason f./1668 – oil on canvas – in a painted oval – 84 x 63.5cm.
(Sotheby's) **$11,935 £7,700**

NEAPOLITAN SCHOOL – The Bay of Naples with Vesuvius erupting – inscribed Eru del 1839 – gouache – 17¼ x 24½in.
(Christie's) **$1,524 £935**

CHARLES JOSEPH NATOIRE (Nimes 1700-1777 Castel Gandolfo) – Ceres – on canvas – 79.8 x 63.5cm.
(Phillips) **$14,670 £9,000**

PIETER NEEFS the YOUNGER (1620-Antwerp-1675) – The interior of a Cathedral, said to be Antwerp – signed Peter Neeffs – on copper – 81.5 x 103cm.
(Phillips) **$89,650 £55,000**

JOHN TRIVETT NETTLESHIP (1841-1902) – Alert after the kill – signed and dated 1901 – 144.7 x 198.1cm. *(Christie's)* **$3,586 £2,200**

CHRISTOPHER RICHARD WYNNE NEVINSON, A.R.A. – Harvest, Sussex – signed – pen and ink and watercolour, heightened with bodycolour – 25 x 35cm. *(Phillips)* **$3,380 £2,000**

CHARLES WYNNE NICHOLLS, R.H.A. – The Elfin haunts – signed twice; signed and inscribed with title on a label on the reverse – oil on panel – 27 x 19cm. *(Sotheby's)* **$2,510 £1,540**

SIR WILLIAM JOHN NEWTON – A young woman drawing – watercolour heightened with bodycolour – 19.5 x 22.5cm. *(Sotheby's)* **$1,459 £858**

CHARLES WYNNE NICHOLLS, R.H.A. – Elfin gambols – signed twice; signed and inscribed with title on a label on the reverse – oil on panel – 27 x 19cm. *(Sotheby's)* **$2,869 £1,760**

NICHOLS

DALE NICHOLS – Evening Before the Witches Ride – signed Dale Nichols, l.l. – inscribed with title on the reverse – oil on canvas – 61 x 76cm.
(Christie's) **$9,350 £5,843**

WINIFRED NICHOLSON (1893-1981) – Pomegrate and Capari – inscribed and dated 1967 on the reverse – oil on board – 40.5 x 56cm.
(Phillips) **$11,410 £7,000**

HENRY HOBART NICHOLS – Snowbound – signed Hobart Nichols, l.r. – oil on canvas – 63.5 x 76cm.
(Christie's) **$4,950 £3,094**

ERSKINE NICOL, R.S.A., A.R.A. – The toothache – signed and dated '71 – oil on canvas – 63.5 x 48cm.
(Sotheby's) **$12,491 £7,480**

EDMUND JOHN NIEMANN, Snr. (1813-1876) – On the Sheaf, Sheffield – signed and dated Sheffield '65 – 46 x 76.5cm.
(Christie's) **$4,372 £2,750**

HENRY HOBART NICHOLS – Snow Fall – inscribed with title on the reverse – oil on canvas – 63.5 x 76cm.
(Christie's) **$14,300 £8,937**

EDMUND JOHN NIEMANN, Snr. (1813-1876) – A view of Nottingham – signed and dated Nottingham '65 – on panel – 20.5 x 48cm.
(Christie's)   **$5,947   £3,740**

ROBERT NIGHTINGALE (1815-1895) – A chesnut hunter in a loose box with a terrier on a blanket – signed and dated 1876 – 41.8 x 52.3cm.
(Christie's)   **$3,048   £1,870**

EDMUND JOHN NIEMANN, Snr. – Bucks damaged by flood, Mapledurham, Berks, morning – signed – inscribed with title and dated 56 – oil on canvas – arched frame – 102 x 127cm.
(Sotheby's)   **$19,723   £12,100**

EDWARD H. NIEMANN, Jnr. – Thorpe, Dovedale – signed and inscribed with title – oil on canvas – 76 x 127cm.
(Sotheby's)   **$4,482   £2,750**

A* NIKOLSKY – A Still Life with red, pink and yellow Roses in a Bowl – signed and dated 1957 – 71 x 91.5cm.
(Bonhams)   **$1,044   £600**

BASIL NIGHTINGALE – Three stallions startled by a passing motor car – signed and dated 1902 – oil on canvas – 92 x 127cm.
(Woolley & Wallis)   **$3,586   £2,200**

THORVALD NISS – On the shore – signed and dated 1874 – oil on canvas – 49 x 69.5cm.
(Sotheby's)   **$2,618   £1,540**

NITTIS

GIUSEPPE DE NITTIS –The Victoria Embankment, London – signed and dated '75 – oil on panel – 19 x 31.1cm.
(Sotheby's) **$319,000 £200,629**

JAMES NOBLE – Anna Zinkiesen Roses in a Glass – signed – on panel – 25.5 x 20.5cm.
(Bonhams) **$1,659 £1,050**

EMIL NOLDE (1867-1956) - Mädchenkopf – signed lower right Nolde – watercolour on paper – 57 x 35cm. – Executed circa 1925
(Christie's) **$30,690 £19,800**

EMIL NOLDE (1867-1956) – Bauernhaus – signed lower right Nolde – watercolour on paper – 34.9 x 47.8cm.
(Christie's) **$81,840 £52,800**

EMIL NOLDE – Rote Mohnblumen – signed watercolour on paper – 34.5 x 47.5cm.
(Sotheby's) **$170,500 £107,233**

EMIL NOLDE - Two horses in a meadow – signed – watercolour and brush and indian ink – 30.7 x 45.7cm.
(Sotheby's) **$82,068 £48,275**

JOSEPH FRANCIS NOLLEKENS (1702-1748) – A musical party – oil on metal – 35.5 x 45.5cm.
(Sotheby's) **$258,720   £154,000**

EMIL NOLDE (1867-1956) – Gefangene – signed lower right Nolde and inscribed on the reverse Gefangene Geraulites Madchen (crossed out) Mädchen u Männes (crossed out) – watercolour, brush and ink on paper – 25.7 x 18.1cm.
(Christie's) **$40,920   £26,400**

JAN VAN NOORDT (1620-Amsterdam-1676) – Portrait of a lady standing before a house surrounded by a moat – on canvas – 84.5 x 67cm.
(Phillips) **$35,860   £22,000**

EMIL NOLDE – Portrait of a woman wearing a yellow earring - signed - watercolour and brush and indian ink – 47.5 x 34.7cm.
(Sotheby's) **$96,724   £56,896**

ORLANDO NORIE – The 12th Lancers – signed – watercolour over traces of pencil with touches of bodycolour – 32.5 x 47cm.
(Sotheby's) **$1,403   £825**

ELIZABETH NOURSE (1859-1938) – Les Heures du Soir
Sior – signed Elizabeth Nourse, l.r. – oil on canvas –
100.3 x 74.9cm. – Painted circa 1912
(Sotheby's) **$82,500** **£52,548**

VILMOS ABA NOVAK – Onarckep – tempera on paper
– signed – 24 x 19cm.
(Mugyujtok Galeriaja Kft) **$974** **£590**

WILLIAM DEGOUVE DE NUNCQUES – A view in Broek op Waterland, in winter - signed with
initials and dated lower right W.D.d.N. 17 - 99.5 x 119.5cm. *(Christie's)* **$37,831 £23,793**

OECONOMOU

LEONARD OCHTMAN – Snowy Landscape – signed Leonard Ochtman and dated 1907, l.l. – oil on canvas – 91.8 x 132cm.
(Christie's) $23,100 £14,437

RODERIC O'CONOR (1860-1940) – Roses in a Blue and White Vase – signed and dated 1921 – oil on panel – 37.5 x 46.5cm.
(Phillips) $57,050 £35,000

OCTAVIUS OAKLEY – A young girl in a plaid cape carrying a handbill – watercolour over pencil heightened with bodycolour – 29.5 x 22.5cm.
(Sotheby's) $1,496 £880

RODERIC O'CONOR – Mother and Child Walking in a Park – signed, and dated '32 – oil on canvas – 41 x 35cm.
(Phillips) $6,720 £4,200

ARISTIDES OECONOMOU (Greek 1821-1887) – A portrait of a young girl – signed and dated 1850 – oil on canvas – 65.5 x 50cm.
(Sotheby's) $25,564 £15,400

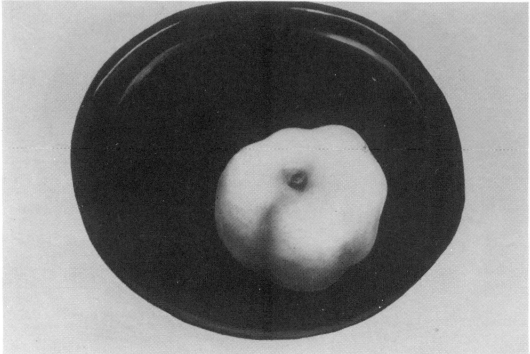

GEORGIA O'KEEFFE (1887-1986) - Still life with apple - inscribed by Georgia O'Keeffe by Alfred Stieglitz on a label affixed to the backing - oil on canvas - 25.4 x 35.5cm - Painted in 1921-22. *(Sotheby's)* **$203,500   £129,618**

OTIS OLDFIELD – The Artist and His Wife – signed Otis Oldfield, u.r. – signed again and inscribed Two Heads and 1405 Montgomery St., San Francisco, Calif. on the stretcher – oil on canvas – 69 x 56cm. *(Christie's)* **$27,500   £17,187**

OTIS OLDFIELD – On the Dock – signed Otis Oldfield, l.r. – bears artist's estate stamp – dated 1926 and inscribed with title and San Francisco Waterfront on the reverse - oil on board – 33 x 41.3cm. *(Christie's)* **$4,400   £2,750**

DANIEL O'NEILL, R.H.A. (1920-1974) – Boats at
Falcarragh – signed – oil on board – 51 x 61cm.
(Phillips) **$13,040 £8,000**

**SIR WILLIAM ORPEN, R.A., R.W.S., R.H.A. (1878-
1931)** – Miss Annie Harmsworth in an Interior – signed
and dated 1907 – oil on canvas – 91.5 x 71cm.
(Phillips) **$130,400 £80,000**

HENRY NELSON O'NEIL, A.R.A. (1817-1880) –
Home again – signed and dated 1859 – 135 x 107cm.
(Christie's) **$258,850 £167,000**

JOSEPH OPPENHEIMER (b. 1876) – Birdcage Walk –
signed lower right Jos Oppenheimer – signed again –
dedicated and dated on the reverse To Ella in gratitude for
your hospitality Josef London 1932 – oil on canvas –
9 x 16in.
(Christie's) **$869 £550**

EMILY MARY OSBORN (fl. 1851-1908) – The basket
of flowers – signed with monogram – 39 x 27.5cm.
(Christie's) **$2,798 £1,760**

OSTADE

ADRIAEN VAN OSTADE, Follower of – A woman greeting a fellow at her door – bears signature and date – oil on panel – 30.5 x 26.8cm.
(Phillips)   **$1,610**   **£1,000**

PIERRE OUTIN – An elegant suitor at the window – signed – oil on canvas – 80 x 64cm.
(Sotheby's)   **$21,505**   **£12,650**

HENRY OTTOMAN - La coiffure - oil on canvas - signed - 60 x 74cm.
(Jean-Claude Anaf)   **$9,575**   **£6,138**

GIUSEPPE PALIZZI (1812-1888) – The shepherd boy –
signed – 62 x 42cm.
(Christie's) **$8,184 £5,280**

PAULINE PALMER (American, 1865-1938) – A
Theatrical Performer – signed – oil on canvas – 45 x 38in.
(Skinner) **$1,800 £1,078**

WALTER LAUNT PALMER – State Building, Albany –
signed Walter L. Palmer and dated 1907, l.r. – oil on
canvas – 57 x 75cm.
(Christie's) **$27,500 £17,187**

WALTER LAUNT PALMER (American, 1854-1932) –
Farm in Winter Twilight, Albany, New York – signed and
dated 1890 – watercolour with gouache on blue
watercolour board – 13 x 17in.
(Skinner) **$4,200 £2,515**

ANTONIO PAOLETTI Jnr. (Italian 1834-1912) –
Feeding the pigeons – signed and inscribed Venezia – oil
on canvas – 60 x 90cm.
(Sotheby's) **$43,824 £26,400**

PATON

SIR JOSEPH NOEL PATON, R.S.A. (1821-1901) –
Fact and Fancy – "Such tricks hath strong imagination" –
(A Midsumer Night's Dream, Act V, Scene 1) – signed
with monogram and dated 1863 – oil on canvas – lunette –
55.2 x 73cm.
(Christie's) **$175,560   £104,500**

HENRY H. PARKER (1858-1930) – A figure with a dog
on a path near a cottage – signed – on canvas laid down on
panel – 20.2 x 29.2cm.
(Christie's) **$1,793   £1,100**

JOHN ANTHONY PARK (1881-1962) – St Ives School
– Unloading the catch from boats in St Ives Harbour –
signed – oil on board – 13 x 16in.
(W. H. Lane & Son) **$4,200   £2,500**

HENRY H. PARKER (English, 1858-1930) –
'Pangbourne on Thames' – signed – signed and inscribed
on reverse – 50.8 x 76.2cm.
(Bonhams) **$18,600   £12,000**

HENRY H. PARKER (1858-1930) – A Surrey cornfield
near Reigate – signed – and signed and inscribed on the
reverse – 61.5 x 91.5cm.
(Christie's) **$12,787   £8,250**

JOHN ANTHONY PARK – The Orange Sail – signed –
oil on canvas – 50 x 61cm.
(Phillips) **$6,760   £4,000**

HENRY H. PARKER (1858-1930) – At Chobham,
Surrey – signed – and signed and inscribed on the reverse –
51 x 76cm.
(Christie's) **$7,346   £4,620**

ATTRIBUTED TO J. PARKER (fl. 1637-1658) – Portrait of Lady Needham – half length, wearing a white dress edged with lace and green ribbons – oil on canvas – in a painted oval – in a carved wood frame – 75 x 62cm.
(Sotheby's)   **$8,525   £5,500**

WILLIAM PARROTT – The carriers cart – A sale of porker – signed and dated '87 – signed and inscribed on the stretcher on the reverse – 30.5 x 46.3cm.
(Christie's)   **$1,194   £715**

BEATRICE PARSONS (1870-1955) – Interior of a Study – signed – watercolour and bodycolour – 25 x 30cm.
(Phillips)   **$2,200   £1,350**

POL PARMENTIER – Tulipes dans un vase Blanc—Tulpen in een Witte Vaas – signed with monogram and dated centre left 16 – oil on canvas — 32 x 24in. – Painted in 1916
(Christie's)   **$5,280   £3,300**

BEATRICE PARSONS – Saxifraga and Primula Kewensis—Kew – watercolour – signed – 22.8 x 30.4cm.
(Bonhams)   **$4,582   £2,900**

JOHN PARTRIDGE (1790-1872) – Portrait of Lord Colborne, with Sir David Wilkie's 'The Parish Beadle' hanging behind – inscribed and dated 1846 – on the relining canvas – 73.7 x 94.3cm. *(Christie's)* $5,738 £3,520

JULES PASCIN (1885-1930) – Les Amoureuses – signed lower right Pascin – watercolour and pencil on paper laid down on board – 28 x 31.7cm.
(Christie's) $17,050 £11,000

JULES PASCIN (1885-1930) – Les Pauvres, Conversation – the studio stamp lower right (L. 2014b) – pen and brush and brown ink on paper – 16 x 21cm.
(Christie's) $6,479 £4,180

JOHN F. PASMORE – Huntsmen's return – signed and dated 1839 – oil on canvas – 89 x 127cm.
(Sotheby's)   **$4,776**   **£2,860**

JAMES McINTOSH PATRICK, R.S.A. – Ballindene, Perthshire, Scotland – signed; signed and inscribed with title on the stretcher – oil on canvas – 63.5 x 76cm.
(Sotheby's)   **$15,614**   **£9,350**

JOSEPH PAULMAN – Haymaking in a Wooded River Landscape – 30.5 x 40cm.
(Bonhams)   **$744**   **£480**

CAROLINE PATERSON (exh. 1880-1899) – Little friends – signed – pencil and watercolour – 30.4 x 22.8cm.
(Christie's)   **$5,738**   **£3,520**

FRANK PATON (1856-1909) – "Canada"; A Bay Hunter – signed – inscribed and dated 1904 – watercolour heightened with white – 22 x 33cm.
(Phillips)   **$782**   **£480**

ANTON PAULSEN, ACTIVE IN STOCKHOLM IN THE 18th C. – Portrait d'homme – oil on canvas – oval – 70 x 60cm.
(Sotheby's)   **$1,978**   **£1,268**

FRITZ PAULSEN – The engagement – signed – oil on canvas – 55 x 73cm.
(Sotheby's)   **$5,610   £3,300**

ELIE ANATOLE PAVIL – A view on a river side, with trees reflecting in the water, at sunset – signed lower left Elie Pavil – 60 x 81cm.
(Christie's)   **$2,118   £1,332**

WILLIAM McGREGOR PAXTON (1861-1941) – Nude in interior – signed Paxton, m.r. – oil on canvas – 43.1 x 35.5cm.
(Sotheby's)   **$110,000   £70,064**

WILLIAM McGREGOR PAXTON – Spring Bouquet – signed Paxton, l.r. – oil on canvas – 51 x 41cm.
(Christie's)   **$16,500   £10,312**

ERNEST PAYNE – A Still Life of mixed Summer Flowers in a stoneware Jug – signed – on canvas – 66.5 x 51cm.
(Bonhams)   **$1,106   £700**

MARGARETTA ANGELICA PEALE – Still Life with Peaches, a Pear and Grapes – signed Margt A. Peale and dated 1864, l.l. – oil on canvas – 33.5 x 46cm.
(Christie's) $12,100 £7,562

HENRY ARTHUR PAYNE (1868-1940) – The Enchanted Sea – signed and dated 1912 – pencil and watercolour heightened with bodycolour and gold – 18 x 13in.
(Christie's) $30,481 £18,700

TITIAN RAMSEY PEALE – Canis Lupus – signed with the artist's initials; also inscribed by Titian R. Peale and titled Canis Lupus in the margin – watercolour on paper – 14.0 x 20.3cm. - executed circa 1819-20
(Sotheby's) $33,000 £20,755

MERVYN PEAKE (1911-1968) – Female Nude – signed and dated lower right Peake 37 – oil on canvas – 29³/₄ x 25in.
(Christie's) $5,562 £3,520

LEONARD PEARMAN – Lions resting in a Wooded Landscape – signed – 63.5 x 76.2cm.
(Bonhams) $626 £360

PARSONS

HERMANN MAX PECHSTEIN – Landscape in the moonlight – signed and dated 1922 – watercolour – 49 x 62.5cm.
(Sotheby's)   **$32,241   £18,965**

BEATRICE PARSONS – Roses in the Garden of Michelgrave House, the Home of Mr. Tiplady at Boscombe – watercolour – signed – 45.2 x 27.8cm.
(Bonhams)   **$4,898   £3,100**

MAX PECHSTEIN (1881-1955) – Kurische Häuser – signed lower left HM Pechstein – inscribed with title on the stretcher Kurische Hauser and dated and numbered 1919 II – oil on canvas – 70 x 80cm.
(Christie's)   **$341,990   £220,000**

MARGUERITE STUBER PEARSON (American, 1898-1978) – Fall Street Scene – signed – oil on canvasboard – 12 x 16in.
(Skinner)   **$1,200   £719**

HERMANN MAX PECHSTEIN – Lake Kos (Eastern Pomerania) - signed and dated 1938 – watercolour heightened with white – 59.5 x 77.5cm.
(Sotheby's)   **$12,896   £7,586**

JOHN PEDDER (1850-1929) – "Burnham Beeches" – signed – also signed and inscribed with title on old label on backboard – watercolour heightened with bodycolour and scratching out over pencil – 56 x 97cm.
(Phillips) **$6,194 £3,800**

MAX PECHSTEIN (1881-1955) – Kurenkahnreihe auf dem Strand – signed and dated upper right H M Pechstein 1919 – watercolour on paper – 48 x 64cm. – Executed in 1919
(Christie's) **$25,575 £16,500**

MAX PECHSTEIN (1881-1955) – Zwei Frauen – signed and dated lower right HMP 1924 – oil on canvas – 120.6 x 144.8cm.
(Christie's) **$410,388 £264,000**

VIGGO PEDERSEN – A lady reading in an interior – signed – oil on canvas – 49 x 53cm.
(Sotheby's) **$3,740 £2,200**

PEEL

JAMES PEEL (1811-1906) – A trout stream, Wensley Dale, near Matlock – signed – inscribed and dated January 1st 1846 on the reverse – 40.5 x 61cm.
(Christie's) **$1,924 £1,210**

JAMES PEEL – Figures in a Wooded River Landscape – 55.9 x 91.4cm.
(Bonhams) **$2,240 £1,400**

WALDO PEIRCE (1884-1970) – Summer of '45 – oil on canvas – signed with conjoined initials W. Peirce and dated '45 lower left – 31 x 43in.
(Bruce D. Collins) **$11,654 £7,150**

THOMAS KENT PELHAM – Gossips at the fountain – signed – 44.5 x 52cm.
(Christie's) **$2,556 £1,540**

THOMAS KENT PELMAN (fl. 1860-1891) – A country girl – signed – 91.4 x 71.2cm.
(Christie's) **$2,152 £1,320**

NARCISSE VIRGILE DIAZ DE LA PEÑA – A still life of flowers in a vase – signed – oil on canvas – 97 x 66cm.
(Sotheby's) **$15,895 £9,350**

JOSEPH PENNELL – West Front of St. Paul's from Ludgate Hill – gouache en grisaille on paper laid down on board – 50.8 x 34.9cm.
(Christie's) **$14,300 £8,937**

JACK PENDER (b. 1918) – Homeward Bound – signed lower right – signed again – dated and inscribed on the reverse Homeward Bound 69 – oil on board – 47¼ x 23¼in.
(Christie's) **$4,171 £2,640**

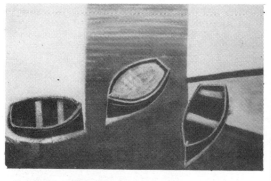

JACK PENDER (b. 1918) – Black Punts waiting – signed and inscribed on the reverse Black Punts Waiting Jack Pender Fishermans Square, Mousehole, Penzance Cornwall – oil on board – 23½ x 35½in.
(Christie's) **$3,824 £2,420**

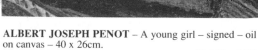

ALBERT JOSEPH PENOT – A young girl – signed – oil on canvas – 40 x 26cm.
(Sotheby's) **$1,309 £770**

PEPLOE

SAMUEL JOHN PEPLOE – Reclining Nude Model –
red chalk – 20 x 27cm.
(Phillips)   **$1,555   £920**

SAMUEL JOHN PEPLOE, R.S.A. – Still life – oil on
canvas – 46 x 41cm.
(Sotheby's)   **$91,850   £55,000**

SANTO PERANDA (1566-Venice-1638) – Portrait of a
young girl, standing beside a table with a vase of flowers –
on canvas – 122 x 95cm.
(Phillips)   **$8,150   £5,000**

SIDNEY RICHARD PERCY – The Conway, North
Wales – signed and dated 1883 – oil on canvas – 48 x
66cm.
(Sotheby's)   **$14,344   £8,800**

SIDNEY RICHARD PERCY (1821-1886) – Cornstooks
in a River Landscape – signed – oil on canvas – 61.5 x
97cm.
(Phillips)   **$17,930   £11,000**

SIDNEY RICHARD PERCY – Early morning, North
Wales – signed and dated 1871; signed and inscribed with
title on the stretcher – oil on canvas – 61 x 96.5cm.
(Sotheby's)   **$32,274   £19,800**

SIDNEY RICHARD PERCY (1821-1886) – Loch
Lomond – signed and dated 1871 – 61 x 96.5cm.
(Christie's)   **$55,968   £35,200**

L. PERICH (late 19th Century) – Portrait of Miss Narisa Sabal – half length in a white dress – signed and inscribed – 53.3 x 39.4cm.
(Christie's) $1,364   £880

PARKER S. PERKINS (American, b. 1862) – Fisherman at Sea – unsigned – oil on canvas with graphite – 27 x 22in.
(Skinner) $400   £240

PARKER S. PERKINS (American, b. 1862) – "A Ship Yard" – signed – identified on verso – oil on canvas – 18 x 22in.
(Skinner) $650   £389

ARTHUR PERIGAL, Jnr., R.S.A., R.S.W. – The Oak tree, near Jedburgh – signed and dated 1884; signed - inscribed with title and dated on a label on the stretcher – oil on canvas – 61 x 50cm.
(Sotheby's) $1,469   £880

PARKER S. PERKINS (American, b. 1862) – Kittens at Play – signed and dated 1899 – oil on canvas – 14$^1/_4$ x 18$^1/_4$ in.
(Skinner) $800   £479

PERMEKE

CONSTANT PERMEKE (1886-1952) – La Dame au
Foulard rose—Vrouw met roze Halsdoek – signed lower
left Permeke – oil on canvas – 75 x 59.7cm. –
Painted circa 1949
(Christie's) **$132,000 £82,500**

CONSTANT PERMEKE (1886-1952) – Nu debout—
Staand Naakt – signed lower left Permeke – black chalk
and black wash on paper laid down on board –
122.5 x 62cm. – Executed circa 1930
(Christie's) **$45,760 £28,600**

CONSTANT PERMEKE (1886-1952) – L'Ecurie—De
Stal – signed lower right Permeke – oil on canvas laid
down on panel – 75.6 x 110.5cm.
(Christie's) **$56,320 £35,200**

ENOCH WOOD PERRY (American, 1831-1915) –
Young Girl with a Water Jug – signed - inscribed and
dated "E. Wood Perry N.Y. '92" – oil on canvas – 20 x
16in.
(Skinner) **$1,800 £1,078**

JANE PETERSON (American, 1876-1965) White Lilies – signed "Jane Peterson", l.r. – oil on board – 23⅝ x 17⅝in.
(Skinner) **$6,000 £3,681**

LILLA CABOT PERRY – Angela – signed and dated 1891 – oil on canvas – 91.4 x 66.0cm.
(Sotheby's) **$31,900 £20,063**

HENRY PETHER (fl. 1828-1865) – Somerset House seen through Waterloo Bridge by moonlight – signed l.l: Henry Pether – oil on canvas – 59 x 89.5cm.
(Sotheby's) **$18,480 £11,000**

ANTOINE PESNE – Paris 1683-1757 Berlin – Le Danseur dand un Paysage – oil on canvas – 78 x 82cm.
(Sotheby's) **$79,159 £50,743**

EDMOND MARIE PETITJEAN (1844-1925) – Scène du village – signed – 46 x 65.5cm.
(Christie's) **$7,672 £4,950**

ROY PETLEY (b. 1951) – A Summer Afternoon – signed
lower left Roy Petley – oil on board – 24 x 36in.
(Christie's) **$24,332 £15,400**

JOHN FREDERICK PETO – Sustenance, a still life
with oranges and a banana – oil on panel – 12.7 x 25.3cm.
(Sotheby's) **$104,500 £65,723**

**AUGUST XAVER CARL RITTER VON
PETTENKOFEN (Austrian 1822-89)** – A portrait of a
child – oil on canvas – 46 x 39cm.
(Sotheby's) **$11,869 £7,150**

PIERRE PEYRON – Aix 1744-1814 Paris – La Mort
d'Alceste ou L'heroisme de l'amour conjugal – Oil on
canvas – 96.5 x 97cm.
(Sotheby's) **$280,354 £179,714**

SAVATORE PETRUOLO (born 1857) – Returning
home, Naples – signed and dated Napoli 1910 –
30 x 45cm.
(Christie's) **$3,187 £1,980**

ROBERT PHILIPP, NA (Am. 1895-1981) - Study for
"On the balcony" – oil on board – signed Robert Philipp –
titled and dated 1953 on the reverse – 4 x 8in.
(Bruce D. Collins) **$550 £344**

ROBERT PHILIPP (American, 1895-1981) – "Champs
Elesé" (sic) – signed – titled and dated 1974 – oil on
canvas – 21 x 27¹/₄ in.
(Skinner)   **$1,400   £838**

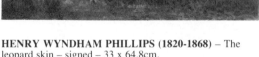

HENRY WYNDHAM PHILLIPS (1820-1868) – The
leopard skin – signed – 33 x 64.8cm.
(Christie's)   **$7,346   £4,620**

THOMAS PHILLIPS, R.A. (1770-1845) – Portrait of
Lieutenant John David Duval (1773-1804) – three quarter
length, standing, wearing uniform of the 19th Light
Dragoons – oil on canvas – 127 x 102cm.
(Sotheby's)   **$33,264   £19,800**

SIR ROBIN PHILIPSON, P.R.S.A., H.R.A., R.S.W. –
Women observed – oil on canvas – 71 x 73cm.
(Sotheby's)   **$6,613   £3,960**

**GIAMBATTISTA PIAZZETTA, Studio of (Pietraossa,
near Venice 1692-1754 Venice)** – A study of two heads,
representing 'Rhetoric' and 'Logic' – on canvas –
43.5 x 36cm.
(Phillips)   **$8,150   £5,000**

PICASSO

PABLO PICASSO – Cruche, Bol et Citron – signed – oil on panel – 64 x 48cm.
(Sotheby's)   **$4,840,000   £3,044,025**

PABLO PICASSO (1881-1973) – Femme à la Broche en Tête de Sphinx – dated upper left 17 Mars 44 – dated again on the reverse 17 Mars 44 – oil on canvas – 80 x 59.7cm.
(Christie's)   **$1,709,950   £1,100,000**

PABLO PICASSO – Au Moulin Rouge – signed – oil on board laid down on cradled panel – 70 x 53.5cm.
(Sotheby's)   **$8,250,000   £5,188,679**

PABLO PICASSO (1881-1947) – Tête de Femme (Portrait de Mlle. Aubrey) – signed upper right Picasso – pastel and pencil on paper – 40 x 29.8cm. – Executed in 1941
(Christie's)   **$255,750   £165,000**

PICKERSGILL

PABLO PICASSO (1881-1974) – Femme attablée – signed upper left Picasso – inscribed and dated on the reverse Vauvenargues 10.4.59 III – oil on canvas – 81 x 100cm.
(Christie's) **$1,402,159 £902,000**

PABLO PICASSO (1881-1973) – Portrait de l'artiste – signed upper left P. Ruiz Picasso – charcoal on paper laid down on board – 47 x 53.2cm. – Drawn in Barcelona, 1899
(Christie's) **$990,000 £620,334**

PABLO PICASSO – Homme et Femme à table: Angel Fernandez de Soto et Son Amie – signed – pastel on paper, laid down on board – 47 x 30.5cm.
(Sotheby's) **$1,540,000 £968,553**

PABLO PICASSO (1881-1973) – Nature morte au Panier de Fruits – signed lower right Picasso – oil on canvas – 73 x 93.5cm.
(Christie's) **$1,453,457 £935,000**

HENRY WILLIAM PICKERSGILL, Follower of – Portrait of George, 11th Earl of Pembroke (1759-1827) – 182.9 x 134.6cm.
(Christie's) **$2,331 £1,430**

PIFFARD

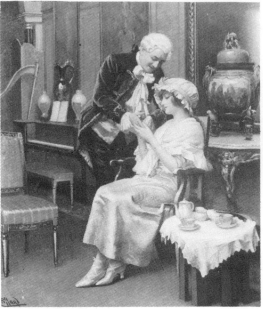

HAROLD H. PIFFARD – Telling his fortune – signed – oil on canvas – 76 x 63.5cm.
(Sotheby's)   **$3,406**   **£2,090**

SERVANDO DEL PILAR - A café scene – signed lower right S. del Pilar – 65 x 53.5cm.
(Christie's)   **$2,775**   **£1,745**

OTTO PILNY (Austrian b. 1866) - A rest en route - signed and dated 1911 - oil on canvas - 120 x 180cm.
(Sotheby's)   **$31,042**   **£18,700**

AUGUSTE DE PINELLI (born 1832) – Flowers for the lady – signed – on panel – 54.5 x 39.5cm.
(Christie's) **$5,456 £3,520**

DOMENICO PIOLA (1628-Genoa-1703) – The creation of man – on canvas – 73.5 x 55cm.
(Phillips) **$6,846 £4,200**

JOHN PIPER, C.H. (born 1903) – Valle Crucis Abbey – signed – inscribed and dated 1940 – on the reverse – oil on linen laid on board – 64 x 76cm.
(Phillips) **$26,080 £16,000**

O*** PINHEIRO – A mother and child – signed – oil on canvas – 108 x 73cm.
(Sotheby's) **$2,838 £1,650**

CAMILLE PISSARRO – Automne, Matin, Temps Gris, Eragny – signed and dated 1900 – oil on canvas – 65 x 81cm.
(Sotheby's) **$2,200,000 £1,383,648**

PISSARRO

CAMILLE PISSARRO – Men unloading a boat – oil on canvas – signed – 19 x 25cm.
(Jean-Claude Anaf) **$231,111 £148,148**

CAMILLE PISSARRO – Les Peupliers, Après-midi à Eragny – signed and dated 99 – oil on canvas – 73 x 92cm.
(Sotheby's) **$2,420,000 £1,522,013**

OROVIDA PISSARRO (1893-1970) – "The Riding Lesson" – signed and dated 1952 – oil on board – 39 x 29½in.
(W. H. Lane & Son) **$4,872 £2,900**

Circle of BONIFAZIO PITATI, called BONIFAZIO VERONESE (1487-1553) – The Holy family with the infant St. John – oil on panel – 49.5 x 65cm.
(Phillips) **$24,300 £15,000**

GIOVANNI BATTISTA PITTONI (1687-Venice-1767) – The continence of Scipio – on canvas – 66 x 96.5cm.
(Phillips) **$252,650 £155,000**

ALFRED PLAUZEAU – Ploughing in springtime – signed – oil on canvas – 48 x 60cm.
(Sotheby's) **$3,406 £1,980**

OGDEN M. PLEISSNER – The Partridge Hunter – signed; also inscribed The Partridge Hunter on the backing – watercolour and gouache on paper – 48.2 x 73.6cm.
(Sotheby's) **$29,700 £18,679**

OGDEN M. PLEISSNER – Red Geraniums - signed; also inscribed Reproduction Rights to the painting expressly reserved by the artist – watercolour and gouache on paper – 45.7 x 71.1cm.
(Sotheby's) **$30,250 £19,025**

NICHOLAS POCOCK (1741-1821) – The defeat of the Dutch fleet off Egerö, Norway, 22 August 1795 – signed l.l: N. Pocock 1796 – oil on canvas – 81.5 x 134.5cm.
(Sotheby's) **$40,656 £24,200**

FRANCESCO PODESTI – King David playing his harp – signed – oil on canvas – 236 x 247.5cm.
(Sotheby's) **$18,700 £11,000**

JAMES POLLARD (1792-1867) – The London-Manchester stage coach 'The Peveril of the Peak' outside the Peacock, Islington – signed J. Pollard 1830 – oil on canvas – 35.5 x 44.5cm.
(Sotheby's) **$17,050 £11,000**

ALFRED POLLENTINE – Ancient Carthage – oil on canvas – 76 x 127cm.
(Sotheby's) **$4,303 £2,640**

HENRI-HORACE ROLAND DE LA PORTE, Circle of (1724-Paris-1793) – A still life with a glass of wine, a plate with half a lemon and sugar cubes standing on a table – on panel – 28 x 23.5cm.
(Phillips) **$7,140 £4,200**

PORTER

MAUD PORTER – A full length Portrait of an Edwardian Lady – pastel on buff paper – signed and dated 1906 – 77.4 x 52.1cm.
(Bonhams) **$214 £140**

JAN PORTIELJE – A young lady with her mandolin – signed l.r. – oil on canvas – unframed – 116.5 x 89.5cm.
(Sotheby's) **$22,704 £13,200**

EDWARD ANTOON PORTIELJE (1861-1949) – The dress makers – signed – 45.7 x 38.2cm.
(Christie's) **$21,979 £14,180**

JOHN FREDERIK PIETER PORTIELJE (1829-1908) – The rose – signed and inscribed ANTWERP – on panel – 60.9 x 49.5cm.
(Christie's) **$20,460 £13,200**

BERNARD POTHAST (British 1882-1966) – The first
step – oil on canvas – signed Pothast lower right –
18 x 22in.
(Bruce D. Collins) **$19,723 £12,100**

JAN FREDERIK PIETER PORTIELJE (1829-1895) –
An oriental beauty – signed and stamped with artist's seal
on the reverse – on panel – 58.5 x 48.5cm.
(Christie's) **$3,188 £1,980**

J. POTTIER (late 19th Century) – A Mediterranean
Street Scene – signed – on panel – 17.5 x 14.5cm.
(Christie's) **$4,427 £2,750**

**HENDRICK GERRITSZ POT (Haarlem 1585 -
Amsterdam 1657)** – Portrait of a lady – bust length,
wearing a golden silk gown with a lace shawl, holding a
pomegranate, a pearl band in her hair – signed with
monogram top right: H.P. – oil on panel – 36.8 x 30.4cm.
(Lawrence) **$28,864 £17,600**

NICOLAS POUSSIN (1594-1665), Circle of – The
Triumph of Neptune and Amphitrite – oil on canvas –
124 x 151cm.
(Phillips) **$6,846 £4,200**

POUSSIN

NICOLAS POUSSIN (Follower of) – The Triumph of Neptune – oil on canvas – 88 x 114cm.
(Phillips) **$2,898 £1,800**

SIR EDWARD JOHN POYNTER, Bt, P.R.A., R.W.S. – Study for "Israel in Egypt" – signed with monogram and dated 1862 – watercolour over pencil – 20 x 42cm.
(Sotheby's) **$6,545 £3,850**

ATTILIO PRATELLA (Italian 1856-1949) – A busy harbour – signed – oil on canvas – 40 x 78cm.
(Sotheby's) **$36,520 £22,000**

ATTILIO PRATELLA (1856-1932) – Fishermen in the bay of Naples – signed – 34.5 x 74cm.
(Christie's) **$16,197 £10,450**

ATTILIO PRATELLA (Italian 1856-1949) – Girls in a poppy field – signed – oil on canvas – 36.5 x 30cm.
(Sotheby's) **$32,868 £19,800**

ATTILIO PRATELLA (1856-1932) – Bringing in the catch, Naples – signed – 38 x 44cm.
(Christie's) **$17,050 £11,000**

MAURICE B. PRENDERGAST (1859-1924) – Figures on the grass – signed Maurice B. Prendergast and dated 1895, l.l. – watercolour and pencil on paper – 25.4 x 34.9cm.
(Sotheby's) **$341,000 £217,197**

MAURICE B. PRENDERGAST (1859-1924) – Canal scene, Venice – signed Prendergast, l.r. – watercolour and pencil on paper – 27.3 x 38.1cm.
(Sotheby's) **$143,000 £91,083**

MAURICE B. PRENDERGAST (1859-1924) – Lady with a red sash – signed Prendergast, l.r. – oil on canvas – 61 x 20.3cm. – Painted circa 1900
(Sotheby's) **$770,000 £490,446**

JOSEF PRESSER (Russian/American, 1914-1967/1907-1967) – Three Girls – signed "Presser" l.l. – watercolour, gouache, pastel and charcoal – 23½ x 17¼in.
(Skinner) **$550 £344**

FRANK CORBYN PRICE – Surrey woodlands – signed, pencil and watercolour heightened with white – 11 x 14in. *(Christie's)* **$1,309 £770**

CARL PROBST (b. 1854) – A Cardinal seated in a pew – signed – on panel – 25.4 x 17.8cm. *(Christie's)* **$1,108 £715**

JOHANNES HENDRIK PRINS (1757-1806) – A woman dressing her children in a chamber – watercolour laid down on card – unframed – and companion – 33 x 26.5cm. *(Phillips)* **$1,932 £1,200**

EDWARD PRITCHETT (fl. 1828-1864) – A view of the Dogana and Santa Maria della Salute, Venice – signed with monogram – 18 x 23cm. *(Christie's)* **$4,198 £2,640**

GIULIO CESARE PROCCACCINI (Bologna circa 1570-1625 Milan) – The Martyrdom of Saint Agnes – on canvas – 123 x 84cm. *(Phillips)* **$244,500 £150,000**

DOD PROCTER, R.A. (1892-1972) – Boy with an Apple – signed – oil on board – 55 x 37cm.
(Phillips) **$30,970 £19,000**

ERNEST PROCTOR, A.R.A., N.E.A.C., I.S. – Mevagissey Harbour, Cornwall – signed and dated '12 – watercolour over pencil – 23 x 34cm.
(Phillips) **$960 £600**

MARGARET FISHER PROUT, A.R.A., R.W.S., R.W.A. (1875-1963) – The Blue Couch – signed – oil on board – 56 x 41cm.
(Phillips) **$5,705 £3,500**

DOD PROCTER, R.A. (1892-1972) – A Mixed Bunch – signed – oil on canvas – 51 x 44cm.
(Phillips) **$27,710 £17,000**

HARALD PRYN – Winter scene – signed – 50 x 70cm.
(P. Herholdt Jensen) **$1,938 £1,189**

PRYN

HARALD PRYN (born 1891) – A wooded winter
landscape – signed and dated Vingenas 1936 –
100 x 134cm.
(Christie's)   **$2,479   £1,540**

HOVSEP PUSHMAN (1877-1966) – Precious
manuscript – signed Pushman, l.r. – oil on panel –
55.2 x 46.3cm.
(Sotheby's)   **$20,900   £13,312**

FRANÇOIS PYCKE (1890-1970) – La Porte ouverte—
De open Deur – signed with monogram lower right – oil on
canvas – 118.2 x 91.4cm.
(Christie's)   **$10,560   £6,600**

FRANÇOIS PYCKE (1890-1970) – Femme au Kimono—Vrouw in Kimono – signed and dated lower right F. Pycke 1922 – the studio stamp on the reverse – oil on canvas – 71.7 x 58.4cm. – Painted in 1922
(Christie's) **$4,928 £3,080**

JAMES PETER QUINN (1871-1951) – An Old Peasant Woman – signed – 60.9 x 50.8cm.
(Christie's) **$1,069 £660**

FRANZ QUAGLIO (1844-1920) – A bay racehorse held by a groom – signed and dated 1876 – 40 x 60cm.
(Christie's) **$6,198 £3,850**

AUGUST QUERFURT (1696-1761) – Peasants resting their horses at a hay trough upon a hill – oil on panel – 16.5 x 23.5cm.
(Phillips) **$6,156 £3,800**

EDOUARD QUITTON – Study of a young lady wearing a lace trimmed sky-blue silk dress, resting on a high back chair – signed and dated 1872 – board – 53 x 40cm.
(Spencer's) **$3,611 £2,300**

RACKHAM

ARTHUR RACKHAM (1867-1939) – An Illustration to Stories of King Arthur: 'King Arthur had hardly spoken, before a white hart ran into the hall' – signed and dated '05 – pencil and watercolour – 8¼ x 6in.
(Christie's)   **$16,137**   **£9,900**

HENRIETTA R. RAE (1859-1928) – Ellen Terry and Henry Irving in Abelard and Heloise – signed – 182 x 136cm.
(Christie's)   **$5,115**   **£3,300**

CASIMIRO RADICE (late 19th Century) - La sagra del paese - signed and dated 78 - 100 x 153cm.
(Christie's)   **$88,660**   **£57,200**

SIR HENRY RAEBURN, R.A., P.R.S.A. (1756-1823) – Portrait of Mrs. John Parish – three quarter length, seated, wearing a white dress with a black sash and green scarf, a landscape beyond – oil on canvas – 127 x 101.5cm.
(Sotheby's) **$71,720   £44,000**

KARL RAHL (1812-1865) – Phoebe and Cupid – signed – unframed – 62 x 50cm.
(Christie's) **$3,188   £1,980**

ATTRIBUTED TO ABRAHAM RAGUENEAU (1623-after 1681) – Portrait of William III, when a boy – half length, wearing armour, and holding a baton – oil on canvas – 74 x 63.5cm.
(Sotheby's) **$11,594   £7,480**

ALLAN RAMSAY (1713-1784) – A portrait of Major Robert Douglas, half length, in the uniform of the 19th Regiment of Foot, later the Green Howards – signed and dated 1754 – painted oval – oil on canvas – 77.5 x 64.7cm.
(Christie's) **$49,896   £29,700**

RAMSAY

JOHAN MATHIAS RANFTL (Austrian 1804-54) –
Two hunters with their spoils playing chess – oil on canvas
– 95 x 110cm.
(Sotheby's) **$12,782 £7,700**

ALLAN RAMSAY (1713-1784) – Portrait of Mrs.
Dundas of Arniston – half length, wearing a red dress
adorned with roses and a black lace shawl and pearl
necklace – inscribed by a later hand with the identity of the
sitter – oil on canvas – in a painted oval – 74.5 x 61.5cm.
(Sotheby's) **$78,430 £50,600**

GUSTAV RANZONI (1868-1956) – The new calf –
signed and dated 1893 – 68.5 x 54.5cm.
(Christie's) **$2,834 £1,760**

ALLAN RAMSAY (1713-1784) – Portrait of Lucy, wife
of Richard Oakeley, Shropshire – half length, wearing a
white dress tied with blue ribbons – oil on canvas laid on
panel – in a painted oval – 76.5 x 62.5cm.
(Sotheby's) **$7,843 £5,060**

HEINRICH RASCH (1840-1913) – On the lagoon,
Venice – signed – on panel – 12.7 x 20.3cm.
(Christie's) **$1,193 £770**

JOHN RATHBONE and GEORGE MORLAND –
Landscape with figures, cattle and goats – oil – signed 'J.
Rathbone & G. Morland' – 34 x 52in.
(Greenslades)   **$18,256   £11,200**

LOUISE RAYNER (1832-1924) - The East Gate,
Warwick – signed – pencil and watercolour heightened
with bodycolour – 15 x 12³/₄in.
(Christie's)   **$17,033   £10,450**

EMILE KARL RAU (born 1858) – The game of cards –
signed – 70 x 55cm.
(Christie's)   **$10,626   £6,600**

JOHAN NEPOMUK RAUCH (Austrian 1804-67) – A
Neapolitan coastal view – signed and dated Naples 1842
oil on canvas – 67 x 104cm.
(Sotheby's)   **$18,260   £11,000**

ODILON REDON – Le Pot de Geraniums – oil on canvas
– 65 x 50cm.
(Sotheby's)   **$990,000   £622,642**

REDPATH

VITTORIO REGGIANINI (Italian b. 1853) – The conversation – signed – oil on canvas – 52.5 x 68.5cm.
(Sotheby's)   **$69,388**   **£41,800**

ANNE REDPATH, R.S.A., A.R.A., A.R.W.S. – White flowers on a black cloth – signed; bears title on a label on the reverse – oil on board – 45 x 56cm.
(Sotheby's)   **$23,881**   **£14,300**

ANNE REDPATH, R.S.A., A.R.A., A.R.W.S. – Village on the coast – signed – watercolour over black chalk – 46 x 57cm.
(Sotheby's)   **$8,082**   **£4,840**

VITTORIO REGGIANINI (b. 1858) – The green dress – signed – 52.7 x 96.2cm.
(Christie's)   **$23,870**   **£15,400**

BABS REDPATH – Autumn table – signed – oil on board – 96.5 x 127cm.
(Sotheby's)   **$5,878**   **£3,520**

CARL REICHERT (1836-1918) – A St. Bernard – signed – on panel – 20.3 x 26cm.
(Christie's)   **$3,740**   **£2,200**

RAMSAY RICHARD REINAGLE, R.A. (1775-1862) – Portrait of two boys – both full length, seated, wearing green and red velvet suits accompanied by their dog, a view of Kirstall Abbey, Yorkshire, and the River Aire beyond – oil on canvas – 100 x 125cm.
(Sotheby's)   **$53,592 £31,900**

PHILIP REISMAN – The Shoe Peddler – signed P. Reisman and dated '38, l.l. – oil on masonite – 45.5 x 35cm.
(Christie's)   **$4,950 £3,094**

REMBRANDT, Manner of – Portrait of an old Man, bust length – oil on panel – 61 x 47cm.
(Bonhams)   **$80,500 £50,000**

REMINGTON

FREDERIC REMINGTON (1861-1909) – Cow Pony –
signed Remington, u.r. – oil on canvas – 50.8 x 60.9cm.
(Sotheby's) **$68,750 £43,790**

FREDERIC REMINGTON (1861-1909) – Attack on the
supply wagons – signed Frederic Remington, l.l. – oil on
canvas – 76.2 x 114.2cm. – Painted circa 1905-1909
(Sotheby's) **$4,730,000 £3,012,739**

PIERRE AUGUSTE RENOIR (1841-1919) – Paysage à
Essoyes – signed lower right Renoir – oil on canvas –
54.5 x 66cm.
(Christie's) **$820,776 £528,000**

PIERRE AUGUSTE RENOIR (1841-1919) – Après le
Bain – signed lower left Renoir – oil on canvas –
56 x 47cm.
(Christie's) **$7,181,790 £4,620,000**

PIERRE AUGUSTE RENOIR (1841-1919) – Tête de
Femme – with signature upper right – oil on canvas –
26 x 19cm.
(Christie's) **$307,791 £198,000**

RENOIR

PIERRE AUGUSTE RENOIR (1841-1919 – Femme de trois-quart – signed lower right Renoir – oil on canvas – 30 x 21.5cm.
(Christie's) **$393,288 £253,000**

PIERRE-AUGUSTE RENOIR – Trois Perdrix – signed - oil on canvas – 32.8 x 41cm.
(Sotheby's) **$550,000 £345,912**

PIERRE AUGUSTE RENOIR (1841-1919) – Paysage de Provence – signed lower right Renoir – oil on canvas – 19.6 x 33.6cm.
(Christie's) **$188,094 £121,000**

PIERRE-AUGUSTE RENOIR – Jeune femme au Corsage rouge – signed – oil on canvas – 65.4 x 54.5cm.
(Sotheby's) **$5,775,000 £3,632,075**

PIERRE-AUGUSTE RENOIR (1841-1919) – Etudes de Tête d'Enfant – signed lower right Renoir – soft pencil on paper – 57.2 x 42.6cm.
(Christie's) **$54,560 £35,200**

PIERRE AUGUSTE RENOIR (1841-1919) – Roses dans un Vase bleu – signed lower left Renoir – oil on canvas – 45 x 37.5cm.
(Christie's) **$649,780 £418,000**

REYNOLDS

SIR JOSHUA REYNOLDS, P.R.A. (1723-1792) -
Portrait of Miss Popham – half length, wearing a white
dress and blue cloak edged with ermine, her left arm
resting on a book – oil on canvas – 75 x 62cm.
(Sotheby's) **$70,224 £41,800**

HENRY MEYNELL RHEAM (1859-1920) – Newlyn
School – Uncle Billie Madder - a bearded gentleman
smoking a pipe before a cottage – signed and dated 1915 –
watercolour – 23 x 14½in.
(W. H. Lane & Son) **$10,080 £6,000**

SIR JOSHUA REYNOLDS, P.R.A. (1723-1792) –
Portrait of Miss Charlotte Fish – three quarter length,
seated, wearing a pink dress with a black shawl and pearl
choker, a landscape beyond – oil on canvas – 127 x 101cm.
(Sotheby's) **$204,600 £132,000**

HENRY MEYNELL RHEAM, R.I. (1859-1920) –
Mother and daughter – watercolour – signed – 10 x 8½in.
(David Lay) **$4,669 £2,900**

LLOBET RIBAS – Reclining nude with mirror – oil on canvas – 73 x 92cm.
(Kunsthaus am Museum) **$2,210 £1,300**

THÉODULE RIBOT (French 1823-91) – The young kitchen maid – signed – oil on canvas – 45 x 37.5cm.
(Sotheby's) **$29,216 £17,600**

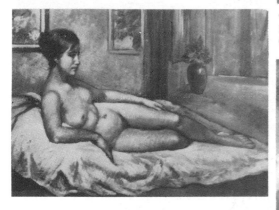

LLOBET RIBAS – Reclining nude – oil on canvas – 73 x 100cm.
(Kunsthaus am Museum) **$1,300 £770**

THÉODULE AUGUSTIN RIBOT (1823-1893) – A woman knitting – signed – 33 x 39.4cm.
(Christie's) **$3,069 £1,980**

PIERRE RIBERA – At the Bal Musette – signed – oil on board – 16 x 24cm.
(Sotheby's) **$11,220 £6,600**

OSCAR RICCIARDI (Italian, b. 1864) – The Bay of Naples with Figures dancing in the Foreground – signed and inscribed 'Napoli' – 40.7 x 61cm.
(Bonhams) **$2,790 £1,800**

RICHARDS

FREDERICK STUART RICHARDSON R.S.A. (1855-1934) – The Morning Catch, Staithes – signed – watercolour over black chalk – 51 x 74cm.
(Phillips) $2,445 £1,500

WILLIAM TROST RICHARDS – Snow Covered Trees – signed Wm. T. Richards and dated 1866, l.l. – oil on canvas laid down on board – 45 x 35cm.
(Christie's) **$176,000 £110,000**

THOMAS MILES RICHARDSON, Jnr. – 'Mount Blanc' – signd and dated 1889 – and indistinctly inscribed on a label on the reverse – 53 x 86cm.
(Anderson & Garland) **$4,080 £2,400**

WILLIAM TROST RICHARDS – Path in the Forest – signed Wm. T. Richards and dated Phil. 1865, l.l. – oil on panel – 46 x 35cm.
(Christie's) **$121,000 £75,625**

HERMAN JEAN JOSEPH RICHIR (Belgian, 1866-1942) – 'La Petite Amazone' (the young horsewoman) – signed – signed and inscribed on label on reverse – 269.2 x 213.4cm.
(Bonhams) **$85,250 £55,000**

RICHTER (1905) – "Young lady holding a bouquet of roses and wearing a feathered hat" – pastel portrait – 27 x 18in.
(Riddetts) **$2,400 £1,500**

HERBERT DAVIS RICHTER – A Still Life with mixed Summer Flowers in a glass Vase beside Oriental Figures on a Table – signed – on canvas – 76 x 63.5cm.
(Bonhams) **$3,160 £2,000**

RICHTER, 19th Century – Szerelmes par – oil on canvas – indistinctly signed – 50 x 36cm.
(Mugyujtok Galeriaja Kft) **$1,297 £786**

MARCEL RIEDER (born 1852) – Scene d'Interieur: sous la lampe – signed – 55 x 45.5cm.
(Christie's) **$4,604 £2,860**

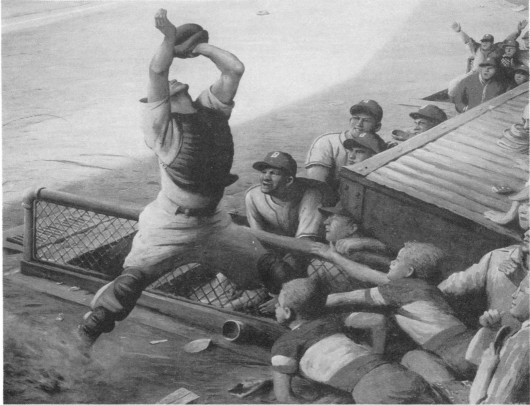

ROBERT RIGGS – Catcher on the Line – signed Riggs, l.r. – oil on panel – 57.5 x 75cm.
(Christie's) **$24,200 £15,125**

REMBRANDT HARMENZ VAN RIJN, After – Self portrait – oil on canvas – 63.5 x 51cm.
(Phillips) **$3,220 £2,000**

JOHN RILEY (1646-1691) – Portrait of Lord Willoughby de Broke (1621-1711) – three quarter length, standing wearing a blue coat and brown mantle – inscribed u.l. : S^r: Rich^d: Verney. L^d: Willoughby de Broke – oil on canvas – in a carved wood frame – 123 x 100.5cm.
(Sotheby's) **$9,377 £6,050**

F. RINALDI (late 19th Century) – The tavern girl –
signed – on panel – 50 x 37cm.
(Christie's)   **$2,479   £1,540**

AIDEN LASSELL RIPLEY (American, 1896-1969) –
Quail Shooting – unsigned – inscribed "...sketch by A.
Lassell Ripley" – watercolour with gouache and graphite
on paper board – 12$^1/_8$ x 18$^1/_2$in.
(Skinner)   **$3,100   £1,938**

JOSEF RIPPL-RONAI (Hungarian 1861-1927) – In the
garden – signed and dated 1919 – oil on canvas – unframed
– 78 x 50cm.
(Sotheby's)   **$45,650   £27,500**

RİPPL-RONAI

BRITON RIVIERE (1840-1920) – Studies of a Jack Russell Terrier – signed with monogram – watercolour and bodycolour – 37 x 53cm.
(Phillips) **$1,011 £620**

JOSEF RIPPL-RONAI (Hungarian 1861-1927) – An elegant lady in a black hat – signed – signed with monogram – oil on canvas – unframed – 41 x 32cm.
(Sotheby's) **$20,086 £12,100**

EDWIN THOMAS ROBERTS – A button short – signed; signed and inscribed with title on the reverse – oil on canvas – 35.5 x 30.5cm.
(Sotheby's) **$3,945 £2,420**

LOUIS RITMAN (1889-1963) – In the garden – signed L. Ritman, l.r. – oil on canvas – 81.3 x 81.3cm.
(Sotheby's) **$110,000 £70,064**

ELIZABETH W. ROBERTS (American, 1871-1927) – Still Life with Orange Chrysanthemums – unsigned – pastels on tan paper – $10^3/_8$ x $8^1/_4$ in.
(Skinner) **$600 £359**

MARKEY ROBINSON – Returning Home from the Market – signed – oil on board – 24 x 49cm.
(Phillips) **$676 £400**

THEODORE ROBINSON (1852-1896) – La Roche-Guyon – signed Th. Robinson, l.r. – pastel and watercolour on paper – 21.0 x 36.8cm. – Executed circa 1891
(Sotheby's) **$71,500 £45,541**

WALFORD GRAHAM ROBERTSON (English, 1867-1948) – A three-quarter length Portrait of a Young Man – signed with monogram and dated 1892 – 101.6 x 50.8cm.
(Bonhams) **$1,008 £650**

EDITH BREAREY ROBINSON (Exh. 1889-93) – The Cottage Garden – signed and dated 1892 – oil on canvas – 25.5 x 30.5cm.
(Phillips) **$1,956 £1,200**

MICHELE ROCCA (Parma 1670/75-1751 Venice) – The mask of truth – on canvas – 66 x 52cm.
(Phillips) **$8,150 £5,000**

ROCHE

ALEXANDER IGNATIUS ROCHE, R.S.A. – A shepherd and his flock – signed – oil on canvas – 72.5 x 98.5cm.
(Sotheby's) **$7,715 £4,620**

ERNEST ROCHER – A young girl reading – signed u.l. and dated '19 – oil on canvas – 64 x 77cm.
(Sotheby's) **$5,676 £3,300**

FERMIN ROCKER – Stepping Out – signed and dated lower left F Rocker 47 – oil on canvas –30 x 24in. – and a print of the same subject – 14³/₄ x 11³/₄in.
(Christie's) **$2,172 £1,375**

NORMAN ROCKWELL – The Wishbone – signed Norman Rockwell, l.l. – oil on canvas – 46 x 42cm.
(Christie's) **$88,000 £55,000**

ALEKSANDR MIKHAILOVICH RODCHENKO (1891-1956) – Photomontage – collection stamp of Dr. Kurt Benedikt on reverse – collage on paper – 39 x 29.5cm. – Executed circa 1920
(Christie's) **$85,008 £52,800**

INGEBORG MARTHA RODE (1865-1932) – The three generations – signed – 112.5 x 83.5cm.
(Christie's) **$3,542   £2,200**

COLIN GRAEME ROE (Late 19th Century) – An Orange Belton English Setter and a Gordon Setter scenting grouse – signed and dated '89 - 40.7 x 61.6cm.
(Christie's) **$4,862   £2,860**

FRED ROE (1899) – 'Checkmate' – Interior Scene with a lady and a gentleman playing chess and an officer looking on – oil – signed – dated and entitled – 17½ x 23in.
(Graves Son & Pilcher) **$4,860   £3,000**

FREDERIC ROE (1864-1947) – Nelson at Church – signed – 49.5 x 65cm.
(Christie's) **$7,346   £4,620**

JAN ROEDE – Springende Meisjes – signed and dated lower right Roëde 46 – and with title on the stretcher – 46 x 55cm.
(Christie's) **$3,026   £1,903**

WILLEM ROELOFS (1822-1897) – A Dutch village in a polder landscape – signed – on panel – 35.5 x 68.5cm.
(Christie's) **$24,794   £15,400**

ROESEN

SEVERIN ROESEN – Tabletop Still Life – signed
Roesen, l.r. – oil on panel – 35 x 45.5cm.
(Christie's) **$28,600 £17,875**

ROIDOT – The chapel at Braine-le-Chateau – mounted
paper – 35 x 47cm.
(Galerie Moderne) **$441 £281**

HENRY LEONIDAS ROLFE – C. Forster – signed –
inscribed with title and indistinctly dated – oil on board –
30.5 x 46cm.
(Sotheby's) **$2,755 £1,650**

CHRISTIAN ROHLFS – Woman and child – signed with
the initials and dated '19 – watercolour and brush and ink
and pencil – 50.7 x 23.5cm.
(Sotheby's) **$22,275 £13,103**

GERARD RÖLING – A still life with fruit, eggs and a
glaze vase on a wooden table – signed with initials and
dated in the centre GR41 – 50 x 67cm.
(Christie's) **$4,035 £2,538**

GEORGE ROMNEY (1734-1802) - Portrait of George Morewood (1720-1792) of Alfreton Park, Derbyshire - full length, standing in a landscape - oil on canvas 203 x 127cm.
(Sotheby's) **$55,440   £33,000**

GEORGE ROMNEY (1734-1802) – Portrait of Mrs. Clay and her son – three-quarter length, seated, wearing a brown dress and a muslin shawl and cap, her child wearing a white dress and blue sash – oil on canvas – 99.5 x 76cm.
(Sotheby's) **$98,890   £63,800**

GEORGE ROMNEY (1734-1802) - Portrait of Elizabeth Grove (1756-1832) - half length - oil on canvas - 76.2 x 62.2cm.
(Sotheby's) **$53,592 £31,900**

GEORGE ROMNEY (1734-1802) – Portrait of a young boy – half length, wearing a red coat and white collar – oil on canvas – 51 x 42cm.
(Sotheby's) **$5,115   £3,300**

ROMNEY

GEORGE ROMNEY (1734-1802) – Portrait of an officer – head and shoulders – a sketch – oil on canvas – 18 x 14cm.
(Sotheby's)   **$8,525**   **£5,500**

GEORGE ROMNEY (1734-1802) – Portrait of Miss Margaret Green – half length, wearing a blue dress with a purple shawl – oil on canvas – 73 x 59cm.
(Sotheby's)   **$20,460**   **£13,200**

ANTON ROOSKENS – Flying animals – 150 x 200cm. – Executed circa 1960
(Christie's)   **$21,185**   **£13,324**

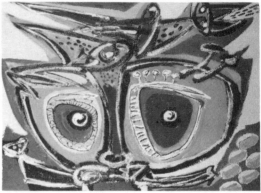

ANTON ROOSKENS – Mask with bird – signed and dated lower right Rooskens 74 – 97 x 130cm.
(Christie's)   **$23,203**   **£14,593**

FÉLICIEN ROPS (1833-1898) – La Femme au Masque – oil on thick paper laid on board – 28 x 13cm.
(Christie's)   **$179,025**   **£115,500**

SALVATOR ROSA, School of (17th Century) – Battle scene – 96 x 150cm.
(P. Herholdt Jensen) **$2,639 £1,619**

ALEXANDER ROSELL – Returning late – signed – oil on canvas – 56 x 76cm.
(Sotheby's) **$2,151 £1,320**

ALEXANDER ROSELL – Who pays? – signed – 56.5 x 76.5cm.
(Christie's) **$2,021 £1,210**

ALEXANDER ROSLIN, Circle of – Portrait of a Lady, half length, wearing a pink and maroon slashed Dress and Cloak, holding a Mask in her Right Hand – oil on canvas – 80 x 63.5cm.
(Bonhams) **$1,449 £900**

W* C* ROSS – Two young Children playing with their Pets in the grounds of a Country House – pencil and watercolour – signed in pencil and dated 1816 – 36.2 x 27.3cm.
(Bonhams) **$642 £420**

PERCIVAL LEONARD ROSSEAU – On the scent –
signed and dated 1919 – oil on canvas – 54.6 x 73.6cm.
(Sotheby's) **$33,000 £20,755**

JACOB VAN ROSSUM (late 19th Century) – Cattle
resting in the shade – signed – signed and inscribed on the
reverse – 60.9 x 81.3cm.
(Christie's) **$1,535 £990**

GEORGES ROUAULT (1871-1958) – Femme assise –
watercolour, gouache and charcoal on paper –
30.5 x 17.7cm.
(Christie's) **$23,870 £15,400**

JAN VAN ROSSUM (Dutch 1630-?) – Portrait of Jasper
Van Lynden, half length, wearing armour – in a painted
oval – signed and indistinctly dated – oil on canvas –
70 x 59cm.
(Phillips) **$4,025 £2,500**

GEORGES ROUAULT (1871-1958) – Auguste: Etude
pour 'Cirque de l'Etoile Filante' – oil and mixed on paper
laid on canvas – 42 x 33.7cm.
(Christie's) **$547,184 £352,000**

W. EDNIE ROUGH (Edinburgh exh. 1926-1935) – The Ferry – signed lower left W. Ednie Rough – watercolour – 35.6 x 48.2cm.
(Lawrence) **$1,118   £682**

CHARLES ROWBOTHAM – Bellaggio – watercolour heightened with bodycolour – signed – inscribed and dated 1883 – 10¹/₂ x 20³/₄in.
(Bearne's) **$2,759   £1,550**

CHARLES ROWBOTHAM – Como – watercolour heightened with bodycolour – signed – inscribed and dated 1885 – 10¹/₂ x 20³/₄in.
(Bearne's) **$2,314   £1,300**

CLAUDE ROWBOTHAM – Picking Blackberries – watercolour – signed – 20¹/₄ x 28¹/₂in.
(Bearne's) **$1,388   £780**

KENNETH ROWNTREE – Fair Isle Jersey – signed with initials – oil on panel – 27 x 19cm.
(Phillips) **$1,920   £1,200**

JULES LE ROY – The cat family – signed – oil on canvas – 73 x 60.5cm.
(Sotheby's) **$7,480   £4,400**

ROY

JULES LE ROY – Cat's cradle – signed – oil on canvas – 24 x 39cm.
(Sotheby's)   **$3,784**   **£2,200**

JULES LE ROY – Two kittens in a basket – signed – oil on canvas – 32 x 39.5cm.
(Sotheby's)   **$5,610**   **£3,300**

PASQUALE RUGGIERO (1851-1916) – A word of advice – signed and inscribed Napoli – 65 x 49cm.
(Christie's)   **$6,820**   **£4,400**

EMIL RUMPF (born 1860) – The arrival – signed and inscribed Cronberg im Taunas – 114 x 178cm.
(Christie's)   **$6,820**   **£4,400**

FERDINAND ROYBET – Admiring his gun – signed – oil on panel – 81 x 53cm.
(Sotheby's)   **$5,676**   **£3,300**

ROBERT RUSS (Austrian 1847-1922) – A garden scene – signed – oil on panel – 17 x 25cm.
(Sotheby's)   **$27,390**   **£16,500**

CHARLES M. RUSSELL (1864-1926) – Pointing out the trail – signed C. M. Russell with skull and dated 1905, l.l. – gouache and watercolour on paper – 33 x 27.3cm. *(Sotheby's)* **$143,000 £91,083**

CHARLES M. RUSSELL (1864-1926) – Return of the war party – signed C. M. Russell with skull – dated 1914 – oil on canvas – 61.6 x 92.1cm. *(Sotheby's)* **$1,100,000 £700,636**

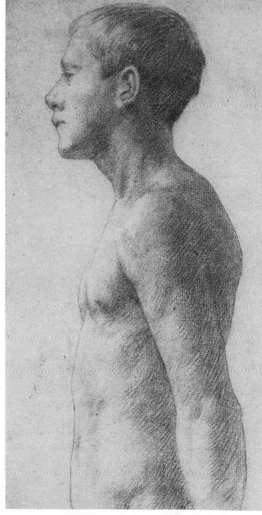

JOHN PETER RUSSELL (1858-1930) – Portrait d'Homme – with inscription R. Tagliana and the number 41 on the reverse – black crayon on white paper watermarked AGM – unframed – 28.3 x 14cm. – Drawn circa 1886
(Christie's) **$2,495 £1,540**

JOHN RUSSELL – Three fresh-run hen salmon on the banks of the Spey near Glen Grant – signed – oil on canvas – 97 x 183cm.
(Christie's) **$31,416 £18,700**

SALOMON VAN RUYSDAEL (Naarden 1600-1670 Haarlem) – Smalships in an estuary with fishermen in a rowing boat hauling in their net – signed with monogram – on panel – 23.5 x 28.5cm.
(Phillips) **$122,250 £75,000**

OTHMAR RUZICKA – A peasant girl with sunflowers
in a garden – signed and dated 1912 – oil on panel –
82 x 69cm.
(Sotheby's)   **$3,740   £2,200**

THÉO VAN RYSSELBERGHE (1862-1926) – Nu Assis
– signed and dated upper right with monogram 08 – oil on
canvas – 100 x 65cm.
(Christie's)   **$44,330   £28,600**

THEO VAN RYSSELBERGHE – Le Canal en Flandre –
signed with monogram and dated 1894 – oil on canvas –
60 x 80cm.
(Sotheby's)   **$770,000   £484,277**

THÉO VAN RYSSELBERGHE (1862-1926) – Vue de
Veere—Zicht op Veere – signed with the artist's
monogram and dated lower left VR 06 – oil on canvas –
59 x 72cm. – Painted in 1906
(Christie's)   **$70,400   £44,000**

HENRY RYLAND – Sunflowers – signed – watercolour
– 30.5 x 20cm.
(Sotheby's)   **$2,805   £1,650**

VALERIUS DE SAEDELEER (1867-1941) – Paysage d'Hiver—Winterlandschap – signed lower right Valerius de Saedeleer – oil on canvas – 40.5 x 50.5cm.
(Christie's) **$42,240 £26,400**

LOUIS SAALBORN – Portrait of a woman, half length, in front of stained glass windows – signed and dated upper right Saalborn 1915 – black chalk and pen and brush and black ink on paper – 70 x 52cm.
(Christie's) **$1,816 £1,142**

CORNELIS SAFTLEVEN (Gorkum 1607-1681 Rotterdam) – An allegory depicting the frailty of life – signed and dated 1663 – on canvas – 60 x 80.5cm.
(Phillips) **$81,500 £50,000**

KATE SADLER (fl. 1878-1894) – News from Abroad – signed and dated '89 – watercolour heightened with bodycolour – 49.5 x 35.5cm.
(Phillips) **$978 £600**

CORNELIS SAFTLEVEN 1607-1681 – Chat dans une Cuisine – oil on panel – 17 x 22cm.
(Sotheby's) **$11,514 £7,400**

SALISBURY

FRANK O. SALISBURY (1874-1962) – Portrait of Miss
Nelson – signed and dated 1928 – oil on canvas –
127 x 101cm.
(Phillips) **$4,564 £2,800**

CARL SALZMANN (1847-1923) – Shipping off a quay –
signed and dated 87 – 52 x 42.5cm.
(Christie's) **$8,525 £5,500**

FRANCISCO RODRIGUEZ SAN CLEMENT – On the
beach – signed – oil on canvas – 67.5 x 87cm.
(Sotheby's) **$4,919 £2,860**

FLORENCE A. SALTMER (fl. 1882-1900) – The
Reapers – signed – oil on canvas – 76 x 51cm.
(Phillips) **$7,172 £4,400**

PAUL SANDBY, R.A. – Sir John Vanbrugh's houses at
Greenwich – pen and grey ink and watercolour over traces
of pencil on laid paper – 14 x 22cm.
(Sotheby's) **$5,610 £3,300**

ALESSANDRO SANI (late 19th Century) – The tethered mouse – signed – 35.6 x 50.8cm.
(Christie's) **$2,557 £1,650**

JOHN SINGER SARGENT (1856-1925) – The little fruit seller – signed John S. Sargent – dated 1879 – and inscribed to my friend Mrs. Contemosi, u.r. – oil on board – 35.6 x 27.3cm.
(Sotheby's) **$258,500 £164,650**

PIETER VAN SANTVOORT, Circle of – Portrait of a young girl, three-quarter length, carrying a basket of fruit – oil on canvas – 76 x 64cm.
(Phillips) **$7,335 £4,500**

EGISTO SARRI, Follower of – Classical Maidens Disporting in a Wooded Glade – 43.2 x 53.3cm.
(Bonhams) **$1,472 £950**

JOHN SINGER SARGENT (1856-1925) – Boy on a rock – watercolour on paper – 40.1 x 53.3cm. – Executed circa 1907-1909
(Sotheby's) **$203,500 £129,618**

ACHILLE VAN SASSENBROUCK – Kerstnacht: a winter landscape with skaters on a frozen river – signed lower right Ach. v. Sassenbrouck – and with inscription and the date 1925 on a label on the reverse – 108 x 130cm.
(Christie's) **$9,585 £6,028**

SAVERIJS

ALBERT SAVERIJS – Village l'hiver – signed lower left Saverijs and inscribed with title on a label on the reverse – on board – 40.5 x 50cm.
(Christie's) **$13,620 £8,566**

HENRY THOMAS SCHAFER – The old cathedral, Limoges – signed and inscribed on the reverse – 25.4 x 20.2cm.
(Christie's) **$919 £550**

HUGH DAVID SAWREY (b. 1923) – Steadying the Leaders, Western Queensland – signed – signed and titled on the stretcher – signed and inscribed on a label on the reverse – 50.8 x 60.9cm.
(Christie's) **$5,346 £3,300**

LUCIEN VICTOR GUIRAND DE SCEVOLA – A still life with flowers and fruit in a bowl – signed – oil on canvas – 54 x 65cm.
(Sotheby's) **$3,740 £2,200**

HENRY SCHAFER (d. c. 1900) – 'Ulm, Bavaria' – signed with monogram and dated 1889 – also signed and inscribed on reverse – oil on canvas – 41 x 30.5cm.
(Phillips) **$1,385 £850**

CORNELIUS VAN DER SCHALCKE (1611-1671) – A dune landscape with figures conversing above a view of Arnhem – oil on panel – 36.2 x 47.8cm.
(Phillips) **$4,830 £3,000**

ANDREAS SCHELFHOUT (Dutch, 1787-1870) – Winter Dutch Coastal Village at Sunset – signed and dated "A. Schelfhout 1855" – oil on panel 16 x 20in.
(Skinner) **$6,000 £3,593**

ALICE SCHILLE (American, d. 1955) – Figures on a Beach – signed "A. Schille" l.r – watercolor on paper – 6$^1/_2$ x 5$^3/_4$ in.
(Skinner) **$5,500 £3,293**

NIELS FREDERIK SCHIOTTZ-JENSEN – Children harvesting – signed and dated 1890 – oil on canvas – 97.5 x 67cm.
(Sotheby's) **$6,433 £3,740**

NIELS FREDERIK SCHIÖTTZ-JENSEN – Ladies on a beach – signed and dated 1916 – oil on canvas – 38.5 x 61cm.
(Sotheby's) **$3,406 £1,980**

HENRI GUILLAUME SCHLESINGER (1814-1893) – Ce n'est pas moi – signed and dated 1872 – 81 x 100.5cm.
(Christie's) **$21,252 £13,200**

SCHLOBACH

WILLY SCHLOBACH (1865-1951) – Les Falaises à Cornwall—Klips te Cornwall – signed with monogram on the stretcher W.S. – oil on canvas – 60.4 x 80cm. – Painted circa 1887-1888
(Christie's) **$10,560 £6,600**

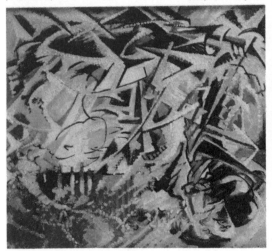

JULES SCHMALZIGAUG (1882-1917) – La Sensation Dynamique de la Danse—Het Dynamische van de Dans – signed and dated lower left Schmalzigaug 1914 – and inscribed with title on a label on the stretcher, Sensation dynamique de la danse interieur de Bar nocturne – oil on canvas – 95 x 105cm. – Painted in Venice in 1914
(Christie's) **$246,400 £154,000**

E* SCHMIDT** – Figures by a windmill in a frozen river landscape – signed l.r. – oil on canvas – 61 x 92cm.
(Sotheby's) **$5,676 £3,300**

EDUARD SCHMIDT – Off the coast – signed – oil on canvas – 69 x 94cm.
(Sotheby's) **$7,854 £4,620**

KARL SCHMIDT-ROTTLUFF – Achillea III – signed and inscribed 6627 – watercolour and brush and indian ink – 69 x 49.5cm.
(Sotheby's) **$29,310 £17,241**

KARL SCHMIDT-ROTTLUFF – Still life with peonies – signed; signed and inscribed Stilleben mit Päonie (5125) – gewachst – on the stretcher – oil on canvas – 65 x 73.5cm.
(Sotheby's) **$99,655 £58,620**

GUIDO SCHMITT (1834-1922) – Portrait of a young boy – signed and dated London 1867 – 50.8 x 38.2cm.
(Christie's) **$2,387 £1,540**

PETRUS SCHOTANUS (1601-circa 1675) – A still life with a duck hanging above a table on which a thrush and a barrel of plums rest – oil on panel – 45 x 32.2cm.
(Phillips) **$2,592 £1,600**

GEORGE SCHMITZ (born 1851) – The port of Hamburg – signed and dated Hamburg 1893 – 24 x 36cm.
(Christie's) **$4,262 £2,750**

PIETER SCHOUBROECK, Attributed to (Hessheim circa 1570-Frankenthal-1607) – Figures on a mountain path leading to a village beyond – on panel – 38.8 x 49.5cm.
(Phillips) **$27,200 £16,000**

WALTER E. SCHOFIELD – North Cliffs – signed; also titled North Cliffs and numbered 147 on the reverse – oil on canvas – 66.0 x 76.2cm.
(Sotheby's) **$12,100 £7,610**

PETER SCHOUBROECK – Helsheimer 1570-1607 Frankenthal – La Fuite de Troie – oil on copper – 23.3 x 29.7cm.
(Sotheby's) **$49,474 £31,714**

SCHOUMAN

AERT SCHOUMAN (1710-1792) – Portrait of a young man, dressed in a green jacket holding a red cape – signed A. Schouman and dated 1734 – oil on canvas – an oval – 81 x 66.5cm.
(Phillips)   **$2,430   £1,500**

GEORG SCHRIMPF – Portrait of a woman – signed and dated '23 – oil on canvas – 54.5 x 47cm.
(Sotheby's)   **$70,345   £41,379**

OTTO MARSEUS VAN SCHRIECK (Nymegan 1619-1678 Amsterdam) – Snakes, a lizard, dragonflies and butterflies clustered around a thistle in a landscape – signed and dated 1664 – on canvas – 69.5 x 53.5cm.
(Phillips)   **$45,640   £28,000**

GEORG SCHRIMPF – Portrait of a woman with a dog – signed and dated '24 – oil on canvas – 75.5 x 58cm.
(Sotheby's)   **$82,068   £48,275**

W*** SCHRODER – Swanage – watercolour – signed
and dated 1890 – 11^1/$_4$ x 15^3/$_4$in.
(Bearne's)   **$836   £470**

LOUIS DE SCHRYVER – Winter time – signed – oil on
canvas – 71.5 x 45cm.
(Sotheby's)   **$10,846   £6,380**

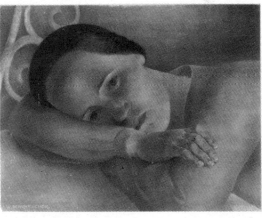

LOUIS DE SCHRYVER – Love – signed – oil on canvas
– 71.5 x 45cm.
(Sotheby's)   **$7,486   £4,400**

WIM SCHUHMACHER – Tête de femme – signed
lower left W. Schuhmacher – and with title on a label on
the stretcher – 35.5 x 45cm.
(Christie's)   **$5,549   £3,490**

SCHUHMACHER

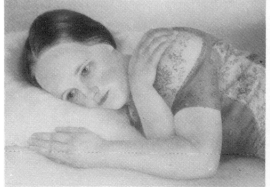

WIM SCHUHMACHER – Vrouwenportret – signed lower left W. Schuhmacher – 33 x 55cm.
(Christie's) **$13,114 £8,248**

JACOBUS SCHUNEMANN (fl. late 17th Century) – Portrait of Robert Makgill, 2nd Viscount Oxenfoord (1651-1705) – half length, wearing a classical tunic and armour – inscribed by a later hand with the identity of the sitter – oil on canvas, in a painted oval – 74 x 62cm.
(Sotheby's) **$9,240 £5,500**

A*** SCHULZE-BIRGE – A portrait of a lady – signed – oil on canvas – 58.5 x 53cm.
(Sotheby's) **$2,081 £1,210**

OTTO SCHULZ-STRADTMANN (German, 20th Century) – A View of Hamburg – signed – 60.3 x 80.7cm.
(Bonhams) **$1,085 £700**

FRANZ SCHUTZE (1842-1907) – Good morning – signed and dated München 1880 – 41.5 x 33.5cm.
(Christie's) **$15,345 £9,900**

JULES SCHYL – Model in black hat – signed and dated – 55 x 47cm.
(Auktionsverket Stockholm)   **$4,734   £2,904**

HENDRIK WILHELM SCHWEICKART (1746-1797) – Jupiter and Ganymede – oil on panel – 205 x 119.5cm.
(Phillips)   **$4,860   £3,000**

CARL SCHWENINGER (1818-1887) – Tete a tete – signed and inscribed Wien – on panel – 33.5 x 26.5cm.
(Christie's)   **$4,959   £3,080**

JOHN SCOTT – A young girl seated in a chair feeding a magpie – signed – watercolour heightened with stopping out – 35.5 x 26cm.
(Woolley & Wallis)   **$1,304   £800**

SCOTT

JOHN SCOTT (1802-1885) – A steam yacht off Whitby
– signed l.r. : J. Scott – oil on canvas – 51 x 74cm.
(Sotheby's)   **$11,935   £7,700**

SAMUEL SCOTT (1703-1772) – The taking of two
French privateers by the Bridgewater and Sheerness in
1745 – Bears later inscription l.c. : The taking of 2 French
Privateers & all their prizes by the Bridgewater and
Sheerness Men of War. 1745 – oil on canvas – 120 x
211cm.
(Sotheby's)   **$73,315   £47,300**

TOM SCOTT – Traquair House, Peebleshire – signed and
dated 1923 – watercolour heightened with stopping out –
45 x 59.5cm.
(Sotheby's)   **$5,878   £3,520**

RICHARD SEEWALD - Church in Ronco – signed and
dated '13 – oil on canvas – 79 x 59cm.
(Sotheby's)   **$10,552   £6,206**

RICHARD SEEWALD – Portrait of Prof. Heinrich –
signed and dated '17 – oil on canvas – 51.5 x 42cm.
(Sotheby's)   **$3,517   £2,069**

ANDRÉ DUNOYER DE SEGONZAC –Nature Morte
avec Vase de fleurs, fruits – signed – India ink and
watercolour on paper – 57 x 77.5cm.
(Sotheby's)   **$52,250   £32,862**

GEORGE SEITZ (1810-1870, Circle of – Still life of
mixed fruit and flowers – with signatute – 42.5 x 52.5cm.
(Christie's)   **$2,387   £1,540**

**ATTRIBUTED TO SIR WILLIAM SEGAR (fl. 1585-
1633)** –Portrait of Gilbert Talbot, 7th Earl of Shrewsbury
(1552-1616) – three quarter length, standing, wearing a
white embroidered doublet with black cap asnd cape and
the Garter Jewel – inscribed u.r. : Aetatis sua 40/ 20: die
novem – oil on panel – unframed – 113.5 x 90.5cm.
(Sotheby's)   **$20,460   £13,200**

F. SERINI (late 19th Century) – The Molo with Doge's
Palace, Venice – signed – 50 x 82cm.
(Christie's)   **$3,751   £2,420**

SERVRANCKX
VICTOR SERVRANCKX (1897-1965) – Opus 40a—
Opus 40a – signed and dated lower right 1922 Servranckx
– inscribed and dated on the stretcher Opus 40a-1922 – oil
on canvas – 39.4 x 69.7cm. – Painted in 1922
(Christie's) **$66,880 £41,800**

JOHN THOMAS SETON (fl. 1758-1806) – Portrait of
the Wallace family – oil on canvas – 132 x 155cm.
(Sotheby's) **$55,440 £33,000**

GINO SEVERINI (1883-1966) – Portrait de monsieur M.
Pautrot – signed lower right G. Severini – pastel on board
– 100 x 76cm.
(Christie's) **$37,510 £24,200**

GEORGES SEURAT (1859-1891) – Paysanne les mains
au sol – conté crayon on paper – 23.5 x 16.5cm. –
Drawn circa 1882
(Christie's) **$407,000 £255,026**

CAROLINE SHARPE, née PATERSON – Under the
laburnum – signed – watercolour heightened with gum
arabic – 27 x 24cm.
(Sotheby's) **$4,675 £2,750**

DOROTHEA SHARP (1874-1955) – Having Fun on the Beach – signed – oil on canvas – 99 x 99cm.
(Phillips) **$73,350 £45,000**

JOSEPH HENRY SHARP (1859-1953) – White Weasel – signed J. H. Sharp, l.l.; also titled White Weasel/Taos and indistinctly inscribed on the backing – oil on canvas – 61.6 x 50.8cm.
(Sotheby's) **$50,600 £32,229**

DOROTHEA SHARP (1874-1955) – Still Life with Spring Flowers – signed – oil on board – 51 x 41cm.
(Phillips) **$8,965 £5,500**

DOROTHEA SHARP (1874-1955) – St Ives School – Front: Children paddling on the foreshore and playing in the waves – Reverse: Children feeding pigeons before an ornate fountain – signed – oil on canvas – 36 x 42in.
(W. H. Lane & Son) **$35,700 £21,000**

SHARP

DOROTHEA SHARP – Picking flowers in the dunes – on board – signed – 12³/₄ x 16in.
(Bearne's)   **$5,070**   **£3,000**

CHARLES L. SHAW – Sitting on a log – signed and dated 1886 – oil on canvas – 51 x 76cm.
(Sotheby's)   **$6,096**   **£3,740**

JOHN BYAM SHAW – 'The Dressmaker's Dummy' – signed and dated 1911 – 32 x 21.5cm.
(Anderson & Garland)   **$646**   **£380**

WALTER SHAW – A High Tide – signed – 67.4 x 102.9cm.
(Bonhams)   **$835**   **£480**

JOHN BYAM LISTON SHAW (1872-1919) – A beauty – signed and dated 1901 – canvas laid down on board – 25.5 x 20cm.
(Christie's)   **$13,992**   **£8,800**

WILLIAM SHAYER, Sr. (English, 1788-1879) – The Supper Break/Landscape with Figures and Plough Horses – signed – oil on canvas – 28 x 36in.
(Skinner)   **$5,500**   **£3,293**

WILLIAM SHAYER, Snr. (1788-1879) – A gypsy
encampment – 46 x 61cm.
(Christie's)   **$7,870   £4,950**

WALTER RICHARD SICKERT, A.R.A. (1860-1942) –
Portrait of Lady Belinda – signed lower right Sickert – oil
on canvas – unframed – 24 x 18$\frac{1}{2}$in.
(Christie's)   **$6,604   £4,180**

WILLIAM SHAYER Snr.(1788-1879) – Outside the inn
– signed – 51 x 76cm.
(Christie's)   **$23,870   £15,400**

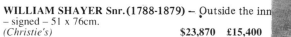

DAVID SHERRIN (English, 19th/20th Century) – Sand
Dunes – signed – 50.8 x 76.2cm.
(Bonhams)   **$341   £220**

SAMUEL SIDLEY (1829-1896) – Primroses and
bluebells – signed – 77 x 64cm.
(Christie's)   **$27,109   £17,050**

SIEBERT

EDWARD SELMAR SIEBERT (American, 1856-1938) – "Summer Afternoon at Chesapeake Bay" – signed and dated "E.S. Siebert May 1927" l.r. – oil on canvas – 26³/₄ x 32⁵/₈ in.
(Skinner) **$18,000 £10,778**

PAUL SIGNAC (1863-1935) – Les Quais (Le Phare), St. Tropez – signed lower right P. Signac – oil on canvas – 18¹/₂ x 21⁵/₈in.
(Christie's) **$1,538,955 £990,000**

PAUL SIGNAC (1863-1935) – Le Pont Marie, Paris – signed and dated lower right P. Signac 1933 – oil on canvas – 46 x 55cm.
(Christie's) **$820,776 £528,000**

PAUL SIGNAC (1863-1935) – Le Café du Casino, Vaison-la-Romaine – the studio stamp lower right P. Signac (L. 2285b) – inscribed and dated lower left Vaison Avril 33 – indistinctly inscribed lower right – watercolour and pencil on paper – 29 x 43.8cm. – Executed in 1933
(Christie's) **$40,920 £26,400**

MAURICE SIJS – A view of the Leie with a moored sailing boat – signed and dated lower right Maurice Sijs 1909 – 80.5 x 100cm.
(Christie's) **$30,264 £19,034**

MAX SILBERT (French, b. 1871) – A Girl reading by Lamplight – signed – 40 x 50.8cm.
(Bonhams) **$1,085 £700**

FRANCIS A. SILVA (1835-1886) – Seascape at sunset –
signed F. A. Silva and dated '74, l.r. – oil on canvas –
35.5 x 66.0cm.
(Sotheby's)   **$60,500   £38,535**

LUCIEN SIMON – The swimming race – signed – oil on
canvas – 60 x 89cm.
(Sotheby's)   **$9,460   £5,500**

FRANCESCO SIMONINI (1686-1753) – A cavalier
mounted upon a prancing horse – oil on canvas – 24.7 x
16.5cm.
(Phillips)   **$3,078   £1,900**

ALFONSO SIMONETTI (1840-1892) - A tinker; and gypsies - signed - inscribed on the reverse -
on panel - 21.6 x 34.3cm.
(Christie's)   **$1,534   £990**

SIMONSEN

NIELS SIMONSEN (Danish 1807-85) – Ship ahoy! – signed and dated 1878 – oil on canvas – 34 x 42cm.
(Sotheby's) **$18,260 £11,000**

CHARLES WALTER SIMPSON – 'Finding the scent -
vale of Belvoir' – signed and inscribed – 23.5 x 32.5cm.
(Anderson & Garland) **$1,190 £700**

CHARLES WALTER SIMPSON (1855-1971) – Ponies
by a river – watercolour – signed – 8 x 10½in.
(David Lay) **$1,007 £650**

ALFRED SISLEY – Le Barrage du Loing-peniches –
signed and dated 85 – oil on canvas – 46 x 55cm.
(Sotheby's) **$1,430,000 £899,371**

ALFRED SISLEY (1839-1899) – Bords de Seine, Saint-Cloud – signed and dated lower left Sisley 79 – oil on canvas – 38 x 46cm.
(Christie's) **$495,885 £319,000**

LAURENCE P. SISSON (American, b. 1928) – "Ode to Grieg"/Winter Harbor – unsigned – oil on masonite – 10$^{1}/_8$ x 14$^{1}/_4$ in.
(Skinner) **$1,500 £898**

ALFRED SISLEY (1839-1899) – La Plaine de Veneux—Vue de Sablons – signed lower right Sisley – oil on canvas – 38.1 x 55.2cm.
(Christie's) **$307,791 £198,000**

NOEL SLANEY, R.S.W. – In the studio – signed – oil on board – unframed – 76 x 102cm.
(Sotheby's) **$1,469 £880**

ALFRED SISLEY – Moret-sur-Loing – signed - oil on canvas – 65 x 92cm. – painted in 1891
(Sotheby's) **$2,530,000 £1,591,195**

CHARLES H. SLATER (fl. 1860-1870) – A Still Life of Plums, an Apple and Grapes on a bank – signed – watercolour and bodycolour – 22.5 x 33.5cm.
(Phillips) **$848 £520**

STEPHEN SLAUGHTER (1697-1765) – Portrait of two young girls – half length, both wearing pink dresses, one with a white lace cap, the other holding a rose – oil on canvas – 62.5 x 75cm.
(Sotheby's) **$9,240 £5,500**

JOHN SLOAN (1871-1951) – Rocks and Weeds, Gloucester – signed John Sloan, l.r.; also titled Rocks and Weeds and inscribed John Sloan/Gloucester, 1914 on the reverse – oil on canvas – 50.8 x 61.0cm.
(Sotheby's) **$34,000 £21,656**

JOHN SLOAN (1871-1951) – Hotel Dance, Santa Fe – signed John Sloan, u.r.,; also titled Hotel Dance in Santa Fe – dated 1919 – oil on canvas – 50.8 x 61.0cm.
(Sotheby's) **$115,500 £73,567**

JOHN SLOAN (1871-1951) – Two little girls – signed
John Sloan, l.r. – oil on canvas – 50.8 x 61.0cm.
(Sotheby's) **$44,000 £28,025**

JAN SLUIJTERS – Portrait of a lady with a hairband –
signed (in monogram) and dated lower right 10 –
35.7 x 32.4cm.
(Christie's) **$42,976 £26,966**

JOHN SLOAN (1871-1951) – Passing through Gloucester
– signed John Sloan and dated '17, l.l; also signed John
Sloan and titled Passing through Gloucester on the
stretcher – oil on canvas – 61.6 x 51.4cm.
(Sotheby's) **$209,000 £133,121**

JAN SLUIJTERS – Maannacht – signed and dated upper
left Jan Sluijters 12 – 80 x 126cm.
(Christie's) **$479,193 £301,379**

JAN SLUIJTERS – Café de nuit – signed lower left J.
Sluijters – on canvas laid down on board – 39.5 x 23cm.
(Christie's) **$8,071 £5,076**

SLUIJTERS

JAN SLUIJTERS – A winter landscape with trees along a country road – signed lower right Jan Sluijters – 40.4 x 50.5cm.
(Christie's) **$37,831 £23,793**

JAN SLUIJTERS – Portrait of a lady in a yellow dress, standing full length, in front of a white cane-chair – signed and dated upper right Jan Sluijters 11 – 53.5 x 50cm.
(Christie's) **$171,501 £107,862**

THEO VAN SLUYS (Belgian, 19th Century) – Hay Manger with Sheep and Hens – signed – oil on canvas – 16 x 23$^{1}/_{4}$ in.
(Skinner) **$3,500 £2,096**

JAN SLUIJTERS – Portrait of the wife of the artist – signed and dated upper right Jan Sluijters 1936 – 127 x 95.5cm.
(Christie's) **$16,142 £10,152**

R. BORLASE SMART R.O.I., R.B.A., R.W.A., R.B.C., S.G.A. (1881-1947) – "St. Michael's Mount from Marazion marshes" – oil on canvas – signed – artist's label to reverse – 17$^{1}/_{2}$ x 23$^{1}/_{2}$in.
(David Lay) **$4,030 £2,600**

FRANS SMEERS (1873-1960) – Fillette au Seau – signed and dated lower right Fr. Smeers 06 – oil on canvas – 72 x 57.5cm.
(Christie's)   **$20,460   £13,200**

GUSTAVE DE SMET (1877-1943) – La jeune Paysanne—Jonge Boerin – signed lower left Gust De Smet – oil on panel – 66.7x 48.2cm. – Painted circa 1935
(Christie's)   **$96,800   £60,500**

GUSTAVE DE SMET (1877-1943) – Paysage d'Hiver—Winterlandscap - signed lower left Gust. de Smet – oil on canvas – 30.5 x 40.6cm.
(Christie's)   **$14,080   £8,800**

GUSTAVE DE SMET (1877-1943) – Paysage Nocturne—Nachtlandschap - signed lower right – oil on canvas – 55 x 65cm. – Painted in 1917
(Christie's)   **$70,400   £44,000**

GUSTAVE DE SMET (1877-1943) – La Ferme Blanche—De Witte Hoeve – signed lower left Gustave De Smet – oil on canvas – 57.2 x 80cm. – Painted circa 1910
(Christie's)   **$56,320   £35,200**

LEON DE SMET – Still life with flowers on a table by a window – signed and dated 1920 – 24³/₄ x 29³/₄in.
(Bearne's)   **$40,750   £25,000**

SMET

LÉON DE SMET – Trees along a road – signed lower right Léon de Smet – 55 x 65cm.
(Christie's)   **$4,792   £3,014**

LEON DE SMET – A still life with dahlias in a vase and a Chinese sugar-bowl, on a table – signed and dated lower left Leon de Smet 1926- 71 x 80cm.
(Christie's)   **$55,486 £34,897**

LÉON DE SMET (1881-1966) – La petite Grisette—Kleine Grisette – signed with monogram and dated LDS 1917 –signed again and inscribed on an old label attached to the stretcher L. de Smet La petite grisette – oil on canvas – 71.2 x 55.8cm. – Painted in 1917
(Christie's)   **$66,880   £41,800**

LÉON DE SMET (1881-1966) – L'Intérieur de la Chaumiére—Bungalowinterieur – signed lower left Leon de Smet – oil on canvas – 68.8 x 79.4cm. – Painted circa 1946
(Christie's)   **$24,640   £15,400**

JAMES SMILLIE – Madison Square Garden – oil on canvas – 101.7 x 61.1cm.
(Christie's)   **$20,900   £13,062**

CARLTON ALFRED SMITH (1853-1946) – The broken vase – signed and dated 1886 – pencil and watercolour – 41.1 x 30.5cm.
(Christie's)   **$3,407**   **£2,090**

ROBERT SMIRKE, R.A. (1753-1845) – The fortune teller – oil on canvas – 118.5 x 94.5cm.
(Sotheby's)   **$11,082**   **£7,150**

CARLTON ALFRED SMITH – A coin for the money box – signed – watercolour over pencil heightened with touches of bodycolour – 27 x 39.5cm.
(Sotheby's)   **$5,984**   **£3,520**

CARLTON A. SMITH – Cottage interior with a lady sitting in contemplation, a letter in her lap – oil - signed – 11 x 9in.
(Graves Son & Pilcher)   **$5,508**   **£3,400**

CARLTON ALFRED SMITH –Shrimps – signed – watercolour – 38 x 26cm.
(Sotheby's)   **$9,724**   **£5,720**

SMITH

GEORGE SMITH (1870-1934) – Feeding the Cattle –
signed lower right George Smith – oil on canvas –
28 x 35½in.
(Christie's) **$4,866 £3,080**

FRANCIS HOPKINSON SMITH (1838-1915) –
Courtyard scene, Inn of William the Conqueror – signed
F. Hopkinson Smith, l.l. – gouache, watercolour and
charcoal on paper – 68.5 x 48.2cm.
(Sotheby's) **$11,000 £7,000**

GEORGE SMITH of CHICHESTER (1714-1776) –
Winter landscape with figures and cattle beside a frozen
stream – signed l.l: G. Smith – oil on canvas – 43 x 62cm.
(Sotheby's) **$14,414 £8,580**

GEORGE SMITH (1829-1901) – Moment of suspense –
signed and dated 1861 – on panel – 40.5 x 35.5cm.
(Christie's) **$12,593 £7,920**

J*** SMITH – Plas Newydd, The Menai Straits - signed
and inscribed on the reverse – 27 x 38cm.
(Anderson & Garland) **$476 £280**

JAMES BURRELL SMITH – Bridge over a gorge –
watercolour heightened with bodycolour – signed and
dated 1895 – 13 x 8³/₄in.
(Bearne's)   **$462**   **£260**

JESSIE WILCOX SMITH (American, 1863-1935) –
"The Grappe (sic) Arbour" – signed 'Jessie Wilcox Smith'
– identified on label on the reverse – oil on charcoal on
board – 25³/₄ x 18¹/₄in.
(Skinner)   **$25,000**   **£15,337**

JESSIE WILCOX SMITH – Rebecca of Sunny Brook
Farm – signed Jessie Wilcox Smith, l.l. – oil and charcoal
on board – 46.7 x 41.6cm.
(Christie's)   **$16,500**   **£10,312**

GEORGE SMITH – Feeding kittens – signed and dated
1875 – oil on panel – 19 x 16cm.
(Sotheby's)   **$2,689**   **£1,650**

SMITH

LOUIS SMITS (mid 19th Century) – A Dutch winter landscape with skaters on a frozen river – signed and dated '60 – 61.5 x 88cm.
(Christie's) $49,588 £30,800

SIR MATTHEW SMITH (1879-1959) – Resting Woman – signed with initials – oil on canvas – 51 x 41cm.
(Phillips) $11,410 £7,000

PIETER SNAYERS, Attributed to (Antwerp 1592-circa 1666 Brussels) – An extensive river landscape with figures on a path, a large chateau in the distance – on canvas – 133 x 183cm.
(Phillips) $8,500 £5,000

SAMUEL SMITH of Worcester (fl. 1811-1838) – A cottage interior with a selection of Worcester 18th century porcelain and a spode blue and white printed tureen – signed and dated 1839 – 38 x 33cm.
(Christie's) $3,751 £2,420

ISAAC SNOWMAN – Portrait of a lady, identified as Madeleine Lemaire – signed and dated 1918 – oil on canvas – 91.5 x 72.5cm.
(Sotheby's) $3,945 £2,420

ANDREA SOLDI (c. 1703-1771) – Portrait of a
gentleman, said to be General Wade – full length, seated,
wearing a blue coat with a red waistcoat – oil on canvas –
164 x 134cm.
(Sotheby's) **$10,230   £6,600**

PAUL VAN SOMER (c. 1577-1621), Attributed to –
Portrait of Henry Brooke, 8th Baron Cobham (1545-1619)
– full length, standing, wearing Garter robes – oil on
canvas – 192.5 x 113cm.
(Sotheby's) **$22,176   £13,200**

SOLOMON JOSEPH SOLOMON, R.A. (1860-1927) –
Portrait of the sculptor George Frampton, as a student
(1860-1928) – 76 x 63.5cm.
(Christie's) **$4,547   £2,860**

THOMAS JACQUES SOMERSCALES (1842-1927) –
A panoramic view of Robin Hood Bay – signed and dated
1918 – 39 x 48cm.
(Christie's) **$3,148   £1,980**

SOMOV

KONSTANTIN ANDREEVICH SOMOV (1869-1939)
– Harlequin and Death – signed in Cyrillic and dated (in ink) top right corner K. Somov 1918 – pencil, pen and ink and watercolour on paper – 28.7 x 22.4cm.
(Christie's)   **$8,501   £5,280**

ROGER SOMVILLE – Figure monumentale 'au' Femme – signed upper right Somville – and signed again and dated 1988 and inscribed with title on the reverse – unframed – 100 x 80.5cm.
(Christie's)   **$5,549   £3,490**

KONSTANTIN ANDREEVICH SOMOV (1869-1939)
– Bathers in the Sun – signed and dated lower left C. Somov 1931 – pencil, watercolour and bodycolour on paper – 25 x 20.5cm.
(Christie's)   **$21,252   £13,200**

WILLIAM SONMANS (fl. 1670s-1708) — Portrait of James Stuart, the Old Pretender, when a boy — three quarter length, standing in a landscape, wearing a red coat and a green cloak — signed W. Sonmans — oil on canvas — 124 x 100cm.
(Sotheby's)   **$18,480 £11,000**

WILLIAM LOUIS SONNTAG – Androscoggin, New Hampshire – signed W. L. Sonntag, l.l. – oil on canvas – 44.5 x 77.5cm.
(Christie's)   **$26,400**   **£16,500**

ISAAK SOREAU (Active in Hanau 1620/38) – A still life of grapes, oranges and peaches in a porcelain bowl upon a table, fruit and a rose rest nearby – on panel – 46 x 54cm.
(Phillips)   **$45,640**   **£28,000**

JOSEPH EDWARD SOUTHALL, R.W.S. – Notre Dame – signed with monogram and dated 1929 – watercolour over pencil – 22.5 x 16.5cm.
(Phillips)   **$4,640**   **£2,900**

FRANK SOUTHGATE – Shellduck and others on a Seashore – monotone watercolour – 14 x 23in.
(G. A. Key)   **$2,558**   **£1,650**

JOHN BALLOCH SOUTER – A Still Life with two Roses in a pewter Vase – signed – on board – 45.5 x 35.5cm.
(Bonhams)   **$711**   **£450**

CHAIM SOUTINE (1893-1943) – La Boulangère – signed lower right C. Soutine – oil on panel – 51.5 x 52.5cm.
(Christie's)   **$410,388**   **£264,000**

SOYER

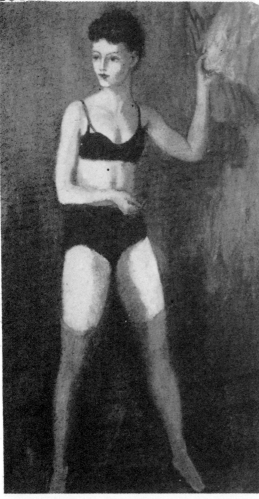

RAPHAEL SOYER (1899-1987) – Woman in slip –
signed Raphael Soyer, l.r. – oil on canvas – 81.2 x 66.0cm.
– Painted in 1963
(Sotheby's) **$15,400 £9,808**

ISAAC SOYER – Red Stockings – signed Isaac Soyer, l.r.
– oil on canvas – 71.4 x 38.2cm.
(Christie's) **$4,400 £2,750**

MOSES SOYER – Dancers in Rehearsal – signed M.
Soyer and dated 51, l.l. – oil on canvas – 76.2 x 91.4cm.
(Christie's) **$16,500 £10,312**

RAPHAEL SOYER - Model with Folded Arms – signed
Raphael Soyer, l.r. – oil on canvas – 50.8 x 40.1cm.
(Christie's) **$11,000 £6,875**

RAPHAEL SOYER (1899-1987) – Broadway and
Fourty-Second Street – signed Raphael Soyer and dated
1935, l.r. – oil on canvas – 52.1 x 43.2cm.
(Sotheby's) **$46,750 £29,777**

RUSKIN SPEAR, R.A. (born 1911) – Hammersmith
Bridge – signed – oil on canvas – 102 x 60cm.
(Phillips) **$19,560 £12,000**

ARTHUR PRINCE SPEAR (American, 1879-1959) –
Twilight Reverie – signed – oil on canvas – 31 x 26in.
(Skinner) **$2,200 £1,317**

RUSKIN SPEAR – Theatre Royal, York – signed – oil on
canvas – 63.5 x 76cm.
(Woolley & Wallis) **$5,705 £3,500**

SPENCELAYH

CHARLES SPENCELAYH – An apple a day – signed –
oil on panel – 23.5 x 18cm.
(Sotheby's)   **$32,274   £19,800**

CHARLES SPENCELAYH – Luxuries – signed – oil on
canvas – 30.5 x 25.5cm.
(Sotheby's)   **$30,481   £18,700**

CHARLES SPENCELAYH - True to his colours - signed - oil on canvas - 25.5 x 30.5cm.
(Sotheby's)   **$29,584   £18,150**

LILLY MARTIN SPENCER – The Picnic – signed Lilly
M. Spencer and dated 1856, l.l. – oil on canvas –
31.1 x 41.2cm.
(Christie's)   **$12,100**   **£7,562**

LÉON SPILLIAERT (1881-1946) – P. G. van Hecke et
Norine—P. G. van Hecke en Norine – signed and dated
lower right Léon Spilliaert 20 – pastel and thick gouache
on paper – 170 x 120cm.
(Christie's)   **$176,000**   **£110,000**

LEON SPILLIAERT (1881-1946) – Rachel – signed
lower left Spilliaert and dated upper left 1909 – pastel and
watercolour on paper – 76 x 46cm. – Executed in 1909
(Christie's)   **$68,200**   **£44,000**

LÉON SPILLIAERT (1881-1946) – Le Paquebot—
Stoomboot – signed and dated lower left L. Spilliaert 09 –
watercolour and coloured crayons on paper – 60 x 70cm. –
Executed in 1909
(Christie's)   **$132,000**   **£82,500**

SPILLIAERT

LÉON SPILLIAERT (1881-1946) – Enfant et Chats—
Kind met Katten – signed and dated Léon Spilliaert 1906 –
signed and dated again on the backboard Léon Spilliaert 20
Janvier 1906 – pastel and watercolour on paper –
48.9 x 38.7cm.
(Christie's) $42,240 £26,400

LÉON SPILLIAERT (1881-1946) – Le Phare
d'Ostende—De Vuurtoren van Oostende – signed and
dated lower left L. Spilliaert '08 – black wash and coloured
crayons heightened with white on paper – 64.6 x 49.5cm. –
Executed in 1908
(Christie's) $96,800 £60,500

CARL SPITZWEG (1808-1885) – Heuernte im Gebirge
– signed with rhombus monogram – 54.5 x 32cm.
(Christie's) $238,700 £154,000

JOHANNES FRANCISCUS SPOHLER (1853-1894) –
A Dutch street scene possibly near the Zuiderkerk,
Amsterdam – signed – on panel – 20 x 16cm.
(Christie's) $6,021 £3,740

LEONARD RUSSELL SQUIRRELL – 'Christmas
morning over Durham Cathedral' – signed and on the
reverse inscribed – 29.5 x 45cm.
(Anderson & Garland) $3,178 £1,950

HARRY STANNARD – Dusk – watercolour – signed –
11½ x 19¾in.
(Bearne's) **$1,157 £650**

NICOLAS DE STAEL (1914-1955) – Mer et nuages –
signed bottom right Stael – signed again and dated on the
reverse Staël 1953 – oil on canvas – 100 x 73cm. –
Painted in 1953
(Christie's) **$1,210,000 £758,186**

HENRY STANNARD – A shepherd with his flock at
sunset - signed – watercolour heightened by scratching out
– 33.75 x 49cm.
(Woolley & Wallis) **$2,295 £1,350**

GEORGE CLARKSON STANFIELD – A North Italian
lake – signed – oil on canvas – 43 x 63cm.
(Sotheby's) **$6,455 £3,960**

HENRY STANNARD (1844-1920) – Grandfathers
cottage; and A cottage garden – signed – pencil and
watercolour heightened with white – 23.4 x 33.7cm.
(Christie's) **$3,048 £1,870**

HENRY JOHN SYLVESTER STANNARD – Late
afternoon glow at Risely, Bedfordshire – signed –

JOHN RODDAM SPENCER STANHOPE (1829-1908)
– The Mill – watercolour and bodycolour – 40 x 60cm.
(Phillips) **$4,890 £3,000**
watercolour heightened with bodycolour and white –
unframed – 11 x 15in.
(Christie's) **$1,496 £935**

STANNARD

HENRY JOHN SYLVESTER STANNARD – Henley-on-Thames, Oxfordshire – signed and inscribed – watercolour over pencil – 17 x 24.5cm.
(Sotheby's)   **$1,964**   **£1,155**

LILIAN STANNARD – Spring Blossom in a garden at Elstow – signed; bears title on a label attached to the backboard – watercolour heightened with white – 25.5 x 35.5cm.
(Sotheby's)   **$8,976**   **£5,280**

LILIAN STANNARD (1877-1944) – A garden path with a pagoda covered in pink roses – signed – pencil and watercolour heightened with white – 25.3 x 34.4cm.
(Christie's)   **$5,738**   **£3,520**

HENRY SYLVESTER STANNARD – A Rectory garden – signed – watercolour over pencil heightened with bodycolour – 33 x 23cm.
(Sotheby's)   **$5,049**   **£2,970**

LILIAN STANNARD (1884-1944) – The Woodland Express – signed – watercolour and bodycolour – 22 x 32cm.
(Phillips)   **$554**   **£340**

WILLIAM JOHN STANNARD – Trompe L'Oeuil – signed and dated 1857 – mixed media – 40 x 32cm.
(Sotheby's)   **$2,805**   **£1,650**

JAN ADRIAENSZ VAN STAVEREN (1625-LEYDEN-1668) – A huntsman resting with his dog at the foot of a tree – on panel – 31.8 x 24.3cm.
(Phillips)   **$14,670   £9,000**

EDWIN STEELE (English, 19th Century) – Still Life with Tulips, Lilies & Fruit – signed and dated "E. Steele 1894" – oil on canvas – 24 x 20in.
(Skinner)   **$12,000   £7,186**

HENDRICK VAN STEENWYCK II, Attributed to (Frankfurt 1580-1649 London) – Saint Jerome in his study – on copper – 10.5 x 12.5cm.
(Phillips)   **$7,650   £4,500**

JOSEPH STELLA – Still Life with Chrysanthemums and Goldfish – signed Joseph Stella, l.l. – oil on canvas – 61 x 51cm.
(Christie's)   **$2,750   £1,718**

PHILIP WILSON STEER, O.M. – The Quayside – signed and dated 1930 – watercolour – 23 x 31cm.
(Phillips)   **$1,217   £720**

STEER

PHILIP WILSON STEER, O.M. – The Old Tin Mine –
signed and dated 1932 – watercolour – 23 x 31cm.
(Phillips) **$980 £580**

G* TERRANCE STEPHENSON (English, Exh. 1906-14) – La Chaumière – signed and dated 1908 – inscribed
on label on reverse – 80.7 x 64.8cm.
(Bonhams) **$1,163 £750**

CARL STEFFECK (1818-1890) – An arab horseman –
signed – 33 x 26cm.
(Christie's) **$2,728 £1,760**

**HANS VON STEGMANN UND STEIN (German, b.
1858)** – Crow Shooting – signed – 71 x 120cm.
(Bonhams) **$1,085 £700**

**CARL AUGUSTE VON STEUBEN (German 1788-
1856)** – Mother and child – signed – oil on canvas –
72.5 x 58.5cm.
(Sotheby's) **$12,782 £7,700**

GEORGE STEVENS – Snipe – signed and dated 1816 – oil on canvas – 42 x 53cm.
(Sotheby's)   **$4,776**   **£2,860**

WILLIAM LESTER STEVENS (American, 1888-1969) – Winter in New England – signed and dated "W. Lester Stevens 1921" – oil on canvas – 25 x 29³/₄in.
(Skinner)   **$3,000**   **£1,875**

WILLIAM LESTER STEVENS (American, 1888-1969) – Farm House in Shade, Autumn – signed and inscribed "W. Lester Stevens N.A." – oil on canvas – 20 x 24in.
(Skinner)   **$800**   **£500**

FRANK ALGERNON STEWART – The Cattistock Hunt on the Scent – signed also inscribed Lancombe Gorse – also annotated verso with details of the landmarks – watercolour and bodycolour – 26.5 x 38cm.
(Phillips)   **$5,868**   **£3,600**

WILLIAM LESTER STEVENS (American, 1888-1969) – The Hayfield – signed "W. Lester Stevens" l.r. – oil on canvas – 24 x 30in.
(Skinner)   **$2,800**   **£1,750**

WALTER FRYER STOCKS – A ruined abbey – signed and dated 1876 – 37.5 x 59cm.
(Anderson & Garland)   **$918**   **£540**

STOLL

LEOPOLD STOLL – A still life of fruit and a bird – signed and dated 1841 – oil on board – 38 x 51cm.
(Sotheby's) **$4,675 £2,750**

SEBASTIAN STOSKOPFF, Attributed to – A Vanitas still life with a bible, skull cluster column candlestick, turret clock and three die on a chair and a calendar pinned to a wall – oil on canvas – 50.8 x 59.6cm.
(Christie's) **$17,556 £10,450**

CLAUDE STRACHAN - Girl with puppy and kitten outside the cottage gate – signed – 6³/₄ x 10in.
(Outhwaite & Litherland) **$5,184 £3,200**

WILLIAM STRANG, R.A., R.E., P.I.S. (1859-1921) – A Summer's Day, Jersey – oil on canvas – 45.7 x 53.3cm.
(Christie's) **$8,316 £4,950**

EDWARD STOTT, A.R.A. (1859-1918) – Connie – inscribed centre left Connie – dated centre right Mars 95 – black crayon, coloured chalks and pastel – unframed – 15¹/₂ x 10¹/₂in.
(Christie's) **$729 £462**

ROGER STREBELLE (1880-1959) – Paysage vu d'un Balcon—Landschap vanaf een Balkon – signed and dated lower left R. Strebelle 1914 – oil on canvas – 26 x 16in. – Painted in 1914
(Christie's) **$8,800 £5,500**

SIR ARTHUR ERNEST STREETON (1867-1943) –
The Creek – signed – 51.1 x 76.8cm.
(Christie's)   **$35,640   £22,000**

FRANCIS STRINGER (fl. late 18th Century) – Samuel
Frith with his huntsmen, Jack Owen, out hunting with his
pack, Chapel-en-le-Frith, Derbyshire – oil on canvas -
155 x 239cm.
(Sotheby's)   **$48,048   £28,600**

PHILIP EUSTACE STRETTON (fl. 1884-1904) – The
best friends — A Pekingese, a German Shepherd and a
terrier – signed and dated 1918 – 76 x 63.5cm.
(Christie's)   **$6,545   £3,850**

FRANCIS STRINGER (fl. 1764-1778) – Little Fox and
Orinoco, two bay hunters with a groom in a landscape –
inscribed: Little Fox/1763 and Orinoco – oil on canvas –
69.5 x 105cm.
(Sotheby's)   **$28,985   £18,700**

JAMES STROUDLEY – Still Life – signed and dated
lower left Stroudley 56 – signed again and inscribed on
thereverse – oil on board – 20 x 35^1/2in.
(Christie's)   **$1,043   £660**

PHILIP EUSTACE STRETTON (fl. 1884-1919) –
Peeping Tom – signed and dated 1895 – 28 x 38cm.
(Christie's)   **$5,984   £3,520**

WILLIAM STRUTT – A swing full of love – signed;
signed and inscribed with title on the reverse – oil on panel
– 43.5 x 34cm.
(Sotheby's)   **$31,377   £19,250**

STRUYKEN

HELENA STURTEVANT (American, 1872-1946) –
Children in Luxembourg Gardens, Paris – signed and dated
1914 – oil on canvas – 25⅛ x 30¼ in.
(Skinner) $25,000 £14,970

PETER STRUYKEN – Cluster II – with title and
inscribed on a label on the reverse – autocryl (Sikkens) on
perspex – unframed – 200 x 133cm. – Executed between
1971 and 1975
(Christie's) $13,114 £8,248

TADE STYKA (French, 1889-1954) – A Head Study of a
pretty Young Woman – signed – 76.2 x 63.5cm.
(Bonhams) $930 £600

WILLIAM STUART – Troops embarking for the Crimea
– signed and dated 1855 – 37 x 53in.
(Bearne's) $8,544 £4,800

GEORGE STUBBS, A.R.A. (1724-1806) – A groom
feeding a Cheshnut Hunter in a landscape – signed l.c. :
Geo. Stubbs/1789 – oil on panel – 57 x 73.5cm.
(Sotheby's) $66,495 £42,900

ALEXANDER VON SUCKOW (born 1855) – On the
beach after the storm – signed – and signed and inscribed
on the reverse – on board – 53 x 83cm.
(Christie's) $4,427 £2,750

SWANWICK

GRAHAM SUTHERLAND, O.M. (1903-1980) – Study of Rocks – signed and dated 1937 – pen and ink and wash – 10.5 x 18cm.
(Phillips) $9,780   £6,000

CARL SUHRLANDT (1828-1919) – A Portrait of Lord Francis Horace Pierrepoint Cecil, seen with two spaniels, a pointer , a roebuck, pheasant and partridge on the hill in the Glentanar Estate, Aberdeenshire – signed 124.5 x 90.2cm.
(Christie's) $3,740   £2,200

BETTY SWANWICK, R.A. – The Scarecrow – watercolour over pencil – 70 x 42cm.
(Phillips) $6,520   £4,000

VASILII IVANOVICH SURIKOV (1848-1916) – The Smoker – signed in Cyrillic lower left – inscribed in Russian upper right – laid on canvas – with two further inscriptions authenticating the work – 44 x 37cm.
(Christie's) $19,481   £12,100

HAROLD SWANWICK, R.I. (1866-1929) – "The Ploughman" – signed – also signed and inscribed on backboard with title and the Lines: "Line after line, along the bursting sod, marks the broad acres where his feet both trod, O. W. Holmes" – watercolour and bodycolour over pencil 59 x 105.5cm.
(Phillips) $9,780   £6,000

GEORGE GARDNER SYMONS – A Hillside Road –
signed Gardner Symons, l.l. – oil on canvas –
63.4 x 76.2cm.
(Christie's)   **$20,900   £13,062**

JOHN GUTTERIDGE SYKES (b. 1866) – Interior, a
farm building – watercolour – 14½ x 10¼in.
(David Lay)   **$961   £620**

GEORGE GARDNER SYMONS – Sunshine – signed
Gardner Symons, l.r. – oil on canvasboard – 37.7 x 45cm.
(Christie's)   **$3,850   £2,406**

GEORGE GARDNER SYMONS – The Creek in Winter
– signed Gardner Symons, l.r. – oil on canvas –
50.8 x 63.5cm.
(Christie's)   **$8,800   £5,500**

WILLIAM CHRISTIAN SYMONS (London 1845-
1911) – A still life of peaches – watercolour and gouache –
25.4 x 35.6cm.
(Lawrence)   **$1,714   £1,045**

WILLIAM CHRISTIAN SYMONS (London 1845-1911) – A Newlyn Fishergirl – watercolour – unframed – 50.8 x 35.6cm.
(Lawrence)   **$577**   **£352**

PAUL VON SZINYEI-MERSE (Hungarian 1854-1920) – A rendez-vous in the shade of a tree – signed and dated 1870 – oil on canvas – unframed – 71.5 x 46cm.
(Sotheby's)   **$29,216**   **£17,600**

ARTHUR FITZWILLIAM TAIT (1819-1905) – Buck in a marsh – signed A.F. Tait and dated N. Y. 83, l.r. – oil on canvas – 36.8 x 50.8cm.
(Sotheby's)   **$14,850**   **£9,459**

TALMAGE

ALGERNON TALMAGE, R.A. (1871-1939) – Summer Mornings, a Milk Maid and Cattle on the Edge of a Field – signed and dated lower left Talmage 1919 – oil on canvas – 25 x 30in.
(Christie's)   **$4,345   £2,750**

PERCY TARRANT – Returning from Market – A farmyard scene, with a group of children surrounding, a donkey cart, a boy lifting a pig from the cart – signed - 45 x 97cm.
(Spencer's)   **$18,745   £11,500**

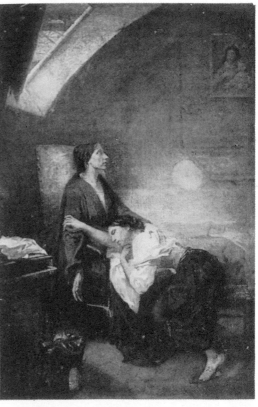

ARNALDO TAMBURINI (b. 1843) – Returning from market – signed and dated 1893 – on panel – 26.7 x 19.1cm.
(Christie's)   **$1,023   £660**

Attributed to OCTAVE TASSAERT - In the garret – indistinctly signed – oil on canvas – 115.5 x 80cm.
(Sotheby's)   **$2,270   £1,320**

ALBERT CHEVALLIER TAYLER (Leytonstone 1862 - London 1925) – Self-portrait of the artist seated in his studio – oil on canvas – 86.9 x 66.6cm.
(Lawrence)   **$5,051 £3,080**

PAUL TAVERNIER – The hunt – signed – oil on canvas – unframed – 60 x 43cm.
(Sotheby's)   **$3,366 £1,980**

ALBERT CHEVALLIER TAYLER – Letters from the Absent – signed and dated '89 – 23¹/₂ x 35in.
(Bearne's)   **$117,480 £66,000**

TAYLOR

H. K. TAYLOR – Coastal scene with fishermen and cottages to the right hand side, sailing vessels on a choppy sea – signed – 60 x 93cm.
(Spencer's) **$5,022 £3,100**

HERMAN TEN KATE – Cavaliers in an Interior – watercolour – signed – 18.4 x 30.4cm.
(Bonhams) **$612 £400**

JEAN-BAPTISTE TENCY (Active 1788-93) – A cat surprising a spaniel – signed and indistinctly dated, Johannes B. J. Tency, F - - - 5 – on panel – 43.6 x 48.5cm.
(Phillips) **$11,410 £7,000**

DAVID TENIERS the YOUNGER (Antwerp 1610-1690 Brussels) – Allegory of Spring – one of the set of the Four Seasons, of which several series were painted by David Teniers the younger – signed with monogram D.T. – on panel – 17.7 x 12.2cm.
(Phillips) **$48,900 £30,000**

JOHAN MARI HENRI TEN KATE (Dutch 1831-1910) – The young thieves – signed – oil on canvas – 71 x 87cm.
(Sotheby's) **$27,390 £16,500**

COSTIA TERECHKOVITCH (Fr. born 1902) – Cecile – oil on canvas – signed C. Terechkovitch lower right – titled on the stretcher – 26½ x 18in.
(Bruce D. Collins) **$4,125 £2,578**

CORNELIUS TERLOUW (late 19th Century) – A vase of roses – signed – 59.7 x 49.5cm.
(Christie's) **$4,092 £2,640**

HENRY HERBERT LA THANGUE, R.A. (1859-1929) – The Black Bonnet – signed – oil on panel – 37 x 23.5cm.
(Phillips) **$11,736 £7,200**

ANTHONY THIEME – Harborside, Gloucester – signed A. Thieme, l.r. – oil on canvas – 81.5 x 92cm.
(Christie's) **$17,600 £11,000**

WILLEM DE FAMARS TESTAS (1834-1896) – An Arab street scene – signed – 80 x 57cm.
(Christie's) **$8,500 £5,280**

ANTHONY THIEME (1888-1954) – West Street in autumn – oil on canvas – 25 x 30in. – signed A. Thieme lower right
(Bruce D. Collins) **$8,250 £4,910**

THIEME

ANTHONY THIEME (American, 1888-1954) - Harbor Scene - signed - fragmentary labels on reverse – oil on canvas - 25 x 30in.
(Skinner)   **$8,000**   **£4,790**

ANTHONY THIEME – Cove Hill – signed A. Thieme, l.l. – inscribed with title on the reverse – oil on canvas – 76.2 x 91.3cm.
(Christie's)   **$36,300**   **£22,687**

ANTHONY THIEME – Peaceful Street – signed A. Thieme, l.r. – inscribed with title on the reverse – oil on canvas – 63.5 x 76.5cm.
(Christie's)   **$5,500**   **£3,437**

Attributed to GERARD THOMAS (1663-1720) – The Alchemist's studio – oil on canvas – 59 x 81cm.
(Phillips) $14,580 £9,000

ATTRIBUTED TO ROBERT STRICKLAND THOMAS (1787-1853) – The steam passenger Packet Vanguard at anchor in Plymouth harbour – indistinctly signed l.r. – oil on canvas – 66.5 x 100cm.
(Sotheby's) $12,787 £8,250

ARCHIBALD THORBURN – Fox in a winter landscape – signed – gouache – 53 x 42cm.
(Sotheby's) $14,696 £8,800

AUGUST THOMSEN – A portrait of Michael Wyller – oil on canvas – painted in 1837 in Lille Toyen Gärd – 90 x 71cm.
(Sotheby's) $24,310 £14,300

ARCHIBALD THORBURN – A French Partridge – watercolour heightened with white – signed – 9^1/$_2$ x 6^3/$_4$in.
(Bearne's) $3,887 £2,300

THORBURN

ARCHIBALD THORBURN – Mallard in flight in snow storm over the sea – signed in pencil to margin – coloured print – 12 x 18in.
(G. A. Key) **$428 £280**

ARCHIBALD THORBURN (1860-1935) – A Hedgehog – signed and dated 1928 – pencil and watercolour heightened with bodycolour – 8⅜ x 6⅜in.
(Christie's) **$9,861 £6,050**

ARCHIBALD THORBURN – Grouse on the moor – signed – watercolour on paper – 55.9 x 78.7cm.
(Sotheby's) **$47,300 £29,748**

ARCHIBALD THORBURN – A goldfinch – watercolour heightened with white – signed and dated 1921 – 7 x 5in.
(Bearne's) **$3,718 £2,200**

ARCHIBALD THORBURN – Pheasants in the woodland – signed and dated 1923 – watercolour heightened with bodycolour – 34 x 55cm.
(Sotheby's) **$64,295 £38,500**

ARCHIBALD THORBURN - Aquila Adalberti (adult) - signed and inscribed - watercolour over touches of pencil, heightened with bodycolour and stopping out - 19 x 26cm.
(Woolley & Wallis) $10,106 £6,200

WILLIAM THORNLEY – Low tide, Isle of Wight – signed – oil on canvas – 25.5 x 40.5cm.
(Sotheby's) $1,793 £1,100

F*** THURLBY – McTavish – signed – inscribed with title and dated 1925 – oil on canvas – 30.5 x 46cm.
(Sotheby's) $1,165 £715

JOHANNES TIELIUS (1660 - 1719) – Portrait of a gentleman, half length, believed to be Willem Van Wassenaer – signed J. Tielius, F. – oil on canvas – an oval – 75 x 63cm.
(Phillips) $1,046 £650

GIOVANNI DOMENICO TIEPOLO (1727-1804) –
David holding a sword – oil on canvas – 60 x 45cm.
(Phillips) **$39,120 £24,000**

FRANCESCO TIRONI, Circle of – A view of the Doge's
Palace from Santa Maria Della Salute – oil on canvas –
65 x 94cm.
(Woolley & Wallis) **$122,400 £72,000**

GILLIS VAN TILBORCH – A wooded Landscape with
a Group of Peasants by a Cottage – oil on canvas –
57.8 x 71.1cm.
(Bonhams) **$6,440 £4,000**

JOHANN HEINRICH TISCHBEIN, the ELDER
(1722-1789), Circle of – Laura – oil on canvas –
71 x 58.5cm.
(Phillips) **$1,467 £900**

GILLIS VAN TILBORCH, circa 1625-1678 – Le
Déjeuner en Plein Air – oil on canvas – 94 x 128cm.
(Sotheby's) **$39,579 £25,371**

DAVID TINDLE – Tea – signed – inscribed and dated
1970 on the reverse – acrylic on canvas – 81 x 101cm.
(Phillips) **$4,056 £2,400**

DAVID TINDLE, R.A. – Balloon Race, Clipston – signed – inscribed with title and dated 1980 – gouache over pencil – 60 x 42cm.
(Phillips) **$6,760 £4,000**

ETTORE TITO (Italian 1859-1941) – The market – signed and dated 1862 – oil on panel – 24.5 x 19.5cm.
(Sotheby's) **$54,780 £33,000**

FELIX ELIE TOBEEN – A Mediterranean landscape with houses and trees – signed lower right Tobeen and signed again on the stretcher – 35 x 46cm.
(Christie's) **$4,035 £2,538**

JAMES JACQUES JOSEPH TISSOT (1836-1902) – Château de Buillon – on board – 51 x 35.5cm.
(Christie's) **$18,755 £12,100**

LOUIS TOCQUE, Follower of – Jiliotte – oil on panel – 20.5 x 18cm.
(Phillips) **$3,542 £2,200**

TODD

RALPH TODD (1856-1932) – Children seated on the steps with chickens in a cottage courtyard – signed and dated 1883 – watercolour – 13½ x 9½in.
(W. H. Lane & Son)   **$4,800 £3,000**

RALPH TODD (fl. 1880- c. 1929) – A Cornish fisherwoman – watercolour – signed – 15 x 10in.
(David Lay)   **$2,898 £1,800**

RALPH TODD (fl. 1880–c. 1929) – A Quiet Moment – signed and dated 1904 – oil on canvas – 25.5 x 35.5cm.
(Phillips)   **$4,075 £2,500**

RALPH TODD (Exh. 1880-1928) – Our London Letter –
signed lower left Ralph Todd – watercolour –
26¼ x 23¼in.
(Christie's) **$7,647 £4,840**

GEORGE TOOKER – Self-Portrait of the Artist – signed
George Tooker, c.r. – signed again – dated 1947 and
inscribed with artist's instructions on the reverse – egg
'tempera on gessoed panel – 47.6cm. diameter
(Christie's) **$330,000 £210,474**

DOMINICUS VAN TOL (1635-1676) – Portrait of
Captain Jacobus Van Der Bergh, standing, three-quarter
length, before the Doeler Poort, Leiden – oil on arch-
topped panel – 41.5 x 31cm.
(Phillips) **$4,050 £2,500**

GEORGE TOOKER – Fiesta – signed Tooker, l.l. – egg
tempera on gessoed panel – 55.8 x 44.4cm.
(Christie's) **$396,000 £252,569**

GEORGE TOOKER - Coney Island – signed Tookerl.l. –
egg tempera on gessoed panel – 48.9 x 66.7cm.
(Christie's) **$341,000 £217,490**

JAN TOOROP – Two peasant girls gathering wood on a
forest road, in Domburg – signed lower right Jh. Toorop –
pencil and coloured crayons on paper – 21.5 x 20cm.
(Christie's) **$6,053 £3,807**

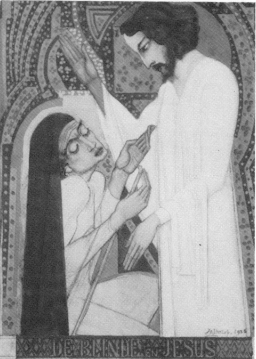

JAN TOOROP (Dutch 1858-1928) – Christ and the blind
man – signed titled and dated 1926 – gouache and pencil –
20.5 x 14.5cm.
(Sotheby's) **$24,651 £14,850**

JAN TOOROP – Two Muses – signed and dedicated lower left Jh. Toorop, aan Marry v/d Elst – pencil on paper – 20.5 x 13cm.
(Christie's)   **$5,549   £3,490**

WOLFGANG ADAM TOPFFER – A Village Fair – signed – inscribed 'Geneve' and dated 1816 – 31⁷/₈ x 40⁷/₈in.
(Bearne's)   **$534,000   £300,000**

FRANK WILLIAM WARWICK TOPHAM (1838-1924) – The taming of the shrew – signed and dated 1879 – 105.5 x 156cm.
(Christie's)   **$19,239   £12,100**

WOLFGANG ADAM TOPFFER – Recruiting – signed – inscribed 'Geneve' and dated 1815 – 31⁷/₈ x 40⁵/₈in.
(Bearne's)   **$729,800   £410,000**

V* TORCY (Continental, early 20th Century)** – A Harem Scene – signed – 57.8 x 73.7cm.
(Bonhams)   **$589   £380**

TORHAMN

GUNNAR TORHAMN – Fishermen at work – signed –
45 x 54cm.
(Auktionsverket Stockholm) **$8,364 £5,131**

GYULA TORNAI – In the Harem – signed – oil on board
– 99 x 139cm.
(Sotheby's) **$4,675 £2,750**

ANTONIO TORRES (Spanish, b. 1851) – A Young
Beauty – signed – 81.3 x 64.8cm.
(Bonhams) **$2,945 £1,900**

**Attributed to FLAMINIO TORRE called DAGLI
ANCINELLI (Bologna 1621 - Modena 1661)** – The
Virgin and Child – oil on canvas – 69.8 x 48.2cm.
(Lawrence) **$1,804 £11,000**

EDOUARD TOUDOUZE – The punishment – signed –
oil on canvas – unframed – 228 x 174cm.
(Sotheby's) **$7,480 £4,400**

HENRI DE TOULOUSE-LAUTREC – Portrait de Comtesse Raymond de Toulouse-Lautrec, née imbert du bosc – signed Monfa and dated 82 – charcoal on paper – 48 x 38cm.
(Sotheby's) **$36,300 £22,830**

FERNAND TOUSSAINT – La Robe Indigo – signed – oil on canvas – 98 x 79cm.
(Sotheby's) **$8,602 £5,060**

HENRI DE TOULOUSE-LAUTREC (1864-1901) – La Clowness assise (Mlle. Cha-u-ka-O) – soft pencil on thin paper laid down on board – 47 x 36.5cm. – Executed in 1896
(Christie's) **$102,300 £66,000**

FERNAND TOUSSAINT (Belgian 1873-1955) – Pink roses in a vase – signed – oil on canvas laid down on board – 46 x 38cm.
(Sotheby's) **$12,782 £7,700**

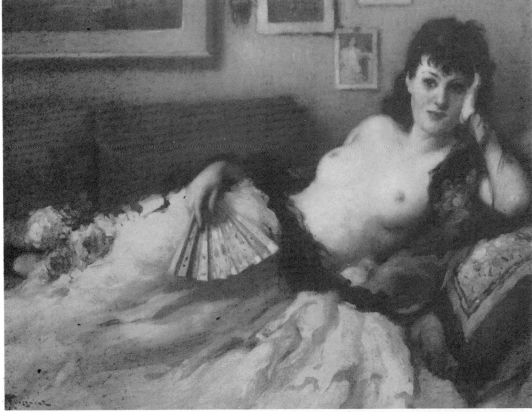

FERNAND TOUSSAINT (1873-1955) – Une Femme
allongée avec Roses et Eventail—Liggende Vrouw met
Rozen en Waaier – signed lower left F. Toussaint – oil on
canvas – 80.6 x 100.4cm.
(Christie's) $52,800 £33,000

CHARLES TOWNE (1781-1854) – A Bay Hunter in a
landscape – signed Chas Towne/1835 – oil on canvas –
51 x 63.5cm.
(Sotheby's) $18,480 £11,000

A. TREVANI (late 19th Century) – A story of a conquest
– signed – on board – 50.8 x 41.9cm.
(Christie's) $1,364 £880

EDWARD TREVOR – Fishermen's cottages by an estuary – on board - signed and dated '84 – 21 x 14¹/₂in.
(Bearne's) **$815 £500**

FRANCOIS DE TROY (Toulouse 1645-1730 Paris) – Portrait of a nobleman, three-quarter length, seated, his right arm across his chest – on canvas – 130 x 98cm.
(Phillips) **$76,500 £45,000**

JEAN-FRANCOIS DE TROY – Paris 1679-1752 Rome – Zéphyr et Flore – oil on canvas – 85 x 153cm.
(Sotheby's) **$140,177 £89,857**

PRINCE PAUL TROUBETSKOI (1866-1938) – Portrait of Joaquin Sorolla y Bastida, seated half length – signed and dated 93 – on panel – 26.5 x 20.3cm.
(Christie's) **$27,280 £17,600**

CONSTANT TROYAN (French, 1810-1865) – The Three Prize Cows – initialed "C.T." – oil on canvas – 32 x 46in.
(Skinner) **$2,500 £1,497**

TROYON

CONSTANT TROYON - The return of the herd - signed - oil on board - 32 x 41cm.
(Sotheby's)   **$10,285   £6,050**

CONSTANT TROYON (1810-1865) – The apple orchard – signed – 52 x 71cm.
(Christie's)   **$32,395   £20,900**

ALBERT TUCKER – Images of Modern Evil – mixed media – signed '72 – 26 x 36cm.
(Australian Art Auctions)   **$6,065   £3,721**

HARRY TUCK – Mousehole – signed – 11½ x 17¼in.
(Bearne's)   **$1,780   £1,000**

RAYMOND TUCKER (Exh. 1882-1903) – "On the Rock, Guernsey" – signed with monogram – also signed and inscribed on old label verso – watercolour – 25 x 35.5cm.
(Phillips)   **$896   £550**

HENRY SCOTT TUKE, R.A., R.W.S. (1858-1929) –
Boy Leaning Against a Rock – signed – watercolour –
20.5 x 13cm.
(Phillips)   **$3,586   £2,200**

HENRY SCOTT TUKE, R.A., R.W.S. (1858-1929) – In
the Rowing Boat – signed and dated '98 – oil on panel –
16 x 24cm.
(Phillips)   **$16,300   £10,000**

HENRY SCOTT TUKE (1858-1929) – The Bather –
signed and dated 1911 – oil on canvas board – 14^{1}/$_{2}$ x 11in.
(W. H. Lane & Son)   **$9,912   £5,900**

HENRY SCOTT TUKE, R.A.,R.W.S. - 'Coral Island' - watercolour - signed and dated 1924 - inscribed on a
label on the back panel - 10 x 14in.
(Bearne's)
                                      $3,586   £2,200

TULK

GEORGE TURNER – Burton-Upon-Trent, near Derby – signed and inscribed with title on a label on the stretcher and bears a copy of the signature and title on the re-lining – oil on canvas – 51 x 76cm.
(Sotheby's) **$7,172 £4,400**

AUGUSTUS TULK – Self portrait – signed and dated '08 – oil on canvas – 76 x 51cm.
(Sotheby's) **$1,345 £825**

AUGUSTUS TULK – Girl with poppies – signed — oil on canvas — 46 x 61cm.
(Sotheby's) **$3,227 £1,980**

GEORGE TURNER (1843-1910) – Near Knowle Hills, Derbyshire – signed and dated 82 – and signed – inscribed and dated 1882 on the reverse – 76 x 122cm.
(Christie's) **$9,095 £5,720**

GEORGE TURNER – Harvesting near Swarkestone, Derbyshire – signed; signed – inscribed with title and dated 1878 on the reverse – oil on canvas – 61 x 91.5cm.
(Sotheby's) **$30,481 £18,700**

CHARLES FREDERICK TUNNICLIFFE – 'Pintail asleep' – signed – watercolour over pencil – 44 x 58cm.
(Woolley & Wallis) **$12,388 £7,600**

GEORGE TURNER (1843-1910) – The cornfield – signed – on board – 30.4 x 50.7cm.
(Christie's) **$6,275 £3,850**

GEORGE TURNER (1843-1910) - Sweet Water Lane, Diseworth, Leicestershire - signed - and inscribed on the reverse - 38.2 x 51.4cm.
(Christie's) $7,172 £4,400

GEORGE TURNER (1843-1910) – 'A forest road, Calk Abbey, Derbyshire' – signed and dated '86 – title on reverse – oil on canvas – 60.5 x 91.5cm.
(Phillips) $8,150 £5,000

GEORGE TURNER (1843-1910) – A lane in the Peak of Derbyshire – signed and dated 83 and signed – inscribed and dated 1883 on the reverse – 51.2 x 76.2cm.
(Christie's) $9,619 £6,050

TURNER

J*** TURNER – Rough shooting – signed and dated 1867 – oil on canvas – 112 x 86.5cm.
(Sotheby's) **$8,068 £4,950**

JOSEPH MALLORD WILLIAM TURNER, R.A. (1775-1851) – Seascape with squall coming up – oil on canvas – 45.5 x 61cm.
(Sotheby's) **$1,071,840 £638,000**

NILS TYDEN – Epabaren – signed – 81 x 116cm.
(Auktionsverket Stockholm) **$7,100 £4,356**

GEORG TYRAHN (1860-1917) – Odalisque – signed – 88 x 43cm.
(Christie's) **$5,667 £3,520**

JOHN H. TWACHTMAN – Canal scene, Holland – signed and dated 1881 – oil on panel – 24.8 x 33.0cm.
(Sotheby's) **$49,500 £31,132**

UDEN

LUCAS VAN UDEN, Circle of (1595-1672) - An extensive wooded river landscape with a drover and cattle on a track - on copper - 11 x 14in.
(Christie's) $3,227 £1,980

ANDREJ GRIGORJEWITSCH UCHTOMSKIJ (Russian 1771-1852) – A Roman street scene – signed on the mount – watercolour over pencil – 24 x 18.5cm.
(Sotheby's) $4,017 £2,420

WALTER UFER - A Singing Indian - signed W. Ufer, 1.1. - oil on canvas - 30 x 25¼in.
(Christie's) $38,500.. £24,555

LUCAS VAN UDEN (1595-1672) - Travellers in a horse-drawn waggon upon a country road leading from a village - oil on canvas - 43 x 68cm.
(Phillips) $3,888 £2,400

UFER

WILLIAM UNDERHILL, Follower of – The harvesters
102.9 x 128.2cm
(Christie's) $7,656 £4,400

WALTER UFER - Fantasies - signed W. Ufer 1.1. - oil on canvas 42 x 38in.

(Christie's) $104,500 £66,650

LEON UNDERWOOD (1890-1978) - Fishermen - signed lower right Leon U - oil on canvas - 11½ x 15½in.
(Christie's) $11,654 £7,150

LEON UNDERWOOD (1890-1978) - Figures on a rope bridge - signed lower right Leon U - oil on canvas - 11½ x 13½in.
(Christie's) $8,068   £4,950

LESSER URY – Forest edge – signed and dated 1902 – pastel – 68 x 48cm.
(Sotheby's) $18,758   £11,034

HUGO UNGEWITTER – Mounted troops in a snowbound town – signed and titled Berlin 1819 – oil on canvas – unframed – 73.5 x 105.5cm.
(Sotheby's) $7,568   £4,400

LESSER URY (1861-1931) - Seelandschaft - signed and dated lower left L. Ury 1898 - pastel on board - 35 x 49cm.
(Christie's) $31,878   £19,800

FRANZ RICHARD UNTERBERGER (Innsbruck 1838 - Neuilly-sur-Seine 1902) – An Alpine Landscape – signed lower left: F. R. Unterberger – oil on canvas – 74.9 x 125.7cm.
(Lawrence) $7,036   £4,290

LESSER URY (1861-1931) – Rheinische Landschaft – signed and dated lower left L. Ury 1893 – pastel on board – 33.5 x 48.2cm.
(Christie's) $13,640   £8,800

URY

LESSER URY – A seated lady reading, in an interior – signed and dated Lesser Ury 1884 – 78.5 x 48.5cm.
(Christie's) **$26,230 £16,497**

ADRIAEN VAN UTRECHT – Anvers 1599-1652 ou 53 – Nature Morte aux Fruits et Singe sur un Entablement – oil on canvas – 75 x 117cm.
(Sotheby's) **$46,176 £29,600**

MAURICE UTRILLO (1883-1955) - Rue de l'Abreuvoir a Montmartre - signed and dated lower right Maurice Utrillo V, 1937 - inscribed with title lower left - oil on canvas - 19¾ x 24in.
(Christie's) **$371,910 £231,000**

MAURICE UTRILLO (1883-1955) – Le Castel du Philosophe a Montmartre - signed and dated - watercolour and gouache on paper - 13 x 19in.
(Christie's) **$70,840 £44,000**

MAURICE UTRILLO (1883-1955) - La Butte Pinson a Montmagny - signed lower right Maurice Utrillo - oil on canvas - 15 x 18½in.
(Christie's) **$230,230 £143,000**

MAURICE UTRILLO (1883-1955) - Eglise de Leynes (Saone-et-Loire) - signed lower right Maurice Utrillo V., - oil on board - 26 x 30¾in.
(Christie's) **$230,230 £143,000**

ANDREA VACCARO (1598-Naples-1670) – Minerva – Painted circa 1640 – on canvas – 125 x 99cm.
(Phillips) **$68,460 £42,000**

AMALIE VALENTINO (fl. circa 1890) – Nu de Dos – signed upper right Amalie Valentino – pastel on canvas – 81.3 x 65.4cm.
(Christie's) **$9,377 £6,050**

H. VALE (fl. early 18th Century) – A Man of War in three positions – signed l.l : H. Vale/1727 – oil on canvas – 93.5 x 155cm.
(Sotheby's) **$36,960 £22,000**

THEODORE V.C. VALENKAMPH (American, 1868-1924) – The Harbour in Winter – signed "T.V.C. Valenkamph" l.r. – oil on canvas – 18¼ x 24¼in.
(Skinner) **$3,800 £2,375**

ANNE VALLAYER-COSTER – Paris 1744-1818 – Portrait D'une Jeune Violoniste – oil on canvas – 117 x 94cm.
(Sotheby's) **$346,320 £222,000**

VALTAT

LOUIS VALTAT – Valtat et son fils - signed with the initials – oil on canvas – 60.6 x 73.6cm. – Painted circa 1918
(Sotheby's)   **$60,500**   **£38,050**

GABRIELE PIETRO GARIBALDI MARIA VARESE – The horse-race – signed lower left Varese – unframed - 53 x 73cm.
(Christie's)   **$1,312**   **£825**

FREDERICK E. VALTER (fl. 1878-1900) – The plough team – signed and dated 1904 – on board – 21.6 x 29.2cm.
(Christie's)   **$1,434**   **£880**

GABRIELE PIETRO GARIBALDI MARIA VARESE – A beach scene with numerous figures – signed lower right Varese – 46.5 x 54.5cm.
(Christie's)   **$808**   **£508**

EMILIO VASSARI - The Gladiators' procession - signed 1.1. - oil on canvas - 74 x 128.5cm.
(Sotheby's)   **$26,488**   **£15,400**

RENÉ VAUQUELIN – A telling off – signed; signed – indistinctly inscribed and dated 1888 on the reverse – oil on panel – 21 x 31.5cm.
(Sotheby's)   **$9,082   £5,280**

BRAM VAN VELDE – Self portrait of the artist, holding a palette, in front of his easel – 108 x 78cm.
(Christie's)   **$8,575   £5,393**

VENETIAN SCHOOL, 18th CENTURY – Portrait of a young naval officer, half length, standing by a window, a man-o'-war at anchor beyond – on canvas – 81.5 x 64.5cm.
(Phillips)   **$6,460   £3,800**

VENNE

JAN VAN DE VENNE ALIAS LE PSEUDO VAN DE VENNE – Mâlines avant 1600-Bruxelles? avant 1651 – Portrait de Femme – oil on panel – 24.5 x 19cm.
(Sotheby's) **$7,421 £4,757**

VENETIAN SCHOOL 16th C. – Vierge à L'enfant avec Saint – oil on canvas – 63 x 91cm.
(Sotheby's) **$4,946 £3,171**

EUGENE VERBOECKHOVEN, Attributed to (Belgian, 1798-1881) – Cattle in a Field – panel – 30.5 x 42cm.
(Bonhams) **$1,318 £850**

LOUIS CHARLES VERBOECKHOVEN – Fishing boats near the coast – signed – oil on canvas – 28.5 x 42cm.
(Sotheby's) **$5,236 £3,080**

RUTGER VERBURGH (1678-c. 1710) – Figures strolling within the Oude Kerk, Delft – signed and dated 1707 – oil on panel – 65 x 53cm.
(Phillips) **$3,260 £2,000**

JAN VERKOLJE (Amsterdam 1650-1693 Delft) – Two children at a window, one holding a silver salver with fruit – signed and dated I. Verkolje 1676 – on canvas – 48.3 x 40cm.
(Phillips) **$23,800 £14,000**

ALPHONSE VERMEIR (20th Century) - Les Masques
de Carnaval—Karnavalsmaskers – signed lower right A.
Vermeir - oil on panel – 96.5 x 79.4cm.
(Christie's)   **$4,928** **£3,080**

ANDREAS FRANCISCUS VERMEULEN (1821-1884)
– A Dutch market scene by candlelight – signed – on panel
– 51 x 42cm.
(Christie's)   **$7,084** **£4,400**

**JAN CORNELISZ. VERMEYEN (circa 1500
Beverwyck-Brussels 1559)** – The Emperor Ferdinand I –
on panel – perhaps bears traces of a monogram –
40.5 x 30.5cm. – Painted in 1530 or 1531
(Phillips)   **$105,950** **£65,000**

PIETER GERARDUS VERTIN – A canal scene; A
street under snow – a pair – both signed and dated '86 – oil
on panel – each 20 x 16cm.
(Sotheby's)   **$7,489** **£4,400**

KEES VERWEY – A still life with bunches of flowers wrapped in paper, in buckets – signed lower left Kees Verwey – watercolour on paper – 49.5 x 67cm.
(Christie's) **$3,026 £1,903**

PIERRE VIDAL – The Young Printmaker – watercolour – signed and dated 1878 – 31.7 x 24.7cm.
(Bonhams) **$581 £380**

EMMANUEL VIÉRIN – Village Zélandois (Ile de Walcheren) – signed and dated lower right Emm. Viérin 1915 – and signed and dated again and inscribed with title on a label on the stretcher – 110 x 119.5cm.
(Christie's) **$9,079 £5,710**

GEORGE VINCENT (1796-1831) – View of the Needles, Isle of Wight, from Christchurch – signed GV (in monogram) 1828 – and inscribed by the artist on a label attached to the reverse – oil on panel – 29 x 39.5cm.
(Sotheby's) **$48,048 £28,600**

DAVID VINCKBOONS, Follower of – Women chasing a young boy from a house while elegant figures are seated nearby – oil on canvas – 81 x 54cm.
(Phillips) **$2,576 £1,600**

E. VITALI – Soldiers farewell – signed and dated 1885 – pencil and watercolour – 18³/4 x 14in.
(Christie's) **$880 £550**

Attributed to WIGERUS VITRINGA (1657-1721) – Figures on a sandy path beside the shore – indistinctly signed – oil on panel – 34 x 52cm.
(Phillips) **$10,044 £6,200**

ASTRUC DE VISSEC, Attributed to (Active Montpellier in the 18th Century) – A still life of flowers in a stone urn, standing on a ledge, a butterfly nearby – on canvas – 40.5 x 33.2cm.
(Phillips) **$10,200 £6,000**

JOHN VITTALY – Grande Course De Haies D'Auteuil, 1897 – signed and dated 1897 – oil on canvas – 60.5 x 128.5cm.
(Sotheby's) **$11,594 £6,820**

VIVIAN

G. VIVIAN (late 19th Century) – Franchetti Palace, Venice – signed – 51.3 x 76.2cm.
(Christie's) $10,230 £6,600

KAREL VAN VOGELAER, Circle of (Maastricht 1653-1695 Rome) – A still life of roses and other flowers in a bronze rococo vase standing on a ledge – on canvas – 68 x 48cm.
(Phillips) $5,100 £3,000

GUILLAUME VOGELS (1836-1896) – Paysage enneigé—Sneeuwlandschap – signed lower right Vogels – oil on canvas – 58.8 x 52.8cm.
(Christie's) $8,800 £5,500

EMIL VOLKERS – A Stallion – signed and dated 1899 – oil on panel – 32 x 41cm.
(Sotheby's) **$3,366 £1,980**

ANTOINE VOLLON (1833-1900) – Still life of lilac in a bowl, a silver ewer, oranges, a book and a glass sweatmeat dish, on a draped table – signed – on panel – 45.2 x 36.2cm.
(Christie's) **$6,092 £2,640**

ANTOINE VOLLON (French 1833-1900) – A still life of eggs, peaches and bread – signed – oil on canvas - unframed – 65 x 81cm.
(Sotheby's) **$21,912 £13,200**

ANTOINE VOLLON – A still life with a tankard and fruit on a table – signed – oil on canvas – 71.5 x 59cm.
(Sotheby's) **$9,350 £5,500**

CORNELIS DE VOS 1585-1651 – Circle of – Portrait de Femme à la Collerette – oil on panel – 63.5 x 53.5cm.
(Sotheby's) **$7,421 £4,757**

VOS

SIMON DE VOS (1603-1676), Attributed to – The reconciliation of Jacob and Esau – oil on copper – 70 x 86cm.
(Phillips)   **$3,586   £2,200**

SEBASTIEN VRANCX – Anvers 1573 ou 78-1647 – Cavaliers Près D'Un Gué – oil on panel – 54 x 92cm.
(Sotheby's)   **$46,176   £29,600**

EDOUARD VUILLARD – Square Vintimille: A pair of paintings – both signed – Détrempre on canvas – Each: 100 x 50cm.
(Sotheby's)   **$2,200,000   £1,383,648**

EDOUARD VUILLARD (1868-1940) – Le Déjeuner au Château des Clayes – the stamp lower right E. V. (L. 909b) – pastel on paper – 33.7 x 46.5cm. – Executed circa 1935
(Christie's)   **$76,725   £49,500**

EDOUARD VUILLARD – Madame Hessel Lisant le journal – stamped with the signature – Détrempre on paper laid down on canvas – 114 x 57cm. – Painted circa 1917
(Sotheby's)   **$506,000   £318,239**

JOHN WAINWRIGHT – Still life of stuffed birds under a bell jar and summer flowers – signed and dated 1863 – oil on canvas – 36 x 45cm.
(Sotheby's)   **$7,172   £4,400**

ERNEST WALBOURN (fl. 1879-1904) – Picking
bluebells – signed – 51 x 76cm.
(Christie's)   **$13,642   £8,580**

JAMES CLARKE WAITE (fl. 1863-1885) – Awaiting
her suitor – signed and dated 1864 – 53.4 x 43.2cm.
(Christie's)   **$986   £605**

ERNEST WALBOURN (late 19th.Century) – Picking
strawberries – signed and dated '99 (?) – on board –
unframed – 30.5 x 40.7cm.
(Christie's)   **$2,152   £1,320**

JAMES CLARKE WAITE (fl. 1863-1885) – Sea side
specimens – signed – and inscribed on an old label on the
reverse – 53.2 x 43cm.
(Christie's)   **$6,820   £4,400**

**FERDINAND GEORG WALDMULLER (Austrian
1793-1865)** – A portrait of the Baroness Managetta –
signed and dated 1840 – oil on panel – oval – 22.5 x 18cm.
(Sotheby's)   **$20,086   £12,100**

ANN WALKE – Portrait of a Young Woman Standing in a Yellow Interior – signed – oil on canvas – 61 x 51cm.
(Phillips) **$1,267 £750**

ROBERT HOLLANDS WALKER – The haybarge crossing the stream – signed – watercolour – 19 x 26in.
(Christie's) **$2,288 £1,430**

FREDERICK WALKER (1840-1875) – Awaiting her Carriage – watercolour heightened with bodycolour – 23.5 x 12.5cm.
(Phillips) **$587 £360**

WILLIAM AIKEN WALKER – Cotton Picker – signed WAWalker with initials conjoined, l.l. – oil on board – 31 x 15.5cm.
(Christie's) **$4,400 £2,750**

ABRAHAM WALKOWITZ – Bather – signed A. Walkowitz on the reverse – oil on canvasboard – 40 x 30.5cm.
(Christie's) **$6,600 £4,125**

TAF WALLET – Still life with cherries – on wood – signed and dated – 50 x 60cm.
(Galerie Moderne) **$2,204 £1,404**

GEORGE STANFIELD WALTERS (1838-1924) – On the Guidecca, Venice – signed – watercolour heightened with bodycolour over traces of pencil – 22.5 x 57cm.
(Phillips) **$1,304 £800**

THOMAS WALLER (1860-1865) - An afternoon in summer - signed and dated 1859 - and signed inscribed and dated 1859 on the reverse - 50.8 x 60.9cm.
(Christie's) **$2,330** **£1,430**

WARD

EDWARD MATTHEW WARD, R.A. – Sir Deighton Probyn in a room in Windsor Castle – signed and dated 1874; bears title on the backboard – watercolour heightened with bodycolour and gum arabic – 50 x 56cm.
(Sotheby's) **$1,496 £880**

JAMES WARD, R.A. (1769-1859) – In the barn – branded on reverse on the stretcher with the artist's cipher – oil on canvas – 68.5 x 88.5cm.
(Sotheby's) **$14,784 £8,800**

EDWARD MATTHEW WARD, R.A. – Lady Teazle, as spinster, playing her father to sleep – School for Scandal – signed and dated 1874 – oil on canvas – 63.5 x 76cm.
(Sotheby's) **$5,020 £3,080**

ARTHUR WARDLE (1864-1949) – Leopards stalking – signed – 31 x 56.5cm.
(Christie's) **$17,490 £11,000**

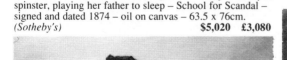

JAMES WARD, R.A. – A Northumberland Mastiff in a landscape – signed with monogram – oil on canvas – 80 x 116.8cm. – This dog was taken when a puppy from Joseph Bonaparte's baggage after the Battle of Vittoria in 1813.
(Sotheby's) **$33,000 £20,755**

ARTHUR WARDLE, R.I., R.B.C., P.S. (1864-1949) – An Irish Wolfhound – signed – on panel – 23.5 x 31.5cm.
(Christie's) **$3,366 £1,980**

ARTHUR WARDLE – On to the next covert – signed –
oil on canvas – 46 x 66cm.
(Sotheby's)   **$10,758   £6,600**

ARTHUR WARDLE, R.I., R.B.C., P.S. (1864-1949) - A
West Highland Terrier – signed – 46 x 33cm.
(Christie's)   **$11,220   £6,600**

ARTHUR WARDLE, R.I., R.B.C., P.S. (1864-1949) – A
Jack Russell Terrier with a rabbit – signed – 51 x 61cm.
(Christie's)   **$2,992   £1,760**

ARTHUR WARDLE, R.I., R.B.C. (1864-1949) – A
Resting Leopard – signed – oil on canvas – 31 x 46cm.
(Phillips)   **$13,040   £8,000**

ARTHUR WARDLE, R.I., R.B.C., P.S. (1864-1949) – A
Scottish Terrier and a Wired Hair Fox Terrier – pencil and
watercolour heightened with bodycolour and white –
unframed – 57.2 x 42cm.
(Christie's)   **$6,545   £3,850**

ARTHUR WARDLE (1864-1949) – A Lion and Lioness at a rocky stream – signed – 45.2 x 65.4cm.
(Christie's) $5,738 £3,520

ANDY WARHOL - Shoe of the evening, beautiful shoe - signed lower right Warhol - and inscribed with title lower centre - brush and ink and watercolour on paper - 22.5 x 35.5cm.
(Christie's) $4,792 £3,014

ANDY WARHOL (1930-1986) – Clockwork Panda
Drummer – each signed and dated on the canvas overlap
Andy Warhol 83 – acrylic and silkscreen on canvas – each
36 x 28cm. – overall 73 x 88cm.
(Christie's)   **$204,600   £132,000**

ARTHUR WASSE – The courtyard – signed and dated
1886 – oil on canvas – 89 x 117cm.
(Sotheby's)   **$20,619   £12,650**

GEORGES WASHINGTON (French 1827-1910) – A
Nomad caravan on the move – signed – oil on canvas –
43 x 61cm.
(Sotheby's)   **$16,434   £9,900**

BILLIE WATERS (born 1896) – The Four Horsemen of
the Apocalypse – signed – oil on canvas – 86 x 112cm.
(Phillips)   **$6,520   £4,000**

ARTHUR WASSE – Fine quality study of figures
conversing by a Continental chalet – signed and
dated 1886 – oil – 34 x 44in.
(G. A. Key)   **$6,273 £4,100**

ISABEL WATKINS – Figures Carrying Pails in a Street
– signed – signed and inscribed "Vreede, Walcheren,
Holland" – oil on canvas – 50 x 60cm.
(Phillips)   **$1,200   £750**

WATSON

ROBERT F. WATSON (fl. 1845-1866) – Cattle watering in a highland landscape – signed and dated 1897 – 50.8 x 76.2cm.
(Christie's) **$1,793 £1,100**

LOUIS-JOSEPH WATTEAU CALLED WATTEAU DE LILLE – Valenciennes 1731-1798 Lille – Scène Galante Devant une Auberge – signé et daté en bas à droite L. Watteau. 1776 – oil on canvas – 39 x 51cm.
(Sotheby's) **$28,035 £17,971**

WALTER J. WATSON – On the Llugwy, North Wales – signed and dated 1921; signed and inscribed with title on the reverse – oil on canvas – 40.5 x 66cm.
(Sotheby's) **$11,654 £7,150**

FREDERICK WATERS WATTS (1800-1862) – At the loch – 86.3 x 127cm.
(Christie's) **$42,625 £27,500**

ANTOINE WATTEAU – Valenciennes 1684-1721 Nogent-sur-Marne – La Promenade – oil on canvas – 36.2 x 32cm.
(Sotheby's) **$626,674 £401,714**

FREDERICK WATERS WATTS (1800-1862) – A wooded river landscape with anglers fishing near a bridge and cottages – oil on canvas – 94 x 119cm.
(Sotheby's) **$98,890 £63,800**

FREDERICK WATERS WATTS (1800-1862) – Tintern Abbey on the River Wye, Monmouthshire – oil on canvas – 88.5 x 130.5cm.
(Sotheby's)   **$14,784   £8,800**

JOHANN GEORG WAXCHLUNGER (Active in Munich circa 1720) – Still life with game and fruit on a ledge – oil on canvas – 88 x 114cm.
(Phillips)   **$10,530   £6,500**

FREDERICK JUDD WAUGH – Breaking Day – signed Waugh, l.r. – oil on canvas – 63.5 x 76cm.
(Christie's)   **$6,600   £4,125**

THOMAS WEAVER (1775-1843) – A Bay Hunter with a hound and a terrier in an extensive river landscape – signed l.r.: T. Weaver. Pinxit/1829 – oil on canvas – 63 x 76cm.
(Sotheby's)   **$12,936   £7,700**

FREDERICK JUDD WAUGH, NA (1861-1940) – Storm surf – charcoal – 9¼ x 13¼in. - signed Waugh lower left
(Bruce D. Collins)   **$990   £589**

JAMES WEBB – Mont St. Michel, Normandy, sunset – signed and dated 1863; bears title on the stretcher – oil on canvas – 61 x 110cm.
(Sotheby's)   **$10,041   £6,160**

WEBB

WILLIAM EDWARD WEBB (c. 1862-1903) – A busy harbour view – signed – oil on canvas – 25.5 x 40.5cm. *(Phillips)*   **$2,282   £1,400**

WILLIAM WEBB – A Cornish fishing village – signed – inscribed on the reverse – 23¹/₂ x 35¹/₂in. *(Bearne's)*   **$7,476   £4,200**

WILLIAM EDWARD WEBB – View on the South Coast, Nr Dover – signed and dated 1885; signed and inscribed with title on the reverse – oil on canvas – 61 x 76cm. *(Sotheby's)*   **$3,586   £2,200**

THEODOR WEBER – Boats returning to port at evening – signed – oil on canvas – 78.5 x 46cm. *(Sotheby's)*   **$4,114   £2,420**

WILLIAM EDWARD WEBB – Ships leaving port – signed and dated '94 – oil on canvas – 41 x 61cm. *(Sotheby's)*   **$6,813   £4,180**

After THOMAS WEBSTER – Going to Market – pencil and watercolour – 52.1 x 71.7cm. *(Bonhams)*   **$765   £500**

WALTER ERNEST WEBSTER (1878-1959) – Ray
Fuller – signed and inscribed on the canvas over lap Ray
Fuller by W E Webster – oil on canvas – 18 x 14in.
(Christie's) **$1,217 £770**

HERBERT WILLIAM WEEKES – Heckling a member
of the commons – signed – oil on canvas – 30.5 x 61cm.
(Sotheby's) **$6,813 £4,180**

JAN-BAPTIST WEENIX – Amsterdam 1621-1663
Deutecum – Berger dans un Paysage Fluvial – oil on
canvas – 67 x 81cm.
(Sotheby's) **$49,474 £31,714**

JOHN REINHARD WEGUELIN (1849-1927) – The
labour of the Danaïds – signed with initials and dated 1878
– and signed and inscribed on an old label on the reverse –
114 x 92cm.
(Christie's) **$42,625 £27,500**

EDWARD HENRY WEHNERT (1813-1868) – The
Rose Bower – signed and dated 1880 – watercolour and
bodycolour – 35.5 x 30.5cm.
(Phillips) **$2,119 £1,300**

WELLS

JOHN WELLS (b. 1907-) – St Ives School – Abstract – inscribed and dated 1972 to verso – oil on canvas – 10 x 11¾in.
(W. H. Lane & Son)   **$2,436   £1,450**

WILLIAM PAGE ATKINSON WELLS, R.B.A. (1872-1923) – The Uplands of Arbory, Isle of Man – signed – oil on canvas – 101.6 x 127cm.
(Christie's)   **$77,616   £46,200**

JOHN S. SANDERSON WELLS – The York coach – signed; signed and inscribed with title on the reverse – oil on panel – 40.5 x 66cm.
(Sotheby's)   **$13,447   £8,250**

STOW WENGENROTH (American, b. 1906) – Lighthouse, Eastern Point, East Gloucester – Bears artist's signature "Stow Wengenroth" l.l. – ink wash with graphite and crayon on board – 18½ x 25in.
(Skinner)   **$1,300   £813**

JOHN S. SANDERSON WELLS - A morning greeting - signed - oil on canvas - 41 x 61cm.
(Sotheby's)   **$13,447   £8,250**

EMIL WENNERWALD (1859-1934) – A view of Capri
– signed and dated Capri 1923 – 61 x 71cm.
(Christie's) **$1,771 £1,100**

WILLIAM WENDT (1865-1946) – Summer landscape –
signed William Wendt and dated 1914, l.r. – oil on canvas
–61.0 x 81.2cm.
(Sotheby's) **$17,600 £11,210**

ADRIAEN VAN DER WERFF, Manner of – A naked
Lady in her Boudoir – oil on canvas – 53.3 x 48.2cm.
(Bonhams) **$1,771 £1,100**

ADRIAEN VAN DER WERFF – Kralinger Ambach 1659-1722 Rotterdam – Vertumne et Pomone – oil on canvas – 53 x 45cm.
(Sotheby's)   **$75,860   £48,628**

JOHN HENRY WEST (c. 1855 - c. 1932) – Fishing fleet "An Easterly Gale" – oil on board – signed – 9 x 29$\frac{1}{2}$in.
(David Lay)   **$465   £300**

BENJAMIN WEST, P.R.A. (1738-1820), Studio of – Portrait of General James Wolfe, when a boy – oil on canvas – 38 x 46.5cm.
(Sotheby's)   **$24,024   £14,300**

CARL WERNER (1808-1894) – A peasant girl in traditional costume – signed – inscribed Costume of Sora, Regno di Napoli and dated Rom 1853 – pencil and watercolour heightened with white – 43.2 x 29.8cm.
(Christie's)   **$852   £550**

WILLIAM WEST (mid 19th Century) – The waterfall – signed and dated 1857 – 86.5 x 71cm.
(Christie's)   **$3,227   £1,980**

JAMES WHEELER – Donkeys feeding – signed – on board – 24.2 x 34.3cm.
(Christie's) **$1,461 £880**

RICHARD WESTALL, R.A. (1765-1836) – Hotspur, Worcester, Mortimer and Owen Glendower in council conspiring to divide the Kingdom in the Archdeacon of Bangor's house in Wales (From Shakespeare's Henry IV Part I, Act III, Scene I) – oil on canvas – unframed – 254 x 185cm.
(Sotheby's) **$93,775 £60,500**

JOHN ALFRED WHEELER – A boy with a donkey and a magpie – signed and dated 1851 – oil on canvas – unframed – 46.5 x 61cm.
(Sotheby's) **$1,434 £800**

GEORGE FAULKNER WETHERBEE (American, 1851-1920) - "The Plough" - board - signed and inscribed on label on reverse - 25.4 x 35.6cm.
(Bonhams) **$2,015 £1,300**

WHEELER

JOHN ARNOLD WHEELER (1821-1904) - Three Fox Terriers - signed - on board - 21.6 x 43.2cm
(Christie's)   **$5,984   £3,520**

ARTHUR WHITE – Fishmarket, St. Ives – oil on canvas
- signed – 28 x 36in.
(David Lay)   **$3,875   £2,500**

FREDERICK JOHN WIDGERY – Holwell Tor near
Haytor – gouache – signed – 20 x 30in.
(Bearne's)   **$2,136   £1,200**

FREDERIC WHITING, R.S.W. – Riding out –
watercolour over pencil – signed – 13¼ x 19in.
(Bearne's)   **$3,026   £1,700**

OLAF CARL WIEGHORST - Only One Chance –
signed O-Wieghorst and inscribed with artist's device, l.l. –
oil on canvas – unframed – 70.1 x 96.6cm.
(Christie's)   **$8,800   £5,500**

GUY CARLETON WIGGINS, ANA (1883-1962) – A windy corner, winter in New York – oil on board – 12 x 9in. – signed Guy Wiggins lower right – signed and titled on the reverse
(Bruce D. Collins)   **$8,250   £4,910**

GUY CARLETON WIGGINS – Fifth Avenue Winter – signed Guy Wiggins N.A., l.r. – signed again and inscribed with title on the reverse – oil on canvasboard – 41 x 30.5cm.
(Christie's)   **$8,800   £5,500**

GUY CARLETON WIGGINS - New York Winter - signed Guy Wiggins, l.l. - signed again and inscribed with title on the reverse - oil on canvasboard - 12.5 x 17.5cm.
(Christie's)   **$5,720   £3,575**

WIGGINS

GUY WIGGINS, N.A. (1883-1962) – St. Patricks in winter – oil on board – signed Guy Wiggins lower right – signed and titled on the reverse – 12 x 9in.
(Bruce D. Collins) **$12,551 £7,700**

IRVING RAMSAY WILES – A Cuban Girl – signed Irving R. Wiles, l.r. – signed again and inscribed with the title on the reverse – oil on panel – 45.8 x 34.9cm.
(Christie's) **$5,720 £3,575**

CHARLES WILDA (Austrian 1854-1907) - The street musician - signed and dated Cairo 1890 - oil on panel - 43 x 58cm.
(Sotheby's) **$52,954 £31,900**

W**** H**** WILKINSON - Drinking Time - watercolour - signed - inscribed on a label on the backboard - 25 x 39¼in.
(Bearne's) $3,295 £1,950

ALBERT WILLIAMS – A Still Life with Peonies and other Spring Flowers in a porcelain Vase – signed – on canvas– 76 x 63.5cm.
(Bonhams) **$6,320 £4,000**

ALBERT WILLIAMS – A Still Life with Roses, Iris, Delphiniums and other Summer Flowers in a crystal Vase – signed – on canvas – 76 x 63.5cm.
(Bonhams) **$4,108 £2,600**

WILLIAMS

EDWARD CHARLES WILLIAMS (1807-1881) – The hunter's rest – signed – 44.4 x 59.6cm.
(Christie's)   **$3,586   £2,200**

TERRICK WILLIAMS, R.A. (1860-1936) – The Harbour, Mevagissey – signed – oil on board – 20 x 27cm.
(Phillips)   **$5,216   £3,200**

EDWARD K. WILLIAMS (American, b. 1870) – "Edge of the Village" – signed "Edward K. Williams" – identified on the reverse – oil on canvas – 24 x 28in.
(Skinner)   **$1,900   £1,188**

TERRICK WILLIAMS, R.A. – Sailing vessels moored in a harbour – signed – 11½ x 17¼in.
(Bearne's)   **$7,832   £4,400**

FREDERICK RONALD WILLIAMS (1927-1982) – Burnt Landscape – signed – 71.1 x 91.4cm.
(Christie's)   **$76,626   £47,300**

TERRICK WILLIAMS – Brixham Trawlers at Sundown – watercolour – signed – signed, inscribed and dated 1928 on the backboard – 10 x 13½in.
(Bearne's)   **$2,619   £1,550**

WALTER WILLIAMS (1835-1906) – 'On the Lledr, North Wales' – signed and dated 1874 – also signed and inscribed on label on reverse – oil on canvas – 53.5 x 94cm.
(Phillips)   **$6,520   £4,000**

WALTER WILLIAMS – View in Kent – signed with monogram and dated 1854; bears title and date on a label attached to the stretcher – oil on canvas – 32 x 49cm.
(Sotheby's)   **$7,530   £4,620**

WALTER WILLIAMS (English, 1835-1906) – The Harvest Field – signed – unframed – 60.3 x 106.7cm.
(Bonhams)   **$8,525   £5,500**

WALTER WILLIAMS (1835-1906) - The Harvesters - oil on canvas - 61 x 107.6cm.
(Christie's)   **$11,154   £6,600**

WALTER WILLIAMS (1824-1903), Attributed to - The Ferry - with signature - 90 x 116cm.
(Christie's)   **$10,144   £6,380**

WILLIAMS

FREDERICK WILLIAMSON – Near Midhurst, Sussex; and Ben a'an Trossachs, - signed - watercolour - 22.8 x 35.5cm.
(Christie's)   **$4,661   £2,860**

WALTER WILLIAMS (1835 - 1906) - The torrent; and by the lake - both signed with initials and dated 72 - 15.8 x 11.4cm.
(Christie's)   **$2,805   £1,650**

FREDERICK WILLIAMSON - Sheep on a moor - signed and dated 1870 - watercolour - 10½ x 17½in.
(Christie's)   **$2,689   £1,650**

WARREN WILLIAMS - A View of Conway Castle - watercolour - signed - 21 x 40cm.
(Bonhams)   **$703   £460**

WALTER WILLIAMSON (19th century) - Herdsman with cattle and sheep in a landscape - 61.5 x 92cm.
(Christie's)   **$2,618   £1,540**

CAREL WILLINK - A selfportrait - signed and dated - pencil on paper - 41.5 x 26cm.
(Christie's)   **$9,088   £5,575**

CAREL WILLINK - A selfportrait - signed and dated - pencil on paper - 41.5 x 26cm.
(Christie's)   **$3,975   £2,439**

CAREL WILLINK - The Poet with a cold - a self-portrait - signed and dated - oil on canvas - 52 x 40cm.
(Christie's)   **$19,312   £11,848**

WILLOUGHBY

W. WILLOUGHBY (fl. 1858-1888) – A Dark Bay Racehorse with jockey, trainer and owner on a race-course – signed W. Willoughby - oil on canvas – 31 x 43cm.
(Sotheby's) **$6,653 £3,960**

WILLIAM WILLOUGHBY (19th century) - The Boston stump from across the River Witham - signed - bears inscription on the reverse - 14 x 19in.
(Christie's) **$1,309 £770**

Attributed to BENJAMIN WILSON (Leeds 1721-1788) – Portrait of Dr. Aston of Dublin – small half-length, wearing a dark coat and stock – in a painted oval – oil on canvas – 74.9 x 63.5cm.
(Lawrence) **$3,608 £2,200**

CHARLES EDWARD WILSON (1870's) - The Weakling - signed - watercolour - 14¼ x 10½in.
(Christie's) **$20,449 £12,100**

CHARLES EDWARD WILSON (1870's) - His Last Investment - signed - watercolour - 14¼ x 10½in.
(Christie's) **$17,660 £10,450**

CHARLES EDWARD WILSON - 'The Sweet Smell of Roses': A Girl at a cottage door - signed - pencil and watercolour - 20¾ x 14in.
(Christie's) **$18,480 £11,000**

CHARLES EDWARD WILSON - Good Companions - signed - pencil and watercolour - 13 x 20in.
(Christie's) **$14,414 £8,580**

CHARLES EDWARD WILSON (Circa 1936) - The Broken Horse - signed - watercolour - 38 x 26.5cm.
(Sotheby's) **$9,600 £6,000**

CHARLES EDWARD WILSON - A Fishergirl with a kitten beside a beached fishing boat - signed and dated - pencil and watercolour - 15 x 10¼in.
(Christie's) **$9,240 £5,500**

WILSON

H. MITTON WILSON (1873-1923) – Norman and Bunty at a nursery table – oil on canvas – 60.9 x 73.6cm.
(Lawrence) **$3,920 £2,420**

JOHN JAMES WILSON – The Port of Leith, Edinburgh from Fife – signed and dated 1870 – oil on canvas – 40.5 x 56cm.
(Sotheby's) **$22,044 £13,200**

H. MITTON WILSON (1873-1923) – A Summer Afternoon – oil on canvas – unframed – 50 x 60cm.
(Phillips) **$5,705 £3,500**

RICHARD WILSON R.A., circle of, (1714-1782) - A river landscape with escarpments and figures in the distance inscribed on the reverse 'Mrs Cockrane no. 18', and 'Wilson pinxit'. - 17½ x 21¼in.
(Christie's) **$1,402 £825**

J. CHESTER WILSON (19th century) – Portrait of a young girl holding a bunch of bluebells – signed and dated 1859 – 62 x 51.8cm.
(Christie's) **$3,740 £2,200**

RICHARD WILSON, R.A., studio of - Anglers on a cliff overlooking the river Arno - oil on canvas - 68 x 101.5cm.
(Sotheby's)

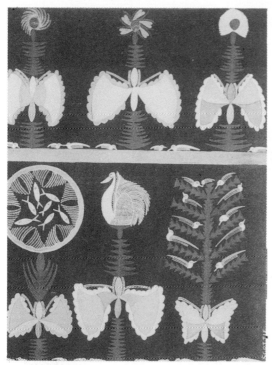

HENRY B. WIMBUSH – Drake's Island, Plymouth – watercolour – signed – 7 x 10½in.
(Bearne's) $1,352   £800

EDMUND MORISON WIMPERIS (1835-1900) - On High Down, Dartmoor - signed with initials and dated 98, - pencil and watercolour - 13¾ x 20¼in.
(Christie's) $1,216   £770

SCOTTIE WILSON - Butterflies, birds, trees, fish and a swan - signed - 48.2 x 35.6cm.
(Christie's) $1,165   £715

EDMUND MORISON WIMPERIS (1835-1900) - Capel Cruig, North Wales - signed with initials - watercolour and pencil - 18¼ x 30in.
(Christie's) $2,045 £1,210

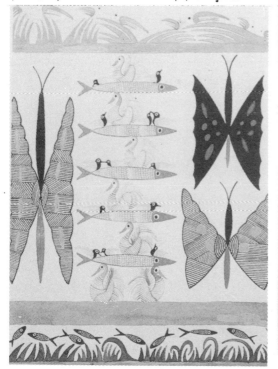

SCOTTIE WILSON - Butterflies, fish, birds and swans - signed - 13 x 9½in.
(Christie's) $1,165 £715

SIR JAMES LAWTON WINGATE, P.R.S.A. (1846-1924) – A spring afternoon – signed and dated 78 – 26.5 x 36.5cm.
(Christie's) $4,547   £2,860

WINGATE

PETER DE WINT (1784-1849) - Country landscape with church beyond - watercolour - 10 x 23 cm.
(Phillips) $7,824 £4,800

SIR JAMES LAWTON WINGATE, P.R.S.A. – Unloading the catch – signed and dated 1885 – oil on canvas – 76 x 107cm.
(Sotheby's) $18,370 £11,000

PETER de WINT (1784-1849) - A still Life with a Wicker Basket and a Jar - pencil and watercolour - 17 x 25cm.
(Christie's) $13,117 £8,250

JAMES DIGMAN WINGFIELD - The painters studio - signed and dated - oil on canvas - 18 x 24in.
(Christie's) $14,872 £8,800

CHARLES ALLEN WINTER - Three-masted ship in lifting fog - monogrammed - signed and dated - 32 x 40in.
(Skinner Inc.) $4,200 £2,500

PETER DE WINT (1784-1849) - An extensive mountain landscape with figures in a field of corn, hay stooks in the foreground - with signature - 45.7 x 60.6cm.
(Christie's) $3,553 £2,090

WILLIAM TATTON WINTER (1855-1928) - A farmyard scene - signed - watercolour - 33.5 x 42.5cm.
(Phillips) $685 £420

FRANZ XAVIER WINTERHALTER (Follower of)
– Selina Ellen Pelly and her two daughters, Gertrude and
Eliza Eugina – oil on canvas – 113 x 144cm.
(Sotheby's)   **$5,379   £3,300**

ARTHUR WINTER-SHAW (born 1869) – The weekly
wash – oil on canvas – 17 x 21in. – signed A. Winter-Shaw
lower left
(Bruce D. Collins)   **$4,125   £2,455**

WILLIAM WISSING, studio of - Portrait of William
III - oil on canvas - 117.5 x 94.5cm.
(Sotheby's)   **$12,012   £7,150**

WIT

JACOB DE WIT (1695-1754) – Obedience and temperance – signed and dated 1725 – oil on canvas – an oval – 126 x 95.5cm.
(Phillips) **$9,454 £5,800**

WILLIAM FREDERICK WITHERINGTON, R.A. (1785-1865) - A scene in Ross-shire - inscribed and dated on the reverse - 71 x 91.5cm.
(Christie's) **$2,869 £1,760**

WILLIAM FREDERICK WITHERINGTON, R.A. (1785-1865) – Part of the Eastern side Bombay Island, from the heights near the Parsee Tombs – signed l.l. : W F Witherington/1827 – oil on canvas – 70 x 105cm.
(Sotheby's) **$39,215 £25,300**

AUGUSTA INNES WITHERS – Still Life of Flowers and Fruit on a marble Ledge – watercolour and gum arabic – signed – 21.7 x 26.8cm.
(Bonhams) **$1,264 £800**

HAROLD C. WOLCOTT (American, 20th Century) – "Bookshop — Rockport Mass" – titled on verso – oil on canvas – 25 x 30in.
(Skinner) **$2,500 £1,497**

EDWARD WOLFE, R.A. (1897-1972) - Landscape, Granada - oil on panel - 12½ x 15½in.
(Christie's) **$3,148 £1,980**

EDWARD WOLFE, R.A. (1897 - 1972) - Pat Nelson - signed lower left Wolfe - oil on canvas - 35 x 27in.
(Christie's)   **$11,368 £7,150**

HENRI VICTOR WOLVENS (1896-1977) – Paysage aux Arbres—Landschap met Bomen – signed lower right H. V. Wolvens – oil on canvas – 39 x 24in.
(Christie's)   **$6,160   £3,850**

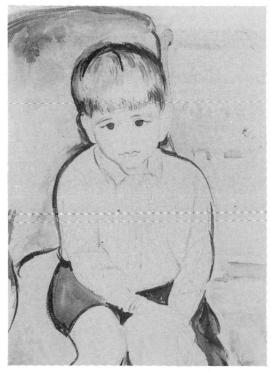

EDWARD WOLFE, R.A. (1897-1972) - Young boy seated - signed lower right Wolfe - watercolour and pencil - 25 x 17in.
(Christie's)   **$3,148   £1,980**

ALFRED WOLMARK (1877-1961) – Village Road with Car – signed and dated lower left Wolmark 39 – oil on panel – 10$\frac{1}{2}$ x 12in.
(Christie's)   **$2,781   £1,760**

WOLMARK

ALFRED WOLMARK (1877-1961) - Studio Interior -
signed - oil on panel - 18½ x 15in.
(Christie's)   **$7,392   £4,620**

ALFRED WOLMARK (1877-1961) – Still Life with
Tulips – signed with monogram and dated lower left 53 –
with studio stamp on the reverse – oil on panel – 19 x 13in.
(Christie's)   **$1,651   £1,045**

ALFRED WOLMARK (1877-1961) - still life with
flowers in a vase - signed - oil on panel - 19¾ x 16½in.
(Christie's)   **$3,632   £3,520**

**GARNET RUSKIN WOLSELEY, A.R.W.A. (1884-
1967)** – Fancy dress – oil on canvas – lined – signed –
30 x 24in.
(David Lay)   **$6,440   £4,000**

CHRISTOPHER WOOD - Bridge and Notre Dame, Paris 1924 - dated - 45.8 x 38.2cm.
(Christie's) **$7,530** **£4,620**

GARNET RUSKIN WOLSELEY (b. 1884) – Newlyn School – Young girl in a red dress at the water's edge – oil on canvas – 14 x 9¹/₂in.
(W. H. Lane & Son) **$2,890** **£1,700**

CHRISTOPHER WOOD – Liner – watercolour over pencil – 19 x 31cm.
(Phillips) **$3,380** **£2,000**

WOOD

CHRISTOPHER WOOD (1901-1930) - Shell, Dish and Fruit - oil on board - 6½ x 12in.
(Christie's) **$8,745 £5,500**

FRANK WATSON WOOD (1862-1953) - The battle of Jutland - signed - 10 x 28¼in.
(Christie's) **$1,394 £825**

FRANK WATSON WOOD - The German High Sea Fleet interned at Scapa Flow, December 1918 - signed and inscribed - 10 x 29½in.
(Christie's) **$2,788 £1,650**

FRANK WATSON WOOD (1862-1953) - Studies of battleships at sea, including Albion, London, Whiting and Janus - all signed and dated 1918 - 7½ x 10¾in.
(Christie's) **$2,788 £1,650**

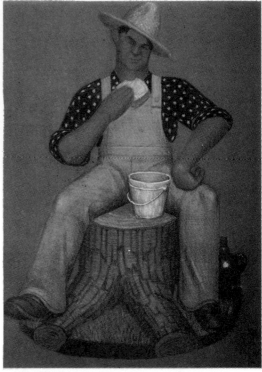

GRANT WOOD – Hired Man – signed Grant Wood, l.c. – gouache and coloured pencil on brown paper – 27.3 x 20.9cm.
(Christie's) **$52,800 £33,000**

LEWIS JOHN WOOD (1813-1901) - Place des Cordeliers dinan, Brittany; and Rue de la Poste Dinan, Brittany - both signed - oil on canvas - 12 x 9in.
(Christie's) **$6,506 £3,850**

THOMAS WATERMAN WOOD – The Secret – signed
T. W. Wood – dated 1886 and inscribed copyrifghted by,
˙ l.r. – oil on canvas – 61 x 45.7cm.
(Christie's) **$11,000 £6,875**

WILLIAM WOODHOUSE – A badger – watercolour
heightened with bodycolour – signed – 9¹/₂ x 14in.
(Bearne's) **$1,487 £880**

DAVID WOODLOCK – Girl in a garden – signed – oil
on canvas – 40.5 x 25.5cm.
(Sotheby's) **$1,524 £935**

WOODLOCK

DAVID WOODLOCK (1842-1929) – 'The Colleoni
Monument, Venice' – signed, inscribed in pencil on
reverse – oil and gouache on board – 44 x 25.5cm –
(Phillips) **$2,145 £1,300**

DAVID WOODLOCK – Cottage Garden at sunset –
signed – 9½ x 13½in.
(Outhwaite & Litherland) **$2,592 £1,600**

DAVID WOODLOCK (1842-1929) - At the Cottage
A Girl with Turkeys near a Tree in Blossom - signed -
watercolour - 19¼ x 7½in.
(Christie's) **$1,912 £1,210**

JOHN ARCHIBALD WOODSIDE, Sr. – Still life with
game in a landscape – signed – oil on canvas –
45.7 x 61.5cm.
(Sotheby's) **$8,800 £5,535**

DAVID WOODLOCK (1842-1929) - Piazza dei San
Marco, Venice - signed - 40 x 24cm.
(Phillips) **$2,119 £1,300**

**ROBERT STRONG WOODWARD (American, 1885-
1960)** – "Passing New England"/Mountain Cabin – signed
– oil on canvas – 30 x 36in.
(Skinner) **$2,500 £1,497**

STANLEY WINGATE WOODWARD (American, 1890-1970) – 'Patrol Waters'/
Distant Steamer Off Rocky Coast – signed –titled on verso – oil on canvas –
28 x 36in. *(Skinner)* **$1,400 £838**

STANLEY WINGATE WOODWARD - The Helmsman
- signed - oil on canvas - 25 x 30in.
(Skinner Inc.)   **$3,780   £2,250**

STANLEY WINGATE WOODWARD (American, 1890-1970) – Beaching in a Rocky Cove – signed – oil on canvas – 25 x 30in.
(Skinner)   **$1,300   £778**

THOMAS WOODWARD (1801-1852) – Billy, Holt Castle's favourite watchdog, the property of John Pickernell, Esq – signed l.r. : TW/1848 – oil on canvas – 137 x 147.5cm.
(Sotheby's)   **$51,150   £33,000**

SAMUEL JOHNSON WOOLF (1880-1948) - The Chicken Yard - signed - oil on canvas - 22 x 30in.
(Sotheby's) **$1,478** **£880**

HENRY A. WOOLLETT — A palomino stallion with a spaniel in a loose box - signed and dated 1863 - 60.9 x 74.9cm.
(Christie's) **$2,869 £1,760**

CHARLES NICHOLLS WOOLNOTH (1815-1906) - On the Severn - signed - watercolour - 13 x 19¼in.
(Christie's) **$1,859 £1,100**

KENNETH E. WOOTON (Exh. 1912) – A Classical Idyll – signed and dated 1912 – oil on canvas – 183 x 76cm.
(Phillips) **$2,771 £1,700**

JOSEPH WOPFNER (1843 Schwaz/Tirol–1927 Munchen) — Harvesting by the Chiemsee — signed — oil on panel — 36.5 x 47cm.
(Sotheby's) **$30,469 £18,693**

RIK WOUTERS (1882-1916) – Nu couché—Liggend
Naakt – signed – dated and inscribed lower right A l'ami
N. Beets Van Harte, Rik Wouters, Amsterdam 1915 –
watercolour, pen and ink on paper – 39.5 x 57cm. –
Executed in 1915
(Christie's)   **$45,760   £28,600**

JULES WORMS (1832-1914) - The Serenade - signed,
– pencil and watercolour - 443 x 279cm.
(Christie's)   **$2,138   £1,320**

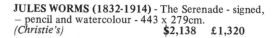

RIK WOUTERS (1882-1916) – Le Village—Het Dorp –
signed and dated lower right Rik Wouters 1910 – gouache
over a printed base – 29.3 x 39.3cm. – Executed in 1910
(Christie's)   **$17,600   £11,000**

FRANS WOUTERS (Liege-1614-1659 Antwerp) –
Charity – on copper – 15.5 x 18cm.
(Phillips)   **$10,595   £6,500**

PHILLIPS WOUWERMAN (1619-Haarlem-1668) –
Peasants on a riverbank with their livestock crossing
a river – indistinctly signed with initials PHW – on
panel – 37.5 x54.5cm.
(Phillips)   **$42,380 £26,000**

GILBERT S. WRIGHT – A stop for the London to
Exeter coach – signed – oil on canvas – 61 x 81.5cm.
(Sotheby's) **$32,274 £19,800**

GEORGE WRIGHT (1860-1942) - A hunter and hounds
in a loose box; and breaking cover - both signed - oil
on canvas - 12 x 14in.
(Christie's) **$6,692 £3,960**

GILBERT SCOTT WRIGHT (1880-1958) - The Master
Changes at a Check - signed - oil on canvas - 72.4 x
52.1cm.
(Christie's) **$13,385 £7,920**

GEORGE WRIGHT (1860-1942) – Away, and Robbed
at the crossroads – both signed – a pair – 26 x 36cm.
(Christie's) **$7,870 £4,950**

GEORGE WRIGHT (1860-1942) - clearing the fence -
signed - oil on canvas - 10 x 18in.
(Christie's) **$22,308 £13,200**

GEORGE WRIGHT (1860-1942) - Moving Off - signed
- 27.5 x 22cm.
(Christie's) **$2,330 £1,430**

JOSEPH WRIGHT of DERBY, A.R.A. (1734-1797) –
Portrait of Miss Jenner – half length, wearing a black dress
with pink sleeves and ribbons – oil on canvas, in a carved
wood frame – 74 x 61.5cm.
(Sotheby's)   **$12,012   £7,150**

JOSEPH WRIGHTof DERBY, A.R.A. (1734-1797) –
Two young gentlemen in the characters of archers – full
length, wearing green and gold draped costumes, holding
bows and arrows, a spaniel at their feet – later inscribed
Francis and Charles Mundy/sons of Frn. Mundy – oil on
canvas – 181.5 x 137cm.
(Sotheby's)   **$147,840   £88,000**

JOSEPH WRIGHT OF DERBY, A.R.A. (1734-1797) –
Portrait of Sir Robert Burdett Bt., of Foremark, Derbyshire
– three quarter length, standing, wearing a grey coat with a
pale blue waistcoat – inscribed by a later hand with the
identity of the sitter – oil on canvas – 125.5 x 100cm.
(Sotheby's)   **$49,445   £31,900**

JOSEPH WRIGHT OF DERBY, A.R.A. (1734-1797) –
Portrait of Master Richard Sale (1781-1845) – head and
shoulders, wearing a yellow jacket and white shirt – oil on
canvas – in a painted oval – 51.5 x 43cm.
(Sotheby's)   **$68,200   £44,000**

JAN WYCK (1645-1700) — A Piebald stallion held by a huntsman in a wooded landscape — bears signature l.l.:j. Wootton — oil on canvas — 133.5 x 166cm.
(Sotheby's) $57,970 £37,400

JAMIE WYETH - We've Got Your Pickle - signed J. Wyeth l.r. — dry brush and mixed media on paper — 37.7 x 50.8cm.
(Christie's) $41,800 £26,660

WYETH

JAMES WYETH – Shark - signed – oil on canvas –
132.0 x 152.3cm.
(Sotheby's)   **$52,250   £32,862**

ANDREW WYETH - The Woodchoppers - signed Andrew
Wyeth, l.r. - watercolour on paper laid down on board -
54.6 x 74.6cm.
(Christie's)   **$104,500   £66,650**

ANDREW WYETH – Water Turtle – signed Andrew
Wyeth, l.r. – watercolour and drybrush on paper laid down
on board – 57 x 76.4cm.
(Christie's)   **$61,600   £38,500**

ANDREW WYETH - Dogwood - signed Andrew Wyeth,
1.1. - watercolour on paper - 48.2 x 69.8cm.
(Christie's)   **$154,000   £98,221**

ANDREW WYETH (b. 1917) – Front room – signed
Andrew Wyeth, l.l. – watercolour on paper –
73.7 x 53.3cm. – Painted in 1946
(Sotheby's) **$93,500 £59,554**

JAMIE WYETH – Rudolf Nureyev – signed J. Wyeth, l.l.
– gouache and pencil on board – 50.8 x 40.6cm.
(Christie's) **$9,350 £5,963**

ANDREW WYETH – Grain barrel – signed - watercolour
on paper – 57.1 x 76.2cm. – Painted in 1961
(Sotheby's) **$143,000 £89,937**

JAMIE WYETH - Marsh Bales - signed Jamie Wyeth l.l.
- watercolour and gouache on paper - 48.6 x 71.7cm.
(Christie's) **$24,200 £15,434**

ANDREW WYETH - Spruce Gun - signed Andrew Wyeth
l.r. - watercolour on paper - 55.2 x 75.8cm.
(Christie's) **$154,000 £98,221**

JOHN ALLAN WYETH - French country landscape
- signed Wyeth l.l. - oil on canvas - 24 x 29in.
(Skinner Inc.) **$2,016 £1,200**

WYETH

NEWELL CONVERS WYETH - young girl with lambs - pen and black ink - 30.3 x 37.1cm.
(Christie's) **$1,980 £1,193**

CHARLES WILLIAM WYLLIE (1859-1923) - Shipping in an estuary - signed - watercolour - 8 x 19in.
(Phillips) **$2,445 £1,500**

NEWELL CONVERS WYETH (1882-1945) - Guns in Flanders - Flanders Guns! (I had a man that worked them once!) - signed - oil on canvas - 34 x 24in.
(Sotheby's) **$18,480 £11,000**

WILLIAM LIONEL WYLLIE, R.A. (1851-1931) –Off Venice – signed with initials – dated Oct. 20th and inscribed "Venice" – oil on card – 19.5 x 27.5cm.
(Phillips) **$4,238 £2,600**

NEWELL CONVERS WYETH (1882-1945) - The Hidden Treasure - signed - oil on canvas - 45 x 40in.
(Sotheby's) **$37,128 £22,100**

WILLIAM LIONEL WYLLIE, R.A. – Review of the fleet, 1911 – signed – oil on canvas – 77 x 153cm.
(Sotheby's) **$30,481 £18,700**

WILLIAM LIONEL WYLLIE, R.A. (1851-1931) - The
Return from the Delhi Durbar, Medina arriving at
Portsmouth - signed and inscribed - watercolour -
8½ x 12¼in.
(Christie's)   **$2,607   £1,650**

WILLIAM LIONEL WYLLIE R.A. – 'Dunottar
Castle" in Rochester Harbour – signed – watercolour
heightened with bodycolour and scratching out over pencil
– 73.5 x 127cm.
(Sotheby's)   **$6,545   £3,850**

BRYAN WYNTER (1915-1975) - Harvest - oil on board -
27¼ x 19¾in.
(Christie's)   **$5,596 £3,520**

BRYAN WYNTER - Freshet - signed - oil on canvas- -
40 x 32in.
(Sotheby's)   **$21,780   £12,100**

BRYAN WYNTER (1915-1975) - Sand Traverse - signed
dated and inscribed on the reverse Bryan Wynter Sand
Traverse 1962 - oil on canvas - 40 x 32in.
(Christie's)   **$8,395   £5,280**

YARNOLD

GEORGE B*** YARNOLD – An angler by a swift-flowing river – signed and dated 1879 – 76 x 125cm.
(Anderson & Garland) **$629 £370**

JACK BUTLER YEATS, R.H.A. (1871-1957) - The Cowboy's Lament - signed - watercolour, pen, brush, black ink and grey wash - 4 x 6in.
(Christie's) **$6,996 £4,400**

WILLIAM YELLOWLEES (1796 - 1856) - Portrait of Sir Walter Scott - 12 x 10in.
(Christie's) **$44,887 £2,640**

HENRY REGINALD YORKE (1803-1871) - View from Hill House - signed and dated - 5 x 7in.
(Christie's) **$595 £352**

JACK BUTLER YEATS, R.H.A. (1871-1957) - The Moon has fallen out of the Sky - signed lower right Jack B. Yeats - oil on canvas - 20¼ x 27¼in.
(Christie's) **$227,370 £143,000**

W. S. YOUNG - Mt. Kearsarge, New Hampshire - signed W. S. Young and dated 1886, 1.1. - oil on canvas - 46 x 76cm.
(Christie's) **$8,250 £5,261**

EUGENIO ZAMPIGHI (1859-1944) – The centre of
attraction – signed – 25 x 35.5cm.
(Christie's)   **$5,667   £3,520**

EUGENIO ZAMPIGHI (1859-1944) – The new vintage
– signed – unframed – 56 x 77.5cm.
(Christie's)   **$12,397   £7,700**

ANNIE MARY YOUNGMAN – Still Life of Carnations
in a small green Jug – watercolour – signed –
45.7 x 29.2cm.
(Bonhams)   **$1,138   £720**

CHRISTIAN ZACHO (1843-1913) - Old Elm trees on the Citadel of Copenhagen - signed and
dated 1884 - 76 x 111cm.
(Christie's)   **$11,935   £7,700**

ZAWISKI

EDOUARD ZAWISKI - At the races - signed - 146 x 113.5cm.
(Christie's) **$34,540 £22,000**

KARL ZERBE - Church Facade - signed - 25½ x 18in.
(Skinner Inc.) **$1,428 £850**

NISSE ZETTERBERG – 'Odette' – signed and dated – 72 x 60cm.
(Auktionsverket Stockholm) **$3,472 £2,130**

FELIX ZIEM (French 1821-1911) – The Grand Canal, Venice – signed – oil on panel – 72 x 104cm.
(Sotheby's) **$32,868 £19,800**

FELIX FRANCOIS GEORGES PHILIBERT ZIEM (1821-1911) – The Bacino, Venice – signed – on panel – 55 x 8cm.
(Christie's) **$15,345 £9,900**

GUSTAV ZIMMER-SCHRODER - The magic wood -
signed - 96 x 77cm.
(Christie's) **$3,108 £1,980**

GUSTAV ZIMMER-SCHRODER - The Orchid
Garden - signed - 188 x 68cm.
(Christie's) **$3,108 £1,980**

GUSTAV ZIMMER-SCHRODER - A still life -
signed - 66 x 51cm.
(Christie's) **$1,208 £770**

ANNA ZINKEISEN - These laid the world away 1939-
45 - signed - 23 x 30in.
(Christie's) **$2,330 £1,430**

ZINKEISEN

DORIS ZINKEISEN – The Black Dress – signed and dated 1937 – oil on canvas – unframed – 86.5 x 106.5cm. *(Phillips)* **$9,600 £6,000**

JOHAN ZOFFANY, R.A. (1733-1810), Circle of – Portrait of a lady, said to be Mrs. Orme, standing half length, in a white dress and lace cap – 35.6 x 28.6cm. *(Christie's)* **$986 £605**

LEOPOLD ZINNOGGER (Austrian 1811-72) – A still life of a butterfly and grapes – signed and dated '839 – watercolour and bodycolour – 70.5 x 52cm. *(Sotheby's)* **$5,478 £3,300**

JOHN ZOFFANY, R.A. (1733-1810) – Portrait of Sir Henry Oxenden, 7th Bt. (1756-1838), when a boy – half length, wearing white Van Dyck dress and a blue cloak – inscribed on the reverse of the original canvas – 75 x 63cm. *(Sotheby's)* **$25,575 £16,500**

JOHANN ZOFFANY, R.A. (1733-1810) – A studio interior with a young boy admiring portraits of his parents – oil on canvas – 74 x 61cm.
(Sotheby's) $36,960 £22,000

ANTONIO ZOPPI (1860-1926) - Paying their respects signed and inscribed Firenze - 69.3 x 88.9cm.
(Christie's) $16,394 £10,120

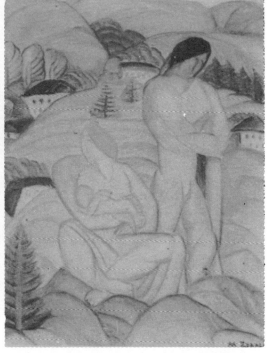

MARGUERITE ZORACH (1887-1968) and WILLIAM ZORACH (1887-1966) - The Zorach family in a landscape and a floral still life - a double sided painting - 23½ x 19½in.
(Sotheby's) $64,680 £38,500

ZORACH

WILLIAM ZORACH (1887-1966) - Field Place - signed - watercolour over pencil - 15 x 22¼in.
(Sotheby's)   **$5,082 £3,025**

FRANCESCO ZUCCARELLI, R.A., circle of -
Italianate landscape - oil on canvas - 125 x 99cm.
(Sotheby's)   **$7,392 £4,400**

JACOPO ZUCCHI, 1541-1589 OU 90 – Attributed to –
Les Trésors de la mer – oil on copper – 52 x 42.5cm.
(Sotheby's)   **$23,912 £15,328**

ANTONIO ZUCCHI, A.R.A. - The Graces - a pair - both oil on canvas - 111 x 94cm.
(Sotheby's) $3,696 £2,200

REINIS ZUSTERS — Down the Harbour - oil on board - signed - 122 x 210cm.
(Australian Art Auctions) $3,032 £1,860